An Introduction to INTERCULTURAL COMMUNICATION

Fourth Edition

The Author's Purpose

My involvement with intercultural communication began with seeing prejudice from the unclouded eyes of a child. It simply made no sense to me. Experiencing prejudice later in life also made no sense to me. My agenda is to facilitate students' development of self-concepts that value their histories and appreciate diversities. My approach is to promote the skills of intercultural communication competence by developing an understanding of how individuals perceive and react to cultural rules. I believe that understandings of the pull to join and the push to make separate are critical for developing intercultural communication competence.

—Fred E. Jandt
California State University, San Bernardino

About the Author

Fred E. Jandt was born of second-generation German immigrants in the multicultural south-central region of Texas. His doctorate in communication is from Bowling Green State University. He has taught and been a student of intercultural communication for more than 30 years, developing his experience through travel and international training and research projects.

While Professor of Communication at State University of New York at Brockport, his reputation as a teacher led to this appointment as SUNY's first director of faculty development. He is currently Professor of Communication at California State University, San Bernardino, and recently was a visiting professor at Victoria University of Wellington in New Zealand.

He has extensive experience in the areas of intercultural and international communication, negotiation and mediation, and computer-mediated communication. He is known for his book *Win-Win Negotiating* (1985), which has been translated into seven languages. The focus of his interest is on the overlap of conflict and culture studies. He edited with Paul B. Pedersen *Constructive Conflict Management: Asia-Pacific Cases* (1996).

Fred E. Jandt
California State University, San Bernardino

An Introduction to
INTERCULTURAL
COMMUNICATION

Identities in a Global Community

Fourth Edition

SAGE Publications
International Educational and Professional Publisher
Thousand Oaks ■ London ■ New Delhi

For information

Sage Publications, Inc.
2455 Teller Road
Thousand Oaks, California 91320
E-mail: order@sagepub.com

Sage Publications Ltd.
6 Bonhill Street
London EC2A 4PU
United Kingdom

Sage Publications India Pvt. Ltd.
B-42, Panchsheel Enclave
Post Box 4109
New Delhi 110 017 India

Printed in the United States of America

Library of Congress Cataloging-in-Publication Data

Jandt, Fred Edmund.
An introduction to intercultural communication: identities in a global community / by Fred E. Jandt.—4th ed.
        p. cm.
Previous editions have title: Intercultural communication.
Includes bibliographical references and index.
ISBN 0-7619-2847-2 (Paper)
   1. Intercultural communication. 2. Intercultural communication-United States. 3. Communication, International. I. Jandt, Fred Edmund. Intercultural communication. II. Title.
GN345.J43 2003
303.48′2—dc211

                                                            2003004599

Printed on acid-free paper

03   04   05   06   07   08   09   10   9   8   7   6   5   4   3   2   1

Acquiring Editor:	Todd R. Armstrong
Editorial Assistant:	Veronica K. Novak
Developmental Editor:	Alicia Carter
Production Editor:	Claudia A. Hoffman
Typesetter:	C&M Digitals (P) Ltd.
Copy Editor:	Kate Peterson
Cover Designer:	Ravi Balasuriya

Contents

To the Student

Two reasonable questions at the beginning of any course are "What is it?" and "Why study it?"

Intercultural communication becomes important for understanding communication among peoples when cultural identifications affect message use. When the Canadian government considers how to explain the legal system to a new generation of immigrants, intercultural communication is important. When a British high-tech firm plans a marketing strategy in India, intercultural communication is important.

Of course, intercultural communication has been a human concern for millennia. Its formal study is generally associated with the publication in 1959 of Edward Hall's *The Silent Language*. Its author showed how culture is critical to understanding intercultural communication.

There have been several approaches to gaining an increased understanding of intercultural communication. One approach is to learn the barriers one would need to overcome. These barriers include such concepts as ethnocentricism, stereotyping, nonverbal misunderstandings, and translation difficulties. Another approach, called ethnography, is to observe the customary behavior of a group to learn the unwritten rules for appropriate behavior in that group. Another approach, called the cultural approach, is to develop an ideal personification of the culture to understand behaviors in that culture. Researchers attempt to understand the relationship between a culture's language and behavior in that culture and to understand the dominant values of individual cultures.

Today's intercultural communication challenges are global. The long-term consequences of colonialism continue to affect indigenous (or native) populations. The widespread use of English as a second language and international marketing increase feelings of nationalism. Increased world migration raises questions of identity. In fact, the study of intercultural communication can be said to be about the definition of self that results from an awareness of a shared consciousness with others. How that shared consciousness affects how you and others communicate defines the subject.

The general goal of this text is to help you develop an understanding of cultures to appreciate the opportunities and challenges that each culture presents to people and to learn how individuals have dealt with those opportunities and challenges. Intercultural communication is fundamentally about individuals communicating with other individuals with whom past experiences have not been shared.

With your course, this text helps you become competent in communication with others of diverse cultural backgrounds by helping you develop the following skills and understandings:

- *Expanding your range of verbal and nonverbal communication skills.* Effective communicators have the ability to select and perform communication behaviors appropriate to various settings.
- *Becoming able to communicate effectively in unfamiliar settings.* We all experience stress in unfamiliar settings. More effective communicators recognize and handle that stress.
- *Recognizing the influence your own culture has had on the way in which you view yourself.* More effective communicators understand how they became who they are and are less threatened by those of other backgrounds.
- *Expanding your knowledge of the ways of other cultures.* More effective communicators know more about the norms and values of other cultures.

As you begin your study, I urge you to avoid the common fallacy that you already know the content of your course from your life experiences. Communication books and courses are unique in that you may have had some experiences with the subject matter before you begin the course. You may have formed some opinions about the subject matter as well. Educators call these skills and beliefs "naïve knowledge"—not naïve as simplistic but naïve as untested in a variety of settings. Rather than use your naïve knowledge as the basis for judging the accuracy of this text and your course, I encourage you to open your naïve knowledge to evaluation. How did you develop your belief? In what situations might that belief not be appropriate? How can you develop the ability to evaluate diverse situations and choose one of many possible ways of communicating?

To the Instructor

This text is written for introductory courses in culture and communication at the sophomore or junior level in departments of communication, business, and anthropology. It assumes little or no previous course work in communication or culture studies. In comparison to earlier editions, you will find in this edition

- One combined chapter on language rather than two and one combined chapter on multiculturalism and the future rather than separate chapters
- Updated examples such as the downing of a U.S. spy plane in China
- Expanded discussions of globalization and intergroup relations particularly as related to the September 11, 2001, attacks on the United States and the 2003 war with Iraq.

Based on e-mail feedback from students and instructors and on formal reviews, popular features of the book have been retained and strengthened. You will continue to find that this text

- Stresses readability by attempting to be reader-centered, interesting, and provocative with chapter summaries written with English as a second language (ESL) students in mind
- Does not use the words *they*, *them*, and *different* when referring to cultures and ethnic groups to avoid putting the reader in the place of an outsider labeling cultures and ethnic groups as "others"
- Attempts to be a textbook for students in any country by using examples from many countries

Two new resources are available for this edition:

There is a new reader, *Intercultural Communication: A Global Reader,* which may be used with this text. The readings were selected to support the major concepts of cultural values, language, identities, peace, and globalization that are presented in this book.

Second, a CD with test questions, student activities, sample syllabus, and resources is available from the publisher.

Thank you for your support of past editions. I work on this book every day. For me, this text, like life itself, is a work in progress. I do appreciate dialogue and do use feedback from students and colleagues.

—Fred E. Jandt
fjandt@csusb.edu

Acknowledgments

Fourth edition:

Marianne Dainton, La Salle University
Min-Sun Kim, University of Hawaii at Manoa
Alex Mwakikoti, University of Texas at Arlington
Mabry M. O'Donnell, Marietta College
Jianglong Wang, Western Washington University

Others/previous editions:

Calvin H. Bowers, Pepperdine University
Richard W. Brislin, University of Hawaii at Manoa
John S. Caputo, Gonzaga University
Rueyling Chuang, California State University, San Bernardino
Fernando P. Delgado, Arizona State University West
Joseph A. DeVito, Hunter College of City University of New York
Mary Fong, California State University, San Bernardino
Howard Frederick, UNITEC Institute of Technology, Auckland, New Zealand
Alberto Gonzalez, Bowling Green State University
Brian M. Harmer, Victoria University of Wellington, New Zealand
Iben Jensen, Roskilde University, Denmark
Michael P. Kelley, California State University, Los Angeles
Ringo Ma, Hong Kong Baptist University
Craig Monroe, California State University, San Bernardino
Michael C. Pounds, California State University, Long Beach
R. Jeffrey Ringer, Akita University, Japan
Rujira Rojjanaprapayon, University of Minnesota, Morris Campus
Edward R. Rothhaar, San Bernardino Valley College
Yosei Sugawara, Pima Community College
Dolores V. Tanno, University of Nevada, Las Vegas
Anita Taylor, George Mason University
Mei Zhong, San Diego State University

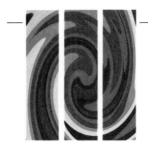

PART I

Culture as Context
for Communication

CHAPTER 1

The Dispute Over Defining Culture

What You Can Learn From This Chapter

Various reactions to globalization

The different meanings of the terms *culture, race, co-culture, subculture,* and *subgroup* and how to critically evaluate the effect of these different meanings

Examples of norms or rules of behavior provided by diverse cultures and subgroups

The last third of the 20th century saw unprecedented improvement in human development: life expectancy 17 years longer than it was in 1960, infant mortality more than halved, and the combined enrollment in primary and secondary schools nearly 1.5 times higher. Among the factors contributing to these advancements was the unprecedented worldwide spread of markets and democracy referred to today as **globalization**.

Proponents of globalization argue that economic systems based on private property and competition are the most efficient and that democracy is the fairest political system the world has ever known (Friedman, 1999). Globalization has given Mexico frappuccinos at Starbucks and the United States the novels of Carlos Fuentes (Cowen, 2002).

Opponents of globalization argue that it has made "the corporation the most powerful institution on earth" (Frank, 2000). Global corporations such as Monsanto, AOL-Time Warner, and McDonald's are seen as undermining local cultures. Because the United States has promoted both free markets and democracy throughout the world, global markets are perceived as reinforcing

Table 1.1   What the World Thinks

Country	Spread of U.S. ideas a "good thing" (%)	Like U.S. music, movies, TV (%)	Like U.S. science and technology (%)
Canada	37	77	76
Britain	39	76	77
Russia	16	42	41
Mexico	22	60	69
South Korea	30	53	81
South Africa	43	71	79
Turkey	11	44	67
Egypt	6	33	51
Jordan	13	30	59
Pakistan	2	4	42

SOURCE: Pew Research Center for the People & the Press, "What the World Thinks in 2002," posted on the Pew Web site: http://www.people-press.org.

U.S. wealth and dominance. Between July and October 2002, the Pew Research Center for the People & the Press surveyed some 38,000 people in 46 languages around the world. In country after country where people like U.S. technology and culture, they are displeased with the spread of U.S. ideas and values (see Table 1.1).

Another reaction to globalization is the growing strength of ethnic identity through the world with a resulting growth of interethnic group hatred (Chua, 2002):

- In 1998, Indonesian mobs looted hundreds of Chinese shops and homes leaving more than 2,000 dead.

- Suicide bombings have become common events in Israel.

- In 2001, Middle Eastern terrorists destroyed the World Trade Center, seen by some as a symbol of greed and cultural humiliation, incinerating its occupants.

Can there be a more critical time to study intercultural communication?

Intercultural communication refers not only to the communication between individuals of diverse cultural identifications but also to the communication between groups of diverse cultural identifications. This text focuses on two equally important aspects of improving intercultural communication: first, that

Farmers, factory workers, human rights activists, environmentalists, and other groups demonstrate against the World Trade Organization, the symbol of globalization.

SOURCE: Photo by Al Crespo.

your effectiveness as an intercultural communicator is in part a function of your knowledge of other peoples and their cultures and, second, that as you learn more about other people from various cultures you also discover more about yourself, which results in an appreciation and tolerance of diversity among people and which makes you a more competent communicator in multicultural settings.

Many classrooms represent a cross section of the diversity of college students—international students, students of various backgrounds and ethnicities, students who see no relevant differences between cultures, and students who have various perspectives on communication among peoples of diverse backgrounds. Many classrooms can be models of the United Nations. Take advantage of the diversity in your classroom to explore various perspectives on the issues presented in this text.

What you can expect to learn of other people begins with your asking questions that affect both of you, jointly examining the issue and mutually benefiting from the experience. When studying with other people, we can examine our shared history, our common challenges and responses, and how we come to perceive one another through media.

In this introductory chapter, you will learn how the definition of the terms *culture, race, subculture, ethnicity, co-culture,* and *subgroup* has changed over the years. Finally, the rules for behavior that these groups provide for their members are described.

CULTURE

Many textbooks begin by defining terms. There is a reason for that: Communication is facilitated by the extent to which we have similar meanings for the terms we use. It should be simple to define terms, but in the area of intercultural communication the terminology can become quite personal because these are the **words** we and others use to refer to ourselves and each other. How these terms are defined can affect how we think of ourselves and how we are seen by others.

Some terms in common use were developed by outsiders to refer to some people who seem to share some features as a group even though the people didn't really see themselves as a group. Other terms developed by outsiders to refer to a group of people carry with them meanings not accepted by that group. And other groups may develop terms to label themselves precisely for the reason of communicating an identity.

The definition of the word *culture* itself is an example of how terminology can become a battlefield.

19th-Century Definition

In the 19th century, the term culture was commonly used as a synonym for Western civilization. The British anthropologist Sir Edward B. Tylor (1871) popularized the idea that all peoples pass through developmental stages, beginning with "savagery," progressing to "barbarism," and culminating in Western "civilization." It's easy to see that such a definition assumes that Western cultures were considered superior. Both Western cultures, beginning with ancient Greece, and Eastern cultures, most notably imperial China, believed that their own way of life was superior.

Today's Definition

The study of multiple cultures without imposing the belief that Western culture was the ultimate goal was slow to develop. Cultures do not respect political boundaries. Border cities such as Juárez, El Paso, Tijuana, and San Diego can develop cultures that in some ways are not like Mexico or the United States. In this text, **culture** refers to the following:

1. A community or population sufficiently large enough to be self-sustaining, that is, large enough to produce new generations of members without relying on outside peoples.

2. The totality of that group's thought, experiences, and patterns of behavior and its concepts, values, and assumptions about life that guide behavior and how those evolve with contact with other cultures. Hofstede (1994) classified these elements of culture into four categories: symbols, rituals, values, and heroes. **Symbols** refer to verbal and nonverbal language. **Rituals** are the socially essential collective activities within a culture. **Values** are the feelings not open for discussion within a culture about what is good or bad, beautiful or ugly, normal or abnormal, that are present in a majority of the members of a culture or at least in those who occupy pivotal positions. **Heroes** are the real or imaginary people who serve as behavior models within a culture. A culture's heroes are expressed in the culture's **myths,** which can be the subject of novels and other forms of literature (Rushing & Frentz, 1978). Janice Hocker Rushing (1983) has argued, for example, that an enduring myth in United States culture as seen in films is the rugged individualist cowboy in the American West.

3. A process of social transmission of these thoughts and behaviors learned from birth in the family and schools over the course of generations.

4. Members who consciously identify themselves with that group, described by Collier and Thomas (1988) as **cultural identity,** or the identification with and perceived acceptance into a group that has a shared system of symbols and meanings as well as norms for conduct.

What does knowing an individual's cultural identity tell you about that individual? If you assume that that individual is like everyone else in that culture, you have stereotyped all the many, various people in that culture into one mold. You know that you are different from others in your culture. Other cultures are as diverse. The diversity within cultures probably exceeds the differences between cultures. So just knowing a person's cultural identity doesn't provide complete or reliable information about that one person.

Knowing another's cultural identity does, however, help you understand the opportunities and challenges that each individual in that culture had to deal with. Growing up in the 21st century presents opportunities and challenges. But how any one person deals with those opportunities and challenges may be quite similar to or quite different from how others do.

We can have no direct knowledge of a culture other than our own. Our experience with and knowledge of other cultures is forever limited by the perceptual bias of our own culture. An adult Canadian will never fully understand the experience of growing up an Australian.

Race

Just as the word *culture* can affect us personally, so does the word *race.* Even more than the term culture, the term race continues to be a battlefield. Race and culture are not synonymous terms. It was popularly believed that differences between peoples were biological or racial. Only recently has it been recognized that one's cultural environment largely influences one's physical and mental characteristics.

From the popular biological perspective, **race** refers to a large body of people characterized by similarity of descent (Campbell, 1976). From this biological definition your race is the result of the mating behavior of your ancestors. Some physical traits and genes occur more frequently in certain human populations than in others, such as some skull and dental features, differences in the processing of alcohol, and inherited diseases such as sickle-cell anemia and cystic fibrosis.

The biological definition is said to derive from Carolus Linnaeus, a Swedish botanist, physician, and taxonomist, who said in 1735 that humans are classified into four types: *Africanus, Americanus, Asiaticus,* and *Europeaeus.* In the 19th century, scientists thought that the races had different kinds of blood, so hospitals segregated blood supplies.

Twentieth-century scientists studying genetics have found no single race-defining gene. Popular indicators of race such as skin color and hair texture were caused by recent evolution in response to climate and diet. Most scientists today have abandoned the concept of biological race as a meaningful scientific concept (Cavalli-Sforza, Menozzi, & Piazza, 1994; Owens & King, 1999; Paabo, 2001).

Another way to define race is as a sociohistorical concept. Racial categories have varied over time and between cultures. Worldwide, skin color alone does not define race. The meaning of race has been debated in societies, and as a consequence, new categories have been formed and others transformed. Dark-skinned natives of India have been classified as Caucasian. People with moderately dark skins in Egypt are identified as White. And in contrast to the

Linnaeus appears on Sweden's 100 kroner currency.

United States, Brazil has a history of intermarriage among native peoples, descendants of African slaves, and immigrants from Europe, the Middle East, and Asia. So in Brazil, where half of the population is Black, there are hundreds of words for skin colors (Robinson, 1999) even though there is an aversion to racial categorization. The biologically based definition understands race as something fixed; the sociohistorically based definition sees race as unstable and socially determined through constant debate (Omi & Winant, 1986).

In relation to culture, then, people may be of the same race but of diverse cultures: Australia and South Africa have very different cultures that include individuals of the same ancestries. Then, too, people can be of the same culture but of different ancestries: The United States is a culture of people of all races (see Box 1.1).

Box 1.1

**OFFICIAL RACIAL DEFINITIONS
HAVE SHIFTED SHARPLY AND OFTEN**

Although the federal government has been collecting information about race for more than 200 years, official racial distinctions . . . changed over time.

. . .

(Continued)

Box 1.1, *Continued*

At the turn of the century, Irish, Italians, and many central European ethnic groups were considered distinct "races" whose alleged hereditary low intelligence and propensity for drunkenness and crime so endangered the public good that Congress imposed immigration quotas on them.

. . .

Over the years, formal racial definitions of white and black each have encompassed the entire spectrum of skin color, changing in every other U.S. census since the Civil War. The U.S. Office of Management and Budget is revising them again [in 1995].

. . .

Depending on the era, American officials classified Chinese immigrants—but not Japanese—as "colored." Armenians were classified as white in some decades, but not in others. People of Mexican ancestry were first classified as a separate race, then as white, and today as Hispanic. To compound the racial confusion, children of mixed ancestry who were considered legally white in one state often were considered legally black in another.

. . .

Ethnic studies experts say the fickle racial status of immigrants from India underscores the absence of any accepted scientific or biological definition of race. In a series of court rulings and administrative decisions since the 1920s, the racial status of Indian immigrants has gone from "Hindu"—a religious designation used as a racial label—to Caucasian, to nonwhite, to white—and then most recently to "Asian Indian," so Indian immigrants and their descendants could qualify legally for minority status. The label is likely to change again before the next U.S. census.

"You can be born one race," said Michael Omi, an ethnic studies expert at UC Berkeley, "and die another."

CULTURAL ELEMENTS

To begin to understand a culture, you need to understand all the experiences that guide its individual members through life, such things as language and gestures; personal appearance and social relationships; religion, philosophy, and values; courtship, marriage, and family customs; food and recreation; work and government; education and communication systems; health, transportation, and government systems; and economic systems. Think of culture as everything you would need to know and do so as not to stand out as a "stranger" in a foreign land. Culture is not a genetic trait. All these cultural elements are learned through interaction with others in the culture (see Box 1.2).

Box 1.2

PERSONALIZING THE CONCEPT

Let's try to develop a personal feeling for what is meant by the term *culture*. I'm going to assume you have a sister, brother, or very close childhood friend. I'd like you to think back to your relationship with that sibling or friend. Probably, you remember how natural and spontaneous your relationship was. Your worlds of experience were so similar; you shared problems and pleasures; you disagreed and even fought, but that didn't mean you couldn't put that behind you because you both knew in some way that you belonged together.

Now let's imagine that your sibling or friend had to leave you for an extended period of time. Perhaps your sister studied abroad for a year or your brother entered the military and served overseas. For some period of time, you were separated.

Time brought you back together again, but you recognized that your relationship had forever changed because of the different experiences you had had during that separation. You still had years of common experiences and memories to reinforce your relationship, but sometimes differences cropped up from your time apart—small differences, but differences nonetheless—that led you both to know that you were more separate than you had been before.

During the time your sister studied abroad she likely acquired new vocabulary, new tastes, and new ideas about values. She uses a foreign-sounding word in casual conversation; she now enjoys fast food or hates packaged food; she now has strong feelings about politics. Of course, these are small things, but they somehow remind you that you don't share as much as you had in the past.

During the time of your separation each of you had different experiences and challenges and had somehow been changed by those experiences and challenges. In a very simple way, this experience can be the beginning point of understanding what is meant today by the term culture. Even so, it illustrates only one aspect of the word's definition—shared experiences.

Canada has modified its currency with raised dots for the subgroup of persons with visual disabilities.

Table 1.2   Currency Exchange Rates

Country	Unit	Equivalent to US $1.00			
		As of August 1994	As of August 1997	As of August 2000	As of August 2002
Australia	Dollar	1.3504	1.3430	1.760	1.837
Canada	Dollar	1.3795	1.3814	1.482	1.556
Colombia	Peso	812.57	1107.50	1957.89	2712.90
Denmark	Krone	6.1000	6.9985	8.2169	7.639
France	Franc	5.3175	6.1940	7.2273	a
Germany	Deutsche Mark	1.5508	1.8366	2.1549	a
Greece	Drachma	234.70	286.85	371.33	a
Hong Kong	Dollar	7.7273	7.7440	7.8003	7.800
Ireland	Punt	.6566	.6858	.8677	a
Italy	Lira	1590.00	1790.00	2133.3	a
Japan	Yen	100.11	118.43	108.67	119.72
Mexico	Peso	3.3968	7.790.00	9.3196	9.827
Singapore	Dollar	1.5060	1.4645	1.7143	1.7585
South Korea	Won	804.30	892.00	1114.8	1205.29
Taiwan	Dollar	26.49	28.48	30.959	34.236
Thailand	Baht	25.04	31.65	40.816	42.280
Venezuela	Bolivar	188.0000	497.0000	689.65	1388.01
		As of January 1999	As of August 2000	As of August 2002	
Europe	Euro	1.167	1.1017	1.0298	

NOTE: Consult the business section of large daily newspapers or the Internet for rates the day you read this chapter. Use key words such as "currency exchange" or "currency calculator." Values changed in the 8-year period shown in the table. Can you speculate as to possible reasons why?
a. Obsolete and no longer legal tender.

Culture, then, refers to the totality of a people's socially transmitted products of work and thought. Thus Irish culture refers to everything commonly thought of as Irish. All these elements are interrelated like a tangled root system. Pull on one, the others move. Change one, the others must change.

Throughout this text, two elements of culture are illustrated: monetary and postal systems. Look at each example as a way of learning more about its culture of origin. For instance, Table 1.2 lists some of the monetary units used in the world.

The euro: "It means there is no turning back from the path toward unification of our continent" (Helmut Kohl, former German chancellor).

On January 1, 2002, 300 million people in 12 Western European nations adopted the euro, the first common currency since the Roman Empire two millennia ago. New bills and coins replaced German marks, French francs, and other national moneys. The euro symbolizes a new European unity. No images of people or specific buildings appear in the designs for the new bank notes. Rather, anonymous architecture was designed to represent the countries' shared culture.

CULTURES WITHIN CULTURES

Now let's look at the definitions of the terms *subculture*, *co-culture*, and *subgroup* as attempts to identify groups that are cultures but that exist within another culture.

Subculture

Complex societies like the United States are made up of a large number of groups with which people identify and from which are derived distinctive values and norms and rules for behavior. These groups have been labeled subcultures. A **subculture** resembles a culture in that it usually encompasses a relatively large number of people and represents the accumulation of generations of human striving. However, subcultures have some important differences: They exist within dominant cultures and are often based on economic or social class, ethnicity, race, or geographic region.

Social Class

It can be argued that social class or socioeconomic status is a subculture (Brislin, 1988). *Social class* has traditionally been defined as a position in society's hierarchy based on income, education, occupation, and neighborhood. Gilbert and Kahl (1982) argue that in the United States the basis of social class is income and that other markers of social class follow from income level. For example, income determines to some extent whom you marry or choose as a lover, your career, and the neighborhood in which you are likely to live.

Kohn (1977) has shown that middle-class and working-class parents emphasize different values when raising children. Middle-class parents emphasize self-control, intellectual curiosity, and consideration for others. The desired outcome of self-direction and empathic understanding transfers easily to professional and managerial jobs that require intellectual curiosity and good social skills.

Working-class parents emphasize obedience, neatness, and good manners. Gilbert and Kahl (1982) argue that this leads to a concern with external standards, such as obedience to authority, acceptance of what other people think, and hesitancy in expressing desires to authority figures. These working-class concerns can be a detriment in schools, which emphasize largely verbal skills. The resulting learned behaviors transfer more directly to supervised wage labor jobs.

Although these observations are based on large numbers of students, they should not be interpreted to apply to one family. Working-class parents who encourage verbal skills through reading and conversation have children who are as successful in school. Although the United States does have social classes that have been shown to have different values, many people in the United States believe that these barriers of social class are easier to transcend in the United States than in other countries.

Ethnicity

Another basis for subcultures is *ethnicity*. The term ethnic group is like the term race in that its definition has changed with time. Its different definitions

Table 1.3   As part of a review of which race and ethnic categories to use in its job statistics, the U.S. Labor Department asked people nationwide in approximately 60,000 households how they prefer to be identified.

A. Percentage responses by people not identifying as Asian-American, American Indian, Black, Hispanic, or multiracial

White	61.7
Caucasian	16.5
European-American	2.4
Anglo	1.0
Some other term	2.0
No preference	16.5

B. Percentage responses by native tribespeople

American Indian	49.8
Native American	37.4
Alaskan Native	3.5
Some other term	3.7
No preference	5.7

SOURCE: U.S. Labor Department, reported in U.S. News & World Report, November 20, 1995, p. 28.

reflect a continuing social debate. **Ethnic group** can refer to a group of people of the same descent and heritage who share a common and distinctive culture passed on through generations (Zenner, 1996). For some, *tribes* would be a more understood term. In Afghanistan, for example, people identify by tribes—Tajiks and Pashtuns. According to some estimates, there are 5,000 ethnic groups in the world (Stavenhagen, 1986). Ethnic groups can exhibit such distinguishing features as language or accent, physical features, family names, customs, and religion. **Ethnic identity** refers to identification with and perceived acceptance into a group with shared heritage and culture (Collier & Thomas, 1988).

Just as definitions of words like *culture* have changed, the way words are written has changed. In U.S. English, ethnic groups are usually referred to in hyphenated terms, such as Italian-American. The hyphen gives the term a meaning of a separate group of people. Most style manuals today have dropped the use of the hyphen, as in Italian American, using Italian as an adjective giving the meaning of "Americans of Italian descent"—a change that puts the emphasis on what Americans share rather than on what makes groups different from one another. This text uses the hyphen to communicate the meaning of a culture within a culture.

What about ethnic groups, such as German-Americans, who are not commonly referred to by a hyphenated term? Does this mean these groups have lost ethnic identities in an assimilated U.S. nationality? Does this imply that the U.S. national identity is only composed of those assimilated groups? To determine what labels to use in its job statistics, the U.S. Labor Department asked people how they prefer to be identified. The results for those people who did not identify as Asian-American, American Indian, Black, Hispanic, or multiracial are shown in Table 1.3A. Very few people chose to use the term "European-American," which would indicate a culturally based identification. Most chose "White" or "Caucasian," which at best is a sociohistorical racial label. This text uses the word "White" in this same sense. The same survey noted that the label preferred by native tribes is American Indian (see Table 1.3B). In a 1977 resolution, the National Congress of American Indians and the National Tribal Chairmen's Association stated that in the absence of a specific tribal designation, the preferred term is American Indian and/or Alaska Native. This text uses that label as it is important to use the label the group itself prefers. (See Box 1.3 for the experience of the Maori of New Zealand—in New Zealand, for voting and land claims, one elects to be Maori.)

Box 1.3

THE MAORI OF NEW ZEALAND

The original inhabitants of what is today known as New Zealand were Polynesians who arrived in a series of migrations more than 1,000 years ago. They named the land Aorearoa, or land of the long white cloud. The original inhabitants' societies revolved around the *iwi* (tribe) or *hapu* (subtribe), which served to differentiate the many tribes of peoples. In 1642, the Dutch explorer Abel Janszoon Tasman sailed up the west coast and christened the land Niuew Zeeland after the Netherlands' province of Zeeland. Later, in 1769, Captain James Cook sailed around the islands and claimed the entire land for the British crown. It was only after the arrival of the Europeans that the term *Maori* was used to describe all the tribes on the land. Those labeled Maori do not necessarily regard themselves as a single people.

The history of the Maori parallels the decline of other indigenous peoples in colonized lands except for the signing of the Treaty of Waitangi in 1840 by more than 500 chiefs. The treaty was recorded in

(Continued)

Box 1.3, *Continued*

Maori and in English. Differences between the two versions caused considerable misunderstandings in later years. The Maori and the English may have had different understandings of the terms governance and sovereignty. In exchange for granting sovereignty to Great Britain, the Maori were promised full exclusive and undisturbed possession of their lands, forests, fisheries, and other properties and the same rights and privileges enjoyed by British subjects. The terms of the treaty were largely ignored as Maori land was appropriated as settlers arrived.

Activism in the late 1960s brought a renaissance of Maori languages, literature, arts, and culture and calls to address Maori land claims as the Treaty of Waitangi became the focus of grievances. In 1975, the government introduced the Waitangi Tribunal to investigate Maori land claims, which resulted in some return of Maori land. In 1994, the government proposed to settle all Maori land claims for $1 billion—a very small percentage of current value.

Today, New Zealand's population by descent is approximately 13% Maori and 78% Pakeha (European). New Zealand is governed under a parliamentary democracy system loosely modeled on that of Great Britain except that there are two separate electoral rolls: one for the election of general members of parliament and one for the election of a small number of Maori members of parliament. Pakeha can enroll on the general roll only; people who consider themselves Maori must choose which one of the two rolls they wish to be on.

The following article appeared in an August 1999 edition of the newspaper *The Dominion*.

WHAT MAKES A MAORI?

The definition of "Maori" for voting purposes . . . is entirely one of self-definition.

The 1956 Electoral Act defined a Maori as "a person belonging to the aboriginal race of New Zealand, and includes a half-caste and a person intermediate in blood between half-castes and persons of pure descent from that race."

In 1975, the Labour government, prompted by then Maori affairs minister Matiu Rata, rewrote the act to define a Maori as "a person of the Maori race of New Zealand, and includes any descendant of such a person who elects to be considered as a Maori for the purposes of this act." Such a person could choose either the Maori roll or the general roll. So, if you are descended from a Maori, then you are Maori and can choose to vote on the Maori roll.

Nigel Roberts, head of Victoria University's School of Political Science and International Relations, says such self-identification is appropriate: "I think that ethnicity is very largely, in the late 20th century, a matter of identification—it is a cultural matter. The world has moved on from classifying people by blood, which was a meaningless definition."

What about Treaty of Waitangi settlements? How does one prove entitlement to the land, fisheries quota, shares, and cash that are being returned to Maoris in compensation for successive Crown breaches?

The definition is different again—and more stringently enforced.

The South Island's Ngai Tahu iwi was awarded $170 million compensation [in 1998] after a gruelling process of Waitangi Tribunal hearings, mandating, and negotiations.

Ngai Tahu *whakapapa* (genealogy) unit spokeswoman Tarlin Prendergast says the iwi is in the fortunate position of having good records from an 1848 census of Ngai Tahu members, just before the Crown's purchase of South Island land.

And in 1920, a group of *kaumatua* had travelled around Ngai Tahu settlements recording the whakapapa of families. "Anyone who is Ngai Tahu must be able to show their lines of descent from a kaumatua alive in 1848.

"That is the basis of our tribal membership," she says.

"It is up to the individuals to align themselves with the *runanga* (area council) that they say they come from and to keep alive their connections. We call it *ahi kaa*—keeping the home fires burning."

SOURCE: Jonathan Milne, "What Makes a Maori?" *The Dominion*, August 6, 1999, p. 9. Reprinted with permission.

That ethnic identity can be the basis of a cultural identity and affect communication with others outside that group has been demonstrated by Taylor, Dubé, and Bellerose (1986). In one study of English and French speakers in Quebec, they found that although interactions between ethnically dissimilar people were perceived to be as agreeable as those between similar people those same encounters were judged less important and less intimate. The researchers concluded that to ensure that interethnic contacts were harmonious, the communicators in their study limited the interactions to relatively superficial encounters.

Co-Culture

Definition

Whereas some define subculture as meaning "a part of the whole," in the same sense that a subdivision is part of—but no less important than—the whole city, other scholars reject the use of the prefix "sub" as applied to the term culture because it seems to imply being under or beneath and being inferior or secondary. As an alternative, the word **co-culture** is suggested to convey the idea that no one culture is inherently superior to other coexisting cultures (Orbe, 1998).

However, mutuality may not be easily established. Assume the case of a homogeneous culture. One of the many elements of a culture is its system of laws. The system of laws in our hypothetical homogeneous culture, then, was derived from and reflects the values of that culture. Now assume immigration of another cultural group into the hypothetical culture. New immigrants may have different understandings of legal theory and the rights and responsibilities that individuals should have in a legal system.

Those understandings may conflict in some ways with the established legal system.

Case Study: American Indians

Can one nation have two legal systems? Can two legal systems coexist equally? There are 309 distinct nations existing by treaty within the territorial limits of the United States. One is the government in Washington, D.C. The remaining 308 are American Indian nations that enjoy some areas of complete sovereignty and some areas of limited sovereignty. By treaty the American Indian nations have their own territory, governmental structure, and laws; collect their own taxes; and are protected by U.S. federal law in the practice of their culture and religion (Dudley & Agard, 1993). The American Indian Religious Freedom Act of 1978 proclaimed "to protect and preserve for American Indians their inherent right to believe, express and exercise the traditional religions."

Recent Supreme Court decisions, however, have negated this law. In 1988 in *Lyng v. Northwest Indian Cemetery Protection Association*, the Supreme Court held that the U.S. Forest Service could build a road through an area sacred to three Indian tribes. And in 1990 in *Employment Division of Oregon v. Smith*, the Court held that the state could deny unemployment benefits to two men fired from their jobs because they ingested peyote as part of their religion.

The *Smith* decision has now been cited in cases involving a Sikh's wearing a turban on the job, a Hmong couple's protesting their son's autopsy, and an Amish man's refusal to post traffic signs.

Nations adopt one system of laws, and that system reflects the cultural values of one culture. But when one is surrounded by a more powerful culture, or exists within the culture of the other, the less powerful culture must accept the laws and legal system of the other, thus subordinating any other understanding of legal systems. At least in this one way the groups are not mutually powerful.

Inaccuracy of the Term

The case of American Indians supports the argument that the term co-culture does not accurately reflect reality in the United States. Just as the term subculture has undesired consequences, so too does co-culture.

In an attempt to avoid misunderstandings, this text avoids using either word. Instead, as much as possible the phrase "cultures within cultures" is used throughout to more accurately represent the reality of contemporary U.S. life.

Subgroup

Definition

Finally, you need to know the concept of **subgroup**, or membership group. Psychologists have long recognized that membership groups have an important influence on the values and attitudes you hold. Like cultures, subgroups provide members with relatively complete sets of values and patterns of behavior and in many ways pose similar communication problems as cultures.

Subgroups exist within a dominant culture and are dependent on that culture. One important subgroup category is occupation. Think of large organizations and of occupations in which most people dress alike, share a common vocabulary and similar values, and are in frequent communication as through magazines and newsletters. These subgroups include nurses and doctors, police officers, and employees of large organizations such as Eastman Kodak and IBM.

Subgroups usually do not involve the same large number of people as cultures and are not necessarily thought of as accumulating values and patterns of behavior over generations in the same way as cultures do.

"Deviant" Label

The term subgroup has at times been unfortunately linked to the word *deviant*. Actually, however, deviant simply means differing from the cultural norm, such as vegetarians in a meat-eating society. Unfortunately, in normal discourse most people associate deviance with undesirable activities. To understand what is meant by subgroups, it is important that you recognize that vegetarians are as deviant as prostitutes—both groups deviate from the norm and both are considered subgroups.

Temporality

Membership in some subgroups is temporary; that is, members may participate for a time and later become inactive or separate from it altogether. For example, there are organizations devoted to Ford cars and trucks. Some people are preoccupied with that for a while and then lose interest and hence relinquish membership in the group. Membership in other subgroups may be longer lasting. One person may be a firefighter for life and another gay.

However, it is a mistake to think of membership in a culture or subgroup as being so exclusive that it precludes participation in other groups. All of us are and have been members of a variety of subgroups. Think of times in your life when you were preoccupied with the concerns of a certain group. At those times, you were a subgroup member. Examples range from Girl Scouts to Alcoholics Anonymous to youth gangs to religious cults to the military.

"Wanna-Be" Behavior

Recognize, too, that individuals can adhere to values and attitudes and behaviors of groups of which they are not a member. The term **reference group** refers to any group to which one aspires to attain membership (Sherif & Sherif, 1953). This behavior is identified in contemporary slang as the "wanna-be," an individual who imitates the behavior of a group he or she desires to belong to. Some people dress like and talk like gang members but are not members of any gang.

RULES AND NORMS

Definition

Every culture and subgroup provides its members with rules of behavior, or what are called rules and norms. **Rules** may refer to socially agreed-on behavior or to individual guidelines for behavior. **Norms** specify appropriate and inappropriate behavior. Travel guides (see, e.g., Braganti & Devine, 1984; DeMente, 1986, 1989) prepare you for a trip by telling you how things are done in the country you're visiting. Individuals are rewarded or punished as they conform to or deviate from the norms. Indeed, the extent to which a person is a member of a culture or subgroup is often gauged by his or her adherence to norms. In communication studies, it is assumed that behavior is governed by socially agreed-on norms or by one's individual guidelines for behavior.

Case Study: The Military

Earlier, this chapter identified the military as a subgroup. An excerpt from the Army's *Drill and Ceremonies* (see Box 1.4) provides an example of a subgroup norm. Notice how complete and detailed the description is.

Box 1.4

NORMS IN THE ARMY: SALUTES

The origin of the hand salute is uncertain. Some historians believe it began in late Roman times when assassinations were common. A citizen who wanted to see a public official had to approach with his right hand raised to show that he did not hold a weapon. Knights in armor raised visors with the right hand when meeting a comrade. The practice gradually became a way of showing respect and, in early American history, sometimes involved removing the hat. By 1820, the motion was modified to touching the hat, and since then it has become the hand salute used today.

Army personnel in uniform are required to salute when they meet and recognize persons entitled (by grade) to salute except when it is

(Continued)

Box 1.4, *Continued*

inappropriate or impractical (in public conveyances such as planes and buses, in public places such as inside theaters, or when driving a vehicle). A salute is also rendered:

- When the United States National Anthem, "To the Color," "Hail to the Chief," or foreign national anthems are played.

- To uncased National Color outdoors.

- On ceremonial occasions [such as reviews and funerals].

- At reveille and retreat ceremonies, during the raising or lowering of the flag.

- During the sounding of honors.

- When pledging allegiance to the U.S. flag outdoors.

- When turning over control of formations.

- When rendering reports.

- To officers of friendly foreign countries.

SOURCE: *Drill and Ceremonies*, FM 22-5, Headquarters, Department of the Army, 1986, p. A-1.

The student body at your college might be considered a subgroup and, as such, has rules of behavior. How well have you learned them? How does being a successful member of the student body involve knowing and complying with norms?

Superstitions

Some cultural customs are often labeled as superstitions. They are the practices believed to influence the course of events. Whether it is rubbing a rabbit's foot for luck or not numbering the 13th floor in a building, they are part of one's cultural identification. We may not follow them, but we recognize them.

The most important of all military norms is the salute.

SOURCE: Department of Defense, 1999.

For example, in Mexican *pulquerias*, saloons where people gather to drink *pulque*, a distillate of cactus, it is considered good fortune to get the worm in your cup.

In Japan, you may see a *maneki neko*, or "beckoning cat" figurine with its front paw raised. The beckoning gesture brings customers into stores and good luck and fortune into homes.

In China, sounds and figures reflect good fortune. The phonetic sound of eight, *baat* in Cantonese and between *pa* and *ba* in Mandarin, is similar to *faat,* meaning prosperity. The number 8, then, is the most fortuitous of numbers portending prosperity.

In Hong Kong, a license plate with the number 8 is quite valuable. But the number 4 can be read as *shi*, which is a homophone for death, so hospitals may not have a Room 4.

Even subgroups can develop shared superstitions. Athletic teams might wear a "winning jersey." Norms and superstitions are only a small part of culture but certainly an interesting part.

FROM THE INTERCULTURAL PERSPECTIVE

Many of us take our culture for granted. The only time that we may ever think about it is when we leave our own country to travel abroad or when we encounter someone with a culture so different from ours that we are forced to examine our own beliefs. Much of what we think is the "right" or "correct" way to act or to do something is actually part of the knowledge that we have learned from our culture. In other words, our culture teaches us rules or norms that tell us how to behave inside our culture. The word *culture* describes everything that makes a large group of people unique. Members of a culture share similar thoughts and experiences. One's culture is part of one's identity and is taught to one's children. Culture also includes all the things that guide a group of people through life, such as myths, language and gestures, ways of communicating, economic systems, what kinds of things to eat, and how to dress.

People identify with being a member of a group. Being a member of a group helps to define who we are. We all are members of groups of different sizes. One of the largest groups that a person can belong to is a culture. Everyone belongs to a culture. No one chooses which culture to belong to. We simply are born into one.

Other groups that people may be a member of are subcultures (sometimes called co-cultures) and subgroups. Subcultures can be based on race, ethnicity, economic or social class, or geographic region. Some people think of race as a group of people descended from the same ancestors. Another definition of race is that it is sociohistorical in that it recognizes how categories of race have changed over time and how different cultures have different racial categories. Because of how the words used to identify people by race have changed, people can be born one race and die another. *Ethnicity* is a word that describes the shared descent or heritage of a group of people. Groups of people with the same ethnicity share the same cultural traits like language, religion, and customs that are passed on to the children. In very homogeneous cultures where there is little difference in race or ethnicity, people might identify with groups that have about the same degree of wealth or that live in the same area as they do.

Subgroups also help define who we are. Subgroups can be as small as a few people or as large as a major religion. For example, a high school student might identify with being a member of the football team or drama club, or a person might identify with being a Christian, a Buddhist, or a Jew. People can be members of many different groups at the same time, so a person might identify with being a Christian, a football player, and a member of the drama club. Subgroups also provide their members with norms that tell people how to behave and even think. So, for instance, a Christian cannot be a Buddhist because Christians have rules that tell them they cannot be members of a different religion. People often make friendships based on their memberships in subgroups.

Business and politics constantly bring people of different cultural groups into contact with each other. Immigration is also a factor that continues to bring different cultures together. Knowledge of the norms of different cultures can help people to better communicate across cultures. It is possible through immigration and marriage to have members of the same family be members of different cultures. One day, your intercultural communication skills might even help you to talk with your in-laws.

KEY TERMS

co-culture	heroes	rules
cultural identity	myths	subculture
culture	norms	subgroup
ethnic group	race	symbols
ethnic identity	reference group	values
globalization	rituals	words

CHAPTER 2

Defining Communication as an Element of Culture

How definitions of communication reflect culture by comparing Western models to a Confucian understanding

What distinguishes intercultural communication from other forms of communication

Applications of ethical systems to intercultural interactions

The skills that make you competent in intercultural communication

You've probably heard many different definitions of the English word **communication**. If you look the word up in a dictionary such as the unabridged edition of the *Random House Dictionary of the English Language*, you'd find that communication is derived from the Latin *communicare*, meaning to share with or to make common, as in giving to another a part or share of your thoughts, hopes, and knowledge. In this chapter, you'll discover that even how communication is defined and used varies by culture.

In Chapter 1, you read how the definitions of the words *culture, race, subculture, ethnicity, co-culture,* and *subgroup* change through continuing social debate. In this chapter, you'll learn how communication itself is a cultural element by studying different models of communication. You'll also learn about the different ways communication and culture are studied and about the skills required to become more effective in intercultural communication.

Because communication is an element of culture, it has often been said that communication and culture are inseparable. As Alfred G. Smith (1966) wrote in his preface to *Communication and Culture*, culture is a code we learn and share, and learning and sharing require communication. Communication requires coding and symbols that must be learned and shared. Godwin C. Chu (1977) observed that every cultural pattern and every single act of social behavior involve communication. To be understood, the two must be studied together. Culture cannot be known without a study of communication, and communication can only be understood with an understanding of the culture it supports.

WESTERN DEFINITIONS OF COMMUNICATION

Origins

The study of communication in Western culture has a recorded history of some 2,500 years and is said to have begun in Greece with Aristotle's *Rhetoric and Poetics*, which described the process of communication as involving a speaker, the speech act, an audience, and a purpose. Study has continued through Roman rhetorical theory, continental traditions, and two centuries in the United States.

Transmission Models

In the United States, the Aristotelian description of communication was adapted by the behavioral sciences to the study of communication in applied settings. Communication was studied as the means of transmitting ideas. For example, agricultural scientists wanted more effective ways of communicating new agricultural technologies to farmers, and the U.S. government wanted effective ways of communicating health information to the peoples of developing countries. The conceptualization of communication at this time could be labeled machinelike or mechanistic. Communication was conceptualized as one-way, top-down, and suited for the transmission media of print, telephones, radio, and television.

Western transmission models emphasized the instrumental function of communication; that is, effectiveness was evaluated in terms of success in the manipulation of others to achieve one's personal goal. One example of this approach is David Berlo's (1960) *The Process of Communication*. Berlo,

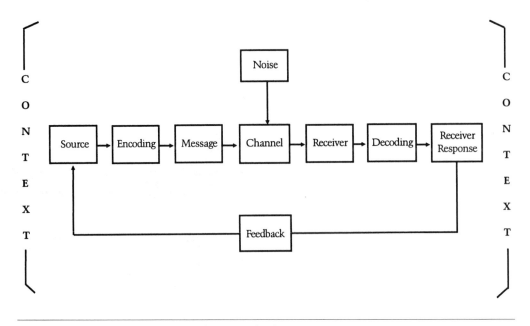

Figure 2.1   Ten components of communication.

though, emphasized that communication is a dynamic process, as the variables in the process are interrelated and influence each other. Berlo didn't see audiences as passive; their actions affected the process.

Components of Communication

Because the transmission models of communication clearly identified components in the communication process, they are particularly useful in beginning a study of communication. You are better able to understand communication when you understand the components of the process (DeVito, 1986). The components of communication, shown in Figure 2.1, are source, encoding, message, channel, noise, receiver, decoding, receiver response, feedback, and context.

Source. The **source** is the person with an idea he or she desires to communicate. Examples are CBS, the White House, your instructor, and your mother.

Encoding. Unfortunately (or perhaps fortunately), humans are not able to share thoughts directly. Your communication is in the form of a symbol representing the idea you desire to communicate. **Encoding** is the process of putting an idea into a symbol.

The symbols into which you encode your thoughts vary. You can encode thoughts into words, and you can also encode thoughts into nonspoken symbols. Tobin and Dobard (1999), for example, have shown how messages were encoded in quilts made by slaves.

Message. The term **message** identifies the encoded thought. Encoding is the process, the verb; the message is the resulting object.

Channel. The term **channel** is used technically to refer to the means by which the encoded message is transmitted. Today, you might feel more comfortable using the word *media*. The channel or medium, then, may be print, electronic, or the light and sound waves of face-to-face communication.

Noise. The term **noise** technically refers to anything that distorts the message the source encodes. Noise can be of many forms:

- External noise can be the sights, sounds, and other stimuli that draw your attention away from the message. Having a radio on while reading is external noise.

- Internal noise refers to your thoughts and feelings that can interfere with the message. For example, being tired or being hungry can distract you from paying complete attention to the message.

- "Semantic noise" refers to how alternative meanings of the source's message symbols can be distracting. For example, a speaker's use of uncalled-for profanity can cause us to wonder why the speaker used profanity and draw attention away from the message itself.

Series of French stamps commemorates *la communication*.

The uniqueness of men—the superiority of men in the world of animals—lies not in his ability to perceive ideas, but to perceive that he perceives, and to transfer his perceptions to others' minds through words.

—Albert Einstein

Receiver. The **receiver** is the person who attends to the message. Receivers may be intentional; that is, they may be the people the source desired to communicate with, or they may be any person who comes upon and attends to the message.

Decoding. **Decoding** is the opposite process of encoding and just as much an active process. The receiver is actively involved in the communication process by assigning meaning to the symbols received.

Receiver response. **Receiver response** refers to anything the receiver does after having attended to and decoded the message. That response can range from doing nothing to taking some action or actions that may or may not be the action desired by the source (see Box 2.1).

Box 2.1

COMPONENTS IN ACTION

Let's use this textbook as an example of the first eight components of communication. As the author of the text, I am the source; I have ideas about intercultural communication I want to communicate. My selecting the words, figures, and pictures to communicate my ideas is encoding. The message is those words, figures, and pictures before you. The channel is the print medium of a book. You are the receiver who decodes as you read. Your decoding might be affected by the noise around you or competing thoughts and feelings. Your responses as the receiver might include highlighting sections for later study and discussing the material with classmates.

These eight components can be conceptualized as a linear model. Communication seems to start with the source and end with a receiver response. These eight components alone describe communication as a one-way process. And much of communication is a one-way process: Some communicators can have no knowledge of the receiver's response. The author of a text may not get information back from readers. A guest on a radio interview show may have no knowledge of audience response.

Feedback. **Feedback** refers to that portion of the receiver response of which the source has knowledge and to which the source attends and assigns meaning. A reader of this text may have many responses, but only when the reader responds to a survey or writes a letter to the author does feedback occur. When a radio interview show host receives enthusiastic telephone calls and invites a guest back, feedback has occurred.

Feedback makes communication a two-way or interactive process. Linear and interactive models seem to suggest that communication is an isolated single discrete act independent of events that preceded or might follow it.

Context. The final component of communication is **context.** Generally, context can be defined as the environment in which the communication takes place and which helps define the communication. If you know the physical context, you can predict with a high degree of accuracy much of the communication. For example, you have certain knowledge and expectations of the communication that occurs within synagogues, mosques, and churches. At times, you intentionally plan a certain physical environment for your communication: You may want to locate your romantic communications in a quiet, dimly lit restaurant or on a secluded beach. The choice of the environment, the context, helps assign the desired meaning to the communicated words.

In social relationships as well, the relationship between the source and receiver may help define much of the meaning of the communication. Again, if you know the context you can predict with a high degree of accuracy much of the communication. For example, knowing that a person is being stopped by a police officer for speeding is enough to predict much of the communication. Certain things are likely to be said and done; other things are very unlikely.

Culture is also context. Every culture has its own worldview; its own way of thinking of activity, time, and human nature; its own way of perceiving self; and its own system of social organization. Knowing each of these helps you assign meaning to the symbols.

The component of context helps you recognize that the extent to which the source and receiver have similar meanings for the communicated symbols and similar understandings of the culture in which the communication takes place are critical to the success of the communication.

Humanistic Models

Other models of communication emphasize a humanistic approach to understanding communication. A transactional model of communication, for example, shows that, in addition to sending and receiving messages simultaneously, communicators take their relationship into account. Recognizing that communication is transactional allows us to understand, for example, that the source can know the intended receiver well enough to incorporate that personal knowledge into the encoding of the message. A transactional understanding of communication helps us recognize that the exact same words can be spoken to diverse people with different meanings.

You have probably had instructors who were one-way communicators, others who were two-way communicators, and others who were transactional communicators. A guest lecturer who reads a prepared text and accepts no questions is a one-way communicator. An instructor who uses information from examinations to adapt lessons and who responds to questions by elaborating on content is a two-way communicator. An instructor who refers to the experiences of specific members of the class to explain concepts is a transactional communicator.

Every textbook on communication, it seems, has its own definition. This seeming lack of agreement reflects the fact that many different approaches are taken to the study of communication (Fisher, 1978), and each approach emphasizes different aspects. If you desire one definition that emphasizes that communication is intentional, symbolic, and involves at least two people, you might say that communication occurs when symbols are manipulated by one person to stimulate meaning in another person (Infante, Rancer, & Womack, 1993).

OTHER DEFINITIONS OF COMMUNICATION

Superior and Subordinate Roles

Some critics within the United States recognized that the way communication was defined reflected important cultural values. For example, semanticist S. I. Hayakawa (1978) noted that decoding—or listening—seems to give the receiver a subordinate role to the source. When someone speaks, others stop what they are doing to listen. Therefore, it would seem that the source is viewed as more active and as more important in the process. Hayakawa's observation makes it clear that cultural beliefs affect how the process of communication is defined.

The transmission models can lead you to think of communication as consisting of an active source and a passive receiver. Speaking may be considered a more noble activity and may demand that others cease other activities to listen. Indeed, in many cultures, listening does place one in a subordinate role to that of the source. In other cultures, where the group's history and knowledge is told and retold verbally, the role of the listener who accurately remembers is critically important.

The story is told that the Puritans, believing to have been called to save heathens, preached to the American Indians. The Indians affirmed conversions to Christianity to the delight of the early settlers. Then the Indians told the Puritans the Indian story of creation and asked the settlers to affirm it. The Indian communication style was not to disagree but to listen and affirm. The Puritans were disappointed that communication, in the Western understanding of communication, had failed. In the American Indian understanding of communication, it had not.

That other cultures define communication in diverse ways demonstrates that communication is an element of culture (Krippendorff, 1993). For example, defining communication from a Confucian perspective emphasizes other uses.

Confucianism

Definitions of communication from many Asian countries stress harmony (Chen & Starosta, 1996). This is most notable in cultures with a Confucian tradition.

The Chinese scholar K'ung-Fu-tzu, a title the Jesuits later Latinized as Confucius (550-478 B.C.E.[1]), lived in a time when the feudal system in China was collapsing. Confucius proposed a government based less on heredity than on morality and merit.

Societies heavily influenced today by Confucian history or tradition are China, North and South Korea, Singapore, and many East Asian countries with large Chinese communities.

Confucius set up an ethical-moral system intended ideally to govern all relationships in the family, community, and state. Confucius taught that society was made up of five relationships: those between ruler and subjects (the relation of righteousness), husband and wife (chaste conduct), father and son (love), elder brother and younger brother (order), and friend and friend (faithfulness).

Three of these five bases of relations occur within the family. The regulating factors in family relationships are extended to the whole community and state. The chief virtue is filial piety, a combination of loyalty and reverence, which demands that the son honor and respect his father and fulfill the demands of his elders.

Confucianism emphasizes virtue, selflessness, duty, patriotism, hard work, and respect for hierarchy, both familial and societal. Just as George Washington and the story of the cherry tree is used in the United States to teach the value of honesty, Confucianism reinforces its lessons about people who represent particular virtues. For example, Chinese children learn about such heroes as Mu Lan, a woman of the 6th century who disguised herself as a man and served 12 years as a soldier so that her ill father would not be disgraced or punished because he could not report for military duty. Mu Lan teaches courage and filial devotion.

Confucianism guides social relationships: "To live in harmony with the universe and with your fellow man through proper behavior." Confucianism considers balance and harmony in human relationships to be the basis of society. June Yum (1988) describes five effects that Confucianism has on interpersonal communication:

1. *Particularism.* There is no universal pattern of rules governing relationships: There are no rules governing interaction with someone whose status is unknown. Instead of applying the same rule to everyone, such factors as status, intimacy, and context create different communication rules for diverse people. In fact, there are several patterns guiding interaction with others whose status is known. In the Confucian country of Korea, it is quite common for strangers to find out each other's age in the first few minutes of conversation and adjust their language to show respect. Koreans are friends (*chingu*) only with those whose age is within a few years of their own. If a male acquaintance is older than this "friendship age range," he must be addressed as *adjussi* and if female as *adjumoni*—terms that equate roughly to "uncle" and "aunt," respectively.

2. *Role of intermediaries.* Rituals should be followed in establishing relationships. In China, it is not unusual to use a third party to negotiate with future in-laws about wedding plans and, in general, to use a third party to avoid direct confrontations and resolve disputes (Gao & Ting-Toomey, 1998).

3. *Reciprocity.* Complementary obligations are the base of relationships. Gratitude and indebtedness are important parts of Chinese culture. For example, a person feels uneasy to be indebted to someone and payback is necessary to achieve balance in the relationship. Reciprocity is the basic rule of interpersonal relationships (Gao & Ting-Toomey, 1998). Obligations in relationships are contrary to Western ideas of individualism.

4. *Ingroup/outgroup distinction.* Scollon and Scollon (1991) argue that the distinction between inside and outside influences every aspect of Chinese culture. **Ingroup** members engage in freer and deeper talk and may find it difficult to develop personal relationships with outgroup members (Gao & Ting-Toomey, 1998). There can even be different language codes for ingroup members.

5. *Overlap of personal and public relationships.* Business and pleasure are mixed. Frequent contacts lead to common experiences. This contrasts with Western patterns of keeping public and private lives separate. There are several Chinese terms for the English word *communication* including *jiao liu* (to exchange), *chuan bo* (to disseminate), and *gou tong* (to connect among people). The Chinese term *he* denotes harmony, peace, unity, and kindness. Seeking harmony with family and others is the goal of communication in Chinese culture (Gao & Ting-Toomey, 1998).

As a consequence of the value placed on balance and social harmony, Chang and Holt (1991) explain how the Chinese have developed many verbal strategies such as compliments, greeting rituals, and so on to maintain good interpersonal relations. Fong (2000), for example, has described the "luck talk" (speech acts related to luck) during the celebration of the Chinese New Year.

Korea adopted Confucianism as a state religion for six centuries. Yum (1987) explains how the Korean language easily accommodates the Confucian rules of relationships. A grammatical form of direct address, called an **honorific**, for example, shows respect. English speakers might vary in how they ask a child, a friend, or a grandparent to sit by using a sentence, whereas Korean speakers would use different forms of the root *ahnta*, meaning to sit or to take a seat:

To a child, younger person, or person of lower rank (informal)	*ahnjo* or *ahnjara*
To a friend or person of equal rank (polite)	*ahnjuseyo*
To an elder, person of higher rank, or honored person (more polite)	*ahnjushipshio*

Korean has special vocabularies for each sex, for different degrees of social status and degrees of intimacy, and for formal occasions. When two people are introduced, they first engage in small talk to determine each other's social position in order to know who should use common language and who should use honorific language. And ironically because Confucianism does not consider relationships with strangers, Koreans are said to ignore—often to the point that some would consider rude—anyone to whom they have not been introduced. In modern Korea, a generation gap exists: Junior business associates may address seniors with familiar rather than honorific language.

The collectivist values of Confucianism mandate a style of communication in which respecting the relationship through communication is more important than the information exchanged. Group harmony, avoidance of loss of face to others and oneself, and a modest presentation of oneself are means of respecting the relationship. One does not say what one actually thinks when it might hurt others in the group.

In some sense, the same ethic can be found in business dealings. Much of commercial life in China is lubricated by *guanxi*, a concept best translated as "connections" or "personal relationships." Guanxi is an alternative to the legal trappings of Western capitalism in that business is cemented by the informal relationships of trust and mutual obligation. Sometimes viewed as bribery, guanxi is less like using professional lobbyists than relying on mutual friends among whom trust can be maintained.

Earlier, you read how communication was defined in the United States in a mechanistic way by components. A Confucian understanding would define communication as an infinite interpretive process where all parties are searching to develop and maintain a social relationship. Carey (1989) describes this as a ritual model of communication that "is directed not toward the extension of messages in space but toward the maintenance of society in time; not the act of imparting information but the representation of shared beliefs" (p. 18).

COMMUNICATION STUDIES APPROACHES

There are many different approaches to the study of communication and culture, among them international, global, cross-cultural, and intercultural.

International

International communication has been used to refer to the study of the flow of mediated communication between and among countries. It has also been used to refer to the study of comparative mass communication systems and to the study of communication between national governments.

Global

Global communication refers to the study of transborder transfer of information and data and opinions and values by groups, institutions, and governments and the issues that arise from the transfer (Frederick, 1993).

Cross-Cultural

Cross-cultural generally refers to comparing phenomena across cultures. Thus, a cross-cultural study of women's roles in society would compare what women actually do in diverse cultures.

Intercultural

Intercultural communication generally refers to face-to-face interactions among people of diverse cultures. Imagine how difficult communication can be if the source and receiver are in different contexts and share few symbols. That's one way of defining intercultural communication.

Origins

The formal study of intercultural communication in the United States originated in 1946 when Congress passed the Foreign Service Act, which established the Foreign Service Institute to provide language and anthropological cultural training for foreign diplomats. Outside the Foreign Service Institute, the study of intercultural communication is generally associated with the publication of Edward T. Hall's book *The Silent Language* in 1959. While associated with the Foreign Service Institute, Hall applied abstract anthropological concepts to the practical world of foreign service and extended the anthropological view of culture to include communication. Later in his popular book, Hall defined culture as basically a communication process (Leeds-Hurwitz, 1990). President John F. Kennedy's creation of the **Peace Corps** in the early 1960s increased interest in knowing more about how people of diverse cultures could communicate more effectively.

Applications of Communication Theories

The German sociologist Georg Simmel's (1858-1918) concepts of "the stranger" and "social distance" were precursors to Berger and Calabrese's (1975) uncertainty reduction theory (Rogers, 1999). This theory assumes that during the initial phase of interaction with another person your primary communication goal is to reduce your uncertainty about that person. Thus you are attempting to discover information about the other person and to share information about yourself. Gudykunst and his colleagues (see, e.g., Gudykunst, 1985) have applied this theory to intercultural communication.

Another communication approach focuses on the bipolarizing tendencies of language and research. Much of it focused on the concept of "the other." **Othering** refers to the labeling and degrading of cultures and groups outside of one's own (Riggins, 1997). Indigenous peoples, women, lesbians and gay men, and ethnic groups have been "othered" by other groups in language. One common way is to represent the Other as the binary opposite, for example, "Colonists were hard-working; natives were lazy" (Jandt & Tanno, 2001).

It seems as people create a category called "us," another category of "not-us" or "them" is created. The collective pronouns "us" and "them" become powerful influences on perception. The names given to "them" can be used to justify suppression and even extermination. Bosmajian (1983) calls this "the language of oppression." The Nazis labeled Jews "bacilli," "parasites," "disease," "demon," and "plague." Why do the words used to refer to "them" matter? It's because although killing another human being may be unthinkable, "exterminating a disease" is not. Segregation was justified when Blacks were considered "chattel" or property. The subjugation of American Indians was defensible when the word "savage" was used. And the words "chicks" and "babes" labeled women as inferior.

In this book you will find no reference to any group as "they" or "them," for it is my belief that doing so encourages you to continue thinking of "them" as different from, and in some way not as good as, "we."

We and They

Father, Mother, and Me,
Sister and Auntie say
All the people like us are We,
And everyone else is They.
And They live over the sea
While we live over the way,
But—would you believe it?
   — They look upon We
As only a sort of They!

We eat pork and beef
With cow-horn-handled knives.
They who gobble Their rice off a leaf

Are horrified out of Their lives;
While They who live up a tree,
Feast on grubs and clay,
(Isn't it scandalous?)
   look upon We
As a simple disgusting They!

We eat kitcheny food.
We have doors that latch.
They drink milk and blood
Under an open thatch. We have
   doctors to fee.
They have wizards to pay.

And (impudent heathen!) They look
　　upon We
As a quite impossible They!

All good people agree,
And all good people say,
All nice people, like us, are We

And everyone else is They:
But if you cross over
　　the sea,
Instead of over the way,
You may end by (think of it!)
　　looking on We
As only a sort of They!

—Rudyard Kipling

INTERCULTURAL COMMUNICATION ETHICS

As a branch of philosophy, ethics addresses the question of how we ought to lead our lives. Andersen (1991) makes clear that ethical theories tend to reflect the culture in which they were produced.

Major Ethical Theories

Western

May and Sharratt (1994) identify four values fundamental to Western ethics:

- *Autonomy.* Being free to act consistent with one's own principles

- *Justice.* Impartiality; giving each person his or her legitimate due or portion of the whole

- *Responsibility.* Accountability for the consequences of one's actions, including a failure to act

- *Care.* Partiality to those who cannot protect themselves and to whom we are in special relationships

Other ethical perspectives stress other values.

African

African ethics stress the well-being of the community and economic considerations over political rights. The well-being of the individual derives from the well-being of the community. As Menkiti (1984) wrote,

Rather, man is defined by reference to the environing community. . . . [T]he reality of the community takes precedence over the reality of individual life histories, whatever these may be. . . . [P]ersons become persons only after a process of incorporation. Without incorporation into this or that community, individuals are considered to be mere danglers, to whom the description "person" does not fully apply. (pp. 171-172)

Buddhist

The Buddhist ethical perspective is individualistic: "The ultimate responsibility for any act rests with the individual" (Beyer, 1974, p. 10). Value is placed on patience, compassion, self-sacrifice, kindness, and love, which are to be pursued for the betterment of the person if not in this life, then in the next. The emphasis on the next life and the rejection of the world as an illusion isolate the individual from family and society (Kim, 1975).

Hindu

Central to Indian Hindu perspectives is ending human suffering through active intervention in this world to make it better. Whereas Buddhism values patience and a passive approach, for Indian philosophers the path to take in ending suffering is as important as the ending of suffering (Sharma, 1965). Hinduism strives for the oneness of reality, for the obliteration of all distinctions including individualism, to merge with the absolute (Dissanayake, 1987).

Islamic

Traditional Islamic perspectives on ethics are based in its religious concepts. There are different rules of ethical conduct for women and for men. Non-Muslims are to be treated differently than Muslims. Islamic ethics, like some Hindu ethics, are highly activist and interventionist.

Ethics Across Cultures

What, though, guides the interactions of people from cultures with diverse ethical perspectives? Are there global values to guide intercultural interactions?

Kale (1997) argues that peace is the fundamental human value. The use of peace applies not only to relationships among countries but to "the right of all people to live at peace with themselves and their surroundings" (p. 450).

From this fundamental value, he developed four ethical principles to guide intercultural interactions:

- Ethical communicators address people of other cultures with the same respect that they would like to receive themselves. Intercultural communicators should not demean or belittle the cultural identity of others through verbal or nonverbal communication.

- Ethical communicators seek to describe the world as they perceive it as accurately as possible. What is perceived to be the truth may vary from one culture to another; truth is socially constructed. This principle means that ethical communicators do not deliberately mislead or deceive.

- Ethical communicators encourage people of other cultures to express themselves in their uniqueness. This principle respects the right of people to expression regardless of how popular or unpopular their ideas may be.

- Ethical communicators strive for identification with people of other cultures. Intercultural communicators should emphasize the commonalities of cultural beliefs and values rather than their differences.

Developing ethical principles to guide intercultural interactions is a difficult task. Even though Kale's principles may be more acceptable in some cultures than in others, they are certainly a beginning step.

INTERCULTURAL COMMUNICATION COMPETENCE

Effective intercultural communication involves more than understanding a group's norms. There have been many attempts to identify the skills needed to be more effective in intercultural communication.

Business Approach

One group concerned with the success of individuals abroad is international business. Mendenhall and Oddou (1985), for example, identify three skill areas:

- Skills related to the maintenance of self (mental health, psychological well-being, stress reduction, feelings of self-confidence)

- Skills related to the fostering of relationships with host nationals
- Cognitive skills that promote a correct perception of the host environment and its social systems

Military Approach

Another group concerned with the success of individuals overseas is the military. The United States Navy ("Overseas Diplomacy," 1979), for example, attempted to assess readiness to serve overseas. The Navy identified eight skills needed for success:

1. *Self-awareness*. Ability to use information about yourself in puzzling situations, to understand how others see you and use that information to cope with difficult situations

2. *Self-respect*. Self-confidence or due respect for yourself, your character, and your conduct

3. *Interaction*. How effectively you communicate with people

4. *Empathy*. Viewing things through another person's eyes or of being aware of other people's feelings

5. *Adaptability*. How fast you adjust to unfamiliar environments or to norms other than your own

6. *Certainty*. Ability to deal with situations that demand that you act in one way even though your feelings tell you something else; the greater your capacity to accept contradictory situations, the more you are able to deal with them

7. *Initiative*. Being open to new experiences

8. *Acceptance*. Tolerance or a willingness to accept things that vary from what you are familiar with

Communication Approach

Definitions of intercultural competence more grounded in communication have tended to stress the development of skills that transform one from a monocultural person into a multicultural person. The multicultural person is one who respects cultures and has tolerance for differences (Belay, 1993; Chen & Starosta, 1996). Chen (1989, 1990), for example, identifies four skill areas: personality strength, communication skills, psychological adjustment, and cultural awareness.

Personality Strength

The main personal traits that affect intercultural communication are self-concept, self-disclosure, self-monitoring, and social relaxation. Self-concept refers to the way in which a person views the self. Self-disclosure refers to willingness of individuals to openly and appropriately reveal information about themselves to their counterparts. Self-monitoring refers to using social comparison information to control and modify your self-presentation and expressive behavior. Social relaxation is the ability to reveal little anxiety in communication. Effective communicators must know themselves well and, through their self-awareness, initiate positive attitudes. Individuals must express a friendly personality to be competent in intercultural communication.

Communication Skills

Individuals must be competent in verbal and nonverbal behaviors. Intercultural communication skills require message skills, behavioral flexibility, interaction management, and social skills. Message skills refer to the ability to understand and use the language and feedback. Behavioral flexibility is the ability to select an appropriate behavior in diverse contexts. Interaction management means handling the procedural aspects of conversation, such as the ability to initiate a conversation. Interaction management emphasizes a person's other-oriented ability to interaction, such as attentiveness and responsiveness. Social skills are empathy and identity maintenance. Empathy is the ability to think the same thoughts and feel the same emotions as the other person. Identity maintenance is the ability to maintain a counterpart's identity by communicating back an accurate understanding of that person's identity. In other words, a competent communicator must be able to deal with diverse people in different situations.

Psychological Adjustment

Effective communicators must be able to acclimate to new environments. They must be able to handle the feelings of "culture shock," such as frustration, stress, and alienation in ambiguous situations caused by new environments.

Cultural Awareness

To be competent in intercultural communication, individuals must understand the social customs and social system of the host culture. Understanding how a people think and behave is essential for effective communication with them.

FROM THE INTERCULTURAL PERSPECTIVE

When communicating with people from different cultures, it is important to remember that culture and communication are strongly connected. The way that people view communication—what it is, how to do it, and reasons for doing it—is part of their culture. The chance of misunderstanding between members of different cultures increases when this important connection is forgotten.

In general, people from Western and Asian cultures have the greatest chance of misunderstanding each other. Much of this misunderstanding comes from the fact that Western and Asian cultures have two very different views of communication. Western cultures, especially the United States, give higher status to the speaker or "source" of information than to the "receiver," the person who pays attention to the information. The source encodes a message (information that the source wants to share with other people) by putting it into symbols (usually words or nonverbal gestures) and then sending it through a channel. A channel can be print media such as magazines and newspapers; electronic media such as television, radio, and the Internet; or sounds traveling through the air when two people speak face-to-face. Sometimes, things make it difficult for the message to reach the receiver. These things are called "noise." Noise can be physical (e.g., loud sound), emotional (e.g., strong feelings like sadness or anxiety), or biological (e.g., being hungry or sick). When receivers get the message, they must "decode" or try to understand it. For example, if the source encodes a message using English, the receivers must use their knowledge of the English language to understand it. Often, the source pays attention to the reactions of the receivers. This information or feedback from the receiver is called "receiver response."

Asian cultures view communication as communicators cooperating to make meaning. This model of communication reflects Confucian collectivist values because respecting the relationship through communication can be more important than the information exchanged.

In intercultural communication situations, it is natural for people to be aware of the potential for various misunderstandings and to want to avoid them. However, despite the best intentions, serious misunderstanding and even

At a bazaar in Iran you can find food, clothing, jewelry, electronics, currency exchange, and more. The experienced bargainer with effective use of spoken language and nonverbal communication can purchase items for half the original price.

SOURCE: Rasheed Irani. Used by permission.

conflicts can occur. One reason for this is that even though people are consciously attempting to avoid problems, they still are making ethical judgments as they are communicating. The values that people hold affect both their communication decisions and interpretation of what others communicate.

Western and Asian cultures often have the greatest misunderstandings when ethics are considered. For example, an Asian who had a Confucian view of communication would think it perfectly acceptable to give gifts to business associates and to hire one's own relatives. Both of these actions help maintain social relationships. However, people in the United States would consider these actions bribery and nepotism, both of which are against the law in the United States. So differing ethics can cause conflicts, especially when what one culture may consider morally wrong, another may actually encourage. When such conflicts occur, people who want to be ethical intercultural communicators should try to understand, respect, and accept each individual's ethical perspective.

Good intercultural communicators have personality strength (strong sense of self and are socially relaxed), communication skills (verbal and nonverbal), psychological adjustment (ability to adapt to new situations), and cultural awareness (understanding how people of different cultures think and act). These areas can be divided into eight different skills: self-awareness (using knowledge about yourself to deal with difficult situations), self-respect (confidence in what you think, feel, and do), interaction (how effectively you communicate with people), empathy (being able to see and feel things from other people's points of view), adaptability (how fast you can adjust to new situations and norms), certainty (the ability to do things opposite to what you feel), initiative (being open to new situations), and acceptance (being tolerant or accepting of unfamiliar things).

NOTE

1. Recently, B.C.E. (before the common era) and C.E. (common era) have been used to avoid the more culturally limited B.C. (before Christ) and A.D. (*anno Domini,* in the year of the Lord).

Key Terms

channel
communication
Confucianism
context
cross-cultural
decoding
encoding
feedback

global communication
honorific
ingroup
intercultural
    communication
international
    communication
message

noise
othering
Peace Corps
receiver
receiver response
source

CHAPTER 3

Culture's Influence on Perception

What You Can Learn From This Chapter

How culture affects sensing

How culture affects each step of the perception process

The distinction between high and low context cultures

The concept of face

How cultural interpretations placed on perceptions such as food reflect other elements of culture

It is a well-known tenet of Buddhism that "this world" is an illusion. The basis of this belief is that knowledge derived from words, from a conceptual understanding, cannot be trusted. Only pure sensation and intuition can be trusted, and knowledge based on sensation and intuition is unutterable. Hinduism also finds language inadequate to comprehend reality. With its belief in the oneness of things, language is seen to categorize reality into forms and structures that are illusionary. Language creates differences that do not exist in reality. In general, Eastern perspectives are as skeptical of language as the way to understand our world as Western perspectives are of intuition.

Nonetheless, it is commonly agreed that language provides the conceptual categories that influence how its speakers' perceptions are encoded and stored. In this chapter, we'll explore this by looking at how culture affects sensation and each step of the perception process. In particular, we'll look at how the language of one's culture provides the symbols to label what is perceived and how cultural values are learned and communicated with language.

SENSING

When you say people "*see* the world differently," what do you mean? Do you mean that people differ culturally in how they physiologically experience the world, or in how they interpret what they experience?

Very few people argue against an external, objective reality. Yet many arguments occur over exactly what that objective reality is. **Sensation** is the neurological process by which you become aware of your environment. Of the human senses, sight, hearing, smell, taste, and touch including pain, temperature, and pressure are the most studied (Gordon, 1971). The world appears quite different to other forms of life with different sensory ranges: A bat, for example, senses the world through ultrasound; a snake does so through infrared light; some fish sense distortions of electrical fields through receptors on the surface of their bodies—none of these directly sensed by humans.

Our Senses and Their Limitations

Sight. More information about the external world comes to us through our eyes than through any other sense. The average person is able to see objects the size of a cantaloupe at a distance of about 1,200 feet. Within that range, the average human gets a workable approximation of objects and actions for most of what exists above the microscopic and below the macroscopic. There is a reasonable degree of consistency between individuals. However, between any object and your mental perception of it are the mechanisms and processes of sight that are themselves less than perfect. It has been estimated that 20% of what is available to be seen is lost or distorted in transit to the human brain.

Hearing. The average person has a workably conscious sound spectrum covering a range from 20 to 20,000 vibration cycles per second—roughly 10 octaves—plus partly conscious "sensing" of higher and lower frequencies often interpreted as "presence" or "richness" of sound. As with sight, there is a normal loss of fidelity estimated at between 22% and 25%, and there is reason to believe that our contemporary noisy world has even further reduced our hearing fidelity.

Smell. The average person can differentiate among about 5,000 different smells down to a threshold of stimulation of as little as 400 molecules of a substance.

But there are inadequacies and problems. It is very unlikely that any two persons will possess the same orchestration of smell capability. The same batches of molecules have triggered diametrically opposed identifications of a simple substance. You might describe a smell as kerosene, whereas another will describe the same smell as perfume. The same person can even identify the same batch of molecules differently at different times. Smell is a less reliable human sense.

Taste. The average nonsmoker has about 10,000 differentiated taste sensations in relation to the basic sensations of bitter, salty, sour, and sweet. A fifth, *umami*, has been well known in Japan for a century. To taste a substance requires about 25,000 times more molecules than are required to smell it. Sense of taste is only an approximate capacity at best. For example, in one study, people were asked to taste the sugar mannose: 15% detected no taste, 20% found it sweet, 10% reported it bitter, and 55% said it was sweet, then bitter, or vice versa.

Touch. Of all human senses, touch, especially as related to pain, temperature, and pressure, relates most directly to automatic, reflex-arc reactions. Virtually all these sensations lead to responses initiated before the brain consciously begins to react. For example, when burned, you pull your hand away before you consciously decide to do so. Nonetheless, in terms of reliability our sense of touch is far from perfect.

Body movements. Two senses give us information about our own body movements. Kinesthesis uses pain and pressure receptors in muscles, joints, and tendons. Equilibrium, or our sense of balance, gives us information to know if we are upright, falling, or rotating.

Even given the limitations of our senses, do two people experience the same sensations? Perhaps because of the way we commonly talk about sensation, we mistakenly believe that there is a direct relationship between what is in the physical world and what we sense is there. We tend to believe that if two people stand at the same place and gaze at the same object they will share a closely similar sensation.

You need to remember that sensation is a neurological process. You are not directly aware of what is in the physical world but, rather, of your own internal sensations. When you report "seeing" a tree, what you are aware of is actually an electrochemical event. Much neural processing takes place between the receipt of a stimulus and your awareness of a sensation (Cherry, 1957).

Effect of Culture on Sensing

How much alike, then, are two persons' sensations? If you are color blind, your sensation of the world is much different from mine. No two of us can assume that our sensations are the same. In fact, we know that very different stimuli can produce the same sensations, that the same stimulus can produce very different sensations, and that the route from stimulus to sensation is in part conditioned by culture. Although the differences are minimal, individuals raised in diverse cultures can behave as though they actually sense different things.

For example, Marshall Segall and his associates (Segall, Campbell, & Herskovits, 1966) found that people who live in forests or in rural areas can sense crooked and slanted lines more accurately than can people who live in urban areas. This demonstrates that the rural and urban groups sense the same event differently as a result of their diverse cultural learnings.

PERCEIVING

Culture has a much greater effect on the **perception** process than on sensation itself (Tajfel, 1969; Triandis, 1964). Human perception is usually thought of as a three-step process of selection, organization, and interpretation. Each of these steps is affected by culture.

Selection

The first step in the perception process is **selection**. Within your physiological limitations you are exposed to more stimuli than you could possibly manage. To use sight as an example, you may feel that you are aware of all stimuli on your retinas, but most of the data from the retinas are handled on a subconscious level by a variety of specialized systems. Parts of our brains produce output from the retinas that we cannot "see." No amount of introspection can make us aware of those processes.

Needs affect what we are more likely to attend to. When we need something, have an interest in it, or want it, we are more likely to sense it out of competing stimuli. When we're hungry, we're more likely to attend to food advertisements.

This demonstrates that even stimuli we can be aware of we do not attend to continually. Being in a busy airport terminal is a good example. While there, you are confronted with many competing stimuli. You simply cannot attend to everything. However, if in the airport terminal an announcement is made asking you by name to report to a courtesy telephone, you would probably hear your name even in that environment of competing stimuli.

Just as you've learned to attend to the sound of your name, you've learned from your culture to select out other stimuli from the environment. A newborn child is a potential speaker of any language. Having heard only those sounds of your own language and having learned to listen to and make only those differentiations necessary, anyone would find it difficult to hear crucial differences in speech sounds in another language.

Examples

Cowboy tracking a villain. The ability to select out certain stimuli can also be learned in a subgroup. Think of a cowboy story. It's the professional scout who sees clues in the environment that make tracking the villain possible. The scout knows what to look for and selects out those clues from other competing stimuli.

Japanese/English difficulties with speech sounds. If you grew up speaking English, there are aspects of the Japanese language that are difficult for you to perceive. There are aspects that do not occur in English, so you didn't learn to listen for them. Because you don't know to listen for them, you literally do not hear them. For example, vowel length doesn't matter in English. You can say "Alabama" or "Alabaaama" and others would know you're referring to a southern U.S. state. Vowel length is important in Japanese. Japanese has short-duration vowels and long-duration vowels. Vowel length in the following pairs of Japanese words actually determines their meanings:

obasan	aunt
obaasan	grandmother
kita	came
kiita	heard

Because vowel length is not a critical attribute in English, perceiving the difference in sounds is a problem for those attempting to understand Japanese.

Other sounds that present difficulties for English speakers are the following:

Doubled consonants:

shita	did
shitta	new

Accent:

kaki	oyster
kaki	persimmon

Pitch:

hashi	bridge
hashi	chopsticks
hashi	corner of a room

If you grew up speaking Japanese, there are aspects of the English language that are difficult for you to perceive. English has some consonant sounds that do not exist in Japanese. If you grew up speaking Japanese, you didn't learn to listen for those consonant sounds. English uses the consonant sounds *f*, *v*, *th* as in *think*, *th* as in *breathe*, *z*, *zh* as in *treasure*, *j* as in the *dge* of *judge*, *r*, and *l*. Thus, if you grew up speaking Japanese, it is difficult to distinguish between the sounds *b* and *v*, *s* and *sh*, *r* and *l*, and so forth, with the result that *lice* and *rice* and *glamour* and *grammar* are frequently pronounced exactly the same way.

Japanese has borrowed thousands of English words. But if you grew up speaking English you'd have difficulty recognizing them. In Japanese, syllables are basically a consonant sound followed by a vowel. Syllables can end only with a vowel sound or an *n*. For example, the Japanese word *iiau* (quarrel) has four syllables—each vowel is pronounced as a separate syllable. A native-born English speaker would not know to do that and would try to pronounce the word as an unsegmented single sound.

An English speaker pronounces the word *thrill* as one syllable. In Japanese, consonant sounds do not exist without vowels, so a Japanese speaker would pronounce all three syllables, something like *sooriroo*. The Japanese *r*, by the way, is difficult for English speakers. It is similar to the Spanish *r* in *pero* or *Roberto*.

From our first language, we learned what sounds are critical to listen for. Because languages can have different critical sounds, learning a new language means learning to attend to new sounds.

Organization

The second step in the perception process is **organization**. Along with selecting stimuli from the environment, you must organize it in some meaningful way. Language provides the conceptual categories that influence how its speakers' perceptions are encoded and stored.

How are perceptions categorized? One argument is that you somehow grasp some set of attributes that things have in common and it is on that basis that they are grouped together in a category. The philosopher Ludwig Wittgenstein (1889-1951), however, concluded that there need be no such set of shared characteristics. Your language provides the symbol to group perceptions of any kind together.

> Language plays a large and significant role in the totality of culture. Far from being simply a technique of communication, it is itself a way of directing the perception of its speakers and it promotes for them habitual modes of analyzing experience into significant categories. And to the extent that languages differ markedly from each other, so should we expect to find significant and formidable barriers to cross-cultural communication and understanding.
>
> —Harry Hoijer, *Language in Culture* (1954)

Examples

Categorizing color. It has been estimated that humans are physiologically capable of sensing 7.5 million different, distinguishable colors. Organizing that wealth of perceptual information is made possible using categories that your language and culture give you. Anthropologists have discovered that the number of basic color terms used in languages varies from only 2 to 11. Let's consider the English words used to refer to color perceptions. Speakers of English divide the color spectrum, as shown in the top row of Figure 3.1.

Speakers of English have learned from their culture to organize color perceptions by grouping certain perceptions together and labeling them with a shared symbol. Do other cultures organize color perceptions differently? Look at the second and third rows in Figure 3.1. The words in the second row are used in Zimbabwe by speakers of Shona, and those in the third row are used in Liberia by speakers of Bassa. Because the categories to organize color sensations are different, are these peoples not aware of the differences that English speakers perceive? Just as you perceive different shades of red and recognize that they are different but still call them all "red," so a speaker of Shona can see different shades of *cipsuka* and call them *cipsuka*.

English

red	orange	yellow	green	blue	purple

Shona

cipsuka	cicena	citema	cipsuka

Bassa

ziza	hui

Figure 3.1   Color categories across cultures.

NOTE: Shona is the language spoken by people in Zimbabwe; Bassa is a tonal language spoken mainly in Liberia.

Can you identify a subgroup that has many different categories for color? Think of interior designers and artists whose subgroups have provided many more categories to organize information about color.

Japanese concept of shibui. Language provides the labels for perceptual categorization, and this categorization can lead us to assume that all items referred to by the same label have certain attributes in common. In Japanese, a word at one time used more commonly to refer to art and individual taste is *shibui*. There is no equivalent term in English, so the concept cannot be easily explained. It has been described as "not showy or gaudy but serene, self-possessed, with presence of mind, austere, understated." Even with this description a non-Japanese does not have enough information to classify an object as being beautiful in a shibui way. You would have to be exposed to a number of objects classified as shibui to determine what the critical attributes are. A Japanese child, however, will learn the concept with little conscious effort just like other concepts of the Japanese culture are learned. Today, the word is more commonly used to mean "cool" or "tasteful," as in "a *shibui* baseball player doesn't dive after balls but expends exactly as much energy as is needed." Or a *shibui kuruma* (car) would be a car that a *shibui hito* (person) would drive.

Interpretation

The third step in the perception process is **interpretation**. This refers to attaching meaning to sense data and is synonymous with decoding. The same situation can be interpreted quite differently by diverse people. A police officer arriving at a crime scene can be experienced by the victim as calming and relief giving but by the criminal as fearsome and threatening.

Here, too, the effect of culture is great. As you encounter people of your own culture you constantly make judgments as to age, social status, educational background, and the like. The cues you use to make these decisions are so subtle that it is often difficult to explain how and why you reach a particular conclusion. Do people in the United States, for example, perceive tall men as more credible? Perhaps.

Many consider dogs as pets. (The author's first dog, Smokey.)

Applying these same cues to someone from another culture may not work. People in the United States, for example, frequently err in guessing the age of Japanese individuals, such as judging a Japanese college student in her mid-20s to be only 14 or 15.

Examples

Dogs as pets or as food. The meanings you attach to your perceptions are greatly determined by your cultural background. Think of how speakers of English categorize life. Most probably use the categories of human life and animal life. Now think of how you typically categorize animal life: probably into wild animals and domesticated animals.

Now think of how you typically categorize domesticated animal life: probably into animals used for food, animals used for sport and recreation, and pets. Look at the picture of the puppy and capture your feelings. Most of us see this puppy in the category of pet for which we have learned to relate warm, loving feelings. Puppies are cute, cuddly, warm, loving creatures.

Now look at the picture on the next page of a man holding up a dog, read the caption, and capture your feelings. Most of us who love dogs find this picture

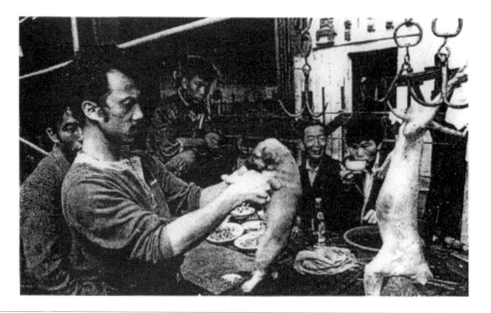

Can you explain your feelings about this photograph?

SOURCE: *Time* magazine, "A Day in the Life of China," October 2, 1989, p. 47, photo by Gerd Ludig. Reprinted with permission.

uncomfortable and disgusting. How can people eat dogs? They're pets, not food! It all depends on where you categorize them. Dogs are pets in some cultures and food in others. In the Arab world, dogs are acceptable as watchdogs and as hunting dogs but are not kept in the home as pets because they are seen as unclean and a low form of life. To call someone a dog is an insult among Arabs.

People in most cultures have strong ideas about which foods are acceptable for human consumption and which are not. People in some countries think the custom in the United States of eating corn on the cob is disgusting because that food is fit only for pigs. The Ukrainian favorite food *salo*, raw pig fat with black bread and vodka, might cause nausea in some, as would knowing that horse meat from California is served in restaurants in Belgium, France, and Japan.

Your reaction of disgust to the second picture is a culturally learned interpretation—and that interpretation can be quite strong. In 1989, California made it a misdemeanor for any person to sell, buy, or accept any animal traditionally kept as a pet with the intent of killing the animal for food. More recently, animal rights groups have protested the sale of live animals, such as turtles, frogs, lobsters, crabs, fish, and chicken, for food at Asian-American markets. Asian tradition is that fresh meat is tastier and more healthful, that the best meat is that "that enters your house still breathing." Animal rights activists contend that the animals are treated inhumanely in the shops and are killed in ways that cause them unnecessary pain. Asian-American groups argue that eating dogs and cats is an extreme rarity among Southeast Asian immigrants and call the law and the animal rights activists racist.

In some cultures, parts of some animals are categorized as medicine. In other cultures, certain animals are considered sacred and would certainly not be eaten. The Hindu elephant-headed God[1] Ganesh is accompanied by a rat whenever he travels. Rats, like cows, are deified in India. No Hindu worship is complete without an offering to Ganesh and his companion, the rat. Rats are fed and rarely killed in India.

Weather vane as Christian cross. The examples so far have been of practices that could offend some English speakers. Let's turn that around with an example of what speakers of English do that could be offensive to others.

Johnston Pump Company, a U.S. company now based in Brookshire, Texas, has been doing business with Saudi Arabia for more than 50 years. By the 1930s, Johnston Pump was well established in California, its pumps having helped change California's arid lands into a leading agricultural area. Johnston's general manager at the time was a world traveler. During a trip to Saudi Arabia, he noted how similar the climate was to areas of California and convinced the Saudi government that vast wastelands could be turned into fertile farmland through the use of Johnston pumps. The first pump was installed in the king's palace.

Over the years, Johnston's success in the kingdom has largely been due to its respect for the country's strict religious customs. All personnel in its international division receive cultural training.

"Making the deserts bloom for 50 years" was Johnston's advertising campaign in 1986. Ads in English and Arabic began appearing in various Middle East publications early in the year. With the success of the campaign, Johnston made large posters of the ads to be distributed throughout the kingdom.

Study the Johnston Pump poster on page 60 and see if you can tell why a Saudi customs inspector would not allow it into the country.

Saudi Arabia allows no public worship of any religion other than Islam. No churches, temples, or any symbols of other religions are permitted. To the customs inspector, the weather vane in the poster looked like a Christian cross and would therefore be prohibited from being displayed. It took intervention by the Minister of Customs to allow the posters into the country.

Johnston Pump poster.

Years later, 10 million bags of potato chips from Thailand were confiscated by the Saudi Ministry of Commerce because toys inside each bag were adorned with crossed triangles that were perceived to be the Star of David. With the perception step of categorization comes a culture's values, and it is those differing categorizations that can so often impede communication, particularly when one group believes its perceptions are right and any other's wrong.

HIGH VERSUS LOW CONTEXT

Another way that culture affects perception is whether the culture is high or low context. The concept of high- and low-context cultures was popularized by Hall (1976). Recall that context was defined in Chapter 2 as the environment in which the communication process takes place and that helps define the communication. Cultures in which little of the meaning is determined by the context because the message is encoded in the explicit code are labeled **low context**. Cultures in which less has to be said or written because more of the meaning is in the physical environment or already shared by people are labeled **high context**.

Think of the difference this way. On meeting a stranger, your verbal communication with that person is highly explicit—or low context—simply because you have no shared experiences. You can't assume anything. However, when you communicate with your sister or brother with whom you have shared a lifetime, your verbal communication is less explicit because you make use of your shared context: For example, the mention of a certain name can lead to laughter. With the stranger you would have to explain in language the story that that name represented. Also, with your sister or brother a certain facial expression can have a shared meaning, such as "There our mother goes again," but the stranger would have no idea what your facial expression communicated. Again, you would have to explain in words that your mother's specific behavior was characteristic, somewhat irritating, but so uniquely her.

In low-context cultures, verbal messages are elaborate and highly specific and tend to also be highly detailed and redundant. Verbal abilities are highly valued. Logic and reasoning are expressed in verbal messages.

In high-context cultures, most of the information is either in the physical context or internalized in the

> High-context cultures make greater distinction between the insiders and outsiders than low-context cultures do. People raised in high-context systems expect more of others than do the participants in low-context systems. When talking about something they have on their minds, a high-context individual will expect his interlocutor to know what's bothering him, so that he does not have to be specific. The result is that he will talk around and around the point, in effect putting all the pieces in place except the crucial one. Placing it properly—this keystone—is the role of his interlocutor.
>
> —E. T. Hall, *Beyond Culture* (1976, p. 98)

Table 3.1   Level of Context, by Culture

High	Low
China	Switzerland
Japan	Germany
Korea	North America, including the United States
American Indian	Nordic states
Most Latin American cultures	
Southern and eastern Mediterranean cultures, such as Greece, Turkey, and Arab states	

person. Very little is in the coded, explicit, transmitted part of the message. High-context cultures decrease the perception of self as separate from the group. High-context cultures are more sensitive to nonverbal messages; hence, they are more likely to provide a context and setting and let the point evolve. Table 3.1 shows examples of both types.

It has been said that language separates people. When understood from the perspective of high and low context, that statement makes sense. In high-context cultures, people are brought closer by the importance of their shared context. Those meanings are often lost in low-context cultures.

I have often shown films of the Japanese tea ceremony to classes in the United States. The tea ceremony reflects the Zen and Taoist traditions celebrating the beauty in the mundane, the superiority of spirit over matter, and tranquility with busy lives. The ceremony united the host and guest in a concert of harmony. Although not as commonly practiced as in the past, the tea ceremony is an excellent example of a high-context experience. Nothing is spoken; all the meanings are in the context of shared experience, the teahouse, the flower arrangement, the calligraphy scroll, the ceramics. A typical response from a low-context observer is, "Hurry up and drink the tea!" Your social experiences over coffee take little meaning from the context and more from the conversation—the words.

THE CONCEPT OF FACE

In Chinese culture, **face** is conceptualized in two ways: *lian* (face) and *mian* or *mian zi* (image). While these are often used interchangeably, they have different meanings. Hu (1944) defines lian as something that "represents the

Japanese tea ceremony.

SOURCE: Photo by Charles W. Wilson. Used by permission of W. Stephen Wilson.

confidence of society in the integrity of ego's moral character, the loss of which makes it impossible to function properly with the community." Mian "stands for the kind of prestige that is emphasized in the U.S., a reputation achieved through life."

Ting-Toomey (1985) has proposed that low-context cultures, such as the United States, with a greater concern for privacy and autonomy, tend to use direct-face negotiation and express more self-face maintenance, whereas high-context cultures, such as China, with a greater concern for interdependence and inclusion tend to use indirect-face negotiation and express more mutual-face or other-face maintenance.

Communication in high-context cultures like China is hence more indirect or implicit and is more likely to use intermediaries. Because social harmony and face maintenance are crucial, communication through intermediaries is especially functional because using intermediaries eliminates face-to-face confrontation and reduces the risk of losing face.

In interviews conducted in central China, Ma (1992) confirmed that unofficial mediation is common in situations involving interpersonal conflict. The mediator is usually a friend of the two parties in conflict or an elderly person respected by both. Intervention by the friend or respected elder is either self-initiated or in response to a request by a person not connected with the competing parties. Impartiality and face maintenance are considered the two key factors in successful mediation.

A CASE STUDY OF PERCEPTION AND FOOD

Perception interpretations provided by a culture can reveal much about that culture. Cultures use food to reinforce and express identities. A recent book's title expresses the importance of cultural identity to food: *You Eat What You Are: People, Culture and Food Traditions* (Barer-Stein, 1999). In the following case study of food in China, identify the elements of culture that are reflected in food preparation.

China has the oldest continuing culture of any nation in the world. About 500 B.C.E., the philosophies of Confucianism and **Taoism** became the prime motivating forces in the development of the cuisine. The counterbalance of these two major philosophies became the basis of Chinese cuisine as an art.

Confucius encouraged a sense of balance and harmony. For example, when meats were used as ingredients, they could not overpower the rice included in the same meal. He also emphasized the aesthetic aspects of cooking and eating. He said a proper dish should appeal to the eye as well as to the palate. For example, intricately carved vegetables are a common decoration.

The distinctive process of preparing Chinese cuisine is based on Confucius and his philosophy of balance. There is a division between *fan*, Chinese for grains and other starch foods, and *chai*, vegetable and meat dishes. A balanced meal, then, must have an appropriate amount of fan and chai.

The main principle of Tao is a life in perfect accord with nature. Taoism as a religion arose from the philosophy of Lao-tzu. Lao-tzu means "old philosopher" or even "old child"—and may have been a Chinese philosopher who lived around the 6th century B.C.E., or it may refer to a line of thought. The basic assumption of Taoism is that there is an underlying pattern or direction of the universe that cannot be explained verbally or intellectually. Lao-tzu cautioned against naming things, for doing so subjugates reality through abstraction and analysis. The Tao is this underlying pattern, commonly known as "the

Way," which can never be captured in words. The Taoist ideal is a person who leads a simple, spontaneous, and meditative life close to nature. Taoists are encouraged to explore roots, fungi, herbs, marine vegetation, and other natural foods to discover their life-giving elements.

There is also a belief in a balance that governs all of life and nature—the **yin** and the **yang**. Originally, yin meant the shady side of a hill and yang the sunny side. Yin is the dark, moist, cool aspect of the cosmos. Females have more yin quality. Yang is the bright, dry, warm aspect. Males have more yang quality.

Foods also have yin and yang qualities. Most water plants, crustaceans, and certain beans are cooling yin foods. Oily and fried foods, pepper-hot flavoring, fatty meat, and oil plant food like peanuts are "warm" yang foods.

The kind of food eaten is related to one's health. When yin and yang forces in the body are not balanced, problems result. Proper amounts of food of one kind or the other must then be eaten to correct this imbalance. For example, a body sore or fever could be due to overeating "warm" foods.

Remember, all elements of a culture interrelate. Half of China is mountainous or unsuited to cultivation. China cannot depend on large animals like cattle that are land intensive. Through necessity, the Chinese have used all forms of edible ingredients—from lotus roots, birds' nests, and sea cucumbers to pig brains and fish lips.

Because of a scarcity of fuel and raw materials, stir-frying was developed. Small pieces of meat, poultry, fish, or vegetables take only a few minutes to cook and thus save fuel.

For at least 5,000 years, rice has been grown in China. Its importance has made it synonymous with food and life. Rice is the symbol of well-being and fertility. Leaving one's job is called breaking one's rice bowl. It is considered bad luck to upset a rice bowl. And the worst of all insults is to take another's bowl of rice and empty it onto the ground.

At the Chinese table, it is the unspoken words that matter. The meal is the message. *Chi fan!*—Dinner is served!

FROM THE INTERCULTURAL PERSPECTIVE

In the past few years in the United States, "magic eye" pictures have become popular. These pictures at first seem to be just a lot of wavy lines. However, if they are looked at in the right way, a hidden picture can be seen. Some people can see the hidden image right away; others take much longer. A few frustrated people never learn to see them. Even though everyone who looks at them sees the same thing (i.e., wavy lines hiding a picture), there are differences in what they perceive (i.e., wavy lines or a picture). In a similar way, cultures affect how people perceive the world. Everyone is able to sense the world in the same way, but cultures teach us how to process and understand the information obtained from our senses.

The information received about the world comes through our physical senses of sight, sound, smell, taste, and touch. Our sense of touch also allows us to feel pressure, temperature, and pain. Imagine how our perceptions might change if we had more acute senses or another kind of sense such as a dolphin's ability to use sonar.

To some degree, cultures affect what people sense, but they have a much greater influence on perceptions. The process of perception can be divided into three stages: selection, organization, and interpretation. In the selection stage, we choose what sensory information to pay attention to. Our senses constantly provide us with an enormous amount of information. We cannot be consciously aware of it all. Therefore, we must choose only the most relevant information for us. Our cultures teach us what is relevant. For example, we pay close attention to the sounds of our native language, but it is more difficult for us to hear and tell the difference between the sounds of foreign languages. Organization is the second stage of the perception process. When we organize information, we place it into categories. Some cultures may categorize certain things in great detail; others might not. The Eskimo culture, for example, has many categories for snow. Interpretation is the third stage in the perception process. In this stage, we give meaning to or "decode" the information that we have selected and organized. People can interpret the same information in completely different ways. A classic example is the glass with water in it. Is it half empty or half full?

Perception can be different in high- and low-context cultures. Cultures with high context generally use fewer words to communicate and rely on shared cultural experience to communicate their meaning. Low-context cultures rely more on words to communicate meaning. The United States is a low-context culture.

Cultural differences in interpretation can be quite dramatic, as in the case of food. What one culture enjoys eating, another culture may find disgusting. It is important to remember that food choice and preparation can be understood in relation to other aspects of culture. The physical geography of a country has a strong effect on culture. It influences clothing, housing, and food. Japanese people, for example, live on a group of islands and consequently eat a lot of fish because it is a food source that is easily available. North Americans eat a lot of beef because the United States has plenty of land on which to graze cattle.

NOTE

1. The word *God* is capped in this text, but no endorsement of any religion is implied. The intent is to honor all religions.

KEY TERMS

face	organization	Taoism
high context	perception	yang
interpretation	selection	yin
low context	sensation	

PART II

Communication Variables

CHAPTER 4

Barriers to Intercultural Communication

What You Can Learn From This Chapter

Ethnographic and cultural approaches to understanding intercultural communication

How barriers impede intercultural communication

Examples of barriers found in a case study of China and the United States

T his chapter begins a series of chapters focused on recognizing and avoiding breakdowns in intercultural communication. In this chapter, you'll read about ethnographic and cultural approaches and then examine anxiety, assuming similarity instead of difference, and ethnocentrism as barriers to effective intercultural communication.

ETHNOGRAPHIC AND CULTURAL APPROACHES

Read the following court transcript (Liberman, 1981) and assess how successful you think the communication was:

Magistrate: Can you read and write?

Defendant: Yes.

Magistrate: Can you sign your name?

Defendant: Yes.

Magistrate: Did you say you cannot read?

Defendant: Hm.

Magistrate: Can you read or not?!

Defendant: No.

Magistrate: [Reads statement.] Do you recall making that statement?

Defendant: Yes.

Magistrate: Is there anything else you want to add to the statement?

Defendant: [No answer.]

Magistrate: Did you want to say anything else!?

Defendant: No.

Magistrate: Is there anything in the statement you want to change?

Defendant: No.

Magistrate: [Reads a second statement.] Do you recall making that statement?

Defendant: Yes.

Magistrate: Do you wish to add to the statement?

Defendant: No.

Magistrate: Do you want to alter the statement in any way?

Defendant: [Slight nod.]

Magistrate: What do you want to alter?

Defendant: [No answer.]

Magistrate: Do you want to change the statement?

Defendant: No.

Of course it is doubtful that the defendant understands the proceedings. Based on this exchange we could also raise doubts about the defendant's "statement."

Now if I told you the defendant was an Aboriginal in Australia, could you say more about the interaction? How you attempt to answer that question illustrates two major approaches to intercultural communication. If you examined the transcript in detail to locate the problems the defendant and the magistrate had in their exchange, your approach was ethnographic. If you asked for information about Aboriginals and the Australian legal system, your approach was cultural.

Ethnography is the direct observation, reporting, and evaluation of the customary behavior of a culture. Ideally, ethnography requires an extended period of residence and study in a community. The ethnographer knows the language of the group, participates in some of the group's activities, and uses a variety of observational and recording techniques. In a sense, the accounts of 15th-century explorers of the unfamiliar cultural practices they encountered were primitive ethnographies.

Modern ethnography tries to avoid questionnaires and formal interviews in artificial settings; observation in natural settings is preferred. The objective is an analysis of cultural patterns to develop a grammar or theory of the rules for appropriate cultural behaviors.

An ethnographic approach to understanding the dialogue between the magistrate and the defendant would use the perspective of the parties themselves to analyze the problems that each faces in the attempt to communicate. Thus, it appears that the Aboriginal defendant is engaged in a strategy of giving the answers "Yes," "No," or "Hm" that will best placate the magistrate (Liberman, 1990a).

A cultural approach attempts to develop an ideal personification of the culture, and then that ideal is used to explain the actions of individuals in the culture. For example, using the cultural approach, it would be important to know that the **Aboriginal** people began arriving on the Australian continent from Southeast Asia 40,000 years before North and South America were inhabited and that it wasn't until 1788 that 11 ships arrived carrying a cargo of human prisoners to begin a new British colony by taking control of the land. Liberman (1990b) describes the unique form of public discourse that evolved among the isolated Aboriginal people of central Australia: Consensus must be preserved through such strategies as unassertiveness, avoidance of direct argumentation, deferral of topics that would produce disharmony, and serial summaries so that the people think together and "speak with one voice." If any dissension is sensed, there are no attempts to force a decision, and the discussion is abandoned. Western European discourse style is direct, confrontational, and individualistic. Thus, it can be said that the Aboriginal defendant in the example finds it difficult to communicate a defense by opposing what has been said and rather frequently concurs with any statement made to him (Liberman, 1990b).

The ethnographic and cultural approaches are complementary and together can help our understanding of breakdowns in intercultural communication.

In Chapter 1, you saw that every culture and subgroup provides its members with rules specifying appropriate and inappropriate behavior. Were you to approach intercultural communication from the perspective of attempting to learn the norms of all cultures and subgroups, it certainly would be an impossible task. There is no way that you could learn all the rules governing appropriate and inappropriate behavior for every culture and subgroup with which you came into contact. You'd always be doing something wrong; you'd always be offending someone. Your communication would likely suffer, as your violation of norms would be a form of noise limiting the effectiveness of your communication.

In fact, you wouldn't even know if you were expected to conform to the other's norms or if you were expected to behave according to your own culture's norms while respecting the other culture's norms.

A better approach is to examine on a general level the barriers to intercultural communication. LaRay M. Barna (1997) has developed a list of six such barriers: anxiety, assuming similarity instead of difference, ethnocentrism, stereotypes and prejudice, nonverbal misinterpretations, and language. His categories of barriers will be used when discussing problems that can arise in intercultural encounters. The first three are discussed in this chapter. Stereotypes and prejudice are discussed separately in Chapter 5. Nonverbal misinterpretations and language are discussed separately in later chapters. Taking these common mistakes into account can help you improve your intercultural communication skills.

ANXIETY

The first barrier is *high* anxiety. When you are anxious because of not knowing what you are expected to do, it is only natural to focus on that feeling and not be totally present in the communication transaction.

For example, you may have experienced anxiety on your very first day on a new college campus or in a new job. You may be so conscious of being new—and out of place—and focus so much of your attention on that feeling that you make common mistakes and appear awkward to others.

Sugawara (1993) surveyed 168 Japanese employees of Japanese companies working in the United States and 135 of their U.S. coworkers. Only 8% of the U.S. coworkers felt impatient with the Japanese coworkers' English. While 19% of the Japanese employees felt their spoken English was poor or very poor and 20% reported feeling nervous when speaking English with U.S. coworkers, 30% of the Japanese employees felt the U.S. coworkers were impatient with their accent, and almost 60% believed that language was the problem in communicating with the U.S. coworkers. For some, anxiety over speaking English properly contributed to avoiding interactions with the U.S. coworkers and limiting interactions both on and off the job to other Japanese only.

ASSUMING SIMILARITY INSTEAD OF DIFFERENCE

The second barrier is *assuming similarity instead of difference*. In 1997, a Danish woman left her 14-month-old baby girl in a stroller outside a Manhattan restaurant while she was inside. Other diners at the restaurant became concerned and called New York City Police. The woman was charged with endangering a child and was jailed for two nights. Her child was placed in foster care. The woman and the Danish consulate explained that leaving children unattended outside cafés is common in Denmark. Pictures were wired to the police showing numerous strollers parked outside cafés while parents were eating inside. The Danish woman had assumed that Copenhagen is similar to New York, that what is commonly done in Copenhagen is also commonly done in New York.

When you assume similarity between cultures you can be caught unaware of important differences. When you have no information about a new culture, it might make sense to assume there are no differences, to behave as you would in your home culture. But each culture *is* different and unique to some degree. Boucher (1974), for example, has shown how cultures differ as to whom it is appropriate to display emotions. If you assume that display of emotions is similar to your culture, you might see people in some circumstances as lacking emotion and others in other circumstances as displaying emotions inappropriately.

The inverse can be a barrier as well. Assuming difference instead of similarity can lead to your not recognizing important things that cultures share in common. It's better to assume nothing. It's better to ask, "What are the customs?" rather than assuming they're the same—or different—everywhere.

ETHNOCENTRISM

Definition

The third barrier to effective intercultural communication is **ethnocentrism**, or negatively judging aspects of another culture by the standards of one's own culture. To be ethnocentric is to believe in the superiority of one's own culture. Everything in a culture is consistent to that culture and makes sense if you understood that culture.

For example, assume that global warming is a fact and, as a result, assume that summers in the United States average 43° C (109° F). It would be logical to make adjustments: Rather than air condition buildings all day, you might close schools and businesses in the afternoons to conserve energy. Such adjustments would make sense. Why then do some people attribute sensible midday siestas in hot climates to laziness?

After reading the comments by Benjamin Franklin (see Box 4.1), who do you think was being ethnocentric?

Box 4.1

**BENJAMIN FRANKLIN'S
REMARKS ON AMERICAN INDIANS**

Savages we call them, because their Manners differ from ours, which we think the Perfection of Civility; they think the same of theirs.

Perhaps, if we could examine the Manners of different Nations with Impartiality, we should find no People so rude, as to be without any Rules of Politeness; nor any so polite, as not to have some Remains of Rudeness.

The Indian Men, when young, are Hunters and Warriors; when old, Counsellors; for all their Government is by Counsel of the Sages; there is no Force, there are no Prisons, no Officers to compel Obedience, or inflict Punishment. Hence they generally study Oratory, the best Speaker having the most influence. The Indian Women till the Ground, dress the Food, nurse and bring up the Children, and preserve and hand down to Posterity the Memory of public Transactions. These Employments of Men and Women are accounted natural and honourable. Having few artificial Wants, they have an abundance of Leisure for Improvement by

Conversation. Our laborious Manner of Life, compared with theirs, they esteem slavish and base; and the Learning, on which we value ourselves, they regard as frivolous and useless. An Instance of this occurred at the Treaty of Lancaster, in Pennsylvania, anno 1744, between the Government of Virginia and the Six Nations. After the principal Business was settled, the Commissioners from Virginia acquainted the Indians by a Speech that there was at Williamsburg a College, with a Fund for Educating Indian youth; and that, if the Six Nations would send down half a dozen of their young Lads to that College, the Government would take care that they should be well provided for, and instructed in all the Learning of the White People. It is one of the Indian Rules of Politeness not to answer a public Proposition the same day that it is made; they think it would be treating it as a light manner, and that they show it Respect by taking time to consider it, as of a Matter important. They therefor deferr'd their Answer till the Day following; when their Speaker began, by expressing their deep Sense of the kindness of the Virginia Government, in making them that Offer; "for we know," says he, "that you highly esteem the kind of Learning taught in those Colleges, and that the Maintenance of our young Men, while with you, would be very expensive to you. We are convinc'd, therefore, that you mean to do us Good by your Proposal; and we thank you heartily. But you, who are wise, must know that different Nations have different Conceptions of things; and you will therefore not take it amiss, if our Ideas of this kind of Education happen not to be the same with yours. We have had some Experience of it; Several of our young People were formerly brought up at the Colleges of the Northern Provinces; they were instructed in all your Sciences; but, when they came back to us, they were bad Runners, ignorant of every means of living in the Woods, unable to bear either Cold or Hunger, knew neither how to build a Cabin, take a Deer, or kill an Enemy, spoke our language imperfectly, were therefore neither fit for Hunters, Warriors, nor Counsellors; they were totally good for nothing. We are however not the less oblig'd by your kind Offer, tho' we decline accepting it; and, to show our grateful Sense of it, if the Gentlemen of Virginia will send us a Dozen of their Sons, we will take great Care of their Education, instruct them in all we know, and make Men of them."

SOURCE: Benjamin Franklin, "Remarks Concerning the Savages of North America" (date of composition uncertain, printed as a pamphlet in 1784), quoted in Mott and Jorgenson (1939).

Another name for ethnocentrism is the anthropological concept of **cultural relativism.** It does not mean that everything is equal. It does mean that we must try to understand other people's behavior in the context of their culture before we judge it. It also means that we recognize the arbitrary nature of our own cultural behaviors and be willing to reexamine them by learning about behaviors in other cultures (Cohen, 1998).

A less extreme form of ethnocentrism can be labeled *cultural nearsightedness,* or taking one's own culture for granted and neglecting other cultures. For example, people in the United States often use the word *Americans* to refer to U.S. citizens, but actually that word is the correct designation of all people in North and South America. Its careless use is a form of ethnocentrism.

Cultural nearsightedness often results in making assumptions that simple things are the same everywhere. Designing forms for something as simple as a person's name is not that simple if you recognize how widely practices vary. For example, in Mexico people may have two surnames, with the first from the father's first surname and the second from the mother's surname. Often, only the first surname is used and the second abbreviated. When a woman marries, she usually retains both of her surnames and adds her husband's first surname. Or consider China with 1.3 billion people and only about 3,100 surnames, with 90% of the population sharing 100 of them. Based on its 1982 census, China has 87 million people sharing the name Li—the most common surname in the world. The name Smith is shared by 2.4 million people in the United States.

Another example is Eurocentric ethnocentrism. This would include, for example, recognizing only Western holidays in schools or basing curriculum only on Western history, music, and art. The terms "the West" and "the East" themselves have been labeled Eurocentric ethnocentrism. Asia is east of Europe, but to call Asia "the East" makes its identity dependent on Europe.

In 1913, members of the Pueblo tribe challenged the degree of control that Congress exercised over tribal affairs. In its decision on *United States v. Sandoval,* the Supreme Court ruled,

"Always living in separate and isolated communities, adhering to primitive modes of life, largely influenced by superstition and fetishism, and chiefly governed according to crude customs inherited from their ancestors, [the Pueblos] are essentially a simple, uninformed and inferior people.... As a superior and civilized nation, [the U.S. government has both] the power and the duty of exercising a fostering care and protection over all dependent Indian communities within its borders."

Negative Effects on Communication

Extreme ethnocentrism leads to a rejection of the richness and knowledge of other cultures. It impedes communication and blocks the exchange of ideas and skills among peoples. Because it excludes other points of view, an ethnocentric orientation is restrictive and limiting.

CASE STUDY OF INTERCULTURAL COMMUNICATION BARRIERS: CHINA AND THE UNITED STATES

In the United States, a lack of knowledge about China and its history contributes to communication barriers. As you read this section and become more familiar with China and its history, identify examples of the intercultural communication barriers that exist between the two cultures. When and how has the United States assumed similarity to China? When and how have both displayed ethnocentrism?

Population

In terms of land area, China is larger than the United States. It is also the most populated country in the world. Its population was estimated to be 1.3 billion in 1999, or about five times as many people as populate the United States. China's population accounts for about one-fifth of the entire human race. Approximately two-thirds of the population are peasants. The average per capita income is $800, but with a large gap between the coastal and urban areas and the less prosperous interior. As the world's second largest economy, China has led the world in economic growth, with $510 billion in imports and exports in 2001.

History

Today's China represents 4,000 years of civilization. Its history was first recorded more than 1,500 years before the beginning of Christianity. For about half its history, China had multiple governments—at times both a southern and a northern regime. Until early in the 20th century, China was ruled by a series of dynasties and through the centuries largely indifferent to the outside world.

Dr. Sun Yat-sen on Chinese and U.S. stamps.

With support from Chinese communities in Hawaii and mainland United States and students in Europe and Japan, Dr. Sun Yat-sen's United League victory in Wuchang was the end of the Ch'ing dynasty. He earned the distinction of being the "father" of modern China.

After Dr. Sun's 1911 revolution, China became fragmented by war lords. In the 1920s, Chiang Kai-shek attempted to reunify the country and establish a nationalist government. Chiang's U.S. support was partly due to the publicity Henry Luce provided through his *Time* magazine, to the popularity of Pearl Buck's novels, and to the images of Chiang as a convert to Methodism and of his Wellesley College-educated wife.

World War II brought Communism and Mao Zedong, who in 1949 defeated Chiang Kai-shek. Chiang fled with his followers to the island of **Taiwan** located about 161 kilometers (100 miles) off the coast of China. Taiwan, which had been occupied by Japan from 1895 until the end of World War II when it was returned to China, is about the size of the states of Massachusetts and Connecticut combined. Only 15% of the island's population were 1949 immigrants, but they dominated Taiwan's government through martial law.

The nationalist government of Taiwan (the Republic of China) considered itself the legal government of all China, whereas the mainland Chinese government claimed Taiwan as part of its territory. Chiang maintained an army of 600,000 in hopes of regaining the mainland. In 1955, the United States agreed to protect Taiwan in case of attack from mainland China.

For more than four decades, Mao was the dominant figure in Chinese life. In the 1950s, the country benefited from land redistribution, introduction of compulsory universal education, adoption of simplified Chinese characters that led to greater literacy, and the introduction of health and welfare reforms. In 1958, Mao launched the Great Leap Forward. This program forced farmers into communes, abolished private property, and set up backyard steel mills to speed China's entry into the industrial age. The program was a catastrophic

Taiwan currency.

failure and brought widespread starvation and the country to bankruptcy. President Liu Shaoqi and Deng Xiaoping, General Secretary of the Communist Party, took over day-to-day control to restore the economy.

Beginning in 1966, Mao led the country through his infamous **Cultural Revolution**. In an attempt to destroy Liu's government and Deng's party, to purify the culture of all outside influences, and to build a new Marxist-Chinese culture, tens of thousands were executed. Millions were exiled to rural labor brigades. During my stays in China, I've spoken with those who were youths during that period. They angrily said their future was stolen from them by Mao. Their only education was Mao's *Red Book (The Thoughts of Chairman Mao)*.

In 1971, the People's Republic of China (mainland China) was admitted to the United Nations in Taiwan's place in spite of U.S. objections. In 1972, a breakthrough in United States-China relations occurred when President Richard Nixon and his national security adviser, Henry Kissinger, established relations with the Chinese government.

On September 9, 1976, Mao died. Shortly after, the Party officially declared Mao's concept of continuing class struggle an ideological mistake, and his call for cultural revolution was commonly believed to have been a terrible disaster.

Post-Mao China was dominated by the leadership of Deng Xiaoping. In 1956, Deng had been fourth in power after Mao. By 1962, he had financial control of the country. Deng's economic approach was reflected in his comment to Mao during an argument over farming policies that became his trademark: "Whether a cat is black or white makes no difference. As long as it catches mice, it is a good cat." Deng replaced Marx and Lenin with a commodity economy and profit incentives, but in 1966, he was denounced as a "capitalist roader" and confined to his compound. At the urging of the dying Chou En-lai, Deng swore loyalty to Mao and was returned to power in 1973.

Starting in 1978, Deng removed aging leaders and opponents and replaced them with younger, well-educated supporters. Later, in a highly significant move under President Jimmy Carter, on January 1, 1979, the United States normalized relations with the People's Republic of China and severed diplomatic relations with Taiwan together with terminating the defense agreement protecting the island.

Deng's **four modernizations**—agriculture, industry, science, and technology—sought to remove the dogmas, irrationality, and inefficiencies of Mao's era and—at a deliberate speed—transformed China into a modern nation. Deng was credited with saying, "To get rich is glorious." The trademark of capitalism, a stock market, was established in 1990 in Shanghai, the most open and cosmopolitan of China's cities. Exporting was promoted as the way to economic growth. By 2001, Wal-Mart alone bought $14 billion in merchandise.

Perhaps in the long term, the village democracy program may prove to be the most important of Deng's modernizations. To the extent that democracy requires conflict between ideas, groups, and parties, some Chinese see it in opposition to Confucianism, which values harmony and cooperation. With the disbanding of the commune system, the village democracy program began in 1987 with the Organic Law on Village Committees as a way to make local leaders more accountable. A 1994 amendment to the law allowed secret ballots. By the end of 1997, 95% of China's 900,000 villages had implemented the program. The program varies greatly from county to county, and some critics say it only transfers unpopular tasks such as tax collection and family planning to the local level. Nonetheless, millions of rural Chinese elect their local leadership.

Regional Differences

Britain's 19th-century conflict with China enabled its traders to continue exchanging Indian opium for Chinese tea and silk, making huge profits while devastating China. Defeated in these wars, China was forced to open ports up and down the coast not only to the opium trade but ultimately to foreign diplomats, residents, missionaries, and traders of every kind. **Hong Kong** island was ceded to Great Britain in perpetuity in 1841, the Kowloon peninsula in 1860, and another slice of the mainland leased in 1898.

Hong Kong is slightly smaller than Los Angeles and home to about 6.7 million people. It is one of the world's great cities with the world's largest containership port, one of the world's largest airports, the best performing stock

Hong Kong's Central District and a restored traditional Chinese sailing junk in Victoria Harbor.

SOURCE: Hong Kong Tourist Association.

exchange in the world, and an impressive trade and financial infrastructure. In 1997, this symbol of free enterprise was returned to China. In a critically important move, in 1990 China promised Hong Kong residents in the Sino-British document known as the Basic Law "one country, two systems." Hong Kong would be a special administrative region of China, with press freedom and continuance of its capitalist economic and social system guaranteed for at least 50 years after the takeover. The Basic Law specified that both Chinese and English would be official languages. By 1998, most public schools switched from teaching in English to Cantonese.

China has made it clear that Hong Kong was never a democracy under British rule. The colony's governor was appointed by the British government. It wasn't until 1991 that Great Britain allowed the first direct election of a portion of the seats in Hong Kong's legislature. Hong Kong's first chief executive after the return, Tung Chee-hwa, was selected by Beijing through a process of indirect elections involving a campaign and vote by 400 business people and community leaders selected themselves by Beijing. Hong Kong's elected

Chinese students celebrate at midnight in Beijing's Tiananmen Square as fireworks explode behind them marking Hong Kong's return.

SOURCE: AP/Wide World Photos.

legislature was replaced by an appointed one. Prior to the return, China wrote a new constitution for Hong Kong reversing some of the civil and democratic rights legislation that were passed after the Basic Law agreement without China's consent. Some believe Hong Kong's leaders will not be able to maintain political distance from Beijing as laws were changed in 2001 so that now the chief executive essentially serves at the pleasure of the mainland government.

By five years after the handover, China's entry into the World Trade Organization ended Hong Kong's historical role as the dominant international commercial trade center. Shanghai and other large trading centers have reduced its prominence.

Macao, the first European settlement in Asia and the last Portuguese-held colony, was returned to China in 1999 after 442 years under Portuguese control. China hopes that these colonies' return will be followed by the reunification of Taiwan and the mainland.

Hong Kong currency.

China is anything but a monolithic communist country, for it has tried dozens of political and economic experiments. China also has significant regional cultural differences. The north, including Beijing, is traditional and conservative. The ancestors of most Chinese in the south migrated from the north, overwhelming the original inhabitants and driving them into what is now Vietnam.

In much the same way that western migration in the United States shaped the character of the west, China's southern migration shaped a different culture in the south. The south is populated with people seeking a better life by escaping the conservatism and poverty of the rural north. Most of China's emigration as well has been from the south as people left China for Hong Kong, Southeast Asia, and the United States.

Chinese in the south are said to be more active, live better, and talk louder and are reasserting their business savvy. Recognizing this difference, Beijing in the late 1970s allowed Guangdong and Fujian provinces to go "one step ahead" in economic reforms. By 1985, this was expanded to the whole Pearl River Delta. Guangdong has emerged as the top producer of goods and services and the biggest exporter. With less than 5% of the population and less than 2% of the land area, it accounts for 11% of China's gross national product. It has attracted more foreign investment than the rest of China put together.

China-U.S. Relationship Issues

The United States and China relations continue to be strained. In 1996, the U.S. Congress created Radio Free Asia to promote democratic values in Asia.

In China, listeners will hear the views of critics of the government. Books such as *The Coming Conflict With China* (Bernstein, 1997) and *China Can Say No*, the 1996 best-seller in China, labeled each the enemy of the other.

The Status of Taiwan

Today, Taiwan is a technologically advanced island of 22 million people with a per capita income of more than $12,000. Taiwan's government has evolved from one-party rule under martial law into a full-fledged democracy. In 1996, Taiwan became the first government in the Chinese-speaking world to have a democratically elected president.

In the past, Taiwan and the mainland disputed which was the legitimate government of one China. Later, Taiwan argued that China is one country with two governments, much like Germany before reunification. On that basis, Taiwan sought greater international recognition and readmission to the United Nations. Although the United States no longer formally recognizes Taiwan, it has sold the Taiwanese jet fighters and dispatched aircraft carriers to the waters off Taiwan when China displayed military force near its shores.

Tiananmen Square Massacre

In 1989, the death of former Communist Party General Secretary Hu Yaobang, who many considered a political reformer, resulted in the student-led demonstration for democracy in Beijing that June. The army crushed the protest, killing hundreds perhaps even thousands on orders believed to have come from Deng (Black & Munro, 1993). Ever since, the Chinese media have blamed the United States for siding with the protesters.

Deng, who saw foreign influence in the uprising, dictated that severe measures, such as martial law, would again be taken in the event of future internal turmoil. Only by these means, he felt, would China's national sovereignty be protected from external interference.

Human Rights

The United States has protested the imprisonment without trial of religious and democracy proponents and the use of prison and child labor in manufacturing and has insisted on human rights improvements in China. The United States has attempted repeatedly, but unsuccessfully, to gain censure for Chinese human rights policies at the United Nations Commission on Human Rights.

Prior to the return of Hong Kong to China, the U.S. Congress passed legislation affirming the human rights of the people of Hong Kong. China views these demands as attacks on its sovereignty, with the United States acting as a global judge of human rights. China has also charged that the U.S. human rights record includes huge prison populations, low voter turnout, and a history of slavery. Rather than viewing this only as a political clash, some would seek explanations based in cultural values. Chinese leaders place a higher premium on social order and a lesser one on individual expression. China emphasizes collective order, whereas Western cultures stress individual liberties (Wasserstrom, 1991).

Tibet

Chinese troops occupied **Tibet** in 1950 and have waged war on the Dalai Lama and Tibetan Buddhism. The Dalai Lama has been seeking autonomy for Tibet since 1959 when he unsuccessfully tried to oust Chinese forces and was forced into exile. The Dalai Lama has proposed autonomy for Tibet while allowing China to retain control over defense and foreign affairs. The major concern has been the elimination of the Tibetan culture as more Chinese move into the region. The India-based Tibetan Government in Exile claims that Chinese immigrants outnumber Tibetans by at least 40 to 1. The United States has protested the treatment of the people and culture of Tibet. China has responded that the Dalai Lama is trying to achieve political objectives under the guise of religion.

International Incidents

In 1999 during the war against Yugoslavia, the North Atlantic Treaty Organization (NATO) approved a CIA proposal to bomb a Yugoslav military supply facility. A U.S. warplane mistakenly bombed the Chinese embassy in Belgrade, killing 3 and injuring 20 others. Chinese protested the bombing in demonstrations in Beijing and other cities. A Kodak Express store was burned, McDonald's restaurants were vandalized and boycotted, and Whirlpool appliances were damaged and pulled from stores in a display of anger directed at U.S. icons.

In April 2001, a U.S. spy plane made an unauthorized emergency landing on Hainan island after colliding with a Chinese fighter jet, killing its pilot. China regards spy planes 8,000 kilometers from their home as unwarranted; the U.S. says it has a legal right to fly over international waters off China. China demanded an apology, which the United States refused to give (see Box 4.2).

Box 4.2

"VERY SORRY" PROVES TO BE KEY PHRASE

Diplomacy: Wording of U.S. letter of regret was thoroughly negotiated. But each side offers different Chinese translation.

When the U.S. declared itself not just "sorry" but "very sorry" for the loss of a Chinese fighter pilot, the government in Beijing finally had a phrase it could translate into a linguistically acceptable apology.

The nuance of language apparently paved the way for the release of the 24-member crew of the American spy plane detained since April 1. And it will go a long way toward determining how the Chinese people perceive the United States' intentions, spelled out in a key letter from U.S. Ambassador Joseph W. Prueher to Chinese Foreign Minister Tang Jiaxuan on Wednesday.

After days of diplomatic negotiations over the wording of the letter, the U.S. side agreed to insert the "very," breaking the stalemate that has kept the crew detained on Hainan island, according to a senior Bush administration official. The letter also said the Americans were "very sorry" that the U.S. Navy EP-3 intruded into Chinese airspace without verbal permission when it made an emergency landing after colliding with the Chinese jet.

But complicating matters, each side issued different Chinese translations of the document.

The version prepared by the U.S. Embassy in Beijing offered *feichang baoqian* as a translation of "very sorry." But state-run Chinese media used *shenbiao qianyi,* a phrase that means "to express profound apology" but could suggest that the speaker is apologizing with some reservations.

Shenbiao qianyi is a "flexible fuzzy" phrase, according to a veteran Chinese language expert, speaking on condition of anonymity.

The word the Chinese wanted, but didn't get, was *daoqian,* which means "to apologize."

"The American side ought to apologize to the Chinese people," Chinese President Jiang Zemin said last week, using the word *daoqian.* Government officials had dismissed as inadequate earlier official U.S. expressions of regret.

"*Daoqian* would be the word Chinese could accept most easily," the language expert said, but added: "Strictly speaking, there is no real difference between *baoqian* and *daoqian.*

"Anyway, without the character *qian* in there, I don't think there would have been a way out of the situation," he said.

The character qian comes from a classical Chinese character that means "bad harvest." The right half of the character means, "to be inadequate" or "to owe something."

In Chinese, *qian* implies that the person delivering the apology is at fault. It also implies that the apology is made sincerely and seriously, not just a casual "Sorry about that."

"It's the sort of thing Japanese people would bow their heads when saying," the language expert said.

The political correctness of language has been serious business in China for millenniums, since the days when it was taboo to use the characters in an emperor's name. Lately, Chinese media have been careful to stick to the official description of the plane debacle, rendered as "the incident of an American military reconnaissance plane crashing into and destroying a Chinese military plane."

After news of the apology broke, China's official media quickly began reporting that some Chinese citizens were not satisfied.

"I think the U.S. government's way of apologizing can't satisfy people," company manager Su Wei told the official People's Daily online edition. Su said U.S. leaders should compensate China for its losses and apologize not in a letter, but in a live, globally televised news conference.

SOURCE: Anthony Kuhn, "Very Sorry" Proves to Be Key Phrase," *Los Angeles Times*, April 12, 2001, p. A14. Used with permission.

Changes in China Today

Soviet communism tried to reform the Soviet Union by loosening the reins on expression while keeping the economy under control. Chinese leaders try the opposite: They allow the economy, particularly in the south, to experiment while they control political speech.

On example is the Internet, which became available in China in 1995. Access was expensive and restricted. Later, the government began to provide computers to universities and state-owned businesses and to encourage Internet use for research and business. Internet usage began to surge. By 2002,

The belief that non-Western peoples should adopt Western values, institutions, and culture is immoral because of what would be necessary to bring it about. . . . If non-Western societies are once again to be shaped by Western culture, it will happen only as a result of expansion, deployment, and impact of Western power. . . . As a maturing civilization, the West no longer has the economic or demographic dynamism required to impose its will on other societies and any effort to do so is also contrary to the Western values of self-determination and democracy.

—Samuel P. Huntington
(1996, p. 310), conservative professor
of political science, Harvard University

some 40 million Chinese were online—mostly young, well educated, and in the eastern cities. Since 1995, more than 60 laws have been enacted governing Internet activities, and periodically material deemed harmful or otherwise critical of the state has been blocked.

China's economic development continues at a fast pace. In 1999, the constitution was amended to include private industry as an "important component" of the nation's economy. In 2000, the U.S. Congress granted China permanent normal trade status. And a year later, the Chinese Communist Party invited capitalist entrepreneurs to join its ranks. China was admitted to the World Trade Organization after agreeing to further open its economy.

Yet communication barriers still exist. What barriers did you identify? What could be done to improve intercultural communication between the peoples of the two cultures?

FROM THE INTERCULTURAL PERSPECTIVE

If you have ever watched street performers, chances are you've seen a mime doing a routine known as "trapped in an imaginary box." At the beginning of the routine, the mime goes in one direction. Suddenly, the mime hits an imaginary wall. Curious, the mime touches the wall and searches for a way around it but cannot find one. The mime then goes in different directions, but after a few steps hits another invisible wall each time. The mime is trapped. The only ways out are either to end the show or to imagine some clever escape. Similarly, in intercultural communication settings, it is all too easy to become trapped by invisible walls or barriers to communication. Although these walls are hard to perceive, they are not imaginary. The only way to "escape" is to learn to see them and avoid making the communication mistakes that come from them.

There are six barriers to communication—anxiety, assuming similarities instead of differences, ethnocentrism, stereotypes and prejudice, nonverbal misinterpretations, and language problems. Anxiety is feeling nervous, which can affect communication when you focus so much on your own feelings that you do not pay attention to what other people are telling you. If you are speaking to someone in your second language, you may worry that the other person may speak too fast or will use words you do not understand. Anxiety may also affect your ability to communicate your ideas to others. If you are in a situation where you feel very nervous, such as talking to your boss, you may find yourself saying awkward things or even making mistakes in grammar that you never do when talking with your friends.

Assuming similarities instead of differences is a natural thing to do if you do not have any information about a culture. Assuming that a culture is similar to your own can cause you to ignore important differences. It does not help to do the opposite—that is, to assume that everything is different—because this will lead to overlooking important similarities between cultures. The best thing to do when you encounter a new culture is to assume nothing and to ask what the customs are.

Ethnocentrism is negatively judging another culture by your own culture's standards. To make ethnocentric judgments is to believe that the ways of your own culture are better than those of others. Although ethnocentrism is considered a barrier to communication, it is common for people experiencing "culture shock" to make these kinds of judgments. When learning a new culture, individuals may go through a stage when they consider everything about the new culture to be worse than their home culture. However, after this stage, individuals usually begin to see one culture as not better or worse than another but as merely different.

Even though modern communication technology allows people access to increasing amounts of information about things happening all over the world, there is still a tendency for people to be more interested in local, state, and national news. In the United States, the most popular news shows do not cover international events in as much detail or accuracy as they do national and local news. It is common for people to form opinions about other countries using only the knowledge acquired through the media. Even though there may be many ties between countries, such as those between the United States and Japan, international travelers still often find that things are very different from what they had expected, which sometimes leads to feelings of anxiety.

Key Terms

Aboriginal	ethnocentrism	Macao
anxiety	ethnography	Taiwan
cultural relativism	four modernizations	Tibet
Cultural Revolution	Hong Kong	

CHAPTER 5

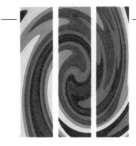

Stereotypes and Prejudice as Barriers

What You Can Learn From This Chapter

How stereotyping and prejudice impede communication

The effect of media stereotyping and prejudice on face-to-face communication

How communication can deal with stereotyping and prejudice

B y the year 1999, there were 6 billion people on earth—no two alike. People can be small and large and in many colors. We wear different clothes and have different ideas of beauty. Many of us believe in one God, others believe in many, and still others believe in none. Some are rich, and many are desperately poor. You can easily see that people from various cultures differ from one another, but how did differences become the basis of prejudice?

Stereotypes and prejudice are a pernicious stumbling block to intercultural communication. The term **stereotype** is the broader term commonly used to refer to negative or positive judgments made about individuals based on any observable or believed group membership, whereas **prejudice** refers to the irrational suspicion or hatred of a particular group, race, religion, or sexual orientation. The terms are related in that they both refer to making judgments about individuals based on group membership.

Figure 5.1   Visual illusion.

NOTE: The moon on the right has been made smaller to simulate the illusion.

STEREOTYPES

Definition

The word *stereotyping* was first used by journalist Walter Lippmann in 1922 to describe judgments made about others on the basis of their ethnic group membership. Today, the term is more broadly used to refer to judgments made on the basis of any group membership.

Psychologists have attempted to explain stereotyping as mistakes our brains make in the perception of other people that are similar to those mistakes our brains make in the perception of visual illusions (Nisbett, 1980).

When information is ambiguous, the brain often reaches the wrong conclusion. As illustrated in Figure 5.1, the moon appears to be much larger when it floats just above the horizon than when it shines overhead. The brain's estimation of distance changes as does the apparent size of the moon.

What we see, the most readily available image, is what we expect to see. We can reject any information that challenges that expectation. In Figure 5.2, a sign appears to read "Paris in the spring," but it actually has an extra "the." As we don't expect to see a double "the," we do not perceive it. In a like manner, if we expect that heads of corporations are tall, slender, White males, we don't see the disabled, women, and people of color in that group.

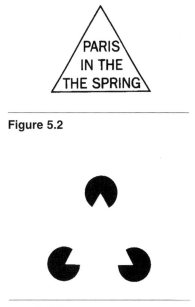

Figure 5.2

In Figure 5.3, a white triangle appears to float in front of three black circles even though no triangle exists. Our brain constructs the triangle; we see something that doesn't exist. We do not so much believe what we see as see what we believe. We tend to discount any perceptions that don't conform to our beliefs.

Who stereotypes? And who is the target of stereotyping? The answer to both questions is that anyone can stereotype and anyone can be the target of stereotyping.

Stereotypes are used by all groups. Until recently, the sign for *Japanese* in American Sign Language was a twist of the little finger at the corner of the eye to denote a slanted eye. The new sign taken from Japanese Sign Language is a hand signal to show the shape of the Japanese islands (Costello, 1995). In Japanese Sign Language, the sign for *foreigner* is the index finger making a circular motion around the eye denoting "round eye."

Figure 5.3

What is the difference between **cultural sensitivity** and ethnic stereotyping? In 1997, American Airlines was criticized for a flight manual that said Latin American customers like to drink before takeoff. Is that cultural information that makes it possible for the airline to provide better customer service, or is it a stereotype? That same flight manual also said that Latin American customers don't expect flights to depart on time and will even call in bomb threats if they are running late and want the flight to be delayed.

Is the practice of **racial profiling** stereotyping? **Profiling** refers to a law enforcement practice of scrutinizing certain individuals based on characteristics thought to indicate a likelihood of criminal behavior. For example, it is believed that a person traveling alone is more likely to engage in terrorist activity. Profiling also refers to, for example, conducting traffic stops based on the vehicle occupant's perceived race, ethnicity, gender, or economic status. The September 11, 2001, attacks on the United States created a climate that gave law enforcement agencies wider latitude to engage in more intensive airport security checks of people who appear to be of Middle Eastern descent. Is profiling a useful and necessary law enforcement tool, or is it a form of stereotyping that unfairly targets minorities?

Although you may think of stereotypes as being negative judgments, they can also be positive. Some people hold positive stereotypes of other individuals based on their professional group membership. For example, some people assume that all doctors are intelligent and wise.

Negative Effects on Communication

Stereotypes are harmful because they impede communication in at least four ways:

- They cause us to assume that a widely held belief is true when it may not be. Research conducted by Gordon Allport (1954) showed, for example, that the prevalent stereotype of Armenians as dishonest was proved false when a credit-reporting association gave the group credit ratings as good as those given others.

- Continued use of the stereotype reinforces the belief. Stereotypes of women as ornaments or of people of color as stupid or licentious or of gay men as promiscuous reinforce a belief that places individual women, African-Americans, and gay men at risk. Popular television may reinforce those stereotypes. Shaheen (1984), for example, has cited the four Western myths about Arabs as shown on television: Arabs are wealthy, barbaric, sex maniacs, and terrorist-minded.

- Stereotypes also impede communication when they cause us to assume that a widely held belief is true of any one individual. For example, if a group is stereotyped as dishonest, that does not mean that any one individual in that group is dishonest. A classic psychology study in the 1970s had two groups of undergraduates read stories about a woman. The stories were identical, except that one had the sentence "Betty is now a lesbian." On a test one week later, individuals in the group that had read that Betty is a lesbian were much more likely than individuals in the other group to recall having read that Betty never dated men. In fact, the story that both groups had read stated that Betty dated men occasionally. The group's stereotype of a lesbian influenced what they recalled having read (Snyder & Uranowitz, 1978).

- The stereotype can become a "self-fulfilling prophecy" for the person stereotyped. Research by psychologists Steele and Aronson (1995) has shown that a negative stereotype creates a threat that can distract the individual stereotyped and lower performance.

When stereotypes lead us to interpret an individual's behavior from the perceptual screen of the stereotype they impede communication. Were you to believe that Armenians are dishonest, when you saw a man you knew to be Armenian taking a package from a car you would be more likely to assume he was stealing it. In 1994, a young man with cigarette burns and the tattoo of an eagle on his arm was arrested by police who cited the burns and tattoo as proof that he was in a Chinese gang. The young man had chosen to get the tattoo, which also showed the words "bird without its flock," following his mother's death to speak of his loneliness living in Iowa. The burns on his arm were self-administered at the time of his mother's death. The young man is Vietnamese.

Case Study: Asian-Americans

Asian-American groups in the United States have experienced stereotyping, which although often positive has impeded communication. The term Asian-American was created by University of California, Los Angeles, historian Yuji Ichioka in the late 1960s to refer to all people of Asian descent in the belief that all Asians shared a common history and struggle in the United States. And up to the 1970s, Asian-Americans were largely born in the United States. The Immigration and Nationality Act amendments of 1965 abandoned the old policy of immigration quotas for each country and established a new system giving preference to relatives of U.S. residents. That change resulted in large numbers of Asians immigrating to the United States between 1981 and 1989. The label Asian-American includes more than 30 ethnicities with family origins extending from East Asia and Southeast Asia to the Indian subcontinent as well as the Philippines and Indonesia. The continued use of the term Asian-American contributes to a stereotype of some 10 million people of Asian ancestry as a single community.

During the civil rights era of the 1960s, "Asian-American" became associated with the stereotype of the "model minority" who achieved success through hard work, perseverance, silent stoicism, strong family ties, and strong support for education. This stereotype seemed to continue the belief that any group can achieve the American Dream if its members "just work hard enough." This stereotype continues in the media. Asian-Americans of all groups are most often portrayed in the press as industrious and intelligent, enterprising and polite, with strong values, and successful in schools and business and in science and engineering.

The 2000 Census showed that Asian-Americans had the highest percentage of households with annual incomes of $75,000 or more. But the stereotype associated with the label hides that Asian-Americans are also the fastest-growing segment on welfare. The rate of households on welfare climbed from 9.7% in 1980 to 12% in 1998. About 40% of Asian-Americans have a college or postgraduate education. And again the stereotype associated with the label hides that one in seven Asian-Americans lacks a high school diploma.

The stereotype is reinforced in news reports that Asian-American students score much higher on math exams than their White counterparts and that the percentage of U.S. scientists who are Asian-American is two to three times the percentage of Asian-Americans in the total population.

Asian-American high school students of all backgrounds complain that teachers often counsel Asian-Americans to go into math and sciences. Some teachers respond that this is done so that immigrants will not have to contend with language problems. Asian-Americans argue that some teachers continue to do this even to those who are fluent in English and that the reason why teachers do this is that Asians are perceived as not being free thinking or extroverted. The "model minority" stereotype is too narrow and confining. A smaller percentage of Asian-American students are encouraged to enter the creative fields of art and theater or the management field.

PREJUDICE

Definition

Whereas stereotypes can be positive or negative, prejudice refers to the irrational dislike, suspicion, or hatred of a particular group, race, religion, or sexual orientation (Rothenberg, 1992). Persons within the group are viewed not in terms of their individual merit but according to the superficial characteristics that make them part of the group.

> The easiest idea to sell anyone is that he is better than someone else.
>
> —Gordon Allport,
> *The Nature of Prejudice* (1954)

Psychologists have identified the highly prejudiced individual as having an **authoritarian personality** (Adorno, Frenkel-Brunswick, Levinson, & Sanford, 1950). Such persons tend to overgeneralize and think in bipolar terms; they are highly conventional, moralistic, and uncritical of higher authority. Highly prejudiced people are unlikely to change their attitudes even when presented with new and conflicting information.

Case Studies

Like stereotyping, anyone can be prejudiced and anyone can experience prejudice. Prejudice exists in cultures around the world.

The Roma

The Roma are believed to have migrated from India more than a millennium ago, settling first in Persia, then arriving in Europe in the 13th or 14th century. The name "Gypsy" was mistakenly applied by medieval Europeans who thought all dark-skinned people came from Egypt. Leading a nomadic life, the Roma were often regarded as tramps and accused of thefts and robberies. From the beginning of the 17th century, attempts were made to forcibly assimilate the Roma people by requiring permanent settlement and banning the Romany language. The Roma were particularly persecuted by Nazi Germany. About 500,000 died in Nazi gas chambers and concentration camps. The Roma now number slightly more than 5 million in Eastern Europe, 2 million more in Western Europe, and about 2 million elsewhere, mainly in North and South America and North Africa. Romania has the largest number—about 1 million.

For decades, Eastern European Communist governments suppressed prejudice against the Roma and banned the nomadic life. As the countries shifted to market economies and many lost jobs, the Roma have again experienced discrimination.

Graffiti have now reappeared on walls: "Gypsies go away" and "Gypsies to the gas." The Roma language and culture including the remembrance of the Holocaust (known in the Roma language as *porraimos*, or "the devouring") are central to Roma identity throughout the world. The European Union states have made better treatment of the Roma a condition for new members. Critics charge that these efforts are for the purpose of reducing migration into the more prosperous Western European nations.

Japan and Korea

Relationships between Japan and Korea reflect deep-seated and long-standing prejudice. Historically, Korea had closer ties to China than did Japan, and both Korea and China tended to view Japan as a "trouble-making" state. This view was reinforced time and again by Japanese incursions into Korean territory and 35 years of Japan's colonial rule. It has only been in recent times that Korean and Japanese governments have signed mutual friendship treaties, established normal diplomatic relations, and entered into joint economic development agreements. In an act of historic symbolism, Korea and Japan cohosted the 2002 World Cup soccer games. Despite economic ties there remains a sense of *han*, or bitter resentment, that many Koreans feel toward the Japanese.

After Japan's annexation of Korea in 1910, thousands of Koreans migrated into Japan seeking employment. Following the great 1923 Kanto earthquake in Japan, it was rumored that Koreans were poisoning water supplies. Mob violence left some 6,000 Koreans dead. Later, between 1939 and 1945, more Koreans were forced to migrate by the Japanese government to work in mines (Weiner, 1994). During World War II, the Koreans in Japan were forced to become Japanese nationals. Japan's surrender to the Allied Forces brought an end to the annexation of Korea, and the majority of Koreans who had been brought to Japan under forced immigration returned to Korea, but some 500,000 to 600,000 Koreans remained in Japan (Fukuoka, 1996).

When the San Francisco Peace Treaty came into effect in 1952, the government of Japan claimed that the Koreans then in Japan should not be granted Japanese nationality. The descendants of the Koreans who remained in Japan who may never have been to Korea and who may not speak Korean are legally foreigners.

As the largest minority group in Japan, Japanese-born Koreans are the victims of social, economic, and political prejudice. Japanese law provides little or no protection against the housing and employment discrimination many Japan-born Koreans experience. In 1974, the National Council for Combating Discrimination against Ethnic Minorities (*Mintohren*) was founded by Korean residents and concerned Japanese to fight for the human and civil rights of the Korean residents in Japan.

United States

Ireland got the potato plant from South America, and by the 1840s one-third of Ireland's tilled land was devoted to potato production. A fungus wiped out 90% of the crop by 1847, and by 1850, one fourth of the population had died or migrated. Some migrated to Australia, and more than 1 million migrated to the United States between 1846 and 1851. Many settled in shanty towns of cities in four states—Illinois, Massachusetts, New York, and Pennsylvania. Many took jobs few other workers would take: The Irish worked in mines and mills and constructed canals and railroad lines. Editorial cartoons depicted the Irish as lazy, "fighting," and drunken. "Job Available" signs in the period often included the phrase "No Irish Need Apply." In the largely segregated Irish communities, the moral values of the Catholic Church were important. With a shared language and a physical appearance similar to the dominant English immigrant culture and with improved economic status and political participation, the Irish assimilated into the dominant culture.

The Jewish religion spans all countries and ethnicities, yet anti-Semitic literature often identifies Jews as a biological race. (Jews and Arabs are Semites, but the term anti-Semitic means anti-Jewish.) Many of the approximately

150,000 German Jews who immigrated to the United States between 1830 and 1860 established small businesses. Cartoon drawings in U.S. publications often characterized Jewish people as money-grubbing shysters with large noses and funny accents. Later, between 1881 and 1924, some 3.5 million eastern European Jews immigrated to escape the anti-Semitic violence in Russia and Poland. Henry Ford published books and articles in the 1920s accusing Jews of causing the Civil War and Lincoln's assassination and of plotting to take over the world. The Ku Klux Klan burned crosses on the front lawns of Jewish families and vandalized synagogues. More recently, Louis Farrakhan of the Nation of Islam charged that Jews ran the slave trade and continue to exploit African-Americans economically. Today, some 6 million of a worldwide population of 13 million Jewish people live in the United States. Media representations of Jewish stereotypes still appear.

Surveys continue to show that prejudiced attitudes exist in the United States (Crosby, Bromley, & Saxe, 1980) and that prejudice exists not only between Whites and minority groups but between minority groups as well.

In 1994, the United States ratified the United Nations' antiracism convention. All countries that ratified the treaty agreed to analyze their own practices. In 2000, the United States reported for the first time to the United Nations Committee on the Elimination of Racial Discrimination that U.S. antibias laws are among the world's most stringent. The report cited affirmative action laws as helping to break down economic barriers. On the other hand, the report cited examples of racial bias in the United States including an African-American man who was dragged to his death in Texas and a Florida hotel that required African-American guests to wear wristbands to identify them as guests.

Media Portrayal of Minorities

It's long been known that negative portrayals by the media increase prejudiced attitudes. In a pioneering study done in the 1930s, Ruth Peterson and Lewis Thurstone (1933) showed that viewing the classic silent film *The Birth of a Nation* (1915), which includes derogatory depictions of African-Americans, increased prejudice toward African-Americans. Yet the portrayal of African-Americans continued to be negative. Writer Langston Hughes created the character Jesse B. Semple, known as "Simple" to his friends in Harlem. Semple once observed, "The only time colored folks is front-page news is when there's been a race riot or a lynching or a whole lot of us have been butchered up or arrested" (Hughes, 1961, p. 230).

To some extent, Hughes's statement is true for everyone. News is about the unusual; it's about the extremes of life—not about normal, everyday life.

Yet the press seems to cover a much broader range of "White life" than of "minority life." Engagement notices, obituaries, and stories about young, middle-class couples struggling to buy their first home are more likely to be about Whites.

Only 15% of the poor in the United States are African-American. Most of the violent criminals, drug users, prostitutes, drunks, illiterates, high school dropouts, juvenile delinquents, jobless, and poor in the United States are neither African-American nor Hispanic but White. The majority of African-Americans and Hispanics are none of the above, yet the press, it is contended, gives African-Americans and Hispanics preponderantly negative coverage.

The Watts riots in Los Angeles in 1965 brought the media under scrutiny for its portrayals of African-Americans. Many critics felt that the media, rather than reporting the social inequalities faced by African-Americans, portrayed African-Americans only as sports heroes, entertainers, and criminals.

The 1992 Los Angeles rioting following the Rodney King verdict again brought the media under scrutiny. Most media images were of White victims and of African-American rioters described by television commentators as "thugs" and "goons." In fact, many rioters were not African-American, but many victims were. One media image after the riot was of lines of African-Americans at post offices. News commentators described the people in line as welfare recipients, when in fact many in the line were there to collect mail that could not be delivered during the rioting. The media coverage, it is argued, reinforced stereotypes of inner-city African-Americans.

RACISM

Definition

In Chapter 1, race was shown to be a nebulous concept. Racism, on the other hand, is a concrete reality.

Racism is any policy, practice, belief, or attitude that attributes characteristics or status to individuals based on their race. Racism involves not only prejudice but the exercise of power over individuals based on their race. Racism can be either conscious or unconscious, intentional or unintentional (Essed, 1991; Rothenberg, 1992; van Dijk, 1987).

Racism exists worldwide. Some Chinese refer to Africans as *hei gwei*, or "black devils," and refer to Whites as "white devils." In Brazil, race is seen as a continuum rather than in mutually exclusive categories. Its long history of intermarriage makes racial definitions ambiguous, yet lighter-skinned

Demonstrations against Abercrombie & Fitch's new T-shirt line.

SOURCE: Asian American Resource Workshop.

Brazilians enjoy higher status and rewards. Racism appears in songs, insults and malicious humor, employment ads written to discourage non-White applicants, advertising with European-looking models, and television that makes Brazil look "whiter than Scandinavia" according to a candidate for deputy mayor of Rio in 1996.

Even though the United States has three centuries of a mixed gene pool, some people see distinct categories (Cose, 1997). Neo-Nazi skinheads, for example, profess to want to awaken other Whites to recognize that Whites are a dying race. Skinheads got their name from some members shaving their heads. The Anti-Defamation League of B'nai B'rith estimates that in the United States in 1992 some 3,500 neo-Nazi skinheads were active in 40 states.

In 2002, Abercrombie & Fitch pulled a line of T-shirts after complaints that they were racist. The T-shirts show Asian cartoon characters. Printed on the shirts were ads for hypothetical businesses: "Rick Shaw's Hoagies and Grinders. Order by the foot. Good meat. Quick feet" and "Wong Brothers Laundry Service—Two Wongs Can Make It White." As senior manager at A&F said, "These graphic T-shirts were designed with the sole purpose of adding humor and levity to our fashion line."

Gobineau: The "Father of Racism"

European views on racism or racial superiority are most often associated with the 19th-century French writer Count Joseph Arthur de Gobineau. Although racism existed before Gobineau, his well-known articulation of White racial superiority, *Essai sur l'inégalité des races humaines*, established his position as the "father of racism" (Biddiss, 1970).

Gobineau makes the shift from simply saying that races are different to arguing that there is evidence for a racial hierarchy. In his hierarchy, the White race is the most advanced, the Black race the least advanced, and the Yellow between the two. Gobineau changed White from one racial group among others to the preferred racial group.

Gobineau used three discursive strategies: categorizing all people into clearly defined groups—the White, the Black, and the Yellow; using appearance for evidence, saying that one could "see" that Whites were the most beautiful; and arguing for drawing boundaries based only on race and not on other factors such as national lines.

Box 5.1

DESPITE ADVANCES, STEREOTYPES STILL USED BY MEDIA

Even the most severe critics of the nation's news media concede that there is now much greater sensitivity in the portrayal of minorities.

But ethnic stereotypes continue to appear.

A *Los Angeles Times* story [in 1989] described a Chinese poker player as "inscrutable" and as a "classically serene Asian," for example, and a *Times* fashion layout showed a Latino model, wearing a Latino designer's clothes—walking alongside a graffiti-scarred wall.

"Do all Latinos live surrounded by graffiti?" asks Alan Acosta, assistant hiring editor at the *Times*.

Racially insensitive and offensive language contributing to harmful stereotypes also remains common:

■ The *New York Times*, *Washington Post*, *Chicago Tribune*, *Time* and *Newsweek*—among others—have used the words "invade" or "invasion" when speaking of the influx of Asian-American immigrants or Asian-American business acquisitions in this country; Asian-Americans say this invokes damaging images and memories of World War II.

■ The *Los Angeles Times*, *Boston Globe*, *Washington Post*, *Philadelphia Inquirer* and *Chicago Tribune*, among others, have used the word "aliens" to describe immigrants who are here illegally; Latinos say this word makes them seem inhuman—strange outcasts from another world. They would rather be called "illegal immigrants" or "undocumented workers."

■ When a woman jogger was beaten and raped in Central Park [in 1989], the *New York Times* and *Washington Post* (among others) called her [alleged] black attackers a "wolf pack," but these papers used no such bestial imagery to describe the whites who murdered blacks in Howard Beach and Bensonhurst.

■ Television sports commentators, in particular, speak of white athletes as being "smart" or "brainy" or as having worked hard; black athletes are often described as "natural" or "pure" athletes, "gifted" with great speed or strength or jumping ability. These formulations ignore the "natural" physical abilities of many white athletes and the demonstrated intelligence of many black athletes—as well as the hours and years of practice many black athletes put in developing their skills.

Andrea Ford, a black reporter at the *Los Angeles Times*, recalls that when Bishop Desmond Tutu of South Africa won the Nobel Peace Prize in 1984, a white colleague at the Detroit Free Press, where she then worked, wrote a caption for a photograph of Tutu dancing in celebration.

The caption said Tutu "broke into a jig."

Ford says she tried to explain that "jig" was a derogatory term for "black" and that it was both ignorant and insulting to suggest that a native of a country with the rich folk

(Continued)

Box 5.1, *Continued*

dance traditions of Africa would break into an Irish dance. Her arguments initially were rejected, Ford says, and she had to appeal to a higher-ranking editor before prevailing.

SOURCE: David Shaw, "Despite Advances, Stereotypes Still Used by Media," *Los Angeles Times*, December 12, 1990, p. 31. Copyright © 1990, Los Angeles Times. Reprinted with permission.

NOTE: This article, written in 1990, calls attention to past practices.

THE ROLE OF COMMUNICATION

Spread of Prejudice and Racism

> The point is that racism has come out of the closet and people are beginning to not be afraid of declaring blatantly racist views and getting away with it.
>
> —South African Archbishop
> Desmond Tutu, December 1991

When studying stereotypes, prejudice, and racism, you may be struck with the role that communication can play in either spreading the beliefs or stopping their spread. Prejudice and racism are commonly viewed as being rooted in the child's early socialization and fostered in communication with other people who are prejudiced or racist (Adorno et al., 1950).

Just overhearing racist comments has been shown to negatively affect the listener's evaluation of the person being spoken about. Research studies have demonstrated this effect (Greenberg & Pyszczynski, 1985; Kirkland, Greenberg, & Pyszczynski, 1987). In the study conducted by Jeff Greenberg and Tom Pyszczynski (1985), groups of White college students observed a debate between a White and an African-American student and were asked to evaluate the skill of the debaters. The debates were staged so that half the time the African-American debater won and half lost. Immediately after the debate and before the evaluations, a confederate either made a derogatory ethnic slur against the African-American debater, criticized the African-American debater in a nonracist manner, or made no comment.

Ethnic slurs did cue prejudiced behavior. The study's results showed that when the audience overheard the derogatory ethnic slur the rating given the African-American debater who lost was significantly lower but not so when the African-American debater won. The researchers comment that evaluations of individual minority group members can be biased by overheard derogatory ethnic labels when the person's behavior is less than perfect.

The Persistence of Prejudice

Researchers have suggested various reasons for the persistence of prejudice:

- *Socialization.* Prejudices are learned. Many prejudices are passed on from parents to children, sometimes in subtle messages such as "we don't associate with people like that" or "be careful when you're with them." Of course, many people shed these prejudices as they discover them to be unfounded. The media can perpetuate derogatory images and stereotypes.

- *Social benefits.* Expressing a prejudice may bring support from others who share that prejudice. It is difficult for people to break away from the prejudices of their families and friends, as rejecting the prejudice can be perceived as breaking away from the association.

- *Economic benefits.* Prejudice can be strong when there is direct competition for jobs. When Chinese immigrants worked on building the transcontinental railroad across the United States when jobs were plentiful, Chinese were perceived as hard-working, industrious, and law-abiding. But after the railroad was completed and jobs dwindled, Chinese were perceived as criminal, crafty, and stupid (Aronson, 1988). In a similar way, the Arab oil embargo of the early 1970s contributed to a rise in prejudice against Arab-Americans, and during trade tensions with Japan, Japanese-Americans became targets.

> There is a myth of the "natural athlete" whose effortless excellence is a kind of spontaneous blooming. That myth is false and pernicious. It dilutes the emulative value of superior performance. It does so by discounting the extent to which character counts in sport. The myth is especially damaging to blacks. . . .
>
> A great ball player received a lot of semi-disparaging praise as a "natural." Willie Mays had just turned 20 when he made his major league debut. His ebullience—his high-pitched laughter, the post-game stickball games in the streets of Harlem—occasioned frequent references to the "childlike" enthusiasm and "instinctive" play of this "natural." Often the condescension was unconscious, but it was nonetheless corrosive. The truth is that Mays was, from the first, a superb craftsman. . . . Mays received much praise for his baserunning "instincts." But again, such praise often is veiled—and not very well veiled—condescension. Mays's "instincts" were actually the result of meticulous work.
>
> —George F. Will, *Men at Work* (1990, pp. 226-227)

Grand Wizard of the Knights of the Ku Klux Klan, Thomas Robb, said in a speech at a rally in Aurora, Colorado, in July 1991, "We've got too many people trying to dissipate our race—the race-mixing, fags, everything."

SOURCE: *Denver Post*, January 21, 1991. Used with permission.

- *Psychological benefits*. Prejudice can be used to generate a feeling of superiority and to explain a complex world in terms of simple causes as in saying that "those people are the source of all our problems."

Hate Speech

Out of such realizations that speech can cue prejudiced behavior in others, some have attempted to restrict that type of speech often referred to as hate speech. **Hate speech** includes threats or verbal slurs directed against specific groups or physical acts such as burning crosses or spray-painting swastikas on public or private property (Walker, 1994).

Does hate speech lead to hate crime? When I was an undergraduate student I first saw this photograph in a textbook. I've never forgotten it. It was taken during the Detroit race riot of 1943. These two young men had come to the aid of a fellow human.

SOURCE: *Detroit Free Press* file photo. Used with permission.

Some cities and colleges have adopted policies attempting to ban hate speech. Strong arguments have been raised that such prohibitions are in violation of the First Amendment, the right from government abridgment of

We cannot overlook the fact . . . that much linguistic expression serves a dual communicative function: it conveys not only ideas capable of relatively precise, detached explication, but otherwise inexpressible emotions as well. In fact, words are often chosen as much for their emotive as their cognitive force. We cannot sanction the view that the Constitution, while solicitous of the cognitive content of individual speech, has little or no regard for that emotive function which, practically speaking, may often be the more important element of the overall message sought to be communicated.

—Justice Harlan, in *Cohen v. California* (1971)

SOURCE: *U.S. Supreme Court Reports*, 29 L. Ed. 2d (1972), quote on p. 294.

freedom of expression other than libel and obscenity. Others counter that hate speech is less like political expression and more like an action, such as a slap in the face (see Haiman, 1994), and that such regulations are necessary to protect equality.

Internationally, the trend since World War II has been to protect individuals and groups from expressions of hatred, hostility, discrimination, and violence. In fact, Australia, Austria, Great Britain, Canada, France, Germany, Italy, the Netherlands, New Zealand, Norway, and Sweden all have statutes or constitutional provisions prohibiting forms of hate speech. The International Covenant of Civil and Political Rights in Article 20(2) expressly provides that "any advocacy of national, racial, or religious hatred that constitutes incitement to discrimination, hostility, or violence shall be prohibited by law." In 1992 when the U.S. Senate ratified this treaty, it stipulated that the United States would not be bound by this provision but would adhere to its own constitution.

First Amendment Rights

Are expressions of racial or ethnic superiority then protected by the First Amendment? In 1991, a federal district judge voided a University of Wisconsin rule against hate speech saying it was unconstitutionally broad. The university's rule barred speech that was intended to create a hostile learning environment through the demeaning of a person's race, sex, religion, color, creed, disability, sexual orientation, or ancestry. In 1992, in *R.A.V. v. St. Paul, Minn.*, the Supreme Court held unanimously that cross burning is protected by the First Amendment. The case involved a Minnesota teenage skinhead who burned a cross on the front lawn of the only African-American family in a working-class neighborhood of St. Paul. The teenager was charged under a city ordinance that banned any action that one knows arouses anger in others on the basis of race, color, creed, religion, or gender. The Court used as precedent its earlier ruling striking down laws against flag burning. The Court's ruling made it clear that speech cannot be limited on the basis of its content.

Cable Television Programming

One form of the electronic media has been accused of inadvertently disseminating hate: Cable television started in the 1940s as a way of extending the reach of television signals into areas out of range of the broadcast signal, such as mountain areas. Later, cable systems moved into other areas and offered signals from distant stations. Most often, local governments award a franchise to a single cable company that allows it to dig up city streets and use utility poles for its cable. In exchange, the cable operator pays a percentage of its receipts to the city and sets aside channels for use by the public, educational institutions, or the government.

The Cable Communications Policy Act of 1984 became the first cable law adopted by Congress. In this act, Congress made cable television the only mass medium required to provide access to its facilities by any member of the public. The act allows cities to require that channels be set aside for government, educational, and public use. Local governments schedule programming such as city council meetings, but they have no control over public use. Even the cable operators themselves have no editorial control providing the programming meets minimum production standards and does not contain obscene content. However, the new cable law passed in 1992 did place limits on indecent and obscene programming on public access channels.

In 1991, an Anti-Defamation League survey labeled 57 programs as preaching racial and religious hatred on public access channels. These were being shown in 24 of the top 100 markets. One example is the series "Another Voice of Freedom" promoted by Ernst Zundel. The Canadian citizen had been imprisoned for violating Canada's hate laws until he was cleared by the Canadian Supreme Court in 1992. Zundel claims the Holocaust was a hoax and distributes his message free over public access cable television in the United States and worldwide over the Internet.

Admittedly, public access programming has very few viewers, but this raises the question of First Amendment rights and racism. Should individuals guaranteed access to cable television mass media have no restrictions on their message content other than obscenity?

The Internet

In April 1995, when the Simon Wiesenthal Center started tracking hate sites on the Internet, it identified one.

In 1996, the U.S. Congress passed the Communications Decency Act, which made it a federal crime to put obscene and indecent words or images on the Internet. The concern was to protect children from pornographic material. The next year, the U.S. Supreme Court invalidated a key provision of the law. The Court ruled that in seeking to protect children the law violated the rights of adults.

In that same year (1997), the Wiesenthal Center identified more than 500 hate sites. Its 1999 report identified 1,426 sites, including an online video game whose objective is to lynch a Black man.

The first federal prosecution of an Internet hate crime occurred in 1996. A 19-year-old male former student at the University of California, Irvine, sent an e-mail message signed "Asian hater" to about 60 Asian students, accusing Asians of being responsible for all crimes on campus and ordering the students to leave the campus or be killed by him. He was convicted in 1998 of interfering with students' civil rights to attend a public university.

In 1997, Germany passed a law under which online providers can be prosecuted for offering a venue for content illegal in Germany, such as Nazi propaganda, if they do so knowingly and if it is technically possible to prevent it. The First Amendment would not permit such a restriction in the United States.

Relation to Hate Crimes

It is argued that such attitudes can erupt into hate crimes. A **hate crime** stems from a fear of differences and results in hostility toward people considered different because of their actual or perceived race, religion, sexual orientation, or ethnicity. (In some jurisdictions, disability and gender are protected.)

Forty-two states and the federal government have hate crime laws of some kind. Under the Hate Crime Statistics Act of 1990, reporting is voluntary.

Attacks against individuals who appear Middle Eastern in the months following the September 11 terrorist attacks are reflected in the 2001 FBI report in Tables 5.1 and 5.2. Attacks against South Asian Americans including Indian- and Pakistani-Americans, especially Sikh Americans (a religious group often mistakenly perceived to be Arab because many of the men wear turbans and long beards), increased significantly.

In making a determination of a hate crime charge, arresting officers are guided by such considerations as a lack of provocation, the absence of any other apparent motive, the attacker's language use, the severity of the attack, and physical evidence of intimidation.

Levin and McDevitt (1993) categorize hate crime perpetrators by their motivation. Almost all hate crimes they found were acts of individuals unaffiliated

Table 5.1   Number of Hate Crime Incidents, by Year

Year	Number of Reporting Agencies	Total Offenses	Race	Religion	Sexual Orientation	Ethnicity/ National Origin	Disability	Multiple Biases
1998	10,730	7,755	4,321	1,390	1,260	754	25	5
1999	12,122	9,301	5,250	1,532	1,487	1,011	21	10
2000	11,690	9,413	5,171	1,556	1,486	1,164	36	17
2001	11,987	9,721	4,367	1,828	1,393	2,098	35	9

SOURCE: FBI Uniform Crime Reports and Hate Crime Statistics, 1998, 1999, 2000, 2001, http://www.fbi.gov/ ucr/01hate.pdf.

Table 5.2   Hate Crime Offenders by Race, by Year

Year	White	Black	American Indian/ Alaskan Native	Asian/Pacific Islander	Multiracial	Unknown
1998	4,970	1,303	54	144	359	659
1999	4,092	947	40	71	178	3973
2000	4,111	1,021	43	82	177	3339
2001	6,054	1,882	59	84	405	755

SOURCE: FBI Uniform Crime Reports and Hate Crime Statistics, 1998, 1999, 2000, 2001, http://www.fbi.gov/ ucr/01hate.pdf.

with any organization. They describe the majority as bored and alienated youths looking for excitement by assaulting someone who is different. There is evidence to suggest that over 50% of hate crimes are committed by people under the age of 21.

Box 5.2

THE CASE OF MATTHEW SHEPARD

Matthew Shepard, 21, a University of Wyoming student, was brutally beaten and left tied to a wooden ranch fence. He was found near death some 18 hours after the attack. He died five days later at a Colorado hospital having never regained

(Continued)

Box 5.2 *Continued*

consciousness. Shepard grew up in Casper and lived abroad until deciding to return to Wyoming to attend his father's alma mater.

Police accused two men of luring Shepard from the Fireside Bar, a campus hangout, by telling him they were gay. Police said that robbery was the chief motive but that the victim was chosen in part because he was gay and that the men made anti-gay remarks after the attack.

In a plea bargain, one pleaded guilty to murder and kidnapping and was sentenced to two life terms. The other's attorneys wanted to stage a "homosexual panic" defense to argue their client lost control after Shepard propositioned him. This legal theory was explored in a 1989 *Harvard Law Review* article which argued "that a person with latent homosexual tendencies will have an extreme and uncontrollably violent reaction when confronted with a homosexual proposition." A year earlier, two Canadian psychiatrists reviewed literature on the subject and concluded in the *Canadian Journal of Psychiatry* that homosexual panic is not a mental disorder but, rather, the culmination of culture's homophobic attitudes.

State District Judge Barton Voigt said that the accused's sexual history was not "appropriate in a case that turns out to be a premeditated gay bashing or robbery poorly disguised as homosexual rage" and prohibited the use of the controversial strategy, reasoning that it was not allowed under state law. The second man was convicted of kidnapping, aggravated robbery, and felony murder.

The New York Lesbian and Gay Anti-Violence Project reported 27 hate-motivated gay murders in the United States in 1996 and 18 in 1997. In June 1998, Senate Majority Leader Trent Lott (R-Mississippi) likened gay people to alcoholics and kleptomaniacs during a nationally televised interview. Shepard's murder increased efforts to pass nationwide hate crime legislation protecting gays. Wyoming, the Equality State, was the first to allow women's suffrage but was 1 of only 8 of the 50 states without a hate crimes law. Efforts in Wyoming had failed repeatedly because critics said it would give homosexuals special rights. A federal hate crimes measure was removed from a budget bill in a congressional conference committee just weeks after the trial with the approval of the Republican congressional leadership.

The following is from a eulogy delivered at a memorial service at the University of Wyoming on Monday, October 12, 1998, the day that Matthew Shepard died:

. . . Matthew was one of MY students. Although I had never had him in class, had never supervised him directly, he was indeed one of MY students.

Matthew was indeed one of OUR students. Like the faculty, staff, and all University of Wyoming students—Matthew was one of US. His loss leaves me feeling personally diminished. . . .

. . . Matthew was the kind of UW student that I came here to be with. Open, caring, unpretentious, vibrant. And, Matthew was gay. He manifest a kind of diversity here in our community that is so essential if we are to learn from each other lessons of love, nurturance, devotion, acceptance, and celebration of diversity. We can't hope to provide a complete and comprehensive educational experience without the Matthew Shepards of this world. We need him as he needed us to become whole.

. . . The one solace I take in all of this is that I find welling up within me a remarkable deep and abiding promise, a commitment, a covenant with myself and with you—that I personally will never be a party to any abusive or harmful conduct, either directly or indirectly, either verbally or behaviorally to any individual or group. My covenant goes beyond that to include finding within me the power of love and nurturance for those about me—especially those who are different from me, different in sexual orientation, gender, ethnicity, or belief. It must start with me, and I am the one to make that happen.

The second part of my covenant is to use all my personal talent and resources in working to assure that our children learn, and we teach each other, fundamental lessons of caring and devotion and commitment to each other's welfare. . . .

SOURCE: Excerpts from eulogy delivered by James C. Hurst, Vice President for Student Affairs, University of Wyoming. Used with permission.

Hate crime laws provide for extra jail terms in the same way that existing laws provide for higher penalties for those who murder the president or a police officer. The Supreme Court has ruled on Wisconsin's law that increases punishment for bias-motivated crimes. In 1989, a young African-American male and his friends were discussing the scene from the movie *Mississippi Burning* showing a White man beating a young African-American youth who was praying. The young African-American male was charged with encouraging his friends to beat up a 14-year-old White male who was walking by. The White male was hospitalized in a coma and suffered permanent brain damage. The African-American male was convicted of aggravated battery. His sentence was increased 4 additional years under Wisconsin's hate crime law. In 1993, in *Wisconsin v. Mitchell*, the Court upheld the enhanced sentence.

Positive Approaches

Cultural Norms

Because laws banning hate speech may not be constitutional in the United States, there are other, more positive approaches to dealing with prejudice and racism. Establishing cultural norms against such behaviors and presenting a more balanced picture of minority life in the media may be more effective.

One research project, for example, demonstrated that hearing other people express strongly antiracist opinions influences both public and private expressions of racist opinions (Blanchard, Lilly, & Vaughn, 1991). In their study, Blanchard et al. (1991) interviewed students on the way to classes. In each interview, three people were involved: the White interviewer, a White confederate, and a naïve White respondent. The interviewer asked the confederate and respondent questions about how their college should respond to anonymous racist notes. The confederate always answered first. The study compared how the respondents answered the questions when the confederate answered with the most antiracist statements to how they answered when the confederate answered with the least antiracist statements.

> He that would make his own liberty secure, must guard even his enemy from oppression, for if he violates this duty, he establishes a precedent that will reach to himself.
>
> —Thomas Paine (1737-1809)

The results showed that hearing the confederate express strongly antiracist opinions produced dramatically stronger antiracist opinions than hearing opinions more accepting of racism. In a second study, Blanchard et al. showed the same results when the respondents expressed their answers privately on paper. On the basis of this research, it can be argued that cultural norms can minimize the public expression of discriminatory or otherwise interracially insensitive behavior. Yum and Park (1990), however, argue that for well-established stereotypes to change, more frequent information and stronger content are needed. What each of us says about racial discrimination really does matter. Your vocal opinions affect what others think and say.

Media

Media have been used as a tool to confront prejudice and racism first by reporting forms of human rights abuses and second by portraying all groups fairly.

One significant example of human rights abuse reporting was done by the British investigative journalist Edmund Dene Morel. For a time, the Congo was the personal possession of King Leopold II of Belgium. The invention of inflatable tires for bicycles and automobiles created a demand for rubber. In the 1890s, the Congo's rain forest was rich with wild rubber. The king's soldiers forced men from the villages to gather the rubber for export, thus destroying the village economy. Hundreds of thousands fled; tens of thousands were killed in rebellions; millions died of starvation and disease. Morel, a mid-20s employee of the British shipping line that carried cargo to and from the Congo, saw that the ships arrived in the Belgian port of Antwerp with ivory and rubber but returned not with trading goods but with guns, ammunition, and soldiers. Morel quit his job and devoted a decade to putting the story of the slavery in European and U.S. newspapers. His reporting convinced Sir Arthur Conan Doyle and Mark Twain to write and lecture on the Congo. Morel himself did slide show lectures. The Congo reform movement became the best-organized and vocal human rights movement for nearly a decade at the beginning of the 20th century.

Another more positive approach to prejudice and racism is to present a more balanced picture of minority life in the media. A number of newspapers have made serious efforts to do just that, but none has been more diligent in its efforts than *USA Today*. Almost every day it publishes four photographs on the top half of the front page. In keeping with the original edict of its founder, Allen Neuharth, at least one of those photos shows a member of an ethnic minority and at least one of the other photos shows a woman. Neuharth wrote in a front-page letter on the first day of the newspaper's publication that "*USA Today* hopes to serve as a forum for better understanding and unity to help make the USA truly one nation."

The paper's efforts go beyond the design of its front page. A determined effort is made to include minorities in every section and element of the newspaper, in stories of fashion and business, and in drawings and charts.

· Disney films have been altered over time to remove their original stereotypes: The 1933 version of the "Three Little Pigs" had the Big Bad Wolf disguising himself as a peddler with a heavy Jewish accent. That was changed and reissued with a falsetto voice. The "Pastorale Symphony" section of *Fantasia* was reedited in 1991 to remove Sunflower, a Black centaurette/shoeshine girl who buffed the other characters' hooves. The lyrics to the opening song in *Aladdin* were changed after the American-Arab Anti-Discrimination Committee registered objections, yet no comment was made on the fact that the Arabian Jasmine and her father speak unaccented, standard American English and the "bad guys" speak with foreign accents.

FROM THE INTERCULTURAL PERSPECTIVE

"Did you hear the one about the _____?" We will not go on. Jokes such as these help maintain a very strong barrier to communication—stereotypes and prejudice. Stereotyping is assuming that a person has certain qualities (good or bad) just because the person is a member of a specific group. An example of a stereotype is the belief that one group of people is stupid or that another produces good athletes. Prejudice is feeling hatred for or expressing suspicion toward people who belong to a certain group, race, religion, or sexual orientation. A specific kind of prejudice, racism, refers to having feelings of hatred for or expressing suspicion toward all members of a particular race and denying this group its rights.

Stereotyping and prejudice both have negative effects on communication. If a stereotype is very common, people may assume that it is true. Even the people who are stereotyped may eventually believe it too. Stereotypes can have a negative effect when people use them to interpret behavior. Prejudice can have very serious effects, for it can lead to discrimination and hate crimes. Hate crime refers to hostile words and/or actions that people say or do against a certain group because that group is different.

Stereotypes, prejudice, and racism are learned from other people or institutions that are prejudiced. Prejudice continues to exist because of socialization and the apparent social, economic, and psychological benefits that come from it. Historically in the United States, there was a lot of prejudice against people who recently immigrated. After the huge wave of immigration that followed the Potato Famine in Ireland, there was much prejudice against Irish people in the United States because earlier immigrants worried that the new immigrants would take their jobs.

Although overtly prejudiced individuals and groups exist, governments, too, have encouraged prejudice in the citizens of their countries through the kinds of policies they have followed. In the United States during World War II, the government's propaganda against Germany and Japan caused much prejudice against people of German and Japanese ancestry. The internment of thousands of Japanese-Americans during the war also served to increase feelings of prejudice against this group. The United States is not the only government to allow such prejudice to exist. The Japanese

> One of the biggest lies out there is that no matter what race or religion you are, it doesn't matter. Now that's a lie, and we all know it. If we don't talk about these problems and take them on, they're going to get much, much worse.
>
> —Spike Lee, movie producer and director

policy of not allowing non-Japanese people to become citizens has created a second-class citizenry among Koreans living in Japan.

Stereotypes, prejudice, and racism continue to have a strong presence in the media. They can be found in print media, ranging from children's books to college brochures, and in electronic media. The movies and television programs of popular culture still portray many minorities and foreign groups in a stereotyped way.

KEY TERMS

authoritarian personality	hate speech	racial profiling
cultural sensitivity	prejudice	racism
hate crime	profiling	stereotype

CHAPTER 6

Nonverbal Communication

What You Can Learn From This Chapter

How nonverbal communication is defined

Types of nonverbal message codes

How nonverbals can be a barrier in intercultural communication

How other aspects of culture are revealed in nonverbal communication behaviors

In Chapter 2, you read how communication as an element of culture is understood differently by cultures. You read that, in the Western transmission models of communication, sources encode ideas into symbols and that symbols can be words or nonspoken symbols. The messages sent without using words are called **nonverbal communication**. The study of nonverbal communication in Western cultures conceptualizes nonverbals as a language system. Gestures, for example, are studied as if they function just like verbal symbols in a language.

Keep in mind that not all nonverbal behavior is nonverbal communication. Communication occurs when we intentionally use symbols—words or nonspoken symbols—to create meaning for others.

This chapter first looks at the different ways that nonverbal communication has been defined. Then nonverbal message codes that have been shown to significantly affect intercultural communication are identified as well as how nonverbal misinterpretations can be a barrier in intercultural communication. Finally, the use of nonverbal messages in a culture will be shown to relate to other factors in that culture.

NONVERBAL BEHAVIORS AS CUES

Some basic nonverbal behaviors seem to be reliable cues as to a person's state of mind because they seem to be "spoken" internationally. Across cultures, people generally recognize the nonverbal cues of pleasure or displeasure, liking or disliking, tension or relaxation, and high status or low status (Buck, 1984).

Charles Darwin (1872/1969), in his classic book *The Expression of the Emotions in Man and Animals*, wrote that our facial expressions, such as smiles and frowns, are not learned but are biologically determined. Studies of children born deaf and blind show that despite the lack of social learning they smile, laugh, and cry in ways virtually identical to infants who can hear and see adults. Most people worldwide correctly identify the facial expressions of anger, disgust, happiness, fear, sadness, and surprise (Ekman, Friesen, & Ellsworth, 1972; Ekman et al., 1987). Researchers have since found evidence for a seventh universal expression of contempt (Ekman & Heider, 1988). In every culture the researchers studied, a large majority of people correctly named the facial expression in pictures of people who were entirely foreign to them. However, in a recent study (Shioiri, Someya, Helmeste, & Tang, 1999) of people in Japan and the United States, the facial expressions of surprise and happiness were well understood by both groups, but those of anger, contempt, disgust, fear, and sadness were not always as well recognized by people in Japan. It was Darwin's idea that these expressions evolved because they allow us to know immediately the difference between strangers who are friendly and those who might attack.

These innate behaviors can change as we grow and learn our culture. For example, even though a smile is universally recognized as a sign of friendliness, it has other meanings that are specific to a culture. Germans smile less than people from the United States, but this doesn't mean that Germans are less friendly. It does mean that people from Germany and the United States have different ideas of when a smile is appropriate.

In a business meeting of people from Germany and the United States, the people from the United States complained that the Germans are cool and aloof; the Germans complained that the people from the United States are excessively cheerful and hide true feelings (Hall & Hall, 1990).

Japanese tradition favors reserved emotional expressions. In photographs, U.S. wives are usually shown smiling at their husbands; Japanese wives are rarely shown smiling. U.S. clerks greet strangers with a smile; Japanese clerks must learn to do so. On the other hand, to maintain reserve, it is said that the Japanese smile to disguise embarrassment, anger, and other negative emotions because the public display of these emotions is considered rude and incorrect in Japanese culture.

NONVERBAL COMMUNICATION AS INTENTIONAL COMMUNICATION

Definition

Exactly what is meant by the term *nonverbal communication* must be specified. Nonverbal communication can be narrowly used to refer to intentional use as in using a nonspoken symbol to communicate a specific message. From this perspective, nonverbal communication refers to a source's actions and attributes that are not purely verbal. For example, communication scholars Judee Burgoon and her colleagues (Burgoon, Boller, & Woodall, 1988) define nonverbal communication as those actions and attributes of humans that have socially shared meaning, are intentionally sent or interpreted as intentional, are consciously sent or consciously received, and have the potential for feedback from the receiver.

The term can be more broadly defined to refer to elements of the environment that communicate by virtue of people's use of them. The color of the walls in the room in which you are interviewed for a job may in some way affect your performance and how you are perceived. Thus, from this perspective, wall color may legitimately be labeled a nonverbal element of communication (Hickson & Stacks, 1989).

Functions

One way to demonstrate how nonverbals can be used to intentionally communicate messages is to look at the functions typically performed through nonverbal communication:

- *Replacing spoken messages.* There are situations in which words cannot be used. In a very noisy manufacturing facility, for example, communicators might use hand gestures to replace spoken messages. Communicators who do not share a language may try to make themselves understood with gestures. Nonverbal symbols can communicate utilitarian messages (Knapp, 1990). A police officer directing the flow of traffic uses nonverbal communication for utilitarian purposes.

Using nonverbal communication in situations where many languages are spoken, such as at international airports or the international Olympics, is addressed in Box 6.1.

Box 6.1

SIGNS AND SYMBOLS

Signs and symbols are used to identify and to direct attention to the things they designate. Signs are sometimes arbitrary in character, sometimes based on a real or fancied analogy, and usually simpler than symbols. For example, arrows are used to point direction. Symbols frequently are based on likeness, metaphor, or comparison. In Japan, for example, the cherry blossom is a symbol of the samurai because it is beautiful, blooms early, and dies soon. Still, symbol use is arbitrary. For example, the color red is a symbol for Christian charity and for communism and class conflict.

As symbols are independent of language, they can be used to communicate across language barriers. For example, symbols were used along ancient roadways. More recently, international events such as the Olympics make extensive use of symbols. In fact, Katzumie Masaru, the art director of the Tokyo Olympics, developed many of the symbols in use today (Modley, 1976). World travel today is facilitated by symbols known to literate and illiterate people alike on highways, at airports; in hospitals, factories, and schools; and on packages and clothing. Almost anyone can function in any international airport. From the symbols, you can find restaurants, rest rooms, and telephones.

Not all symbols, however, are universally understood. What is commonly called the swastika in the United States and Europe has long been understood in other parts of the world as a symbol for blessings and when posted outside is meant to bestow good wishes on passersby. It is a commonly used symbol to mark Buddhist temples throughout Asia and is often used on maps to designate the locations of Buddhist temples. In this sense, it is similar to the cross in Christianity. Imagine the misunderstanding if one does not know the symbol's diverse meanings.

Symbols continue to be invented. In 1992, Jeremy Irons was the first celebrity to wear the red AIDS ribbon at that year's televised Tony Awards. It was the idea of a

(Continued)

Box 6.1, *Continued*

New York group, Visual AIDS, to bring attention to the AIDS epidemic. Later in 1992, during the Emmy Awards telecast, Jamie Lee Curtis explained the meaning of the symbol, and by the next year the red AIDS ribbon had become one of the most recognized symbols worldwide. It was so successful as a symbol that soon there were pink ribbons for breast cancer, lavender ribbons for abused women, and so on. Its use then declined, but it raised the public's awareness of AIDS.

National flags can be a powerful symbol. The Union Jack is a familiar red-white-and-blue symbol of Britain worldwide. Recently, there has been a resurgence in popularity for displaying the English flag, the St. George's flag. Some explain its resurgence by its use at events such as the Queen's Golden Jubilee and the World Cup. Others explain it as a symbol of English nationalism since Scotland and Wales now have their own parliaments.

■ *Sending uncomfortable messages.* Some messages are awkward or difficult to express in words, but the meaning can be conveyed with nonverbals without hurt feelings or embarrassment. Imagine being on your way home and being stopped by an acquaintance who wants to talk. The message in your mind that you want to communicate is, "Don't bother me, I don't have time for you now." You may not want to say those words, but you can communicate that meaning by slowly continuing to walk away. Your nonverbal communication followed by the verbal message of "I really have to go" is received without bad feelings because it's clear you really do have to leave. Likewise, you may find it difficult or awkward to say, "I love you," but eye contact, touch, and close proximity deliver the message.

■ *Forming impressions that guide communication.* We all attempt at times to manage the impressions that others have of us. Think about how you would give some thought to what you would wear to a job interview. You intentionally choose to wear certain clothes and groom in a certain way to send a message about who you are to the employer.

■ *Making relationships clear.* Communication messages have both content and relationship information. Content refers to the subject matter of the message. Relationship information refers to the relationship between the communicators. As relationship information might be uncomfortable if spoken, nonverbal communication removes the threat. For example, think of the nonverbal messages on the job that replace the spoken words "I am your boss and you do as I say, even though you may not like it." In the United States, most nonverbal communication at work reinforces power. According to Mehrabian (1981), status manifests itself by a relaxed posture and way of interacting. Those of lower status display more rigidity.

■ *Regulating interaction.* Have you ever considered how you know when it's your turn to talk in a conversation? If you didn't know when to start talking, you'd be interrupting others all the time. Directing turn-taking is an example of how nonverbal communication regulates people's interaction. Box 6.2 shows how important turn-taking nonverbals can be in intercultural communication.

Box 6.2

IT'S YOUR TURN TO TALK

After I was married and had lived in Japan for a while, my Japanese gradually improved to the point where I could take part in simple conversations with my husband and his friends and family. And I began to notice that often, when I joined in, the others would look startled, and the conversational topic would come to a halt. After this happened several times, it became clear to me that I was doing something wrong. But for a long time, I didn't know what it was.

Finally, after listening carefully to many Japanese conversations, I discovered what my problem was. Even though I was speaking Japanese, I was handling the conversation in a western way.

Japanese-style conversations develop quite differently from western-style conversations. And the difference isn't only in the languages. I realized that just as I kept trying to hold western-style conversations even when I was speaking Japanese. . . .

A western-style conversation between two people is like a game of tennis. If I introduce a topic, a conversation ball, I expect you to hit it back. If you agree with me, I don't expect you simply to agree and do nothing more. I expect you to add something—a reason for agreeing, another example, or an elaboration to carry the idea further. But I don't expect you always to agree. I am just as happy if you question me, or challenge me, or completely disagree with me. Whether you agree or disagree, your response will return the ball to me.

And then it is my turn again. I don't serve a new ball from my original starting line. I hit your ball back again from where it has bounced. I carry your idea further, or answer your question or objections, or challenge or question you. And so the ball goes back and forth, an original spin, a powerful smash. . . .

If there are more than two people in the conversation, then it is like doubles in tennis, or like volleyball. There's no waiting in line. Whoever is nearest and quickest hits the ball, and if you step back, someone else will hit it. No one stops the game to give you a turn. You're responsible for taking your own turn. . . .

A Japanese-style conversation, however, is not at all like tennis or volleyball. It's like bowling. You wait for your turn. And you always know your place in line. It depends on such things as whether you are older or younger, a close friend or a relative stranger to the previous speaker, in a senior or junior position, and so on.

When your turn comes, you step up to the starting line with your bowling ball, and carefully bowl it. Everyone else stands back and watches politely, murmuring encouragement. Everyone waits until the ball has reached the end of the alley, and watches to see if it knocks down all the pins, or only some of them, or none of them. There is a pause, while everyone registers your score.

Then, after everyone is sure that you have completely finished your turn, the next person in line steps up to the same starting line, with a different ball. He doesn't return your ball, and he does not begin from where your ball stopped. There is no back and forth at all. All the balls run parallel. And there is always a suitable pause between turns. There is no rush, no excitement, no scramble for the ball.

No wonder everyone looked started when I took part in Japanese conversations. I paid no attention to whose turn it was, and kept snatching the ball halfway down the alley and throwing it back at the bowler. Of course the conversation died. I was playing the wrong game.

SOURCE: Nancy Sakamoto and Reiko Naotsuka, *Polite Fictions: Why Japanese and Americans Seem Rude to Each Other.* Tokyo: Kinseido, 1982, pp. 80-83. Reprinted with permission.

- *Reinforcing and modifying verbal messages.* Nonverbal cues can be metamessages that affect the decoding of the spoken message. Nonverbal messages can reinforce the verbal message. You can use your hands to indicate how close another car came to hitting your car as you say the same message in words. Nonverbal messages can also modify—and even negate—the meaning of the verbal message.

KNOWING CULTURE THROUGH NONVERBAL MESSAGES

Some nonverbal messages can be clearly identified with a culture. Min-Sun Kim (1992), for example, has demonstrated how the nonverbal messages shown in Korean and United States print media advertising clearly reflect the culture. Culture can be conceptualized as an interrelated system: Each aspect of culture is related to other aspects of that culture. For example, it is said that in Europe body language is an important indicator of one's level of education and good manners—a relationship not seen as often in the United States. You'll see that many nonverbal messages used in a culture are related to and consistent with other aspects of the culture. In one sense, then, other aspects of a culture are revealed in the nonverbal code. In the next two chapters, you'll see how the same is true for language.

In Chapter 2 you read that Alfred G. Smith wrote that communication and culture are inseparable, that culture is a code we learn and share that requires communication, and that communication coding and symbols must be learned and shared. As some of those symbols are nonverbal, it is partially through the nonverbal messages that we experience the culture.

NONVERBAL MISINTERPRETATIONS AS A BARRIER

In Chapter 4, you identified *nonverbal misinterpretations* as a barrier in intercultural communication. While we expect languages to be different, we are less likely to expect and recognize how the nonverbal symbols are different.

Often when people do not share the same language, some resort to hand gestures to communicate. In such situations, people discover that the belief that hand signals and bodily expressions are universal is not true.

Many nonverbal expressions vary from culture to culture, and it is just those variations that make nonverbal misinterpretation a barrier. Judee Burgoon (1986) has identified two perspectives on nonverbal communication: She writes that much nonverbal communication does have consensually recognized meanings and consistent usage within a culture and as such forms a vocabulary of nonverbal symbols. In the United States, for example, many gestures are commonly recognized across the country. She also contends that some nonverbal communication, even in the same culture, is so ambiguous that its interpretation is mediated by context. For example, in the United States, the meaning of a touch can often be ambiguous. Comparing observations and interpretations of nonverbal symbols often will reveal their ambiguity.

The example is given of a technical instructor in Iran from the United States who complained that his students weren't paying any attention to him. The basis of the instructor's inference was that his Iranian students were passively sitting and staring at him instead of taking notes on the important points of his lecture. On the basis of his experience with students in the United States who expect lectures to supplement texts, he believed that note taking is a nonverbal cue signaling interest and the lack of note taking a cue signaling boredom or distraction. He failed to learn that Iranian students expect lectures to correspond exactly to the text so there is no need to take notes.

NONVERBAL MESSAGE CODES

Another way to define nonverbal communication is by category. Perhaps you've experienced that a nonverbal symbol can mean different things depending on where you are. The kinds of nonverbal communication given the most attention by travelers and researchers alike are proxemics, kinesics, chronemics, paralanguage, silence, haptics, clothing and physical appearance, territoriality, olfactics, and oculesics. Each of these nonverbal message codes is discussed below.

Proxemics

The term given to the study of our use of personal space is **proxemics**. Edward Hall's (1959) work has demonstrated clearly that cultures differ substantially in their use of personal space.

His general theory is that we exist inside an invisible "bubble" or personal space. How much space we each want between ourselves and others depends on our cultural learning, our upbringing in our families, the specific situation, and our relationship with the people to whom we're talking. Although the physical distance we want between ourselves and others does vary, Hall reports the range is fairly consistent for most people in North America (see Table 6.1).

Experience shows that these distances vary in diverse cultures. In India, there are elaborate rules about how closely members of each caste may approach other castes, and Arabs of the same sex do stand much closer than North Americans. North Americans in an elevator maintain personal space if the physical space permits it. An Arab entering an elevator may stand right next to another person and be touching even though no one else is in the elevator.

Queuing means how you form a line while waiting. The traditional first-come, first-served line was typical in 19th-century France, but today, along with the Italians and Spaniards, the French are among the least queue-conscious in Europe. Until recently, the British were known to stand in queues for taxis, for food, and for tickets. Even in shops and pubs, customers were served in order. The practice may be dying in Great Britain, but people in the United States still stand in line—usually—and have elaborate "rules of queuing" (i.e., "cutting in line," "saving places," etc.).

Table 6.1   Proxemics

	Distance	Description	Voice
Intimate	Touching to 18 inches	Private situations with people who are emotionally close. If others invade this space we feel threatened.	Whisper
Personal	18 inches to 4 feet	The lower end is "handshake" distance—the distance most couples stand in public.	Soft voice
Casual	4 feet to 12 feet	The lower end is the distance between salespeople and customers and between people who work together in business.	Full voice
Public	Greater than 12 feet	Situations such as teaching in a classroom or delivering a speech.	Loud voice

SOURCE: Adapted from Hall (1959).

Some explain the absence of queues in Europe and in Mediterranean areas as a sign of feelings against unwarranted regulation and interference. Hall (1959) argues that queues are more likely to be found in cultures whose people are treated as equals.

Kinesics

Gestures, body movements, facial expressions, and eye contact are behaviors termed **kinesics.** In his landmark book *Gestures,* Desmond Morris (1979) wrote that communication depends heavily on the actions, postures, movements, and expressions of our bodies. In a later book titled *Bodytalk,* Morris (1995) explained that gestures can be intentional or unconscious. For example, lower classes in ancient Rome used four fingers and thumb to pick up food; upper classes used two fingers and thumb. The difference may have been unconscious, but it clearly communicated class distinctions.

Morris and his colleagues studied the use of 20 of the most familiar European gestures to map their use across national boundaries. For example, they found the thumbs-up gesture commonly used in the United States by hitchhikers to be more widely understood to mean "okay." But in Greece and

Sardinia, it more accurately communicates the idea of "get stuffed." And in Australia, Iran, and Nigeria, it has similar obscene connotations.

The forefinger-to-thumb gesture forming a circle can mean "okay" in the United States. In France, it means zero or worthless. In Japan, the same gesture can mean "money," but it is a symbol many times more offensive than the raised middle finger in Brazil. Curling the middle three fingers into the palm, extending the thumb and little finger, and then twisting the hand back and forth from the wrist is the Hawaiian greeting "hang loose." To the University of Texas Longhorn fans, the pinkie and index finger raised up with the middle two fingers and thumb folded into the palm means "Hook 'em horns." But in parts of Africa the same gesture is a curse, and to Italians it is the *cornuto* signaling that one's wife is being unfaithful. Extending one hand, palm forward, means "stop!" in the United States, but in Greece it's the *moutza* or hand push, a sign of confrontation. In West Africa, the same gesture is more insulting than the upraised middle finger (Axtell, 1991).

Morris and his colleagues found wide variations even with such universal rituals as nodding agreement and greeting friends. Although most cultures do indicate "yes" by an up-and-down nod of the head and "no" by shaking it from side to side, there are variations: In Albania and Bulgaria, the yes-no gestures are reversed. In Ceylon, a yes answer to a specific question is indicated by a nod of the head, whereas general agreement is indicated by a slow sideways swaying of the head.

For greetings, in the United States a firm handshake is appropriate. In France, where the traditional U.S. handshake is considered too rough and rude, a quick handshake with only slight pressure is preferred. In Latin America, a hearty embrace is common among women and men alike, and men may follow it with a friendly slap on the back. In Ecuador, to greet a person without a handshake is a sign of special respect. In India, the handshake may be used by Westernized citizens, but the preferred greeting is the *namaste*—placing the palms together and nodding one's head. In Japan, the traditional form of greeting is a bow or several bows.

Likewise, waving good-bye varies among cultures. In Italy, Colombia, and China, people may wave good-bye by moving the palm and fingers back and forth, a gesture that more likely means "come here" in the United States. But in Malaysia, beckoning someone by moving the forefingers back and forth would be taken as an insult.

Even seemingly obvious gestures can be misunderstood. Using fingers to indicate numbers can vary. In the United States, most people would indicate "1" by holding up the forefinger. In parts of Europe, "1" is indicated by using the thumb, "2" by the thumb and forefinger.

U.S. soldiers were warned against using the "V for victory" or peace sign in Bosnia-Herzegovina. Serbs would find it offensive to see the peacekeeping troops making this sign, as the Croats use it as an informal greeting.

The "V for victory" sign made popular during World War II by Winston Churchill is appropriately made by showing the palm. In the United States in the late 1960s, the same gesture became a symbol for peace (Dresser, 1996). When former British Prime Minister Margaret Thatcher made a "V for victory" sign during an election campaign, she showed the back of her hand. That gesture signifies at least nine different obscenities!

And the list continues: Some Japanese point a forefinger to the face to indicate referring to self, whereas in the United States, people are more likely to point to the chest. And it is said that at least some Japanese women stick out the tongue to indicate embarrassment.

In Brazil, people may add emphasis to statements by snapping the fingers with a whiplike motion of the hands. Brushing the tips of fingers forward under the chin may indicate "I don't know." Indians in Delhi may use hands to grasp the ears as a gesture meaning repentance or sincerity. Fijians may fold the arms as a sign of respect when talking to another person.

Patterns of eye contact learned in childhood seem to be relatively unaffected by later experiences. One study showed that Arabs, Latin Americans, and Southern Europeans gaze on the eyes or face of conversational partners, whereas Asians, Indians and Pakistanis, and Northern Europeans tend to show peripheral gaze or no gaze at all (Harper, Wiens, & Matarazzo, 1978). Duration of eye contact varies in diverse cultures (Shuter, 1979). In the United States, the average length of time that two people gaze at each other is 1.18 seconds (Argyle, 1988; Argyle & Ingham, 1972). Any less than that and we may think the person is shy, uninterested, or preoccupied. Any more than that and we may think the person is communicating unusually high interest.

People from Asian, Latin American, Caribbean, and American Indian backgrounds may offer respect by avoiding eye contact. Looking someone directly in the eyes may be interpreted as a provocation that can lead to violence. In parts of the United States, such as Appalachia, more people have heard of the belief in the "evil eye"—the power attributed to certain persons of inflicting injury or bad luck by a look. One communication professor new to the area worked hard to maintain eye contact with students during lectures only to be told that some students perceived him as having the evil eye.

It is said that Spanish men even today in more rural areas may use eye contact to make "passes" toward women on the street. Returning the stare is accepted as a gesture indicating that the man may attempt conversation. It is also said that Spaniards snap the eyelids when angry or impatient. Psychologist Monica Moore (1995) has studied the nonverbals of heterosexual flirting. She says that in Western cultures women control the process by making the initial choice of the man. To attract men, Moore has noted that women most often smile, glance, primp, laugh, giggle, toss the head, flip the hair, and whisper.

Chronemics

Next is the study of **chronemics,** or the study of our use of time. Many American Indian peoples understood time to be cyclical, whereas Western cultures think of time in the linear sense of a flow from the past to the present to the future. (Yet Western science accepts Einstein's and other physicists' concepts of quantum physics in which there is no definite past, present, or future but only possibilities of position, in which particles can move backward in time as well as forward and in which what happened in the past can be altered by energy events in the future.) It is said that the idea of linear time became commonly accepted as we became more aware of change—that is, aware that things were different before change and after change. Acceptance of some religious beliefs necessitates the acceptance of the understanding of time as linear. For example, the Christian belief that Christ's birth and death were unrepeatable events necessitates the acceptance of the understanding of time as linear. It existed in the past of our present, and since it could only occur then, it could not be repeated in our future.

Humans marked time with calendars centuries before Christ. Calendars have been based on the sun or the moon. The ancient Britons may have used Stonehenge as a calendar. Mayan astronomers had determined that a year was precisely 365.24 days long. The **Hijrah** calendar divided the year into 354 days and 12 lunar months. The Sumerians divided the year into 360 days—12 lunar months of 30 days each. The Egyptians extended this calendar year by adding 5 days at the end of the year.

The original Roman calendar was composed of 10 months and 304 days. Two months and one day were added later. The Julian calendar, devised by Julius Caesar, became the basis for what is used today. Coming at the time of the Reformation, reforms instituted by Pope Gregory XIII in 1582 created the

SOURCE: Dorene Yamaguchi. Used by permission.

Gregorian calendar year in use today. Pope Gregory's reforms were not immediately adopted in Protestant countries: The Gregorian calendar was adopted in Germany in 1700, in Sweden in 1753, in Britain in 1752, in Russia in 1918, and in China in 1912 but not widely so until the Communist victory in 1949 (Duncan, 1998).

The marking of a day also has a long history. In the 11th century, the Chinese scholar Su Sung built an early water clock. In the 13th century, English monasteries had mechanical clocks driven by weights. The bells on these devices were known as "cloks." Precision timekeeping came with the invention of the pendulum clock by Dutch scientist Christian Huygens. The clock introduced a new consciousness—the clock, rather than the sun, became the arbiter of time for everyone.

Our technological world demands even more accurate timekeeping. Since 1948, we have used atomic clocks accurate to within 1 second in 300,000 years. Still, we have demanded more accurate marking of time: microsecond (one millionth of a second), nanosecond (one billionth of a second), picosecond (one trillionth of a second), and femtosecond (one thousandth of a picosecond). Consider this: There are more femtoseconds in 1 second than there are seconds in 31 million years.

How we use time varies from culture to culture. That cultures use time differently can be a barrier to intercultural communication. What time you are expected to arrive for an 8 p.m. party varies as to where the party is. How long you should be kept waiting—if at all—for a business appointment varies as well. And once a meeting has begun, it varies how much informal conversation there is before the actual business discussion begins. Arabs, for example, engage in up to half an hour of informal conversation before turning to business.

Paralanguage

The nonverbal elements of the voice are referred to as **paralanguage** and include the following:

- Vocal characterizers, such as laughter and sobs

- Vocal qualifiers, such as intensity (loud/soft), pitch (high/low), and extent (drawl and clipping)

- Vocal segregates, such as "uh," "um," and "uh-huh"

The sounds of "psst" and of whistling are examples of vocal characterizers. "Psst" is an acceptable way of calling a waiter in Spain. In India, whistling is considered offensive.

Thais speak in a very soft and gentle voice and manner. This is based on the cultural belief that speaking in a soft voice is how one shows good manners and an educated character. Voices are raised only to show the emotion of anger or in an argument or confrontation. When first hearing persons in the United States speak, some Thais believe the speakers are rude or angry or even don't like Thais because people from the United States speak so loudly.

Another example is tonal languages. Speakers of English do use tone to some extent but most often to express emotion. Think of how you would say "thank you" to convey a degree of sarcasm. However, in true tonal languages such as Mandarin Chinese and Vietnamese, the denotative meaning of some words depends on the context and how the word is said. Japanese is replete with homophones, where the meanings of many words are distinguished only by stress and intonation, which in turn convey the emotional nuances of anger, surprise, sincerity, and displeasure.

Accent may be considered an aspect of paralanguage. British ears can detect a speaker's educational background in the accent. It can be said that everyone has an accent; it's just that some accents are more accepted than others. Accent may present problems and even lead to charges of racism (Ryan, 1974). One study in San Antonio, Texas (de la Zerda & Hopper, 1979), had employment interviewers listen to taped speech samples of males speaking with varying degrees of accent and make a hiring prediction. Standard speakers were significantly favored for supervisory positions and accented speakers for semiskilled positions. Collier (1988) as well has shown that Whites note Hispanics' inability to speak English as socially inappropriate. In recalling conversations, Whites cite examples of Spanish language use and "broken English" as inappropriate and difficult to understand.

Midlevel Asian-American employees can find promotion to management closed—particularly if spoken English is perceived as nonfluent. In Honolulu, a Filipino man was denied a job as a city clerk. He sued on the basis of racial discrimination. Attorneys for the city argued that his heavy Filipino accent would have kept him from working effectively as a clerk. The case was appealed to the Supreme Court, and in *Fragante v. City and County of Honolulu,* the Court let stand a federal appeals court decision supporting the city.

In Massachusetts, parents petitioned their local school board to ban first- and second-grade teachers with pronounced accents. The opposition argued that such a ban would be discrimination based on national origin and would violate the Fourteenth Amendment, which provides equal protection for everyone under the law. In Anaheim (Orange County), California, a radio station contest was based on telephoning convenience-store clerks and asking listeners to identify the clerks' nationalities. Some refugee organizations charged the contest was racism disguised as humor.

Silence

We should also consider the use of **silence** in communication. Rather than a void of communication, silence can communicate agreement, apathy, awe,

Moo-sol-jon is a traditional-style lecture hall in Bulguksa, a Buddhist temple located on the outskirts of Geongju, the old capital of the Unified Shilla Kingdom in Korea. The plaque reads in part: "The Moo-sol-jon is a hall for lecturing. Though it is a place to give lectures on sutras, it is called the 'Moo-sol' (no-word/non-lecturing) hall because it is impossible to express and reach the essence of the Buddha's teachings or the depth of Truth through language."

confusion, contemplation, disagreement, embarrassment, obligation, regret, repressed hostility, respect, sadness, thoughtfulness, or any number of meanings. Traditionally, Eastern societies such as India, China, and Japan have valued silence more than Western societies. Oliver (1971) observed that "silence in Asia has commonly been entirely acceptable, whereas in the West silence has generally been considered socially disagreeable" (p. 264). In the Confucian context, silence, not talking, is a virtue.

In India (Jain & Matukumalli, 1993), on the individual level, silence can be viewed as a state of being, allowing you to experience the highest truth and bliss. On the interpersonal level, silence is used to promote harmony, cooperation, and other collectivistic values; it is a sign of interpersonal sensitivity, mutual respect, personal dignity, affirmation, and wisdom. On the level of social movements, silence can be protest, as demonstrated by Mohandas (Mahatma) Gandhi in his struggle for India's independence through nonviolence.

To most people in the United States, silence means lack of attention and lack of initiative. A person must speak up to participate. In contrast, to the Chinese, silence means agreement. You should talk only if you have something important to add. You should always let the other talk first.

Silence can mean one is fearful of communicating. This form of silence is associated with the communication variable commonly studied in the United States known as **communication apprehension**, or, more commonly, stage fright. Communication apprehension refers to an individual's fear or anxiety associated with either real or anticipated communication with another person or persons. James McCroskey's (1990) studies of communication apprehension led him to label it the most common handicap that people suffer from today. McCroskey also suggests that U.S. society stresses verbal performance so much that U.S. speakers may experience more pressure than those from other cultures. For example, he has shown that Swedish students consider themselves more competent communicators but are less prone to initiate communication than are U.S. students.

Haptics

Less well studied is **haptics**, or the study of our use of touch to communicate. Again, there are examples to support that the use of touch to communicate varies from culture to culture. In India, for example, it is considered rude to touch women. In Thailand and Laos, it is rude for a stranger or acquaintance to touch a child on the top of the head because the head is regarded as the home of the spirit or soul. It is believed that a child's spirit or soul is not strong enough to be touched and has a tendency to become ill if patted (Smutkupt & Barna, 1976).

Compared with other cultures, people in the United States are touch deprived, having one of the lowest rates of casual touch in the world. If you are talking with a friend in a coffee shop in the United States, you might touch each other once or twice an hour. If you were British and in a London coffee shop, you probably won't touch each other at all. But if you were French and in a Parisian café, it is said that you might touch each other a hundred times in an hour.

In many cultures, adult male friends walk hand in hand—a behavior frequently misunderstood by people from the United States who assume the friends are gay. In other cultures, one does not offer anything to another with the left hand, as the left hand is used to clean one's self after using the toilet.

In the United States, more touching may take place in preschool or kindergarten than during any other period. Touching is lowest during the early to midteens. The first comprehensive study of communication and touch in the United States was conducted by Jones and Yarbrough (1985). Their study of university students at a western U.S. university showed 12 meanings communicated with touch: affection, announcing a response, appreciation, attention getting, compliance, departures, greetings inclusion, playful affection, playful aggression, sexual interest or intent, and support as well as hybrid meanings such as departure/affection and greetings/affection.

In his consulting with businesses, Jones (1993) says that employees are more aware of inappropriate touching and sexual harassment. At least in the United States, most touching has symbolic content, but contextual factors are critical to the meaning. What is appropriate touching in a 4-person psychotherapy clinic may not be appropriate in a 200-person insurance office.

Clothing and Physical Appearance

More obvious is the use of **clothing** and physical **appearance**. What we wear varies so much across the world as does the meaning conveyed by the clothes. Clothing can reflect cultural heritage.

Men in Saudi Arabia may wear a **thawb**, a loose-fitting, ankle-length, usually white shirt; the **ghutrah**, the white or red-and-white-check cloth covering the head; and the **iqual** or *agal*, the double ring of black rope or cord used to hold the ghutrah.

Clothing can also reflect subcultural and subgroup identity—medical professionals and military, for example, often wear uniforms outside of work.

The entrance of the MGM casino in Las Vegas was designed to be consistent with feng shui.

SOURCE: MGM Grand. Used by permission.

Earlier, we mentioned color use as symbols. We communicate when we integrate clothing and symbols into our clothing: Red is a good-luck color for the Chinese, but it signifies bad luck to many Koreans. To others, red is associated with fertility, but in Ghana, it is associated with sorrow. In Western societies, black is the color of mourning. Asians traditionally wear white to funerals because it is the color of sadness.

Territoriality

Territory is the space that an individual claims whether permanently or temporarily. **Territoriality** refers to how space can be used to communicate messages.

Sennett (1999) has described how spaces can encourage democracy. From roughly 600 to 350 B.C.E., Athens used two very different spaces—the theater and the town square—for its democratic practices. The *Pnyx*, an open-air theater, focused attention on a single speaker at a time, yet it was still possible to gauge others' reactions. The space supported a verbal order, "the unfolding of argument." The *agora* was the town square used for many simultaneous activities. Rather than each group being isolated and segregated, the agora was the place in the city where citizens became accustomed to diversity.

Chinese geomancy, *feng shui* (pronounced fung SCHWAY), is the art of manipulating the physical environment to establish harmony with the natural environment to achieve happiness, prosperity, and health. It is used in site planning and design of buildings for the greatest compatibility with nature. Feng shui also has principles for designing homes and placing furniture.

A home with good feng shui has a balance of comfort and style and radiates serenity. Location, room shape, color, plants, artwork, and furniture are arranged for positive energy and balance.

Olfactics

The study of communication via smell is called **olfactics**. Smell remains one of the least understood senses. The amount of the human brain devoted to olfaction is very large. We do know that odor is first detected by the olfactory epithelium in the nose. This starts a chain of events that leads to an information flow to the olfactory bulb and limbic system of the brain, which plays a key role in regulating body functions and the emotions. Smell is the only sense linked directly into the limbic system, which may be evidence of its being our most basic, primitive sense. In all cultures, women can detect odors in lower concentrations, identify them more accurately, and remember them longer than men (Doty et al., 1984).

Scientists have also identified a tiny organ in the nasal cavity that responds to chemicals known as pheromones, natural substances believed to play a role in basic human emotions such as fear, hunger, and, most notably, those related to sex. Recently, scientists have uncovered evidence of human pheromones (Weller, 1998).

The ancient Romans were obsessed with roses. They were worn in garlands, used in pillows, medicines, and love potions, and displayed at banquets and orgies. In the 16th century, lovers exchanged "love apples," peeled apples kept in the armpit until they were saturated with sweat and then given to a lover to inhale. In ancient Hawaii when meeting, traditional Hawaiians inhaled one another's breath. Although many people today consider *haole* (outsider) a derogatory word, in Hawaiian it originally meant "not of the same breath."

Aromatherapy is the use of oils of flowers, herbs, and plants to make people feel better. Aromatherapy was widely practiced in ancient Chinese, Egyptian, and Indian civilizations and is widely practiced today in Belgium, England, France, Germany, and Switzerland. In Japan, fragrance is used in the workplace. The architectural and construction firm Shimizu has developed computerized techniques to deliver scents through air-conditioning ducts to enhance efficiency and reduce stress among office workers.

Advertisers believe smell is important. Fragrance strips in magazines enable consumers to sample a perfume by pulling open a strip, releasing tiny fragrance capsules glued inside. British stores use smells such as freshly dried linen, chocolate, and musk in the air-conditioning system to put customers in the mood for their products.

Smell also refers to body odor. Some cultures are sensitive to any body odor; others mask body odor with perfumes and colognes; others find the odor of perfumes and colognes distasteful. Some say that body odor is affected by the food you eat and that meat eaters have a distinctive body odor.

Oculesics

The study of communications sent by the eyes, termed **oculesics**, has not received as much study, but real differences between cultures have been noted. Considerable research has been done on pupil dilation, or pupillometrics (Hess, 1975). In 15th- and 16th-century Italy, women put drops of belladonna (literally "beautiful woman") into their eyes to dilate the pupils. Dilated pupils were thought to be more attractive.

CASE STUDY: THE *WAI* IN THAILAND

In Thailand, the **wai** is a nonverbal gesture used to communicate greeting, bidding farewell, deep and sincere respect, and appreciation (Smutkupt & Barna, 1976). The palms of both hands are placed together and held vertically slightly under the chin followed by a slight head bow, chin toward the fingertips. There is no eye contact because the head is bowed. The wai is not accompanied by verbal communication. Usually the younger person or subordinate initiates the wai, and the older person or higher-ranking person responds with a wai as well (Rojjanaprapayon, 1997).

The wai is consistent with other elements of the Thai culture. Children absorb its nuances along with learning the Thai spoken language that has a hierarchy of honorific titles and a special language of self-debasement to be used when speaking to royalty. The first nonverbal teaching the Thai child receives is this gesture of obeisance. The mother holds her infant, puts its palms together between her own, and raises the hands to the chin or the forehead—the higher the hands, the greater the degree of deference. Before the child is taken from the house, its hands will be put in the proper position to greet guests. When its mother takes the child to the temple, she raises its palms to pay homage to Buddha. The child is constantly directed to wai on every appropriate occasion until it becomes a regular component of behavior. Children never fail to wai parents and the family's elders before leaving for school in the morning. In the classroom, children stand and perform the wai upon the teacher's arrival. When school ends, the students wai to thank the teacher. On returning home, the children greet all parents and elders with the wai. The day ends with paying homage to Buddha by performing the wai in front of the family's altar.

Thus, the wai is a representation of the cultural values, including respect for parents and elders, that the child learns while learning the nonverbal code. By understanding the wai we can also understand part of the Thai culture.

FROM THE INTERCULTURAL PERSPECTIVE

When we learn to communicate, we learn not only a spoken language but also the various other ways that people communicate meaning within our culture. Communicators use both verbal and nonverbal modes to communicate, and listeners expect to receive both kinds of messages during a conversation. If a speaker uses nonverbal codes poorly or inappropriately, a listener may consider the person a poor speaker. Because speakers and listeners expect nonverbal codes they both know, misunderstandings can occur when the speakers and listeners are from different cultures that generally do not share the same nonverbal codes.

Nonverbal communication codes can be divided into different types:

Proxemics is the way we use fixed space and personal space. Cultures vary in such things as how living space is arranged and how close to stand together.

Kinesics are behaviors such as gestures, body movements, facial expressions, and eye contact. Certain facial expressions like smiles are universal, but many gestures are not. What may be an innocent gesture in one culture may be insulting in another.

Chronemics is how we perceive and use time. Chronemics also includes ideas about politeness that are related to time, such as whether or not you can be late for an appointment.

Paralanguage refers to sounds and other nonverbal elements that can be produced by the mouth and voice. Sounds like laughter or "uh," "um," and "psst"; how loudly or softly we speak; how high or low we speak; and how long or short we say vowel sounds in words are all examples of paralanguage. Paralanguage can change the meaning of what we say. Consider the polite expression "Excuse me." Depending on how it is said, its meaning can range from a polite apology to an insulting exclamation.

Silence can be used to communicate a lot of different meanings that often depend on culture. In general, Eastern cultures value silence more than Western cultures do. In the United States, silence is often seen negatively. If a person is silent, many people think that the person is not paying attention or is not interested. Many U.S. citizens feel uncomfortable during extended periods of silence, and they often try to "fill" the silence by talking.

Haptics is communicating by touch. Touch can communicate a wide variety of messages. The meaning of touch depends on the kind of touch (hard, gentle, etc.) and the context. Different societies have different norms for touching. These rules determine the kinds of touching that are appropriate for certain situations and social relationships.

Clothing and physical appearance can communicate meaning. What we wear commonly communicates information such as group or subgroup membership and marital status. The significance of certain articles of clothing and the symbols that may be used in clothing are unique to each culture.

Territoriality refers to how space can be used to communicate. For example, physical space, such as a home, office, or public area, can be arranged to encourage conversation. Feng shui is the Chinese art of placement to create a balanced environment in a building, home, or office.

Olfactics is communicating by smell. Many companies, for example, use scents to advertise their products. Cultures have different opinions about what smells good or bad. People in the United States do not like the body's natural smell, so they bathe often and wear fragrances that cover up this odor.

Oculesics is communicating with the eyes. What the eyes communicate often depends on the culture. In the United States, it is usual for people to maintain eye contact. If a person tries to avoid eye contact in a conversation, the other person may think that person is dishonest. In some Asian cultures such as Japan, students will often avoid making eye contact with their instructors as a sign of respect.

It is important to remember that all cultures do not share the same nonverbal behaviors or the same interpretation of them. Although crying is a nonverbal behavior that exists in many cultures, each culture may have different rules about it, such as when and where it is appropriate and who may do it. For example, in a society that has the norm "men do not cry," a man who cries may be considered emotionally weak.

KEY TERMS

appearance	haptics	paralanguage
chronemics	Hijrah	proxemics
clothing	iqual	silence
communication	kinesics	territoriality
apprehension	nonverbal	thawb
feng shui	communication	wai
ghutrah	oculesics	
Gregorian	olfactics	

CHAPTER 7

Language as a Barrier

What You Can Learn From This Chapter

The relationship between language and culture

How translation problems impede intercultural communication

Ways of communicating when there is no shared language

Language as nationalism, including the arguments on whether the United States should have an official language

From Chapter 4, you know that language is a barrier to intercultural communication. In this chapter, you'll first look at how linguists study languages and the development of spoken languages and of writing. As was done with nonverbals, language will be shown to relate to other factors in that culture. The Sapir-Whorf hypothesis is discussed; this hypothesis states that the world as you know it is largely predetermined by the language of your culture.

This chapter also deals with two ways in which language affects intercultural communication: translation problems between languages and language as nationalism. Like nonverbals, words as symbols become barriers when their full meaning is not shared. Even speakers of the same language do not share exactly the same meaning for every word. That problem is compounded when you attempt translation between languages. The second way that language becomes a barrier is linguistic imperialism when the use of a particular language is forced on a people by those with more power.

Language is central to national identity. In 1846, Jacob Grimm, one of the Grimm brothers known for fairy tales and a forerunner of modern comparative and historical linguistics, said that "a nation is the totality of people who speak the same language." When Norway, Eire (Ireland), and Israel became independent states, each adopted a largely defunct language (Norse, Gaelic, and Hebrew, respectively) as an official language as necessary for national identity. Citizens of the former Yugoslavia spoke roughly the same language, Serbo-Croat, with regional differences. Today, the nationalist regimes that rule Muslim, Serbian, and Croatian parts of Bosnia are adding new words and changing spellings and pronunciations to distinguish their language and national identity.

What, then, is language? One definition of **language** is that it is a set of symbols shared by a community to communicate meaning and experience. The symbols may be sounds or gestures as in ASL (American Sign Language). Language, then, has a direct relationship to culture. Language bonds a people together and reflects what those people saw, ate, and thought.

STUDY OF LANGUAGE ORIGINS

Some linguists, particularly scholars in the former Soviet Union, study language from an anthropological or cultural perspective. These scholars are attempting to trace the origins of all the world's languages back to a **mother tongue** or even back to humans' first language.

Their study of the origins of languages is based on two assumptions: that languages are dynamic and ever changing and that the relationship between the sound of a word and its meaning is arbitrary.

The first assumption, that languages are dynamic and ever changing, can easily be seen from these examples of English:

- 8th-century Old English: "Hwaet! We Gar-Dena, in geardagum." (Beowulf)

- 14th-century Middle English: "Whan that Aprille with his shoursesote." (Chaucer)

- 16th-century English: "Shall I compare thee to a summer's day?" (Shakespeare)

- 20th-century English: "Don't have a cow, man." (Bart Simpson)

Cat, *chat, katze, katte, kot.*

The second assumption, that the relationship between the sound of a word—the symbol—and its meaning is arbitrary, deals with how words mean. With the exception of onomatopoeic words like *sizzle*, the sound of a word has no connection to its meaning. Words represent symbols that a language community uses to refer to other things. In this sense, words are not the thing they refer to, and the use of any word symbol is arbitrary. For example, English uses the word *cat* to refer to a furry domesticated carnivorous mammal having four legs and a tail and noted for its skill at catching mice and rats. Tomorrow, all English speakers could as easily agree to use the word *yahtzee* instead of *cat*.

Linguists study the words in languages and then look for similar sounding words with similar meanings in different languages. So as to be able to read Hindu legal texts, Sir William Jones, a judge in Calcutta at the end of the

Table 7.1   Basic Word Order

Word Order	Sample Languages
SVO "cats eat mice"	English, Chinese, Swahili
SOV "cats mice eat"	Japanese, Korean
VSO "eat cats mice"	Classical Arabic, Welsh, Samoan
VOS "eat mice cats"	Tzotzil (a Mayan language)
OSV "mice cats eat"	Kabardian (a language of the northern Caucasus)
OVS "mice eat cats"	Hixkaryana (a language of Brazil)

SOURCE: Matthews, Polinsky, and Comrie (1996).

NOTE: S = subject, V = verb, O = object.

18th century, began to study Sanskrit, the ancient language of northern India. He found similarities between Sanskrit words and ancient Greek and Latin words and argued that the languages were derived from a common mother tongue. Scholars in the 19th century were inspired by this suggestion and began studying languages for their common ancestors.

Another important aspect of language is **syntax**, or how words are arranged to convey meaning—the order of subject (S), verb (V), and object (O). Table 7.1 shows the six possible combinations. The first three are overwhelmingly more frequent. Basic word order is often reflected in the order of names. In SOV languages, such as Japanese and Korean, the surname comes first as in *MATSUMOTO Tada*. This also applies to titles as in *Yamata sensei*— "Professor Yamata."

SAPIR-WHORF HYPOTHESIS

Development of the Hypothesis

Many academic disciplines refer to the **Sapir-Whorf hypothesis** (also known as the Whorfian thesis) when accounting for the differences in languages across cultures (Carroll, 1956). Benjamin L. Whorf (1897-1941), a successful fire prevention engineer at the Hartford Fire Insurance Company, came into contact with the noted linguistic anthropologist Edward Sapir (1884-1939) through a course that Sapir (1921) was teaching at Yale. Largely self-taught, Whorf had studied ancient Hebraic, Aztec, and Mayan cultures and in the 1930s went to the U.S. Southwest to study the Hopi's Uto-Aztecan language. Among Whorf's observations were that the Hopi

- do not pluralize nouns referring to time, such as days and years. Instead, time is viewed as a duration.

- do not use words denoting phases of a cycle, such as summer as a phase of a year, as nouns. Whorf suggested that the Hopi view of time is the perpetual "getting later" of it.

- do not see time as linear in that there are no tenses in the language. Whorf observed that the Hopi have no words, no grammatical forms, constructions, or expressions that refer to time.

> Human beings do not live in the objective world alone, nor alone in the world of social activity as ordinarily understood, but are very much at the mercy of the particular language which has become the medium of expression for their society.
>
> —Edward Sapir, *Selected Writings in Language, Culture, and Personality* (1949, p. 162)

Whorf's papers written in the 1930s on the Hopi language produced exact and documented expression of the Sapir-Whorf hypothesis that reality for a culture is discoverable in its language.

Linguistic Determinism

After Whorf's studies, scholars divided the hypothesis into the linguistic determinist interpretation and the linguistic relativity interpretation. The linguistic determinist view is that language structure controls thought and cultural norms. Each of us lives not in the midst of the whole world but only in that part of the world that our language permits us to know. Thus, the world as each of us knows it is to a large extent predetermined by the language of our culture. And the differences between languages represent basic differences in the worldview of diverse cultures.

> Learn a new language and get a new soul.
>
> —Czech proverb

Linguistic Relativity

Subsequent research did not support all the claims made by linguistic determinist researchers (Fishman, 1972; Hoijer, 1954). In 1983, for example, Ekkehart Malotki, a Northern Arizona University professor of languages who standardized a writing system for the Hopi, documented many references to *time* he had found in the Hopi language.

Even though Whorf's Hopi example might not stand, the Sapir-Whorf hypothesis does offer a useful way of thinking about the relationship between language and culture in the linguistic relativity view. In this interpretation, linguistic characteristics and cultural norms influence each other.

The hypothesis may be expressed, then, as follows: Culture is controlled by *and* controls language.

In this interpretation, language provides the conceptual categories that influence how its speakers' perceptions are encoded and stored. Steinfatt (1989), in an extensive review of the literature, argues that the basis of linguistic relativity is that the difference between languages is not what can be said but what is relatively easy to say.

Applications

Vocabulary

One level of the Sapir-Whorf hypothesis is vocabulary. You can assume that if a language has a particularly rich vocabulary for a thing or activity in comparison to other languages, that thing or activity is important in that culture. The most commonly used example is Eskimo and snow—although this example also has been challenged.

The name Eskimo was first applied to the peoples of the Arctic by a Jesuit who heard people using the word *eskimantsik*, which means "eaters of raw meat or fish." Alaska has three native groups: the Aleuts in the Alaska Peninsula and islands beyond; Indians such as the Athapaskan, Haida, and Tlingit; and Eskimo groups such as the Chugach, the Koniag, the Yupik, and the Inupiat known as the Inuit in Canada and the Inupik in Siberia. It was said that Eskimo languages have many words for different kinds of snow:

qana	falling snow; snowflakes
akilukak	fluffy fallen snow
aput	snow on the ground
kaguklaich	snow drifted in rows
piqsirpoq	drifting snow
qimuqsuq	snowdrift

Notice that the language has many separate single words to refer to different kinds of snow; hence snow must be an important part of these groups' lives (Birke-Smith, 1959). Notice, too, that other languages, such as English, may require several words to refer to the same thing. Speakers of diverse languages can perceive all these different conditions of snow—it's just that the Eskimo peoples have more separate single words to refer to these different conditions. The challenge of this example contends that single English words such as *blizzard*, *dusting*, and *avalanche* exist as equivalents to the Eskimo words.

In a like way, the Hanunov tribe has 92 separate single words to refer to rice. In fact, in most of the languages of Asia, one word means both *food* and *rice*. Using the Sapir-Whorf hypothesis, you can assume that rice is important in these cultures.

In a similar way, you might assume that a language with a paucity of terms in comparison to other languages to refer to a thing or activity reflects a culture in which that thing or activity is absent or not important. The Yanomamo of southern Venezuela are one of the few societies in the world with a primitive technology. The Yanomamo language has only three numbers that correspond to "one," "two," and "more than two" in English. The development of technology requires a language that can symbolize mathematics.

> It is said that when a Japanese writes a letter, it always begins with a remark on the weather and the season. It will say things like "It is already mid-May, and the young foliage is fresh and green . . ."

Compared to English, Japanese has a rich vocabulary of words to identify seasons of the year. The four seasons are divided into 24 subseasons according to the traditional lunar calendar. And each subseason is divided into the beginning, middle, and end.

Grammar and Syntax

The second level of the Sapir-Whorf hypothesis is grammar and syntax. Whorf felt that **grammar** had an even greater influence than vocabulary. For example, it has been observed that in the Eskimo language there is a consistent use of the word *if* rather than *when* in reference to the future. Think of the difference between "When I graduate from college . . ." and "If I graduate from college . . ." In this example, *when* seems to indicate more certainty than *if*. Linguists have associated the more common use of *if* in the Eskimo language with the harsh environment that Eskimos live in where life is fragile and there is little control over nature (Chance, 1966).

English word order is typically SVO (see Table 7.1). English places emphasis on a doer, on an action taker. Only about a third of English sentences lack a subject. In contrast, 75% of Japanese sentences lack a subject. For example, you are more likely to hear, "I brought my textbook with me" in the United

States and hear "Brought book" in Japan. The subject is known by context. Similarly, if you have hiked for a day into a deserted canyon you might say to yourself, "I feel lonesome." A Japanese hiker would say only "Samishii," identifying the experience lonesome without the need to identify the subject. Yes, in English, we sometimes speak in abbreviated forms, but we're conscious of it being a shortened version of a more detailed statement. The Japanese speaker is not abbreviating; Japanese does not require the specification of a subject.

Case Study: Arabic and the Arab Culture

As a demonstration of the Sapir-Whorf hypothesis, you can use the following case study to learn about Arab culture from the characteristics of the **Arabic** language that are presented. As you read this section, identify elements of Arab culture that you see in the following description of the language.

Arabic is spoken in one form or another by more than 200 million people. Because Arabic is strongly interconnected with the religion **Islam**, the Sapir-Whorf hypothesis explains the critical importance of the religion to the culture. The **Koran** is the ultimate standard for Arabic style and grammar. Islam has had major effects on both written Arabic and the spoken language. Classical Arabic, the language of the Koran, is the accepted standard for the written language (Asuncion-Lande, 1983). As Islam spread throughout the world, so too did spoken Arabic, as all Muslims, regardless of nationality, must use Arabic in their daily prayers.

Like any language, spoken Arabic continues to evolve and does vary from country to country. In classical Arabic, the number 2 is *ithnayn,* but *tween* is used in Lebanon, *itneen* in Egypt, and *ithneen* in Kuwait. Perhaps because of the influences of the Koran, Arabic withstood Turkish-Ottoman occupation and colonial empires and changed less than would have been expected. Advocates of Arab unity continue to work to unify and purify the spoken language. Modern standard Arabic is used, for example, at Arab League meetings, in radio and television news broadcasts, and in books and newspapers. Nonetheless, English or French is still the second language in the region.

Arabic style attempts to go beyond reflecting human experience to transcending the human experience. As Merriam (1974) noted, Al-Sakkaki divided rhetoric into three parts: *al ma'ani* is the part dealing with grammatical forms and kinds of sentences; *al-bayan* refers to modes for achieving lucid style and clarity of expression; and *al-badi* (literally "the science of metaphors") refers to the beautification of style and the embellishment of speech.

Skillful use of language commands prestige. Arabic vocabulary is rich. For example, there are 3,000 words for camel, 800 for sword, 500 for lion, and 200 for snake. Translated into English, Arabic statements often sound exaggerated. Instead of "We missed you," the statement may be "You made us desolate with your absence." It is said that because of the love of language the Arab is swayed more by words than by ideas and more by ideas than by facts.

Arabic emphasizes creative artistry through repetition, metaphor, and simile in part because of the poetic influences of the Koran. The role that formal poetry, prose, and oratory play is missing today in Western culture. Westerners often find it difficult to locate the main idea of an Arabic message; Arabs often fault Westerners for being insensitive to linguistic artistry.

Arabic makes more use of paralanguage—pitch, rhythm, intonation, and inflection—than other languages. The language rhythm can be magical and hypnotic. Higher pitch and greater emotional intonation are natural to Arabic speakers.

Speakers of Arabic may talk with a lot of noise and emotion. The rhetoric of confrontation—verbal threats and flamboyant language—is common. What may appear to be a heated argument may just be two friends having a chat. A speaker of Arabic uses language as a mode of aggression. Such verbal aggression essentially diffuses and prevents actual violence.

It is said that when an Arab says yes, he means maybe. When he says maybe, he means no. An Arab seldom says no because it may be considered impolite and close off options. Instead of no, an Arab may say *inshallah*, or "if God is willing." Inshallah is used when mentioning a future event of any kind as it is considered sacrilegious to presume to control future events. To mean yes, one must be both repetitive and emphatic.

TRANSLATION PROBLEMS

Even when cultures speak the same language—as do Australia and the United States—there can be vocabulary differences. When cultures speak different languages, translation is critical—but always imperfect. When President Jimmy Carter greeted the people of Poland on his 1977 trip there, the translator said, "The President says he is pleased to be here in Poland grasping your secret parts" (Axtell, 1994). Sechrest, Fay, and Zaidi (1972) have identified five translation problems that can become barriers to intercultural communication. Each of these is discussed below.

Vocabulary Equivalence

First is the lack of *vocabulary equivalence*. Recall the discussions of the Sapir-Whorf hypothesis and the example given that Eskimo languages have many different words to refer to snow. Were you to translate on a word-for-word basis, you would translate all those different words into the one English word *snow*. Much of the meaning of the more specific and more descriptive words—for example, qualities of slushiness or hardness or newness—would be lost in a word-for-word translation.

As another example, imagine having to translate all shades of pink, burgundy, orange-red, and so on into the one word *red*. As you might imagine, such a limitation would be frustrating to you if you were accustomed to using more descriptive words.

One frequently quoted example of the lack of vocabulary equivalence is from World War II. The Allies had issued the Potsdam Ultimatum demanding the surrender of the Japanese military to end the war. At a

> No one when he uses a word has in mind exactly the same thing that another has, and the difference, however tiny, sends its tremors throughout language. . . . All understanding, therefore, is always at the same time a misunderstanding. . . . and all agreement of feelings and thoughts is at the same time a means for growing apart.
>
> —Wilhelm von Humboldt (1767-1835)
> (quoted in Cowan, 1963)

press conference, Prime Minister Suzuki was asked for his opinion. He responded, "The government does not see much value in it. All we have to do is *mokusatsu* it." The Japanese cabinet had carefully chosen that word to convey their intended meaning. Later, Japanese cabinet officials said they intended to convey a bland "no comment" at that time, as there was interest in negotiating a surrender and more time was required for discussions. Unfortunately, the word *mokusatsu* can mean anything from "ignore" to "treat with silent contempt." Western translators used the latter meaning, and the Potsdam Ultimatum was then considered to have been rejected. After-the-fact reasoning argues that that translation led to the continuation of the war and the first use of atomic weapons.

Languages that are different often lack words that are directly translatable. Consider the number of English words with different meanings: A U.S. businessperson might write a letter to be translated into Japanese with the sentence "We wonder if you would prepare an agenda for our meeting." The word *wonder* and the construction of this sentence may have been intended as a polite way of telling the Japanese counterpart to prepare the agenda. The word wonder could be translated with the Japanese word *gimon*, which most commonly means doubt. The translated sentence now would read, "We doubt that you would prepare an agenda for our meeting" (Axtell, 1994).

Idiomatic Equivalence

The second barrier to successful translation is the problem of *idiomatic equivalence*. The English language is particularly replete with the **idiom**. Take the simple example of "the old man kicked the bucket." Native speakers know that this idiom means the old man died. If the sentence is translated word for word, the meaning conveyed would be literally that the old man kicked the bucket—quite different from the intended meaning. You can no doubt think of many other examples. Just think of how the idioms "out to lunch" and "toss your cookies" could cause communication problems!

It's easy to think of many idioms in common use in spoken U.S. English that can be misunderstood: "break a leg," "read between the lines," "hold your horses," and "raining cats and dogs." This is one reason why English is a difficult language to learn as a second language. However, learning the idioms of a language can be an effective way of learning the culture (Lee, 1994).

Grammatical-Syntactical Equivalence

Third is the problem of *grammatical-syntactical equivalence*. This simply means that languages do not necessarily have the same grammar. Often, you need to understand a language's grammar to understand the meaning of words.

For example, words in English can be nouns or verbs or adjectives depending on their position in a sentence. In English you can say "plan a table" and "table a plan" or "book a place" and "place a book" or "lift a thumb" and "thumb a lift."

Experiential Equivalence

Fourth is the problem of *experiential equivalence*. If an object or experience does not exist in your culture, it is difficult to translate words referring to that object or experience into that language when no words may exist for them. Think of objects or experiences that exist in your culture and not in another. "Department store" and "shopping mall" may be as difficult to translate into some languages as "wind surfing" is into others. The 2000 U.S. Census attempted to be sensitive to Vietnamese immigrants' experience with Vietnam's government tracking of individuals. Instead of using the Vietnamese words for census that translate "investigation of the population" the phrase *Thong ke dan so* or "survey of population" was used.

Conceptual Equivalence

Fifth, the problem of *conceptual equivalence* refers to abstract ideas that may not exist in the same fashion in different languages. For example, people in the United States have a unique meaning for the word *freedom*. That meaning is not universally shared. Speakers of other languages may say they are free and be correct in their culture, but the freedom they refer to is not equivalent to what you experience as freedom in the United States.

The English word *corruption* translates as the Korean word *pup'ae*, but the words are not conceptually equivalent. For both people in the United States and Korea, the word connotes negative, bad, improper behavior, but in the United States, corruption is a crime and wrong on moral grounds, whereas in Korean, corruption is not morally wrong. It is wrong in the sense that it interferes with the proper functioning of government and is bad in its social consequences. Even though the word is negative and has similar interpretations, there are sufficient conceptual differences to create intercultural communication misunderstandings (Szalay, Moon, & Bryson, 1971).

A similar misunderstanding can occur with the word *democracy*. To both people in the United States and Korea, democracy means freedom and liberty. In the United States, the meaning of the word places strong emphasis on procedures such as elections, campaigning, and voting, whereas in Korea, the word democracy is an abstract ideal. Think of how post-Communist Russians readily embraced the words *democracy*, *congress*, and *president*, but having just broken with the totalitarian tradition many had trouble understanding the underlying concepts.

In a 1994 interview, former President Jimmy Carter identified conceptual equivalence problems with the term *human rights*. According to Carter, each country defines the term by what it has. In the United States, human rights refers to the Bill of Rights (e.g., freedom of speech, right to a fair trial). In other countries, the term refers to adequate housing or universal health care.

One way to improve translation is to use **back translation**. Back translation involves first translating into the second language, then translating back into the first language, and then comparing the result to the original. Often, the

In French, "solitude" is intimate, so intimate perhaps that the lips want to conceal, in pronouncing it, the very word they name. But in Spanish, "soledad" is immense, an overwhelming condition. . . . Thus one can be a little sad in one language but desperate in another.

—Hector Bianciotti, *Hopscotch*, Winter 2000 (http://www.hopscotch.org)

NOTE: Bianciotti, novelist and critic, the son of Italian immigrants, grew up in Argentina, where he was first exposed to French literature in the seminary. His first novels were in Spanish. He now writes exclusively in French.

process can prevent amusing translation problems. For example, on a trip to see Hitler's Eagle's Nest I was given a ticket for my return trip down the mountain. On the back of the ticket I found this message in English: "The indicated return time must be strictly adhered to. A later return is determined by the disposable bus seats." The misuse of the word *disposable* would probably be caught if the sentence was translated back into German and then compared to the original German sentence. (See Box 7.1 for more examples.)

Even with these problems in translation, successful computer translating programs have been developed. A translating program first analyzes the syntax of a sentence to identify subject, verb, object, and modifiers. Then, using a dictionary, the words are translated into another language. Finally, the program analyzes the result and generates an intelligible sentence in the new language based on the rules of that language's syntax. Several Internet sites provide usable instant translation. Machine translation of the spoken voice is more difficult. One-way handheld voice translators were used by the U.S. military in Afghanistan in 2002. Two-way voice translators are possible, but not perfect.

Box 7.1

SPECIALIST IN WOMEN AND OTHER DISEASES

One of the 84 known subcategories of humor is the commercial sign written in a language not native to the country in which the sign is found. A recent list of prime examples has been making its way through the computer networks; allegedly, its origin is an Air France memo.

It's hard to know how real these signs are. Almost certainly many have been shortened or rephrased to make them funnier; a few may be outright inventions. Nevertheless, as any traveler knows, this art form does exist.

Nor, of course, are English speakers innocent of provoking the same merriment in other countries. One only has to remember the multimillion-dollar campaign that introduced Coca-Cola to China a few years ago. Its proud slogan, emblazoned everywhere, trumpeted: "Bite the wax tadpole."

Thus and herewith:

- From a Tokyo Hotel: "Is forbidden to steal hotel towels please. If you are not a person to do such a thing is please not to read notis."

- In a Bucharest hotel lobby: "The lift is being fixed for the next day. During that time we regret that you will be unbearable."

- In a Yugoslavian hotel: "The flattening of underwear with pleasure is the job of the chambermaid."

- On the menu of a Swiss restaurant: "Our wines leave you nothing to hope for."

- In an advertisement by a Hong Kong dentist: "Teeth extracted by the latest Methodists."

- In a Belgrade hotel elevator: "To move the cabin, push button for wishing floor. If the cabin should enter more persons, each one should press a number of wishing floor. Driving is then going alphabetically by national order."

- In a Rhodes tailor shop: "Order your summer suit. Because is big rush we will execute customers in strict rotation."

- In an Austrian hotel catering to skiers: "Not to perambulate the corridors during the hours of repose in the boots of ascension."

- In a Bangkok temple: "It is forbidden to enter a woman even a foreigner if dressed as a man."

- In a Norwegian cocktail lounge: "Ladies are requested not to have children at the bar."

- In a Copenhagen airline office: "We take your bags and send them in all directions."

- In an Acapulco hotel: "The manager has personally passed all the water served here."

- On the menu of a Polish hotel: "Salad a firm's own make; limpid red better soup with cheesy dumplings in the form of a finger; roasted duck let loose; beef rashers beaten up in the country people's fashion."

(Continued)

Box 7.1, *Continued*

- In a Zurich hotel: "Because of the impropriety of entertaining guests of the opposite sex in the bedroom, it is suggested that the lobby be used for that purpose."

- A sign posted in a German park: "It is strictly forbidden on our black forest camping site that people of different sex, for instance, men and women, live together in one tent unless they are married with each other for that purpose."

- On the door of a Moscow hotel room: "If this is your first visit to the USSR, you are welcome to it."

- In a Macao store: "Sorry! Midgets will always be available tomorrow!"

- From a brochure from a car rental firm in Tokyo: "When passenger on foot heave in sight, tootle the horn. Trumpet him melodiously at first, but if he still obstacles your passage then tootle him with vigor."

The headline of this column, by the way, is a sign outside a doctor's office in Rome.

SOURCE: Jon Carroll, "A Specialist in Women and Other Diseases," *San Francisco Chronicle*, July 30, 1990, p. F10. Copyright © 1990, San Francisco Chronicle. Reprinted with permission.

PIDGINS, CREOLES, AND UNIVERSAL LANGUAGES

When cultures with no shared language came in contact, such as through international trade or during colonialism, one way to communicate was through the development of pidgins and creoles. Once thought of as crude nonstandard languages, they are now central to the study of linguistic development (Holm, 1989; Romaine, 1988).

Pidgins

A **pidgin** is the mixture of two or more languages to form a new language originally used for restricted purposes such as trade. As a contact language between diverse language groups, pidgins have widespread use in West Africa. Cameroon used a pidgin drawn from English, German, French, and local words to facilitate communication among some 285 tribal languages. In the western Pacific, European traders, whalers, and missionaries and the hundreds of tribes there developed a pidgin based on English, German, and a local language with a distinctly Melanesian grammar and sentence structure. Melanesian Pidgin English is a pidgin language based on English. Use of Pidgin English became widespread when colonial European plantations were established in the 19th century in Samoa, Fiji, and other places using laborers from New Guinea and the Solomon Islands, an archipelago of several hundred islands spread over 1,000 miles and over 50 languages. In the 20th century, Pidgin English died out in the monolingual communities of Samoa and Fiji but continued to be used in the multilingual communities of Papua New Guinea and the Solomons (Keesing, 1988).

The Papua New Guinea constitution recognizes three "national" languages—English, Hiri Motu, and Tok Pisin. English is the major language of education and written communication. Hiri Motu is the language of the southern provinces of the mainland. Its use is declining as the use of Tok Pisin expands. Tok Pisin is used in speeches and reports in the National Parliament and in social interaction among people of diverse language backgrounds. It was spoken when Prince Charles opened Papua New Guinea's National Parliament during independence celebrations in 1975. And in 1984, Pope John Paul II celebrated Mass in New Guinea in pidgin (Romaine, 1992).

The development of a pidgin is not inevitable. One example from East Africa is Swahili, the language used by the coast tribes that settled in eastern Tanzania. In the 1800s, Arab traders searching for slaves migrated down the coast, spreading Arabic. Over time, 50% of Swahili was derived from Arabic. Later, British colonial rule brought English, but Swahili continued as the unifying language of the country's 120 diverse tribes. African nationalism in the 1960s reinforced the use of Swahili over English. Today, it is not unusual for people to switch back and forth from Swahili to English to communicate ideas.

Creoles

Today, a **creole** is defined as a new language developed from prolonged contact of two or more languages (Bickerton, 1981). Whereas a pidgin can be thought of as a second language, a creole is acquired by children as their first language. Creoles were largely the product of the colonial era. Creoles are concentrated in areas where slave labor was used—the Caribbean, the Indian Ocean, and Pacific islands. Typically, creoles incorporate the vocabulary of the dominant language with the grammar and some words from the subordinate language to become the new language of the subordinate group.

The most well known creoles are Jamaican Patois, a mixture of English and West African languages, with more than 2 million speakers and French-based Haitian with some 5 million speakers. These are increasingly used in newspapers and radio.

In Macao, a patois, or **dialect**, developed from Portuguese and Cantonese words in combinations like *compra som*, meaning to buy groceries from the Portuguese *compra* and the Cantonese *som*, and *avo gong*, which joins together the Portuguese and Cantonese terms for grandfather.

Esperanto

Would communication between individuals of diverse cultures be improved if we all spoke one language? There have been attempts to construct such a universal language. The only moderately successful attempt was **Esperanto**, devised in 1887 by Polish oculist and philologist Lazarus Zamenhof when 19 years old. Zamenhof wrote under the name of Dr. Esperanto, or "one who hopes."

Esperanto is a simplified, regular language with Latin-type grammar and European vocabulary. It is claimed that you can learn the language in 100 hours or less. Estimates of the number of speakers of Esperanto today range from 1 million to 16 million worldwide. Vatican Radio and China broadcast programs in Esperanto, and on its 100th anniversary, an Esperanto version of the play *The Importance of Being Earnest* was presented in London.

When Esperanto was devised, English was the language of commerce, French of diplomacy, and German of science. Today, English, rather than Esperanto, has become the universal language of all three.

Esperanto and other attempts at universal languages are not successful precisely for the reasons described earlier in this chapter as characteristics of language itself. Universal languages are artificial languages; they have no relationship to a culture—hence they are static and don't change and evolve as a culture changes and evolves. Nor do universal languages reflect the worldview of any culture. Any universal first language would probably begin to develop unique regional vocabularies and pronunciations over time and would then again begin to reflect cultural differences as the regional dialects grew further apart.

LANGUAGE AS NATIONALISM

A second way that language can be a barrier relates to the Sapir-Whorf hypothesis discussed earlier. When a group with more power enforces the use of its language on another group, it is also making its culture dominant. The Brazilian Paulo Freire (1992) used the term **cultural invasion** to refer to one group penetrating the culture of another group to impose its own view of the world. Cultural invasion can be physical and overt as in war and political takeover or it can be indirect or even in the form of helping. The spread of a language to common use around a region also means the spreading influence of the culture native to that language.

English: A History of Borrowed Words

As the use of English becomes increasingly worldwide, more concerns are voiced that it carries "the baggage" of one culture.

English did not exist when Julius Caesar invaded Britain in 55 B.C.E. The Celts spoke languages that survive today as Welsh, Gaelic, and Breton. In the mid 5th century, the Jutes (modern Denmark) and the Saxons (Germany) migrated to the south of Britain, and the Angles (Germany) migrated to the north and east of Britain. Pope Gregory's monks brought some Latin and Greek words. The Vikings from Scandinavia arrived in the late 8th century and enriched the vocabulary. (*Rear* a child is Anglo-Saxon; *raise* a child is Norse.) The Norman French conquered England in 1066. English kept its relatively simple Germanic structure while adding a huge vocabulary of French words. Even before Columbus, English had borrowed words from 50 languages.

Anglo-Saxon	French	Latin
end	finish	conclude
fair	beautiful	attractive
fear	terror	trepidation

Borrowed words tend to be pronounced the same as in their original language.

The printing press and the European Renaissance added thousands of words to the English vocabulary. In 1780, John Adams moved for the creation of an academy to keep the English language pure. His proposal died in the Continental Congress. The *Oxford English Dictionary* contains more than 600,000 English words. By comparison, German has fewer than one-third that number and French fewer than one-sixth. Today, half of the world's published books are in English.

> The English language hasn't got where it is by being pure.
>
> —Carl Sandburg

This 1970 British stamp honors the *Mayflower* leaving Plymouth.

The Spread of English

Even though at one time it could not have been predicted, of particular concern today is the spread of American English. In 449, the Jutes first arrived on the Kent coast. The Germanic dialect of the Jutes along with those of the Angles and the Saxons was soon to become known as English. The Germanic invaders took little from the language of the Celts they displaced, but soon began its characteristic assimilation of words from other languages—first Latin from Christian missionaries arriving in 597, then Old Norse from Danish invaders, then French from Norman rule (Stevenson, 1999).

In 1582, a scholar observed, "The English tongue is of small account, stretching no further than this island of ours, nay not there over all." In little more than 25 years, English had spread across the ocean and has not stopped expanding since. In early colonial days, some 5 million people spoke English. By 1930, the number had risen to 200 million. By the mid-1960s, counting those who used English as a second language, the number of people speaking English had doubled to 400 million. By 1990, that number had risen to about 750 million, or 1 in every 7 people.

English is the native language in 12 countries and an official or semiofficial language in 33 others. Its study is required or popular in at least 56 other countries (see Table 7.2). Consider this: An Argentine pilot landing in Turkey speaks to the air traffic controller in English. English is the de facto language of aviation worldwide. A German physicist publishes findings in English-language journals. Japanese executives conduct business in Mexico in English. It is the most widely studied and most borrowed-from language in the world.

English has grown to dominate in the areas of science, technology, commerce, tourism, diplomacy, and pop culture. CNN International and MTV broadcast in English. Some 80% of the world's electronic databases and communication networks are in English.

The Internet was developed in the United States, and the overwhelming majority of World Wide Web sites, newsgroups, and chat rooms are based in the United States. Internet search engines are largely in English. Even computer keyboards are typically based on the English alphabet. French President Jacques Chirac told la Francophonie, a group formed in France to preserve the use of French in cyberspace, "If in this new medium our language, our programs,

Table 7.2 English Spoken Here . . . and Here . . . and Here

English as the Native Language	*English as the Official or Semiofficial Language*	
North America	Africa	Asia/Pacific
Canada, except Quebec	Botswana	Bangladesh
United States	Cameroon	Burma (Myanmar)
South America	Ethiopia	Fiji
Guyana	Gambia	India
Caribbean	Ghana	Malaysia
Bahamas	Kenya	Pakistan
Barbados	Lesotho	Philippines
Grenada	Liberia	Singapore
Jamaica	Malawi	Sri Lanka
Trinidad and Tobago	Mauritius	Tonga
Europe	Namibia	Western Samoa
Ireland	Nigeria	Mideast, Mediterranean
Great Britain	Sierra Leone	Israel
Pacific	South Africa	Malta
Australia	Sudan	
New Zealand	Swaziland	
	Tanzania	
	Uganda	
	Zambia	
	Zimbabwe	

Countries Where English Is Studied Widely

North America	Luxembourg	Nigeria
Mexico	The Netherlands	Senegal
Central America, Caribbean	Norway	Togo
Costa Rica	Portugal	Zaire
Cuba	Romania	Mideast
Dominican Republic	Russia	Egypt
Honduras	Sweden	Jordan
South America	Switzerland	North Yemen
Brazil	Africa	Saudi Arabia
Colombia	Algeria	Syria
Venezuela	Angola	Turkey
Europe	Burkina Faso	Asia
Austria	Burundi	Afghanistan
Belgium	Central African Republic	China
Denmark	Chad	Hong Kong
Germany	Gabon	Indonesia
Finland	Guinea	Japan
France	Ivory Coast	Nepal
Greece	Libya	South Korea
Iceland	Madagascar	Thailand
Italy	Morocco	

SOURCE: Adapted from *U.S. News & World Report*, February 18, 1995, pp. 50-51. Copyright © 1995 by *U.S. News & World Report*. Used with permission.

our creations don't have a strong presence, our future generations will be economically and culturally marginalized."

India

A more extreme case of the spread of English is India, the world's second most populated country, approaching 1 billion people. India is a country of diversity: a multiplicity of languages as well as religions, castes, and living conditions. Since its independence in 1947, India has struggled to maintain a society that values the country's diverse linguistic, religious, and historic groups.

India's people speak 20 major languages and hundreds of dialects. When India became an independent country in 1947, Hindi was slated to become the national language by 1965. But as 1965 approached, the use of Hindi had not spread. Hindi speakers concentrated in the north claim that English is elitist and a holdover from the colonial past. India is slowly eradicating the legacy of British colonial rule by renaming cities and streets. Madras is now Chennai, Bombay is now Mumbai, and Calcutta is now Kolkata. English speakers largely in the south argue that Hindi as an official language would exclude those who don't speak it.

Using English would at least give everyone an equal handicap. From among India's officially recognized languages, individual states are free to adopt their own language of administration and education. Every citizen has the right to petition the government in any of the official languages.

South Africa

The first Dutch settlement on the southern tip of Africa dates back to 1652 with the arrival of Dutch, German, and French Huguenot immigrants (later known as Afrikaners or as Boers by the British). Dutch became the official language of that colony, but within 150 years it had been replaced with Afrikaans, perhaps the world's youngest language and the only Germanic language born outside Europe.

Afrikaans was derived from 17th-century Dutch and reflects the influences of Malay, Portuguese, German, French, English, and native African languages. It represents a cultural tradition of self-sufficiency and Calvinist morality. For many years, speakers of Afrikaans were the oppressed under British colonial rule. But in 1925, Afrikaans joined English as the country's two official languages and from then on earned the reputation among Blacks as the language of oppression. The most widely known word in the Afrikaans vocabulary is *apartheid*—*literally apart-hood* or separateness—government-sanctioned segregation of racial and ethnic groups that ended with Nelson Mandela's election in 1994.

The most commonly spoken languages in South Africa are Zulu (22% of the population) and Xhosa (18%), followed by Afrikaans (15%), Tswana, Northern Sotho, English (perceived as the language of colonial heritage), and Southern Sotho. English is the first language for only 9% of the population, but it is gaining popularity as the second language. The multitude of languages became a major factor in developing a new constitution. English and Afrikaans will now join nine others as official languages.

English may play a role in bridging South Africa's divides, as can be seen with the changes taking place on South Africa's state radio. The English-speaking elite were the audience for the state-owned radio station known as Radio South Africa. Now known as SAfm, the radio of the new South Africa, African-accented English is becoming the norm just as African-accented English is becoming the lingua franca of the country.

Australia and New Zealand

The continent of Australia with the island state of Tasmania is approximately equal in area to the continental United States. The first inhabitants of Australia were the Aboriginals, who migrated there at least 40,000 years ago from Southeast Asia. It is estimated that there may have been a half million to a million Aboriginals at the time of European contact. Today, Aboriginals number about 1% of the total population of 18.7 million.

The first English speakers to arrive in number in Australia were convicts and their guards put ashore in 1788 at the penal colony of Botany Bay. (Convicted under the penal code of the day, their offenses would be considered minor today.) The convict argot was known as flash and was so incomprehensible to speakers of Standard English that an interpreter was sometimes needed in the courts. Flash began to die out as former convicts joined new English and Irish immigrants in developing a unique Australian English with some words borrowed from the Aboriginals (Stevenson, 1999).

New Zealand English shares much with Australia, but each has unique words and idioms. After seal and

*Haka/*Maori war dance.

Köhanga reo mäpihi pounamu (treasured language nest).

Whänau ana te tamaiti, mauria atu ka whaka-mau ki te ü, ä, hei reira tonu ka tïmata te körero Mäori atu ki a ia.

Translation: "When a child is born, take it, put it to the breast, and begin speaking Maori at that point."

—Kaumatua Hui, 1980,
Te Köhanga Reo National Trust
(http://www.kohanga.ac.nz)

whale hunters came other European traders and merchants, primarily British, attracted by flax, forests, and trade with the Maori. Maori, the indigenous language of New Zealand, and English are recognized as official languages in New Zealand. The Maori comprise about 9% of the nation's 3.7 million population. Maori is an Austronesian language similiar to Hawaiian and Samoan and particularly close to the language of the Cook Islands and Tahiti. There were regional dialects, some of which diverged radically but which have lost influence to a standard dialect. On the South Island, which is dominated by one tribe, the Southern dialect persists.

The final two decades of the 20th century saw an enthusiasm for the survival of the Maori language. Most notable were the efforts of Maori women to establish *köhanga reo* (language nests) where preschool children are introduced to the language. The first köhanga reo was established in 1982. There are now more than 700 providing immersion education for over 13,000 children. In addition, a number of Maori universities have been established.

Canada's stamps reflect its two-language policy.

Canada

The situation in Canada is unique. More than 200 years ago, Canada's French settlers were defeated by the British army on a Quebec field called the Plains of Abraham. New France then became British, but the French settlers were permitted to maintain their language (French) and religion (Roman Catholicism). By itself, Quebec would be the world's 18th largest country in size. Its population is about 7.3 million, one-quarter of Canada's population.

SOURCE: Editorial cartoon by Mike Thompson from *La Opinión*, November 20, 1995. Reprinted with permission of Copley News Service.

Though the years, Quebec has maintained a vision of itself as a French-speaking society. Several generations chose to keep their language and culture. Canadian French has retained characteristics of the language of the 18th century. To the modern French, Canadian French has a somewhat monotonous intonation and lacks articulation (Stevenson, 1999). Colloquialism, slang, and accents differ widely. Quebec supports French-language artists, newspapers, radio, and television. More than 80% of its population speak French as the first language. In the 1950s, Quebec began to protest the use of English. In response, the federal government appointed the Royal Commission on Bilingualism and Biculturalism. The commission first recommended that Canadians of French origin be brought into full participation in Canadian life and later included all other cultural groups. In 1971, the prime minister announced officially that Canada would be bilingual and multicultural.

Officially a two-language country, Canada continues to deal with a strong separatist movement in Quebec. Quebec has never ratified the Canadian constitution because it is believed that it fails to protect the province's minority French language and culture. In 1977, Quebec established a French-only policy enforced by 400 "language police." Its inhabitants refer to the rest of Canada as "English Canada" and propose withdrawing from English-speaking Canada. The phrase *nous et les autres* (us and the others) united Quebeckers against the English-speaking Canadians and the fast-growing immigrant population that claims neither French nor English as its first language.

United States

Whereas Canada has two official languages and India many, the United States has none. Nowhere does the U.S. Constitution provide for an official language, although having one was seriously considered. German, French, Greek, and Hebrew were suggested. At the time of independence, the second language in the United States was a form of German known as Pennsylvania Dutch or Pennsylvania German. Half the population of Pennsylvania spoke German. Even an 1863 Pennsylvania law mandated that all official notices appear in German-language newspapers. German was the country's most common second language during the 19th century.

After independence, there have been times when some have pressed to make English the official language of the United States. In the 1870s, faced with large numbers of Chinese immigrants, California considered English-only laws. Later, with the large number of central and southeastern Europe immigrants at the turn of the century, the United States made oral English literacy a requirement for naturalization in 1906. Still later, during and after World War I, anti-German sentiment led some states to ban German, remove German-language books from libraries, and close German-language theaters (Crawford, 1992). Those laws were declared unconstitutional. During World War II, German-speaking residents of the United States experienced humiliation and insult because of their accents. Since 1950, the requirement for citizenship has been "to read, write and speak words in ordinary English."

Even so, the United States has had a long history of non-English-speaking immigrants. (See Table 7.3 for current language use in U.S. homes.) In

> Until recent times, perhaps the U.S. has been the only country in which to speak two languages was a mark of low status.
>
> —Edward C. Stewart,
> *American Cultural Patterns* (1972)

Table 7.3   Language Use in U.S. Homes

State	Percentage Who Speak a Language Other Than English at Home
California	39.5
New Mexico	36.5
Texas	32
New York	28
Hawaii	26.6
Arizona	25.9
New Jersey	25.5
Florida	23.1
U.S. average	17.9

SOURCE: U.S. Census Bureau, 2000 Census.

1848, Cincinnati, Ohio, had the first bilingual school to serve the German-American community. In the early 1900s, a dozen states had bilingual education, with at least 4% of students receiving all or part of their instruction in German. At one time more than 4,100 schools taught German (Grosjean, 1982). By 1920, 75% of the population of some cities were foreign born. Several cities and states printed some official documents in languages other than English (Crawford, 1992).

Before 1980, only two states had official-English laws: Nebraska in 1920 and Illinois in 1923. By the 1950s, Spanish had effectively become the second language. In the 1980s, the official-English movement became active, due in large part to the large numbers of Hispanic immigrants, some of whom have not assimilated as quickly as earlier immigrants. Immigrant children have been taught the Pledge of Allegiance in foreign languages, and the Immigration and Naturalization Service has conducted citizenship ceremonies in Spanish. Residents of southern Florida and southern California could use a 1040 tax return printed in Spanish. (The form was discontinued when only 718 were returned out of a half-million distributed.) A 1992 amendment to the federal Voting Rights Act requires counties to supply voting materials for Hispanic, Asian-American, American Indian, and Alaskan minority groups that number 10,000 or more, speak little or no English, and have a **literacy rate** below the national average.

Today, Miami is the only major U.S. city with a Hispanic majority. It is said that it is possible to live a full life in Miami without ever learning English. Miami has bilingual stores and restaurants, Spanish print and electronic media, and jobs for which only Spanish is required. Miami had an English-only ordinance but has since repealed it.

Persian, English, and Irish: Iranian immigrant Mashti Shirvani adds his name to the former Mugsy Malone ice cream store and creates a blend of languages and cultures.
Photograph © Karen Wiley. Used by permission.

In 1969, the federal government began providing funds for programs to help children with limited English. In 1974, the Supreme Court ruled in *Lau v. Nichols*, a class-action suit against the San Francisco Unified School District, that schools that do not provide special help for children with limited English are violating these students' civil rights. In the Court's language,

> The failure of the San Francisco school system to provide English language instruction to approximately 1,800 students of Chinese ancestry who do not speak English, or to provide them with other adequate instructional procedures, denies them a meaningful opportunity to participate in the public educational program and thus violates . . . the Civil Rights Act of 1964. (*Lau v. Nichols*, 1974, p. 203)

In effect, the Court held that there is no equality of treatment of students who do not understand English.

As their ruling did not specify what form this help should take, the Court did not require bilingual education. The Federal Bilingual Education Act of 1978 defined bilingual education as a program of instruction designed for children of limited English proficiency to achieve competence in English and to progress effectively through the education system.

Other arguments to make English the official language point to the millions spent on bilingual education, bilingual ballots, high school equivalency diploma tests, driving tests in foreign languages, and instant translation of court proceedings for defendants who do not speak English. Emergency and health care organizations would face a burden of providing information in all the languages spoken in the United States.

One of the organizations supporting official-English laws was founded with the guidance of U.S. Senator (1977-1982) Hayakawa. U.S. English, a political lobbying organization, argues that because of the influx of Hispanic immigrants the United States risks becoming divided linguistically and culturally like Canada. During the 1996 election campaign, the U.S. House of Representatives passed the English Language Empowerment Act that would make English the official language. Between 1984 and 1988, 13 states passed resolutions making English the official language. By 1997, 23 states and some 40 cities had passed measures making English the official language, and legislation was pending in 10 others. Generally, the laws don't affect what language is spoken in homes or in neighborhoods; the laws do prohibit the states from

In 1981, California Senator S. I. Hayakawa introduced an amendment to the United States Constitution that would make English the official language of the United States. The new article would state,

Section 1. The English language shall be the official language of the United States.

Section 2. The Congress shall have the power to enforce this article by appropriate legislation.

The following comments were made by Hayakawa and quoted in a speech by Senator Symms in the *Congressional Record*, January 22, 1985:

Language is a powerful tool. A common language can unify, separate languages can fracture and fragment a society. The American "melting pot" has succeeded in creating a vibrant new culture among peoples of many diverse cultural backgrounds largely because of the widespread use of common language, English.

The ability to force unity from diversity makes our society strong. We need all the elements. Germans, Hispanics, Hellenes, Italians, Chinese, all the cultures that make our Nation unique. Unless we have a common basis for communicating and sharing ideas, we all lose. The purpose of this proposal is to insure that American democracy always strives to include in its mainstream everyone who aspires to citizenship.

printing documents, such as voter information pamphlets, in other languages.

So far, courts have shown a tendency to reverse restrictions from official-English ordinances. In 1988, Arizona voters approved by 50.5% an initiative that made English the official language of the state and the language of "all government functions and actions." A lawsuit was filed by a Spanish-speaking state employee saying the measure barred her from speaking Spanish to Spanish-speaking people. In 1990, a federal district court ruled that Arizona's English-only law violated First Amendment guarantees of free speech. The federal judge ruled that the law curtailed government employees' free-speech rights by prohibiting them from using other languages when dealing with the non-English-speaking population. The citizens group that sponsored the initiative appealed the decision to the 9th Circuit Court of Appeals that affirmed the district court ruling. The case was then appealed to the Supreme Court, which ruled in 1997 on procedural problems. As the Arizona state employee who had originally sued had long since resigned, the Supreme Court said that the federal district court had no jurisdiction in the case (*Arizonans for Official English v. Arizona*), which has the effect of returning the issue to the Arizona state courts. Until that case, or another, reaches the Supreme

Court, the state laws stand. The next year, the State Supreme Court ruled that the 1988 voter-approved law provision requiring that official state and local business be conducted only in English violates constitutional free-speech rights and the Fourteenth Amendment's equal-protection clause (Crawford, 1992).

In private employment, though, the court has supported English-only job rules. Since 1970, the U.S. Equal Employment Opportunity Commission has told employers they may not enforce English-only rules except in cases of business necessity. This ruling was tested in 1991 when two employees sued their employer, a South San Francisco meat processing plant, after having been accused of making racist remarks in Spanish about two coworkers. They alleged that their employer's English-only rule violated a federal law barring on-the-job bias based on national origin. A federal appeals court ruled in favor of the employer, and in 1994 the Supreme Court declined to hear the case, thus leaving the appeals court decision as binding law in nine western states. (First Amendment rights do not apply in this case. Remember, the First Amendment applies to the government, not to private employers. For example, a private employer can prohibit union slogans on T-shirts.)

The other side of the issue is the weakening and disappearance of languages. Hawaiian language and culture, for example, are on the verge of extinction. The same can be said of some indigenous American Indian languages.

The Situation in Hawaii

The Hawaiians had no written language. Centuries of history, genealogies, legends, and religious teachings were passed from generation to generation orally. New England Christian missionaries who first arrived in 1820 devised a written language based on five vowels and seven consonants (*h*, *k*, *1*, *m*, *n*, *p*, and *w*). The glottal stop, the short break between the pronunciation of two vowels, was acknowledged but not denoted. It later became marked with the "backward apostrophe" as in *u'ina*, the word for glottal stop. The written language that was developed by the missionaries was not Hawaiian as the Hawaiians know it; it reflected what the New England English speakers perceived (Allen, 1982).

After the overthrow of the Hawaiian monarchy in 1893 by U.S. sugar planters and businessmen, Hawaii became a republic and sought

Hawaii (in Hawaiian: Hawai'i) was an independent kingdom until 1893, a republic from 1893 to 1898, and annexed to the United States in 1898 at the request of the inhabitants. This 1894 stamp honors King Kamehameha I.

Notice the words "Leper colony disinfected." By royal decree, lepers were sent to the island of Molokai and became a subgroup based on disease.

admission to the United States. The Hawaiian language was officially suppressed when the United States annexed the islands. In 1880, there were 150 schools teaching in Hawaiian. A decade later, there were none. Public school regulations written at the turn of the 20th century prohibited the use of Hawaiian in the schools.

By 1990, only about 1,000 native Hawaiian speakers remained, and 200 of those lived on Nihau, the privately owned island that is home to the last self-contained community of full-blooded Hawaiians. The language survived primarily through music and a few popular phrases. Nonetheless, at the 1978 constitutional convention Hawaiian was made an official language of the state along with English.

Hawaiians make up less than 20% of the state's 1.2 million population and are the fourth largest ethnic group behind Whites, Japanese-Americans, and Filipino-Americans. Recognizing that the loss of the language also means the loss of the culture, Hawaiians started a private preschool language immersion program in 1984. Inspired by the Maori of New Zealand and the Mohawks of Canada, a nonprofit foundation Aha Punano Leo, which means "language nest" in Hawaiian, was established. In 1986, the state legislature lifted the century-old ban on schools teaching only in Hawaiian. The language immersion

Table 7.4   Status of American Indian Languages

	Number	Examples
Spoken in homes by children	20	Navajo, Western Apache, Hopi, Zuni
Spoken by parents and elders	30	Crow, Cheyenne, Mesquakie
Spoken only by elders	70	Tlingit, Passamaquoddy, Winnebago, Comanche, Nez Percé, Yakima
Spoken by fewer than 10 elders	55	Eyak, Pawnee, Wichita, Omaha, Washoe

program then spread to the public school system. Controversy surrounds the program: Some argue that the program is a chance to save the language and recapture a lost cultural identity; others argue that it is the first step toward a separated society like the French in Canada. Support for that argument is found in the movement for the formation of native Hawaiian government within the framework of United States laws along the lines of other indigenous groups (Dudley & Agard, 1993).

Loss of American Indian Languages

In colonial times, more than 300 indigenous languages were spoken in North America. Today, only about 175 remain, with Navajo having the most speakers, approximately 148,530 (see Table 7.4). From the 1860s until about the 1950s, federal policy and local practice combined to discourage and eliminate American Indian languages from schools and public settings. In the 1920s, students in federal boarding schools were beaten for using their own language. Yet during World War II, U.S. Marines used Navajo "code talkers" at Guadalcanal and Iwo Jima; the Japanese were never able to decipher signals encoded in the Navajo language.

In 1990, the U.S. Congress passed the Native American Language Act, legislation sponsored by Hawaii Senator Daniel Inouye. The act endorses the preservation of indigenous languages and encourages the use of American Indian languages as languages of instruction. The languages remain used in tribal politics and religious ceremonies and on radio stations. It was said that movement to make English the official U.S. language mobilized many tribes in the recognition that linguistic survival is the same as cultural or tribal survival.

Puerto Rico and Statehood

Another story is being played out in Puerto Rico, where the official language has been a part of the argument over statehood. The island was made a U.S.

territory after Spain ceded it to the United States in 1898. Residents became U.S. citizens in 1917, and in 1952 Puerto Rico became a commonwealth. Residents cannot vote and pay no federal income tax. A 1967 nonbinding plebiscite had 60.4% voting for commonwealth status, 39% for statehood, and 0.6% for independence. A 1993 nonbinding plebiscite had 48.6% voting for commonwealth status, 46.3% for statehood, and 4.4% for independence. Most recently, a 1998 plebiscite had 46.5% voting for statehood and 50.2% voting "none of the above," which was the commonwealth option. Spanish was made the island's official language in 1991 with the backing of statehood opponents. Proponents of statehood were successful in passing a new law in 1993 that made English and Spanish official languages of the territory.

FROM THE INTERCULTURAL PERSPECTIVE

Language can be defined as the set of symbols shared by a community to communicate meaning and experience. The idea that culture and language are connected may not be obvious at first. When we learned our native language, we also unconsciously learned our culture. However, if a person learns another language or grows up speaking more than one language, the person may become aware of the different ways that each language allows a speaker to perceive and describe reality. These differences in perception are differences in culture. So the relationship between language and culture is that they are like mirrors to each other. Each one reflects and is reflected by the other.

Linguists have studied the relationship between language and culture, and it is described in the Sapir-Whorf hypothesis. This theory says that cultural elements can be seen in the vocabulary and grammar of a language. If a language has a rich vocabulary for certain things or ideas, it is easy to describe those things or ideas in that language. If the language makes it easy to express such things or ideas, they must be important to the culture. A similar relationship exists between the grammar of a language and a culture. Grammar allows the expression of ideas such as time and mood. If the grammar of a language does not allow a speaker to describe certain relationships, either that culture must not perceive them or does not consider them important.

Unique aspects of cultures are reflected in the languages spoken by their populations. Language can become a barrier to communication when these unique aspects interfere with translation. It can also become a barrier when a group of people is forced to speak a language it does not want to.

Five elements that typically cause problems in translation are the lack of equivalences in vocabulary, idioms, grammar and syntax, experiences, and concepts. Sometimes, translations cannot be made on a word-for-word basis because words that exist in one language may not exist in another. Idioms present a similar problem in that they, too, cannot be translated word for word.

The words that make up an idiomatic expression normally do not make sense at a literal level. Languages also do not all share the same grammar and syntax. Translations that have incorrect grammar and syntax can be confusing or even change the meaning from what was originally intended. Cultures often do not share the same experiences. Translation becomes problematic when one culture has certain experiences and another does not. Last, cultures may not understand concepts in the same way. Concepts such as "equality" and "freedom" mean different things in different cultures. One way to avoid translation problems is to "back translate," which is to first translate the concept into one language and then translate it back into the original language. Doing so makes it possible to check a translation for accuracy.

When cultures have contact but share no common language, a number of things may occur. First, a pidgin may develop. A pidgin is a trade language that has elements of the dominant language or languages, but with a greatly reduced vocabulary and grammar. Pidgins have no native speakers. Second, a creole may develop. Creoles are pidgins that have become "nativized." They have native speakers, and their vocabulary and grammar are expanded to the point of being complete languages. A third possibility is that the cultures will simply choose a language to use for communication purposes. In modern times, one of the most commonly chosen languages for this purpose is English. An artificial language, Esperanto, was developed as a universal second language, but its use is not widespread.

Language can be a barrier when it becomes an issue of nationalism. Because language carries elements of culture, many countries fear the influence on their own culture that the introduction of a new language may have. One response to this concern is to limit the influence of nondominant languages within a country. Examples of this type of action are the "English only" movement in the United States and the French Academy's efforts to keep the French language pure of foreign words.

National bilingualism can also have certain problems, as the separatist movement in Canada shows. One negative effect of language nationalism is the loss of language and culture of nondominant groups within a country.

KEY TERMS

Arabic	grammar	mother tongue
back translation	idiom	pidgin
creole	Islam	Sapir-Whorf hypothesis
cultural invasion	Koran	syntax
dialect	language	
Esperanto	literacy rate	

PART III

Cultural Values

CHAPTER 8

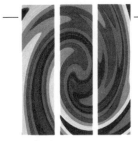

Dimensions of Culture

I n 1980, the Dutch management researcher Geert Hofstede first published
the results of his study of more than 100,000 employees of the multinational
IBM in 40 countries (Hofstede, 1980, 1983, 1984, 1991, 1997, 2001). Hofstede
was attempting to locate value dimensions across which cultures vary. His
dimensions have been frequently used to describe cultures.

Hofstede identified four dimensions that he labeled individualism, masculinity, power distance, and uncertainty avoidance. His individualism-collectivism
dimension describes cultures from loosely structured to tightly integrated. The
masculinity-femininity dimension describes how a culture's dominant values are
assertive or nurturing. Power distance refers to the distribution of influence
within a culture. And uncertainty avoidance reflects a culture's tolerance of
ambiguity and acceptance of risk.

Hofstede and Bond (1984; also see Chinese Culture Connection, 1987)
identified a fifth dimension, a Confucian dynamism labeled long-term orientation versus short-term orientation to life. The Confucian dynamism dimension
describes cultures that range from short-term values with respect for tradition

and reciprocity in social relations to long-term values with persistence and ordering relationships by status.

When reading this chapter, and particularly when reading the lists of countries that exhibit or fail to exhibit each dimension, you might think of exceptions: individuals from a culture who do not act as might be implied by these lists. These lists reflect an overall average; no one person should be expected to fit that average exactly. Indeed, to expect so would be stereotyping.

INDIVIDUALISM VERSUS COLLECTIVISM

First is **individualism** versus **collectivism**. This dimension refers to how people define themselves and their relationships with others. In an individualist culture, the interest of the individual prevails over the interests of the group. Ties between individuals are loose. People look after themselves and their immediate families. Masakazu (1994) defines modern individualism as "a view of humanity that justifies inner beliefs and unilateral self-assertion, as well as competition based on these" (p. 127). In a collectivist culture, the interest of the group prevails over the interest of the individual. People are integrated into strong, cohesive in-groups that continue throughout a lifetime to protect in exchange for unquestioning loyalty (Hofstede, 1997). One difference is reflected in who is taken into account when you set goals. In individualist cultures, goals are set with minimal consideration given to groups other than perhaps your immediate family. In collectivist cultures, other groups are taken into account in a major way when goals are set. Individualist cultures are loosely integrated; collectivist cultures are tightly integrated.

In individualist cultures such as the United States, for example, when meeting a new person you want to know what that person does. You tend to define people by what they have done, their accomplishments, what kind of car they drive, or where they live. Individualist cultures are more remote and distant (see examples in Table 8.1).

Cultures characterized by collectivism emphasize relationships among people to a greater degree. Collectivist cultures stress interdependent activities and suppressing individual aims for the group's welfare.

Often, it is difficult for individuals from highly individualist cultures to understand collectivist values. This example may help: A student from Colombia may study in the United States and earn a Ph.D., teach at a distinguished university, and publish important books, but when he returns to visit Colombia, people to whom he is introduced will want to know to whom he is related. Colombians want to know who his family is because that places

Table 8.1   Individualism Rankings for 50 Countries and Three Regions

1	United States	28	Turkey
2	Australia	29	Uruguay
3	Great Britain	30	Greece
4/5	Canada	31	Philippines
4/5	The Netherlands	32	Mexico
6	New Zealand	33/35	East Africa
7	Italy	33/35	Yugoslavia
8	Belgium	33/35	Portugal
9	Denmark	36	Malaysia
10/11	Sweden	37	Hong Kong
10/11	France	38	Chile
12	Ireland	39/41	West Africa
13	Norway	39/41	Singapore
14	Switzerland	39/41	Thailand
15	Germany (F.R.)	42	El Salvador
16	South Africa	43	South Korea
17	Finland	44	Taiwan
18	Austria	45	Peru
19	Israel	46	Costa Rica
20	Spain	47/48	Pakistan
21	India	47/48	Indonesia
22/23	Japan	49	Colombia
22/23	Argentina	50	Venezuela
24	Iran	51	Panama
25	Jamaica	52	Ecuador
26/27	Brazil	53	Guatemala
26/27	Arab countries		

SOURCE: Hofstede (2001, Exhibit 5.1, p. 215).

him in society much more so than any of his accomplishments in the United States.

In the United States, there are few family names—perhaps only Rockefeller, Kennedy, DuPont, Getty—that carry such defining meaning. You are not socially defined by your family name but by your individual accomplishments. A generation ago, people were introduced by family name, and a new acquaintance then asked permission to use one's given name. The asking and giving of permission was an important stage in the development of a friendship. Today's introduction by one's given name only makes no reference to one's family. Individualism is so strong in the United States that you might even have difficulty appreciating how people might feel content in a collectivist culture. Contentment comes from knowing your place and from knowing you have a place.

In the workplace, in individualist cultures, the employer-employee relationship tends to be established by contract, and hiring and promotion decisions are based on skills and rules; in collectivist cultures, the employer-employee relationship is perceived in moral terms, like a family link, and hiring and promotion decisions take the employee's in-group into account.

Hofstede's data revealed several associations with this dimension:

- *Wealth.* There is a strong relationship between a nation's wealth and individualism.

- *Geography.* Countries with moderate and cold climates tend to show more individualism.

- *Birth rates.* Countries with higher birth rates tend to be collectivist.

- *History.* Confucian countries are collectivist. Migrants from Europe who populated North America, Australia, and New Zealand tended to be sufficiently individualist to leave their native countries.

Another interesting association with inheritance practices was developed by Knighton (1999). Those cultures that have rules for equal partition of parental property among all offspring tend to be collectivist; those that have rules permitting unequal partition and those that have historically allowed parents to have full freedom in deciding who will inherit tend to be individualist.

Individualism and collectivism have been associated with direct and indirect styles of communication—that is, the extent to which speakers reveal intentions through explicit verbal communication. In the direct style, associated with individualism, the wants, needs, and desires of the speaker are embodied in the spoken message. In the indirect style, associated with collectivism, the wants, needs, and goals of the speaker are not obvious in the spoken message. Rojjanaprapayon (1997), for example, demonstrated specific communication strategies in Thai communication: Thais do not use specific names when they express negative feelings; Thais tend to use words and phrases expressing probability, such as "maybe," "probably," "sometimes," "likely," and "I would say so, but I am not sure"; Thais do not show their feelings if doing so would make the other person feel bad; and Thais also use indirect nonverbal communication of less or avoidance of eye contact and greater personal distance.

Case Study: Japan as a Homogeneous Culture

From Hofstede's (1983) research, Japan is placed about in the middle between individualism and collectivism. Yet Japan is popularly stereotyped as a group-oriented culture.

In a 1995 study of Japanese students using the original Hofstede questionnaires, Woodring found that students scored higher on individualism and lower on power distance than Hofstede's original sample. Woodring explained that the higher individualism and lower power distance score might be explained by age; that is, Japanese college students may value individualism and equality more than Japanese society does as a whole.

Hofstede's longitudinal study did show that national wealth and individualism were related. About 1990, the term *shin jin rui* (literally "new human beings") was applied to youths 25 years old and younger who were described by older Japanese as "selfish, self-centered, and disrespectful of elders and tradition."

Hofstede's study suggested that the Japanese were group oriented, hierarchical, and formal. There are reasons to suggest that at least younger Japanese prefer moderately egalitarian distribution of power and feel moderately independent of collective thought and action. This demonstrates that we should avoid allowing the Hofstede research to become a stereotype.

In 1986, Prime Minister Yasuhiro Nakasone described Japan as being a "homogeneous" country—a widely held view by Japanese society at large.

In the following descriptions of Japan's history, religion, and cultural patterns, identify specific ways that homogeneity affects communication.

History

Japan is an archipelago formed by four large islands and more than 3,000 small islands covering 377,835 square km, roughly the size of California. More than 80% of the land surface is hilly or mountainous, leaving only 20% that is flat enough for farming. Hence, Japan imports a large amount of its food and relies heavily on the ocean. Seafood is a staple in the Japanese diet, and Japan is the world's leading producer of fish. As an island nation, Japan will never be fully self-sufficient. It must export in order to import materials it needs to survive.

The population of Japan is approximately 126 million, equivalent to about half of the U.S. population, and inhabits only 4% of the land area, which translates to a population density of about 850 people per square mile; in the United States, the comparable density is 58. Japan is divided into 47 administrative

Mt. Fuji.

units or prefectures. Over 78% of Japan's population live in urban areas, with approximately 45% of the population living in the three major metropolitan areas of Tokyo (the largest city in the world), Osaka, and Nagoya.

Japan's origins are not clear. It is thought that Chinese culture as it passed through Korea was seminal. Japan is known as the Land of the Rising Sun, as is symbolized on its flag. Founded early in the Christian era, Japan has been ruled by a line of emperors that continues to the present. According to legend, all Japanese are genealogically related to the emperor at some distant point. In pre–World War II Japan, the emperor was worshiped as a living god. Hirohito was the emperor from 1926 until his death in 1989. Tradition dictated that a full year of mourning pass followed by a full season to plant and harvest a crop of sacred rice before his son Akihito could be formally enthroned as a symbolic constitutional monarch in 1990.

Two key points characterize Japanese history: more than 10,000 years of culture continuity and the ability to adapt imported culture and technology to the traditional culture. After Perry's arrival with battleships, Japan transformed itself from a feudal country into an industrialized nation by adapting

Western technology. Later, from the mid-1920s to the mid-1930s, urban Japanese experienced U.S. fashions, movies, and music. Following World War II, Japan again adopted more Western culture. The postwar constitution drafted by Allied occupation authorities and approved by the Japanese Parliament made Japan a constitutional monarchy.

The new constitution also renounced war and forbade the use of military forces for offensive purposes. Again because of the U.S.-inspired postwar constitution, Japan maintains only a defense force; over the period 1960-1988, 0.9% of its gross national product was spent on defense. (In the same period, the United States spent 6.4%.) Japan now pays several billion dollars annually to subsidize U.S. military bases in Japan. In response to criticism for not providing troops in the 1991 Gulf War, Japan approved providing troops for the United Nations' peacekeeping operations in noncombat roles and is becoming more engaged in world security issues.

Even after a decade of poor economic performance, Japan remains the world's second or third largest economy with several world-class companies that are technological leaders and household names. Japan is a major foreign investor and a major foreign aid donor.

Japanese life and language are Westernized. U.S. popular culture reaches Japan more quickly than it reaches parts of the United States. English loan words in the Japanese language grow at a fast rate. Japan's Westernization has been criticized by some Asian countries.

Religion

Japan is one of the most homogeneous countries in the world: More than 95% of its population is Japanese; Koreans, Chinese, and native Ainu constitute the remaining 5%. In 1997, Japan's parliament voted to replace a century-old law that forced the Ainu to assimilate. The Ainu were recognized by the United Nations as a native people in 1992 but still face discrimination in Japan.

Except among the older people, religion is not a strong force. Christianity was brought to Japan by Jesuit missionaries in 1549. Although less than 1% of the population is Christian, Christian lifestyles, moral codes, and ethics have become part of Japanese life. The majority of the population traditionally practices a syncretistic combination of Shinto and Buddhism.

Shinto is exclusively nationalistic. It was the state religion from the Meiji Restoration of 1868 until the end of World War II. It is not so much a creed as it is a link to ancestors and Gods. Shinto means "the way of the Gods" and has three predominant ideas: worship of the Gods of Japan, loyalty to Japan, and cultivation of a pure Japanese spirit. Almost all Japanese are born Shinto. It is said that to be Japanese and to be a Shintoist are synonymous. There are two types of Shintoism: Popular Shinto, which has its strength in the home, and Sect Shinto, which believes in reincarnation and service to humanity as service to God. A third type, State Shinto, which taught that the Japanese were separate from other races, excelling in virtue, intelligence, and courage, was abolished by order of the Allies in 1945.

Buddhism came to Japan from Korea in the mid-6th century. There are more than 200 sects of Buddhism in Japan, with wide differences in doctrines. Buddhism has been called the "adopted faith of Japan" and centers around the temple and the family altar. Most households observe some ceremonies of both religions, such as a Shinto wedding and a Buddhist funeral. Overall, though, religion is more a social tradition than a conviction. Some charge that due to a lack of religious beliefs the Japanese have no principles. Meditation, aesthetic appreciation, ritual cleansing, and a respect for nature's beauty and humans' part in it are important cultural beliefs.

Box 8.1

BUDDHISM WORLDWIDE

Siddhartha Gautama (563-483 B.C.) was born in southern Nepal. He sought supreme truth in meditation and became Buddha, "the enlightened one."

Buddhist doctrine first took hold in northern India. Over the centuries, monks spread the religion throughout much of Asia. Today, Buddhism includes a wide variety of sects grouped into three primary branches: Hinayana, Mahayana (including Zen), and Tantrism. With 350 million adherents, Buddhism is the world's fourth largest religion behind Christianity, Islam, and Hinduism.

Buddhism accepted the basic concepts of Hinduism—including reincarnation and the law of karma, which holds that one's actions directly control one's destiny—but opposed the rituals and hardening caste system of Hinduism.

Buddhism stresses ethics as the means to salvation. It offers the "middle way" that avoids the extremes of mortification and indulgence. Following the "noble eightfold path" of right living and actions frees the adherent of self who can then achieve nirvana—the state of bliss in which humans escape the law of reincarnation.

| Country | Largest Buddhist Populations | |
	Buddhist Population (in millions)	Percentage of Total Population
Japan	91.0[a]	74
China	63.3	6
Thailand	52.5	94
Burma (Myanmar)	36.5	88
Vietnam	36.1	51
South Korea	15.4	37

SOURCE: Compiled from the *Los Angeles Times*, October 8, 1991, p. H6.

a. Includes Japanese who adhere to both Shintoism and Buddhism.

A study by Hajime Nakamura (1964) of the National Institute of Science and Technology Policy in Japan asked citizens to name aspects of their country of which they were proudest. Topping that list was Japan's maintenance of social order, followed by its natural beauty, its history and traditions, the diligence and talent of its people, the high level of education, the country's prosperity, and its culture and arts.

Cultural Patterns

Critical to understanding the cultural patterns of Japan is the homogeneity of its population, although some would argue that Japan is not all that homogeneous. However, the cultural myth of homogeneity is believed and therefore is an important cultural concept.

Because it is an island country and hence borders on no other countries, Japan had been little affected by foreign influence until 1853. Japan's isolation means that its history is its own. Everyone shares the same ideas and, lacking outside influences, has no reason to doubt them.

In addition, as a small, densely populated country, its ideas and information are easily shared. Even the tradition of rice growing contributes to a society based on cooperation, minimizing conflict, and enhanced cooperation, which, like the rice, are all necessary for survival.

Japan's homogeneity contributes to its people's "communication without language" (Tsujimura, 1968, 1987). It is said that being monolingual and

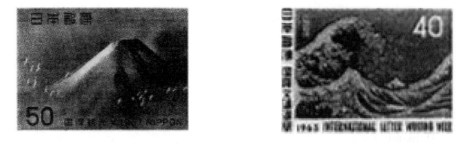

Japanese stamps reflect the country's beauty. Sacred Mt. Fuji (left) is by Taidan Yokoyama, and Great Wave off Kanagawa (right) is by the famous artist Hokusai.

monoracial makes it easy for Japanese to understand each other with few words. The United States, with its high level of diversity, is verbose—more talking is required to overcome diverse languages, diverse lifestyles, and diverse ways of feeling and thinking. Japanese axioms teach that verbosity is dangerous: "Least said, soonest mended" and "Out of the mouth comes evil."

Today, the education system maintains those same cultural values. All schools have the same curriculum. Schools have uniforms and encourage students to take part in after-school group activities.

Japanese worldview is consistent with that of an isolated island. There is no differentiation: People from the United States, Europe, and other parts of Asia are foreigners. The world is divided into Japan and others: *gaikoku*, or outside nation, and **gaijin**, or outside person.

Japan has often been described as a society in which conflict is avoided by emphasizing homogeneity and dismissing differentness as incidental. The Japanese do not have the same perception of self as an individual that is typical in the United States; instead, the Japanese feel most comfortable with others who empathize. To be completely understood, people have to cooperate in the same context, and in doing so, there can be no differentiation of individuals. In such an extremely homogeneous society, you are not seen as an individual, nor do you regard individualism as a positive trait.

It has been said that group life is to the Japanese what individualism is to the United States. Homogeneity is the core value of society that substantially defines other values and permeates all areas of life. This social interdependence has been referred to by Takeo Doi (1956, 1973) as **amae** (noun that comes from the verb *amaeru*, which means to look to others for support and affection).

Amae is the feeling of nurturing for and dependence on another. Amae is a sense of complete dependence based on a wish to be loved and cared for unconditionally. It develops in the relationship between mother and child and later transfers to the child's teachers and others in positions of authority. Amae is a reciprocal relationship. Just as the child is dependent on the mother, the mother is dependent on the child, which arises from the need to be needed. Amae, with its emphasis on interdependence, contrasts sharply with individualism. (See Box 8.2 for a description of how the game of baseball reflects Japanese cultural patterns.)

Japan is changing. The younger generation is more independent and worldly. Perhaps Japan is beginning to recognize that it is not as homogeneous as the cultural myth suggests. Japan is beginning to identify itself more in terms of nationality rather than ethnicity. Traditional mores are becoming less important as Japan becomes more international. Many feel that modern Japan cannot continue to value the communication subtleties that are not easily understood by non-Japanese.

Box 8.2

SPORTY JAPANESE IMPORT

Baseball is not new to Japan. It dates back to 1873, when American teachers and missionaries organized the first formal game. It spread throughout schools, for the Japanese felt it taught self-denial and moral discipline. Some teams included Zen meditation and emphasized purity of spirit.

American teams such as the Giants and the Chicago White Sox came to Japan in 1910, which increased public interest. In 1934 when Babe Ruth came to Tokyo, 65,000 fans squeezed into Jingu Stadium for his first game. They lined the streets of the Ginza for miles and greeted him like a hero.

After World War II, the Allies encouraged baseball in Japan as a vehicle for boosting morale, and the country's passion for the game was rekindled.

Today, there are two pro leagues in Japan, the Central and the Pacific, and competition is fierce. Some say the game of baseball is uniquely suited to Japan, with its emphasis on perfection, sacrifice for the common good, and in the individual confrontation between pitcher and batter, not unlike that of sumo wrestlers.

One of Japan's top baseball teams comes to Yuma, Arizona, for spring training.

Each morning a throng of Japanese reporters waits for the Yakult Swallows to burst from their locker room at the Ray Kroc Baseball Complex in Yuma, Arizona. To feed baseball frenzy, representatives of six Japanese TV stations, two radio stations, two news agencies, six all-sports dailies, and two general newspapers are

(Continued)

Box 8.2, *Continued*

on hand to record the Swallows' every move. Each night in February the team members appear on television screens all over Japan. Among viewers, Yuma is the best-known city in the United States.

The Swallows make the 5,000-mile trip to Yuma chiefly for the weather; February is Japan's coldest month. The team also comes because in crowded Japan, four practice fields are out of the question.

Some of the Japanese media's attention is centered on team member Kazushiege Nagashima, the son of one of Japan's most famous players. Fans at home are anxious to know if the youngster can measure up to his father.

Hideaki "Chief" Kawako, the Swallows' Seattle-born chief interpreter and public relations official, watched the cameras swarm around Nagashima and remarked, "Bloodlines are important in Japan."

Although the Swallows are playing the all-American sport, there are many subtle differences in their approach to the game that make it distinctly Japanese. Everything from the way the players respectfully doff their caps when addressed by their coach to their strategy and philosophy of the game is infused with elements of Japanese culture.

The Swallows' day begins at dawn with a jog, followed by conditioning exercises. "They do everything as a team, which is part of the Japanese culture," Kawako says. Five abreast, the players trot down the field and chant in unison.

There is little room for individualism in Japanese baseball, as opposed to American baseball. The Americans like to do their own thing. Some observers say the stifling of initiative hampers Japanese baseball, but others say obedience, discipline, and respect for authority simply reflect their country's culture.

American players have traditionally found it difficult to adjust to baseball in Japan. They face a different pitching style, different strike zones, inconsistent umpires, and a different philosophy and strategy.

Kawako says, "In Japan, coaches think it's easier to win while their team is ahead, so we like to go for runs in the early innings and get our players in scoring position. American hardhitters are told to bunt, and they resent that. Also, we don't like to mount a big score against another team. It's best to let them save face."

At the end of the season, the Swallows form a circle and in Shinto ceremony give thanks for a good and safe spring training.

Kawako watched the ceaseless practice and said, "Still, you see, we Japanese have a secret weapon. We try harder."

SOURCE: Jean Gillette, "Sporty Japanese Import," in *Westways*. Copyright © 1991, Automobile Club of Southern California. Article reprinted by permission, courtesy of *Westways*.

MASCULINITY VERSUS FEMININITY

The second dimension across which cultures vary is **masculinity** versus **femininity**. Hofstede (1980) found that women's social role varied less from culture to culture than men's. He labeled as masculine cultures those that strive for maximal distinction between what women and men are expected to do. Cultures that place high values on masculine traits stress assertiveness, competition, and material success. Those labeled as feminine cultures are those that permit more overlapping social roles for the sexes. Cultures that place high value on feminine traits stress quality of life, interpersonal relationships, and concern for the weak. Table 8.2 shows examples of both types.

It is important to understand that these traits apply to both women and men; that is, both women and men learn to be ambitious and competitive in masculine cultures, and both women and men learn to be modest in feminine cultures.

From his study of Thais in the United States, Rojjanaprapayon (1997) notes that masculinity in all cultures is not the same as Hofstede's Western concept of masculinity as assertiveness, aggressiveness, and goal orientation. Thais can be very aggressive and goal oriented in some situations but are expected to be attentive, supportive, and yielding. Rojjanaprapayon suggests labeling this dimension more appropriately as affection.

In the workplace, in masculine cultures, managers are expected to be decisive and assertive; in feminine cultures, managers use intuition and strive for consensus. Solidarity and quality of life are stressed.

Hofstede's data revealed two associations with this dimension:

- *Geography.* Feminine cultures are somewhat more likely in colder climates.

- *Birth rates.* In feminine cultures, the woman has a stronger say in the number of children. In masculine cultures, the man determines family size.

POWER DISTANCE

The third dimension is **power distance,** or the way the culture deals with inequalities. Hofstede (1997) defines power distance as "the extent to which less powerful members of institutions and organizations within a country expect and accept that power is distributed unequally" (p. 28). Hofstede believes that power distance is learned early in families. In high power distance cultures, children are expected to be obedient toward parents versus being treated more or less as equals. In high power distance cultures, people are

Table 8.2   Masculinity Rankings for 50 Countries and Three Regions

1	Japan	28	Singapore
2	Austria	29	Israel
3	Venezuela	30/31	Indonesia
4/5	Italy	30/31	West Africa
4/5	Switzerland	32/33	Turkey
6	Mexico	32/33	Taiwan
7/8	Ireland	34	Panama
7/8	Jamaica	35/36	Iran
9/10	Great Britain	35/36	France
9/10	Germany	37/38	Spain
11/12	Philippines	37/38	Peru
11/12	Colombia	39	East Africa
13/14	South Africa	40	El Salvador
13/14	Ecuador	41	South Korea
15	United States	42	Uruguay
16	Australia	43	Guatemala
17	New Zealand	44	Thailand
18/19	Greece	45	Portugal
18/19	Hong Kong	46	Chile
20/21	Argentina	47	Finland
20/21	India	48/49	Yugoslavia
22	Belgium	48/49	Costa Rica
23	Arab countries	50	Denmark
24	Canada	51	The Netherlands
25/26	Malaysia	52	Norway
25/26	Pakistan	53	Sweden
27	Brazil		

SOURCE: Hofstede (2001, Exhibit 6.3, p. 286).

expected to display respect for those of higher status. For example, in countries such as Burma (Myanmar), Cambodia, Laos, and Thailand, people are expected to display respect for monks by greeting and taking leave of monks with ritualistic greetings, removing hats in the presence of a monk, dressing modestly, seating monks at a higher level, and using a vocabulary that shows respect.

Power distance also refers to the extent to which power, prestige, and wealth are distributed within a culture. Cultures with high power distance have power and influence concentrated in the hands of a few rather than distributed throughout the population. These countries tend to be more authoritarian and may communicate in a way to limit interaction and reinforce the differences between people.

In the high power distance workplace, superiors and subordinates consider each other existentially unequal. Power is centralized, and there is a wide salary gap between the top and bottom of the organization.

In cultures high in power distance, for example, corporate presidents' offices are more likely to be luxurious, with controlled access. Company bosses are "kings" and employees "loyal subjects" who don't speak out. In the low power distance workplace, subordinates expect to be consulted, and ideal bosses are democratic. In more democratic organizations, leaders are physically more accessible. Table 8.3 shows examples of both types.

The United States is becoming higher in power distance. The year 2002 was the year of Enron and other corporate scandals. Their chief executive officers (CEOs) had taken excessive compensation. In the United States in 1980, the average CEO salary was 42 times as much as the average worker. In 1990, it was 85 times as much. In 2000, it was 531 times as much. Japan began to worry when its CEOs were making more than 8 times the factory worker's wage. In 1977, the top 1% in the United States had an after-tax income equal to the bottom 49 million; in 1999, the top 1% had an after-tax income equal to the bottom 100 million. Brazil has one of the largest gaps: The poor constitute half the population but earn only 12% of the national income.

Hofstede notes four interesting associations with power distance:

- *Geographic latitude.* Higher latitudes are associated with lower power distance.

- *Population.* Large population is associated with high power distance.

- *Wealth.* National wealth is associated with lower power distance.

- *History.* Countries with a Romance language (Spanish, Portuguese, Italian, French) score medium to high as do Confucian cultural inheritance countries, whereas countries with a Germanic language (German, English, Dutch, Danish, Norwegian, Swedish) score low. Both the Romance language countries and the Confucian cultural inheritance countries were ruled from a single power center, whereas the Germanic language countries remained "barbaric" during Roman days.

UNCERTAINTY AVOIDANCE

Hofstede's (1980) fourth dimension is **uncertainty avoidance**, the extent to which people in a culture feel threatened by uncertain or unknown situations. Hofstede explains that this feeling is expressed through nervous stress and in a

Table 8.3   Power Distance Rankings for 50 Countries and Three Regions

1	Malaysia	27/28	South Korea
2/3	Guatemala	29/30	Iran
2/3	Panama	29/30	Taiwan
4	Philippines	31	Spain
5/6	Mexico	32	Pakistan
5/6	Venezuela	33	Japan
7	Arab countries	34	Italy
8/9	Ecuador	35/36	Argentina
8/9	Indonesia	35/36	South Africa
10/11	India	37	Jamaica
10/11	West Africa	38	United States
12	Yugoslavia	39	Canada
13	Singapore	40	The Netherlands
14	Brazil	41	Australia
15/16	France	42/44	Costa Rica
15/16	Hong Kong	42/44	Germany (F.R.)
17	Colombia	42/44	Great Britain
18/19	El Salvador	45	Switzerland
18/19	Turkey	46	Finland
20	Belgium	47/48	Norway
21/23	East Africa	47/48	Sweden
21/23	Peru	49	Ireland
21/23	Thailand	50	New Zealand
24/25	Chile	51	Denmark
24/25	Portugal	52	Israel
26	Uruguay	53	Austria
27/28	Greece		

SOURCE: Hofstede (2001, Exhibit 3.1, p. 87).

need for predictability or a need for written and unwritten rules (Hofstede, 1997). In these cultures, such situations are avoided by maintaining strict codes of behavior and a belief in absolute truths. Cultures strong in uncertainty avoidance are active, aggressive, emotional, compulsive, security seeking, and intolerant; cultures weak in uncertainty avoidance are contemplative, less aggressive, unemotional, relaxed, accepting personal risks, and relatively tolerant. (See Table 8.4.)

Students from high uncertainty avoidance cultures expect their teachers to be experts who have all the answers. And in the workplace, there is an inner need to work hard, and there is a need for rules, precision, and punctuality.

Table 8.4   Uncertainty Avoidance Rankings for 50 Countries and Three Regions

1	Greece	28	Ecuador
2	Portugal	29	Germany (F.R.)
3	Guatemala	30	Thailand
4	Uruguay	31/32	Iran
5/6	Belgium	31/32	Finland
5/6	El Salvador	33	Switzerland
7	Japan	34	West Africa
8	Yugoslavia	35	The Netherlands
9	Peru	36	East Africa
10/15	France	37	Australia
10/15	Chile	38	Norway
10/15	Spain	39/40	South Africa
10/15	Costa Rica	39/40	New Zealand
10/15	Panama	41/42	Indonesia
10/15	Argentina	41/42	Canada
16/17	Turkey	43	United States
16/17	South Korea	44	Philippines
18	Mexico	45	India
19	Israel	46	Malaysia
20	Colombia	47/48	Great Britain
21/22	Venezuela	47/48	Ireland
21/22	Brazil	49/50	Hong Kong
23	Italy	49/50	Sweden
24/25	Pakistan	51	Denmark
24/25	Austria	52	Jamaica
26	Taiwan	53	Singapore
27	Arab countries		

SOURCE: Hofstede (2001, Exhibit 4.1, p. 151).

Students from low uncertainty avoidance cultures accept teachers who admit to not knowing all the answers. And in the workplace, employees work hard only when needed, there are no more rules than are necessary, and precision and punctuality have to be learned.

Hofstede notes two interesting associations with uncertainty avoidance:

- *Religion.* Orthodox and Roman Catholic Christian cultures (except the Philippines and Ireland) score high. Judaic and Muslim cultures tend to score in the middle. Protestant Christian cultures score low. Eastern religions score medium to very low (except Japan).

■ *History.* Cultures with a Romance language and history of Roman codified laws score high uncertainty avoidance. Cultures with Chinese-speaking populations and Confucian tradition tend to score lower.

LONG-TERM VERSUS SHORT-TERM ORIENTATION

In 1987, the "Chinese Culture Connection," composed of Michael H. Bond and others, extended Hofstede's work to include a new dimension they labeled **Confucian work dynamism,** now more commonly called **long-term orientation** versus **short-term orientation** to life. This dimension includes such values as thrift, persistence, having a sense of shame, and ordering relationships. Confucian work dynamism refers to dedicated, motivated, responsible, and educated individuals with a sense of commitment and organizational identity and loyalty.

Countries high in Confucian work dynamism are Hong Kong, Taiwan, Japan, South Korea, and Singapore—popularly referred to as the Five Economic Dragons. Long-term orientation encourages thrift, savings, perseverance toward results, and a willingness to subordinate oneself for a purpose. Short-term orientation is consistent with spending to keep up with social pressure, less savings, preference for quick results, and a concern with face. (See Table 8.5.)

Case Study: Singapore

Singapore is an island nation of 540 square kilometers, the smallest, but one of the most prosperous in Southeast Asia. Various groups of people have migrated to Singapore. Its 2.9 million population is 78% Chinese. Today, Singapore is a multiracial, multicultural society with a dynamic economy.

Lee Kuan Yew, prime minister from 1959 to 1990, is now officially a senior minister. He remains the most powerful figure in Singapore. Yew's government has been strict and paternalistic, steadily building the country into an economic and trade powerhouse that has education and income levels comparable to those in the United States. The island nation is clean, efficient, and law-abiding.

While on a trip there in 1987, I came across a newspaper editorial in which Confucianism is considered in juxtaposition to individualism (see Box 8.3).

Table 8.5   Long-Term Orientation Rankings for 23 Countries

1   China
2   Hong Kong
3   Taiwan
4   Japan
5   South Korea
6   Brazil
7   India
8   Thailand
9   Singapore
10 The Netherlands
11 Bangladesh
12 Sweden
13 Poland
14 Germany (F.R.)
15 Australia
16 New Zealand
17 Unites States
18 Great Britain
19 Zimbabwe
20 Canada
21 Philippines
22 Nigeria
23 Pakistan

SOURCE: Hofstede (2001, Exhibit 7.1, p. 356).

Box 8.3

FINDING THE GOLDEN MEAN

Confucianism is once again in the news. Its role in Singapore's progress was the theme of the Prime Minister's recent interview with the *New York Times*. And several distinguished scholars are in Singapore this week to discuss the part Confucianism has played in the economic success of East Asian nations. At the heart of this debate is a fundamental question that has exercised the minds of philosophers and kings for ages: How should a society organize itself? The goal has always been to find an effective way to control the passions of people so they can live in harmony among themselves and in peace with their neighbours. The quest is not only for sound

(Continued)

political systems but, more importantly, for better social and economic systems.

Whatever the arguments about the State and the individual, the Prime Minister was unequivocal about one of the driving forces behind Singapore's success, namely, the basic Confucian concept of placing the good of society above that of the individual. A related factor was social cohesion. Given Singapore's mix of races, cultures and religions, its fragile harmony cannot withstand what the Prime Minister called the "untrammelled individualism" of the West. There is good reason why these two concepts have been such a constant preoccupation of Singapore's leadership. For while Singaporeans may accept the notion of sacrificing individual interests for a larger common good and to preserve social harmony, several factors make this especially difficult to apply in real life.

One of these stems from the wrenching changes that cultures in Singapore have undergone, all in one generation. In many families now, children who are Western-educated and English-speaking find it difficult to accept the mores of their dialect-speaking and more traditional parents. As families are the basic units of Asian societies, the cultural strains that this imposes are enormous. Unfortunately, the individualist genie, once unloosed, cannot be easily coaxed back into the lamp. But on the other hand, some traditional social norms die hard no matter how badly changes are needed. Witness how even English-educated men in Singapore still have the Eastern preference for submissive wives.

An even bigger paradox arises when trying to preserve Confucian ethics and other Asian traditions within a modern capitalist economy. For capitalism is based essentially on the pursuit of individual gains. The political philosophers of Keynes' day justified capitalism on the grounds that money-making was less of an avarice than, and could in fact countervail, other more dangerous passions and vices. Individuals pursuing relentlessly their own interests will, in fact, further the common good. Or so the theory goes. Added to this, of course, is the colonial legacy of a democratic political system in which is enshrined each individual's right to vote.

So the task is to balance Confucian ethics, and its emphasis on the common good, with the individualism inherent in a capitalist economy and in a one-man, one-vote political system. Certainly selfish individualism and abrasive dissent have no place if there is to be order and harmony. Singapore has no margin for error. Still, room must be given for creativity and innovativeness. For Singapore cannot achieve the excellence it seeks as a society if there is no open-mindedness to new, and sometimes opposing, ideas. The government's important role is not so much to deliver the goods but more to inspire the people to accept what it takes to achieve the good life—and for them to work at getting there. Singaporeans must themselves find the golden mean that suits their circumstances for, in the end, they can only be their own selves.

SOURCE: "Finding the Golden Mean," *The Straits Times*, January 9, 1987, p. 24.
Copyright © 1987, The Straits Times Press (1975) Limited. Reprinted with permission.

Case Study: Commercial Airline Pilots

Merritt and Helmreich (1996) surveyed 9,000 male commercial airline pilots in a study to replicate Hofstede's study originally conducted in the late 1960s and early 1970s. Merritt and Helmreich selected airlines that were owned, managed, and operated by members of the same national culture and pilots at those airlines whose nationality at birth and current nationality matched the nationality of the airline.

The dimensions of individualism and power distance were replicated successfully. The pilots did have higher scores on individualism than in Hofstede's data. Merritt and Helmreich attributed this to either a worldwide shift toward more greater individualism or that people who become pilots are more individualistic than their country counterparts. Pilots from the United States, Britain, and Ireland had the highest individualism scores; pilots from Taiwan and Korea had the lowest. Pilots from Brazil, Korea, Mexico, and the Philippines had the highest power distance scores; pilots from New Zealand, Australia, and South Africa had the lowest.

Masculinity-femininity and uncertainty avoidance were only moderately replicated: Merritt and Helmreich noted that since both masculine and feminine items (good working relationships and opportunity for high earnings) define the pilot environment this dimension does not discriminate within the pilot profession. A subset of the uncertainty avoidance items dealing with attitudes toward automation did indicate that cultures that endorse rules and procedures as a way of resolving uncertainty also endorse the use of automation. Pilots from Taiwan and Korea had the highest uncertainty avoidance scores; pilots from Hong Kong (British pilots), New Zealand, the United States, and Ireland had the lowest.

Merritt and Helmreich found power distance and uncertainty avoidance to have the most relevance for aviation. One example is attitudes toward automation in the cockpit. Anglo pilots with low power distance and uncertainty avoidance scores show the least inclination to accept and trust automation but are also drawn to it. They dislike the lack of individual control and inflexibility that automation dictates, yet may enjoy learning to work with new technology. Pilots with high power distance and uncertainty avoidance scores were enthusiastic about automation because automation is perceived as authoritative and brings a reassuring level of certainty to flight management.

Case Study: China

Values

Cultural values are relatively stable, but as we have suggested with Japan they can change over the course of generations from contact with other cultures. China provides an example of changing cultural values resulting from internal political change. The Chinese Communist Party founded the People's Republic of China in 1949 and brought political change and has affected religion and traditional cultural values.

Religion does not hold a high place in Chinese society. Most Chinese practice a syncretistic combination of Confucianism, Taoism, and Buddhism as a practical guide for living. Christianity, Islam, and folk religions still remain and are practiced by some. The ideology of Communism in China endorses atheism. Under the Communist government, organized religious activity is usually discouraged. However, citizens are given the right to "believe or not believe in religion."

Chu and Ju (1993) conducted a survey of rural and urban Chinese in the late 1980s. They presented their respondents with a list of 18 traditional Chinese Confucian values and then asked which ones the respondents felt proud of, which ones should be discarded, and

Religious shrine in China.

SOURCE: Photo by Matthew V. Pollack, 1987. Reprinted with permission.

Table 8.6   Endorsement and Rejection of Traditional Chinese Values

Traditional Chinese Value	Endorsement Index
Long historical heritage	89.7
Diligence and frugality	86.2
Loyalty and devotion to state	67.5
Benevolent father, filial son	48.0
Generosity and virtues	39.8
Respect for traditions	38.5
Submission to authority	33.2
Preciousness of harmony	29.5
Tolerance, propriety, deference	25.3
Chastity for women	−13.5
Glory to ancestors	−23.8
A house full of sons and grandsons	−35.5
Farmers high, merchants low	−43.3
Pleasing superiors	−48.9
Discretion for self-preservation	−85.9
Differentiation between women and men	−59.2
Way of the golden mean	−59.6
Three obediences and four virtues	−64.0

SOURCE: Chu and Ju (1993, p. 222).

which ones they were not sure of. To calculate an index of endorsement, Chu and Ju subtracted the percentage who said a value should be discarded from the percentage who said they were proud of it. The results are shown in Table 8.6.

Chu and Ju speculate that a century ago nearly all values would have received a positive high rating, but in this survey there is evidence that relationships between women and men have changed, that attitudes about large families have changed, and that the traditional Confucian precepts of harmony and tolerance are no longer as strongly endorsed. Chu and Ju see in the data mounting frustrations and rising aspirations, the result of changes brought about by the Communist Revolution and modernization.

FROM THE INTERCULTURAL PERSPECTIVE

How tall are you? How much do you weigh? Whatever you answer, you will be using some kind of measurement to describe these characteristics about yourself. We often use measurements to compare things. For example, if we want to know if one room is bigger than another one, we measure its length and width to find out. These measurements are called dimensions. In a similar way, cultures can be compared by measuring their dimensions. However, the dimensions used to compare cultures are generally not physical measurements but, instead, are measures of the values and attitudes that different cultures have. These are called value dimensions.

Geert Hofstede originally identified four dimensions of culture: individualism (versus collectivism), masculinity (versus femininity), power distance, and uncertainty avoidance. Individualistic cultures give more importance to individuals' needs when they do things such as setting goals. Collectivist cultures, on the other hand, give more importance to the needs of the group. The masculinity-femininity dimension measures a culture's dominant values ranging from aggressive (masculine trait) to nurturing (feminine trait). Also, masculine cultures generally keep masculine and feminine behaviors separate and value assertiveness, competition, and material wealth. Feminine cultures may have overlapping gender roles and focus on quality of life, interpersonal relationships, and concern for the weak. Power distance describes the distribution of influence within the culture. Is power held by just a few people, or is it held by many? Uncertainty avoidance measures how much ambiguity people will endure and how much risk they like to take. Cultures that are high in uncertainty avoidance are aggressive, emotional, compulsive, and intolerant, whereas cultures that are low in uncertainty avoidance are thoughtful, relaxed, less aggressive, accepting of risks, and generally tolerant.

There are other value dimensions besides the four mentioned above. One of these is called Confucian work dynamism, now called long-term versus short-term orientation. The Confucian dynamism dimension emphasizes thrift (spending money wisely), persistence and hard work, having a sense of shame, and ordering relationships (i.e., a system for giving certain relationships more or less importance). Singapore is a country with high Confucian work dynamism.

KEY TERMS

amae	gaijin	Shinto
collectivism	individualism	short-term orientation
Confucian work	long-term orientation	uncertainty avoidance
dynamism	masculinity	
femininity	power distance	

CHAPTER 9

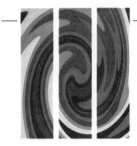

Dominant U.S. Cultural Patterns

Using Value Orientation Theory

What You Can Learn From This Chapter

Categories useful for describing cultural patterns

Use of that category system to describe dominant U.S. cultural patterns

How U.S. cultural patterns can affect intercultural communication

A **value** is a central and basic motivating belief that shapes our goals and motivations (Rokeach & Ball-Rokeach, 1989). An **attitude** is an outgrowth of a value. Our *attitudes* about current controversial issues often depend on the larger *values* we hold. For example, a person's attitude about immigration issues can relate to humanitarian values.

We learn what is moral, what is competent, and what is desirable behavior from our culture. This type of learning is called **emic** knowledge, or knowledge of the culture learned from the inside. Emic knowledge constitutes the rules known from inside the culture and as such are seldom organized or consciously discussed (Stewart, 1982). (When a culture is learned by an outsider, the stranger tends to acquire theoretical and normative information called **etic** knowledge.) Because culture is widely shared and taken for granted, we have little experience in discussing how cultural values affect our behavior.

Of course, not everyone in a culture acts in accordance with the culture's values all the time. Nonetheless, dominant cultural values or patterns of behavior can be identified that make it possible to compare cultures in a meaningful way.

Intercultural communication competence requires understanding dominant cultural values and understanding how our own cultural values affect the way we perceive ourselves and others.

In this chapter, the origins of U.S. cultural patterns are presented, and the forces that tended to shape a national character from several regional groups are described. Then, what have been labeled the dominant U.S. cultural patterns are described. Finally, the forces that are contributing to new regional groups are described.

ORIGINS OF U.S. CULTURAL PATTERNS

Pre-16th-Century Indigenous Americans

Before the time when Columbus arrived, North America was home to a diverse population of some 10 million people. Indigenous Americans spoke hundreds of languages. Three centuries before the creation of the U.S. Constitution, the Iroquois had a Congress-like council, exercised the veto, protected freedom of speech, and ran a classless society. The American Indian nations had elaborate social structures but very little bureaucratic or centralized government.

European Enlightenment

The society that evolved and is dominant today grew from European roots. The scientific method, democracy, and capitalism are institutions of Western cultures. The dominant language, the system of representative government, the structure of law, and the emphasis on individual liberty all derive from the Enlightenment ideals formulated in England. Other important U.S. ideals, such as the separation of powers, derive from the French philosopher Montesquieu. These values, established early in U.S. history, remain strong.

Regional Differences Resulting From Immigration

The United States is a country of immigrants from all over the world, each person immigrating with his or her own cultural values. Many arrived in groups and tended to remain settled in the same area.

Brandeis University historian David Hackett Fischer (1989) argues that the early immigrants from England established distinctive regional cultures that remain today. He further argues that the United States has been a society of diversity—not homogeneity—from its very beginning.

The Puritans came from eastern England to Massachusetts between 1629 and 1641. A small number of Royalist elite and large numbers of indentured servants from southern and western England settled in the Chesapeake region between 1642 and 1675. Quakers from England's north midlands and Wales settled in the Delaware Valley between 1675 and 1725. The final group from Northern Ireland, Scotland, and the border area of northern England settled in Appalachia between 1717 and 1775. Each of these groups had diverse dialects and attitudes, and all retained a degree of separateness. Even Henry Adams's *History of the United States* had separate chapters on the "intellect" of New England, the Middle States, and the South in 1800.

Zelinsky (1973) examined regional patterns in language, religion, food habits, architecture, place names, and the culture of the inhabitants who established the first effective settlements and identified five regions: New England, the Midland, the Middle West, the South, and the West. More recently, Bigelow (1980) examined ethnicity, religion, party affiliation, and dialect and identified these regions: Northeast, Border South, Deep South, Midwest, Mexicano, Southwest, Colorado, Mormondom, Pacific Northwest, Northern California, and Southern California.

These analyses clearly show that the United States may never have been a completely homogeneous culture. In 1831, then 26-year-old French aristocrat Alexis de Tocqueville (1805-1859) toured the United States and saw the country as composed of almost separate little nations (Tocqueville, 1835 and 1840/1945; see also Mayer, 1981).

Communication Markers of Regions

Variations make each region psychologically and behaviorally distinct (Andersen, Lustig, & Andersen, 1987). In relation to communication differences, Andersen et al. (1987) suggest regional differences in three areas:

- *Verbal control and dominance.* New Englanders are more likely to be introverts; those in the Mid-Atlantic region are characterized as not particularly talkative or verbally dominant.

- *Affiliativeness and immediacy.* People from Texas, Oklahoma, Arkansas, and Louisiana visit more neighbors and rate friends higher than do people in other regions. Pacific Coast residents report the most isolation from friends, least acquaintance with their neighbors, greatest distance from relatives, and lowest frequency of interactions with confidants.

- *Arousal or activation.* New Englanders employ a nondramatic and reserved communication style. The South and the Northwest are slow and relaxed compared to the fast pace of the urban Northeast.

FORCES TOWARD THE DEVELOPMENT OF A DOMINANT CULTURE

Tocqueville predicted that the United States would be a great power. The reasons he gave were the country's large geographic size, abundant natural resources, a growing population, and a vibrant national character.

Historians have charted the series of events that resulted in a dominant national culture:

- Opening of the Erie Canal in 1825 and the emergence of New York as the financial and corporate capital of an integrated industrial complex stretching from the Northeast to the upper Midwest

- Defeat of the South and the passage of the Thirteenth, Fourteenth, and Fifteenth Amendments that established national citizenship over state citizenship

- Development of Theodore Roosevelt's "new nationalism" that provided the intellectual foundations for an activist national government

- Passage of the Immigration Restriction Act of 1924 that permitted a degree of homogenization of the population

- Development of radio and television that nationalized politics and popular culture

- The automobile and interstate highway system that made the country internally mobile

- The Great Depression, World War II, and the onset of the Cold War, all of which increased the need for a strong centralized national government

These forces contributed to an exceptional uniformity that characterized the U.S. society in the early post-World War II period (Clough, 1997).

Another perspective is to recognize that the various groups comprising the United States have, to some extent, diverse cultural patterns. They may overlap, but they do differ. To talk about a dominant cultural pattern from this perspective is to talk about the cultural patterns of the group that controls the society. This perspective is developed in much more detail in Chapter 18, which examines multiculturalism.

International opinion polls continue to show that U.S. residents have values different from those of other cultures. It was Tocqueville who coined the phrase "American Exceptionalism" to express the idea that the United States *is* different. Understanding these values and their development contributes to improved intercultural communication, for as you learn to understand and accept your own culture, your intercultural communication improves.

As you go through this chapter, then, you must keep in mind that it is generalizing the values of an entire culture. You may find that you as an individual do not agree with all the values identified as typical in the United States, and you will surely know of others who would not agree. This chapter is about the dominant cultural values said to be characteristic of the majority of U.S. citizens.

As you examine these values, remember too how everything that occurs in a culture is related to and consistent with other things in that culture. None of the values presented is discrete—all are related to and reinforce each other.

VALUE ORIENTATION THEORY

Kluckhohn and Strodtbeck (1961) argue that all human cultures are confronted with universally shared problems emerging from relationships with fellow beings, time, activities, and nature. These five basic problems are as follows:

- What is a human being's relation to nature? (man-nature orientation)

- What is the modality of human activity? (activity orientation)

- What is the temporal focus of human life? (time orientation)

- What is the character of innate human nature? (human nature orientation)

- What is the relationship of the individual to others? (relational)

Kluckhohn and Strodtbeck's (1961) value orientation theory suggests that cultures develop unique positions in these five value orientations: man-nature, activity, time, human nature, and relational. Man-nature is described here as worldview (after Samovar, Porter, & Jain, 1981) and considers how humans dominate, live with, or are subjugated to nature. Activity orientation deals with people in the culture "being" (passively accepting), "being-in-becoming" (transforming), or "doing" (initiating action). Time orientation deals with the emphasis the culture places on the past, the present, or the future. Human nature orientation considers whether humans are primarily evil, primarily good, or a mixture of both. And relational orientation considers the way the culture organizes interpersonal relationships: linear hierarchy, group identification, or individualism.

There have been many excellent descriptions of United States cultural patterns (Kohls, 1984; Samovar et al., 1981; Stewart, 1972). The one used in this chapter is based on Kluckhohn and Strodtbeck's (1961) value orientations and modifies and adds to their categories as necessary to describe the cultural patterns that are characteristic of the majority of U.S. citizens and have an influence on communication. The Kluckhohn and Strodtbeck value orientations can be used to describe other cultures and provide, then, a systematic way of comparing cultural values.

WHAT IS A HUMAN BEING'S RELATION TO NATURE?

The term **worldview** deals with a culture's most fundamental beliefs about its place in the cosmos, beliefs about God, and beliefs about the nature of humanity and nature. Worldview refers to the philosophical ideas of being.

Huntington (1993, 1996) has argued that the world can be divided into eight major "cultural zones" that have been shaped by religious tradition still powerful today. The zones are Western Christianity, the Orthodox world, the Islamic world, and the Confucian, Japanese, Hindu, African, and Latin American zones.

Throughout the 19th century, religious discourse in the United States was dominated by White male Protestant conservatives of European heritage (Eck, 1993). In the 20th century, the United States became a meeting place for all the world's religions.

Sociologist Seymour Martin Lipset (1990) argues that because the United States separates church and state, thus making religion totally voluntary, people in the United States are more likely to believe that religion provides spiritual needs. In countries with a state religion, that religion is in many ways a person's only choice, whereas in the United States the wide diversity of religious options provides more opportunities for an individual to identify with a religious denomination.

Among the world's industrialized nations, the United States is the most religious. U.S. citizens are more likely to believe in heaven, hell, the Devil, and life after death. In fact, 95% of U.S. citizens believe there is a God or universal spirit. This compares dramatically with England's 31% and Sweden's 19%. Another study comparing the United States with European countries found that 87% of U.S. citizens report never having doubted the existence of God. A 2002 *U.S. News & World Report* article showed that nearly two-thirds of people in the United States say religion is very important in their lives and close to half say they attend worship services at least once a week—the highest percentage since the 1960s.

> There is no country in the world where the Christian religion retains a greater influence over the souls of men.
>
> —Alexis de Tocqueville, *Democracy in America* (1835 and 1840/1945)
>
> The U.S. "now has a greater diversity of religious groups than any country in recorded history."
>
> —J. Gordon Melton, *Encyclopedia of American Religions* (1991)

Consistent with previous research, a recent analysis of the World Values Survey clearly shows again that the United States continues to have a much more traditional value system than any other advanced industrial society. In fact, the United States has levels of religiosity and national pride comparable to those found in developing societies (Inglehart & Baker, 2000). (See Table 9.1 for a survey on moral values in the United States.)

Samovar et al. (1981) identified three parts to worldview: the individual-and-nature relationship, science and technology, and materialism.

The Individual-and-Nature Relationship

In the United States, people typically make a clear and separate distinction between human life and nature, valuing nature but clearly placing a higher value on human life.

This belief that humans have "dominion over nature" has made it possible for the United States to change the course of rivers, harvest forests for wood and paper, breed cattle for increased meat production, and destroy disease-causing bacteria. There can be little doubt that this belief has contributed to the material wealth of the United States.

The environmental movement and the animal rights movement are not contradictory to this belief. Both movements share the basic assumption that humans have a responsibility to protect nature. For the most part, these

Table 9.1   Survey on Moral Values in the United States (in percentages)

Question: Would you say you are satisfied or dissatisfied with moral values these days?

Satisfied	20
Dissatisfied	78
Neutral/Don't know	2

Question to those who answered dissatisfied: Why are you dissatisfied with the nation's moral values? (Note: Two answers accepted)

Breakdown in family	47
Lack of community involvement	34
Crime	12
Too much sex/violence in movies/TV	11
Lack of religion	5
Schools not strict enough/should teach civics	5

SOURCE: Adapted from the *Los Angeles Times,* May 26, 1996, p. A21.

NOTE: Poll of 1,374 adults nationwide. Margin of error is plus or minus 3 percentage points.

activists agree that humans should act to protect nature—that is, that humans are different from the rest of nature and in some ways superior to it. Having a responsibility to protect nature implies a dominant role.

Other views are that humans are a part of nature and should attempt to live in harmony with it—not exploit or protect it—and that humans are subjugated by nature.

Science and Technology

People in the United States have a strong faith in the **scientific method** of solving problems. In the United States it is a common belief that events have causes, that those causes can be discovered, and that humans can and should alter that relationship.

That events have causes rather than being random has a long tradition. The early colonists felt that nothing that occurred in the world was a random event but, rather, was the product of intent by some mover. A New England earthquake in 1727 "filled the houses of God" and contributed to the first Great Awakening. Pennsylvania's Johnstown Flood in 1889, the sinking of *Titanic* in 1912, and the Great Depression of the 1930s were all attributed to the wrath of God.

Modern acceptance of the scientific method is reflected in much communication and logic. Objectivity, empirical evidence, and facts are valued. Consider the majority approach to the AIDS epidemic. Most people in the United States recognized that the disease had a viral cause and that the virus could be identified and eradicated as polio had been.

The United States has strong faith in science and technology. The 1939 World's Fair celebrated technology in the United States. Also in 1939, the U.S. Army numbered 175,000 officers and men, 16th largest in the world, right behind Romania. World War II changed that. In 1945, Germany built 40,593 aircraft and Japan 28,180. The United States built 96,318. By 1945, half of all ships afloat in the world had been built in the United States. U.S. industry made the military the best equipped in the world.

This faith in science and technology is reflected in politics ("Star Wars" as a Cold War bargaining chip), in advertising (DuPont's "Better Living Through Chemistry" and ARCO gasoline's Clean Air campaign), and in genetically modified food. In fact, 58% believe that science will help humanity. Among Europeans, 35% hold the same belief.

Materialism

If there is one value that most of the rest of the world attributes to the United States it is **materialism,** or the belief that possessions are important in life. In *Democracy in America*, de Tocqueville (1835 and 1840/1945) wrote about how materialistic people in the United States were even in 1831.

In many ways, the miracle of the economic system of the United States is that most people have jobs that provide an income sufficient to buy things and services and in turn create jobs for others. The system is dynamic and depends on the constant circulation of money to ensure full employment.

The U.S. system encourages people to buy things and then to buy the "new improved" versions as new things quickly become obsolete. It is said that a man is a boy with more expensive toys. Others are judged by their possessions: Where do they live? What kind of car does she drive? What did he wear to the party? You can even express positive feelings about yourself by acquiring and showing things. The difference between clothes and designer clothes is price and how you feel about yourself when you wear them. (See Table 9.2 for a list of home electronics found in most U.S. homes in 1995.)

A materialistic system encourages high turnover, disposability, and "supersizing." Last season's styles are not as desirable. Last year's toys are in the attic. The phonograph is in the garage to make space for the CD player. The

Table 9.2   Percentage of U.S. Households With Selected Electronic Products, 1995

Product	Percentage
Television	98
Home radio	98
VCR	85
Telephone answering machine	54
Home CD player	44
Personal computer	33
Camcorder	20
Portable CD player	19
Home fax machine	6

SOURCE: Electronic Industries Association, Washington, D.C.

landfill is the final resting point for yesterday's materialistic purchases still unpaid on today's credit card statement. Ford Excursions are 19 feet long, Double Gulp drinks are 64 ounces, MacDonald's has SuperSize portions, and Starbucks has Venti cappuccino.

The annual survey conducted by the Higher Education Research Institute at the University of California, Los Angeles (see http://www.gseis.ucla.edu/heri/heri.html), shows that the number of college freshmen who said it was essential or very important to be very well off financially grew from 41% in 1968 to 73% in 2001. During the same time period, the number who said "developing a meaningful philosophy of life" was a top priority fell from 83% to 41%.

> When do you have enough in America? Never! It's a culture of excess, a permanently nouveau riche mentality. We want the biggest, the most extreme of everything.
>
> —G. Clotaire Rapaille, French anthropologist (quoted in *Los Angeles Times Magazine*, June 9, 2002, p. 12)

The desire to have possessions is also related to the high level of consumer debt in the United States. Borrowing money has a long history, but for the most part money was loaned only to start businesses because those businesses would generate profits to repay the loans. Consumer loans, which make instant gratification possible by using borrowed money to buy things, is a much more recent innovation. Gasoline and store charge cards were the standard until 1950 when Diners Club established the first credit card. In 1986, the average cardholder debt was

$900. By 1996 the average cardholder debt was $2,900; it's now estimated to be more than $6,000 per household. U.S. households averaged 11 credit cards per household in 1998. About 70% of college students have at least one credit card. Debt on these cards averages more than $2,000.

That people are evaluated by their possessions can be seen in reactions to occasional stories of individuals who die in poor surroundings yet whose mattresses are stuffed with cash. The popular reaction is that these people must have been crazy.

Yet the genius of the U.S. economic system is that materialism makes high employment and a standard of living possible for a vast number of people and the huge middle class.

WHAT IS THE MODALITY OF HUMAN ACTIVITY?

The term **activity orientation** refers to the use of time for self-expression and play, self-improvement and development, and work. Most visitors to the United States find it a hectic, busy culture. You can see this in the following three aspects.

Activity and Work

It would seem from the preceding section that people in the United States work only to earn money to buy more things. Yet people in the United States have a special feeling about jobs, defining self and others by occupation. Work becomes part of one's identity. About half of U.S. citizens agree that a "feeling of accomplishment" is the most important aspect of work. This is about twice the agreement rate in other countries where work is a means to get money and where self-identity and self-accomplishment come more from what one does outside work.

Work is taken very seriously in the United States. It is separated from play, which is something done outside work. To support that, a complex recreation industry has been developed to provide play away from work.

Efficiency and Practicality

People in the United States are perceived as placing such a high value on time that "efficiency experts," whose emphasis is on getting things done on time, cause lives to be organized for efficiency so that the most can get done. How many people organize their lives according to lists? Or at least think about organizing the day to get the most done?

It is possible that the emphasis on efficiency results in losing sight of other values such as contemplation and aesthetic values. For example, most people plan commutes for the shortest possible drive time. Rarely would a person think about going the scenic route—unless on vacation and "has time to kill."

Practicality refers here to a preference for short-time goals over long-term goals. This means planning for what works best for the short time—the most practical. As a culture, the United States is less likely to make short-term sacrifices for long-term gain because progress is judged so much by monthly and quarterly goals. Meaningful 10-year goals, much less 100-year goals, are very unlikely.

> Democratic nations will habitually prefer the useful to the beautiful, and they will require that the beautiful should be useful.
>
> —Alexis de Tocqueville, *Democracy in America* (1835 and 1840/1945)

It may appear that education is a long-term activity. However, a college education is divided into 40 or so courses. Education is viewed as a series of courses, each of which must be completed successfully.

The focus on short-term practicality may appear shortsighted, but tomorrow is another day with new problems and new opportunities.

Progress and Change

Related to practicality and to materialism is an unwavering fundamental faith in the future. The belief is that **change** is basically good, that the new is better than the old. New Tide detergent is better than old Tide detergent.

Not only is the new viewed as better, the new is often adopted without critically examining its effect on other aspects of the culture. For example, the microwave oven does make food preparation faster, but it may also lessen even more the time that families spend together. Such consequences are usually not considered in the adoption of the new.

Perhaps the willingness to accept change also explains why the United States has one of the highest moving rates in the world. Each year, nearly one in five U.S. households moves.

The belief that progress and change are good is associated with technological developments. Some observers, however, contend that the faith in progress and change is also being applied to values.

U.S. values or standards of what is right and wrong do change, and most would agree that these changes are proper. For example, I am old enough to have attended segregated public schools in Texas: Integration is not that old, but you'd agree that that change was right.

Because social beliefs are changed so easily and so frequently in the United States, some say there are no longer any beliefs that are permanent.

> [In the United States] they all consider society as a body in a state of improvement, humanity as a changing scene, in which nothing is, or ought to be, permanent; and they admit that what appears to them today to be good, may be superseded by something better tomorrow.
>
> —Alexis de Tocqueville, *Democracy in America* (1835 and 1840/1945, chap. 18)

WHAT IS THE TEMPORAL FOCUS OF HUMAN LIFE?

Cultures differ widely in their conceptions of time, as was first mentioned in Chapter 6's Chronemics section.

First of all, in the United States, time is viewed as a commodity. Such phrases as "time is money," "how much time do you have?" "don't waste time," and "budget your time" are common. Think about the conception of time as a commodity and the consequences of that belief.

When time is thought of as a commodity, one needs to be constantly aware of it. Time clocks are everywhere: In homes, cars, work sites, on wrists, at organized play sites. Many people report feeling uncomfortable not knowing the time. Perhaps only camping in the woods—without a radio and clocks— can one be free of time awareness in the United States.

When time is considered a resource, it becomes something to be managed and used responsibly. It can become a master if one becomes a slave to it. How many people do you know who carry schedules of their day, week, year?

Second, when time is viewed in a linear fashion, it obviously has a past, a present, and a future. Most will admit to being motivated by the future in how to act in the present: going to school to get a degree and a satisfying job, work- ing to be able to provide for oneself and one's family in the future, dieting so as to have a better figure and more friends in the future, training so as to be better at sports in the future, and living the future in the present.

Some would say that, because of living the future in the present, one is less aware of the present, having less time and appreciation for what is happening in the moment. Some would even say that living the future in the present is an illusion because the future is not yet here—it is unreal. In living for something that is not real, one misses much of the reality of the present.

WHAT IS THE CHARACTER OF INNATE HUMAN NATURE?

What does it mean to be human? What is human nature? What are human rights and responsibilities? These are the types of questions meant by human nature orientation.

Goodness

This area refers to the question of the innate nature of humans. Are we born good? Evil? With the potential for both?

It has been argued that the Puritan ancestry of the United States suggests a view that people are born evil but have the potential to be good. To achieve good in this view, one must control and discipline the self.

Others argue that contemporary beliefs in the United States are that people are born with a mixture of or a potential for both good and evil.

Rationality

Related to the concept of the innate nature of humans is **rationality**. To believe that humans are rational is to believe that humans act on the basis of reason. In other words, if you believe that humans have the potential for both good and evil, you also believe that humans have free choice and therefore responsibility for their actions. However, if you believe that humans are innately evil and lacking in rationality, you also believe that human evil is natural.

A belief in rationality, then, is consistent with a belief in the scientific method. Truth can be discovered through human reason. That being accepted, democracy, trial by jury, and a free enterprise system are all consistent beliefs because they assume that individuals can be trusted to make decisions for themselves.

Several high-profile criminal defenses would suggest that we as humans are not responsible for our actions: In 1978, the man who killed San Francisco Mayor George Moscone and Supervisor Harvey Milk blamed his crime on eating too much junk food.

Mutability

The term **mutability** means subject to change. This then refers to the belief that human nature can be changed by society. This is reflected in the belief that education is a positive force in improving human nature.

It is also fundamental to the belief that the prison system can rehabilitate wrongdoers, that although an individual chose to do evil, that individual can be changed by society to choose to do good.

Through science, this belief is now open to renewed public debate. In studies linking biology and human behavior, some scientists believe they are finding a substantial genetic underpinning for human behavior, having now demonstrated a genetic role in intelligence, aggression, and homosexuality (LeVay, 1993), and the personality trait "novelty seeking." Genetic determinism diminishes the power of one's capacity to choose and accept responsibility for those choices. Is the alcoholic a helpless victim of biology, or a willful agent with control over behavior?

Public debate also extends to whether unhealthy circumstances can lead individuals to do evil. Notice a contradiction here to the belief in rationality if you believe that a person who was abused as a child is more likely to abuse children and allow that fact in court to mitigate the individual's responsibility to have chosen rationally not to be abusive.

> Every adult, no matter how unfortunate a childhood he had or how habit-ridden he may be, is free to make choices about his life. To say of Hitler, to say of the criminal, that he did not choose to be bad but was a victim of his upbringing is to make all morality, all discussion of right and wrong, impossible. It leaves unanswered the question of why people in similar circumstances did not all become Hitlers. But worse, to say "It is not his fault; he was not free to choose" is to rob a person of his humanity, and reduce him to the level of an animal who is bound by instinct.
>
> —Harold S. Kushner, *When Bad Things Happen to Good People* (1982)

WHAT IS THE RELATIONSHIP OF THE INDIVIDUAL TO OTHERS?

This cultural pattern refers to perceptions of the self and the ways society is organized.

Persons of diverse cultures tend to have differing perceptions of the self. In U.S. culture, people tend to define the self in terms of one's role and responsibilities in the society. Generally, people in the United States define self in terms of occupation rather than in terms of family or other relationships.

Individualism

Remember, as was discussed in the preceding chapter, the United States is characterized to a high degree by individualism as opposed to collectivism. In fact, surveys in the industrialized nations during the 1980s clearly show that the most distinctive and perhaps permanent characteristics of the U.S. character are independence and individuality. Yet the word *individualism* did not enter the English vocabulary until 1835 when Tocqueville used it to describe what he found in the United States.

Those characteristics are echoes of constitutional guarantees of free speech and free press. Freedom for people in the United States is the freedom to be an individual. People in the United States have a passion for freedom. Patterson (1991) links this passion with the country's history of slavery. The concept of freedom that emerged from slave-holding Virginia was mass based and egalitarian.

This value is enforced early. According to a Chinese proverb, "You have to have the right name to do the right thing." In some cultures, names given to children have traditional or family meaning. Today, in the United States, names are more likely chosen by sound alone. Instead of tradition or family, children's names help reinforce individualism. Months-old infants are put in cribs in rooms separate from other people, and crying is tolerated because of the importance placed on learning to be an individual. In contrast, in virtually all preindustrial societies, mothers sleep with babies for many months—and might well consider the U.S. practice cruel or certainly not attentive to the child's needs. Children are encouraged to be autonomous, to make independent decisions, solve problems independently, and generally to view the world from the point of view of the self.

In the United States, adults maintain a separate self-concept when working in groups and organizations and are encouraged to accept responsibility as separate, independent individuals. Keep in mind, however, that independent individuals can cooperate—or compete—according to what maximizes benefits for the individual relative to costs.

A concern for individualism relates to views on love and marriage. In other cultures, marriage decisions are too important to be left to the individuals because, where families are most important, marriages present opportunities for alliances between families. Love develops after the marriage. Only in cultures that value individualism is romantic love the reason for marriage.

In contrast to some cultures, the emphasis on individuality may make it somewhat difficult to experience the comfort and security of association that other cultures experience. It may also explain a weaker family structure than is found in other cultures. One-fourth of U.S. households consist of a single person. And families in the United States are likely to be nontraditional: It is estimated that less than 10% of households now are made up of career fathers, homemaker mothers, and school-age children and that one-third of all U.S. families are single-parent ones.

Tocqueville predicted that the United States would succumb to the excesses of individualism, which he called egoism. Glendon (1991) calls this **hyperindividualism**, a withdrawing into individual private shells.

Self-Motivation

The value of individualism in the United States is reflected in the belief that individuals should set their own goals and then pursue them independently. Motivation should originate in the individual; individuals have the power to determine their own destiny. Rather than favoring group decisions or having others decide for the person most affected, individual responsibility for decision making is favored.

A possible explanation for the emphasis on individualism and self-motivation can be seen in the history of Western religion and industrialization. What may appear to be an unlikely relationship has been clearly described by David McClelland (1976).

In medieval Europe, society was rigidly structured. A person's place in society, or birthright, was defined by gender, social class, and lineage. The most holy life that one could aspire to on earth was to be a part of the church as a brother or nun and, in a sense, to be apart from the world. In medieval Catholicism, priests, nuns, saints, and rituals interceded with God for the masses.

The Protestant Reformation changed this view. Protestant religious beliefs influenced attitudes toward work and relationships with God. Martin Luther taught that all forms of work are legitimate; that is, earthly work was not subordinate to spiritual work. Calvin and others taught that it was godly to be hard-working and that success was evidence of one's godliness. Within the Catholic Church, the Council of Trent (1545-1563) eliminated the abuses identified by the Protestant Reformers. These actions represented a significant shift in attitude. Whereas in the distant past a talented person might find opportunity in the church apart from the world, after the Reformation a talented person who worked hard might succeed in business. Success in the world became consistent with religious beliefs.

In addition, Protestantism of every kind argued for the private nature of religion. Protestantism sought to diminish the gap between people and God, thus supporting the growing individualism. Another influence was the

In October 1517, Martin Luther challenged the world to debate the 95 theses he had posted on the Wittenberg Church door. The Reformation diverted into secular life the energies that had been given in monastic life.

Industrial Revolution. In the agricultural lifestyle, sons did what their fathers had done and daughters did what their mothers had done generation after generation. The Reformation and the Industrial Age made entrepreneurism, winning, personal ambition, and individualism a good thing.

McClelland (1976) labeled the consequences of this shift a "need for achievement." Individuals in cultures with a high **need for achievement** want to excel because of the feeling of accomplishment that it brings. McClelland showed that economic development in the West was largely built by individuals so motivated.

A particularly interesting part of McClelland's study was to use popular literature as an indicator of a culture's degree of need for achievement at any time. He studied the prevailing ideas and concerns in popular stories, songs, poems, plays, and speeches to index a culture's degree of need for achievement at any one time. He then correlated industrial activity in the culture to the presence of the achievement theme in popular literature. Not surprising was his finding that a peak in U.S. industrial activity was also a peak of this theme in popular literature, such as the Horatio Alger stories of the 1850s. Most of the 135 books that Horatio Alger wrote for boys in the 19th century stressed that a bright, self-reliant boy with hard work can go from "rags to riches."

The majority of the popular literature of the United States continues to stress the theme that an individual who works hard can succeed. The United States is called the land of opportunity, the country where people believe that if you work hard you succeed. Many mistakenly believe that the saying "God helps those who help themselves" is from the Bible. Actually, the saying is attributed to Benjamin Franklin.

The class structure that the United States has places strong emphasis on status-defining boundaries of power, money, and involvement in influential social circles. This contrasts sharply with the French, who define class boundaries based more on intelligence, cosmopolitanism, and refinement.

The actual data appear to contradict the myth. The period from 1955 through 1974 was an era of economic growth. The income of all groups rose. It was also the era of the greatest equality of incomes. In 1974, the top 10% of U.S. households had incomes 31 times those of the poorest 10% and 4 times those of median-income households. And in 1974, chief executive officers (CEOs) of U.S. corporations made $35 for every worker's dollar. Since that time, the gap between the rich and the poor has grown rapidly. By 1994, the top 10% of U.S. households had incomes 55 times those of the poorest 10% and 6 times those of median-income households. And in 1995, CEOs of U.S. corporations made $224 for every worker's dollar. In comparison, CEOs of German corporations made about 21 deutsche marks for every 1 earned by workers (Fischer, Hout, Jankowski, Swidler, & Lucas, 1996). The top 20% of the U.S. population controls 9 times as much wealth as the bottom 20%—the biggest gap in any industrial country. The percentage of U.S. children living in poverty is more than double the percentage in the developed world and more than quadruple the rate in Western Europe. But the important thing is the belief in the cultural myth—work hard and thus

Table 9.3   Support for the Welfare State, by Country: Affirmative Responses

Country	Percentage
Italy	81
Hungary	77
The Netherlands	64
Great Britain	62.9
All	58.6
West Germany	55.6
Australia	41.6
United States	27.9

SOURCE: Adapted from *U.S. News & World Report,* August 7, 1989. Copyright © 1989, *U.S. News & World Report.* Reprinted with permission.

succeed. (See Table 9.3 for a comparison of support for the welfare state, by country.)

This drive for individual achievement is still reflected in our popular culture. The success of the movies *Wall Street* and *Rocky* and television shows like *Lifestyles of the Rich and Famous* carry the message that through hard work the American Dream of success is still possible.

Closely related to individualism and self-motivation is the presence of competition. Competition is a part of life from early childhood. Children play games in which only one person can win. Video games are competitive. Schools are competitive. And that competition is carried into the workplace. The overwhelming presence of competition in U.S. society can be seen in the ever present sports metaphor. Many human endeavors are spoken of in sports language: a playing field, competitors, scores, winners, rankings. A good book or a good movie is ranked No. 1 by the newspapers. Presidential candidates are given daily scores by the media—one candidate is so many points ahead of the competition.

Surveys suggest that because of individualistic values, U.S. citizens are less likely to vote on the basis of economic class. U.S. citizens are less likely to favor government redistributing income from rich to poor or providing jobs for all. In fact, surveys show that only 23% of U.S. citizens favor the state taking care of the poor. The next lowest in Europe is Germany at 50%. People in the United States, though, are far more likely to do volunteer work. More than half do. People in the United States prefer to help the needy independently. And, as an opportunity society, the United States ranks first among nations believing that people should have the chance to attend college.

Social Organization

This cultural pattern refers to ways the society is organized. For example, the United States separates religion and state. Other cultures integrate church and state.

Two major social organization patterns—equality and conformity—may explain many others characteristic of the United States.

Equality

Equality is an important cultural myth in the United States, although beliefs may appear contradictory to actions. The U.S. legal system promises equal treatment, yet evidence can be cited that questions this assertion. It is popularly said, though, that everyone should be treated equally.

The United States has "equal opportunity" laws. That choice of words is clearly important: Everyone should have the same opportunity to work hard and succeed. It is in the area of employment that the laws struggle to define equality. Employment decisions cannot be made on the basis of age, ancestry or ethnicity,

> There are those who are asking the devotees of civil rights, "When will you be satisfied?" We can never be satisfied as long as our bodies, heavy with the fatigue of travel, cannot gain lodging in the motels of the highways and the hotels of the cities. We cannot be satisfied as long as the Negro's basic mobility is from a smaller ghetto to a larger one. We can never be satisfied as long as our children are stripped of their selfhood and robbed of their dignity by signs stating "for Whites only."
>
> —Martin Luther King, Jr., "I Have a Dream" speech, Washington, D.C., August 28, 1963 (quoted in McCroskey, 1968)

disability, marital or parental status, race, religion, or sex. Again, though, evidence can be cited that demonstrates that people are different in achievements, successes, and rewards. (See Table 9.4 for a comparison of the importance of equality and freedom, by country.)

The struggle for an Equal Rights Amendment highlights a very real struggle in the United States to define equality of the sexes.

The sense of equality extends to freedom to decide with whom to associate and occasional disregard for hierarchical structures. Most call each other by first names. Employees associate with bosses off the job, and all feel— perhaps mistakenly—that it is a "right" to go to the "top" to deal directly with the boss.

Table 9.4   Importance of Equality and Freedom, by Country: Affirmative Responses

	Importance of	
Country	Equality (in percentages)	Freedom (in percentages)
United States	20	72
Great Britain	23	69
France	32	54
Ireland	38	46
Italy	45	43
West Germany	39	37
Japan	32	37
Spain	39	36

SOURCE: Adapted from *U.S. News & World Report,* August 7, 1989. Copyright ©1989, *U.S. News & World Report.* Reprinted with permission.

Conformity

Cultures differ in the content or type of conformity. Some emphasize **conformity** to traditional or past-oriented norms, whereas others exhibit conformity to modern or future-oriented norms. People in the United States tend to emphasize conformity to modern norms. U.S. citizens seem to conform to what is "in."

Although these fads may be short-lived, they involve much of the society in some way. Consider the following: name-brand athletic shoes, designer jeans, haircut styles, bottled water, exercise and food trends, television programs from *American Idol* to *Survivor*, and Super Bowl Sunday.

Overall, people in the United States exhibit an unusual confidence in U.S. institutions, such as schools, the military, and the judiciary. U.S. citizens have an 80% rate of confidence compared to about 50% in major European nations.

U.S. citizens are also unusually patriotic. Fully 80% are proud to be a citizen—some polls have placed that figure at 97%. The average in Europe is 38%. In some polls, 71% of U.S. citizens would be willing to fight for the country. Other polls show a lower percentage but still a majority. The all-Europe average is 43%; Japan's is 22%.

While Tocqueville praised the United States, he also wrote that he knew of no other country with "less independence of mind and true freedom of discussion."

FORCES TOWARD THE
DEVELOPMENT OF REGIONAL CULTURES

You've read about the various events that resulted in the development of a national culture during the early post-World War II period. Today, that national unity is fragmenting into new cultural regions.

Let's look at the forces fragmenting a national culture:

- The old industrial heartland is being replaced with new regional economic centers in the South and West while at the same time the United States is becoming part of an integrated global economy.

- Integration and equal rights have resulted in recognition and acceptance of social and cultural differences.

- Immigration has eroded the homogeneity of the U.S. population and created ties between U.S. society and other societies around the world.

- As national media have grown into global media, new forms of local, special interest, and multilanguage media have appeared.

- International air transportation makes it easier and less expensive to travel abroad than to rural U.S. locations.

- The end of the Cold War lessened for a time the need for a large national security establishment.

These forces are still in their beginning stages, but the trend is becoming increasingly clear that the United States is returning to a country of distinct, relatively independent regions (Clough, 1997).

Consistent with regionalism is the growing strength of regional dialects in the United States. Recent research (Labov, Ash, & Boberg, 1997) found in Philadelphia, the cities of the Great Lakes region, and most of the South that accents are getting stronger. The dialects of U.S. cities are more different from each other now than 50 or 100 years ago.

> There is a fashionable intellectual perception that America is becoming more and more alike from one end to the other, that it's all covered with interstate highways and Howard Johnsons. Horsepucky. The most amazing thing about this country is its diversity, and the persistence of its regional and cultural differences.
>
> —Molly Ivins, journalist (1991, p. 123)

From Sea to See

Contrary to common perceptions that regional
dialects are slowly disappearing into a homogenized
stew, the dialects of North America are actually a
dynamic mosaic of still-evolving pronunciation
patterns, separated by unusually sharp boundaries.

Regional Dialects

The map illustrates dialect boundaries and pronunciation
changes over the last century in their most extreme form.

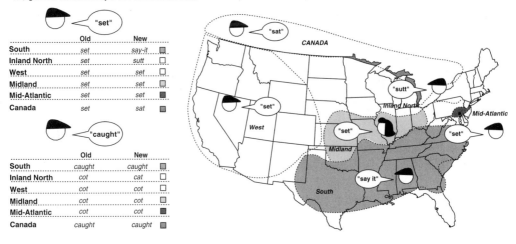

	Old	New
South	set	say-it ☐
Inland North	set	sutt ☐
West	set	set ☐
Midland	set	set ☐
Mid-Atlantic	set	set ■
Canada	set	sat ■

	Old	New
South	caught	caught ☐
Inland North	cot	cat ☐
West	cot	cot ☐
Midland	cot	cot ☐
Mid-Atlantic	cot	cot ■
Canada	caught	caught ■

From sea to see.

SOURCE: *Los Angeles Times*, June 24, 2002, p. A12.

The New Regions

Nearly 25 years ago, Garreau (1981) described what he called the "nine nations" of North America. Today, it is possible to imagine even more. Some of the metropolitan areas that have taken on distinct cultures within the larger U.S. culture include the following:

■ Atlanta (Georgia), site of leading global corporations (Coca-Cola and Delta Airlines) and CNN headquarters, has strong ties to developing countries from the presence of the Centers for Disease Control and Prevention and CARE, the world's largest relief organization, and interest in Africa by the city's African-American majority.

■ Charlotte (South Carolina), the center of a new southern industrial belt dominated by manufacturing and banking, has close ties to Europe, especially Germany.

- Miami (Florida) is heavily linked to Cuba, Haiti, and Latin America and has diverse Hispanic and Caribbean immigrant populations.

- Houston (and the rest of Texas and the Southwest) is an oil producer with increasing ties to Mexico as its culture and economic interests become ever more distinct from those of other parts of the United States.

- Los Angeles (and southern California), with the nation's largest and most ethnically diverse immigrant community and global entertainment and tourist industries, is the leading entry port for trade with Asia.

- San Francisco's Bay Area is the capital of the world's high-tech industry.

- Seattle (Washington), site of Starbucks and Microsoft, has economic ties to Asia.

FROM THE INTERCULTURAL PERSPECTIVE

Although human beings live in different geographic areas, speak different languages, and wear different kinds of clothes, everyone shares the same basic problems. Every culture deals with these universal problems in a unique way and has its own philosophy about them. The problems that all cultures face are the relationship between humans and nature (man-nature orientation), how we engage in our daily activities (activity orientation), how we use and perceive time (temporal orientation), questions about our own nature (human nature orientation), and the relationship between an individual and other people (relational).

Man-nature orientation can also be called worldview and describes how people view their relation to nature. Do they see themselves as superior to nature and try to control it? Do they try to work in harmony with nature? Or are they the victims of nature? Activity orientation describes how people do, don't do, or change things. In other words, people either passively accept events, change events that are already happening, or initiate events on their own. Time orientation describes how people in a culture focus more on the past, present, or future. Human nature orientation relates to a culture's beliefs about humans being naturally good, bad, or both. Relational orientation looks at how cultures organize relationships between people. Is it based on a hierarchy, on group identification, or on individualism?

By using the five value orientation categories, it is possible to describe the cultural patterns of a country. The United States may be becoming more regionalized; that is, its cultural patterns may be a little different in different parts of the country. However, some general observations can still be made. People in the United States generally believe in a supreme God or universal spirit and believe that they can control nature. They have a lot of faith in science and technology and are materialistic. They get a sense of identity from work and generally separate work from play. People in the United States are efficient, practical, and see progress and change as a good thing. They place a high value on time and have a future time orientation, although they often divide it into short-term goals.

People in the United States do not agree about whether humans are naturally good, bad, or a mixture of both. However, two beliefs related to human nature—rationality and mutability—are still believed by many in the United States. Rationality is the belief that people are reasonable and can make decisions for themselves. Mutability is the belief that people can change. For example, a criminal can learn to be a good citizen. One of the most fundamental beliefs of people in the United States is individualism. Associated with this belief are the ideas of self-motivation, competition, and responsibility for one's own actions. People in the United States also have an unshakable belief in equality. They do not believe that everyone is the same, but they do believe that everyone does or should have the same opportunities as everyone else. This is the basis of the American Dream. Last, people in the United States are conformist—it is important to stay in touch with the latest fashions in hair, clothing, and so forth.

KEY TERMS

activity orientation	equality	need for achievement
attitude	etic	rationality
change	hyperindividualism	scientific method
conformity	materialism	value
emic	mutability	worldview

CHAPTER 10

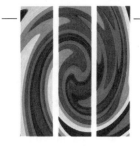

Comparative Cultural Patterns

Arab Culture

What You Can Learn From This Chapter

What defines Arab culture

The major beliefs of the Islamic faith

How Arab and U.S. cultural values compare

The difficulties in intercultural communication between Arab and Western cultures

Any two cultures could be compared as a way of learning more about both. Knowledge of other cultures is critical. You remember that cultural awareness is identified as a critical intercultural communication skill. In this chapter, the same categories used to describe dominant U.S. cultural values are used to learn more about Arab culture—a culture often misunderstood in the United States.

This chapter is devoted to how religion and language define Arab culture and then extends that with an examination of the conservative Arab state Saudi Arabia and the more tolerant state Oman. The chapter concludes by identifying some of the communication barriers among the Arab states and the United States.

As you study this chapter, make comparisons to the previous chapter on dominant U.S. cultural values. What intercultural communication problems could arise between individuals from these diverse cultures?

THE ARAB STATES

There is much diversity in the Arab world today, composed of 22 countries with a total population of 280 million. The population per country ranges from 600,000 in Qatar in 2001 to 65 million in Egypt in 2001. Iran is not considered an Arab country because its language is Persian (Farsi). Life expectancy in Arab countries ranges from 45 years in Djibouti to 76 in Kuwait. Annual per capita **gross domestic product (GDP)** ranges from $278 in Comoros to more than $19,000 in Qatar. Literacy rates range from 27% in Somalia to 89% in Jordan (see Table 10.1).

The design of this Saudi stamp issued in 1917 is adapted from stucco work above the entrance to the Cairo railroad station. T. E. Lawrence (Lawrence of Arabia) was responsible for the design of early Saudi stamps.

The Arab world's history spans more than 5,000 years. Yet from the time of Napoleon, who invaded Egypt in 1798, until the end of World War I, European countries conquered close to 90% of the Arab world by military force. After World War I, the European colonial powers began a slow retreat.

THE ISLAMIC FAITH

The strength of the Arab culture is demonstrated in its history. A family from southern Arabia could move to Spain, and its descendants 6 centuries later could move back and find familiar surroundings. The Arab culture transcends time and space, particularly through its language and its Islamic faith, the second largest in the world after Christianity, with some 1.2 billion followers, or about 20% of the world's population. **Arabs,** the ethnic group that originally spread **Islam,** are now a minority in the religion. The **Muslim** religion extends far beyond the Arab world from Africa to Europe to Asia, including the republics of the former Soviet Union that had experienced suppression of religion and language since the time of the Russian czars. Today, some 75 countries have large Muslim populations. Just as the Muslim religion includes more than Arabs, not all Arabs are Muslim. The Arab world, however, is connected by a shared culture that developed in the Islamic faith.

Table 10.1   Overview of 22 Arab Countries

Country	Population (millions)	Life Expectancy (years)	Adult Literacy (%)	GDP per Capita ($)
Algeria	30.4	68.9	66.6	1,566
Bahrain	.07	72.9	87.1	9,714
Comoros	.69	58.8	59.2	278
Djibouti	.66	45.5	63.4	802
Egypt	64.5	66.3	54.6	1,380
Iraq	23.0	58.7	54.6[a]	574
Jordan	6.5	69.7	89.2	1,154
Kuwait	2.1	75.9	81.9	14,076
Lebanon	3.3	72.6	85.6	5,030
Libya	6.2	70.0	79.1	4,501
Mauritania	2.4	50.5	41.6	402
Morocco	28.3	66.6	48.0	1,283
Oman	2.3	70.5	70.3	6,200
Palestine[b]				
Qatar	.60	68.9	80.8	19,669
Saudi Arabia	19.9	70.9	76.1	7,005
Somalia	7.2	46.9	27.0[a]	600
Sudan	28.4	55.0	56.9	346
Syria	16.1	70.5	73.6	1,006
Tunisia	9.5	69.5	69.9	2,189
United Arab Emirates	2.9	74.6	75.1	17,965
Yemen	17.7	59.4	45.2	384

SOURCE: Population and GDP per capita: ArabDataNet, http://www.arabdatanet.com (1999 data); life expectancy and adult literacy: United Nations Development Programme, *Arab Human Development Report, 2001.*

a. 1995 data.
b. No data available.

People who practice this religion are called Muslims (literally "submitters" to the will of God). Islam is a nonhierarchical religion; there is no priesthood. No one institution or individual speaks for Muslims. Rather than churches, there are places to pray.

Muhammad, the Prophet

The prophet **Muhammad** (born circa 570, died 632) founded the religion in the early 7th century in Arabia. Orphaned at an early age, Muhammad ibn

The number of Muslims in the United States is a matter of dispute. Estimates range from 1.6 to 6 million.

The first Muslims in the Americas were enslaved Africans brought over in the 17th century. African-Americans account for the majority of all converts to Islam in the United States. Among African-Americans, the Nation of Islam grew most rapidly in the 1960s. Most of its mosques underwent reforms after 1975 to join conventional Islam. Today, the Nation of Islam represents a small fraction of Islams in the United States.

Today, Islam is one of the fastest growing religions in the United States. Islam's presence is being felt in the United States: Casio markets a watch that sounds an electronic call to prayer, some banks have set up "Islamic accounts" in response to the Muslim prohibition against paying or receiving interest, and Warith Deen was the first Muslim to open the U.S. Senate with a prayer.

SOURCE: Smith (2000) and Dannin (2002).

Abdullah was a businessman when, in 610, it is said he received his first revelations through the angel Gabriel. These continued for another 20 years to form the Koran, the holy book of Islam.

The Koran

The Koran (often spelled Quran) was revealed by God to the prophet Muhammad in Arabic and is considered to contain the literal words of Allah, or God. The Koran contains stories, admonitions, verse and prophetic segments, and social, political, and economic laws. The Koran embraces all areas of human affairs from the most personal to international relations. Not only is it unique in its completeness, it also deals with human transactions in such a way as to make God's presence felt in every human transaction. There is no separation of church and state as in the United States. The Koran is a spiritual guide, a system of law, a code of ethics, and a way of life. Islam is the only world religion that offers rules by which to govern a state as well as a set of spiritual beliefs.

Religious Practices

Westerners once called Islam "Muhammadanism," but Muslims dislike the term because Muhammad is not regarded as divine. He is considered the last and most important prophet in a line that includes Abraham, Noah, Moses, and Jesus. The accounts of Muhammad's life and teachings are second only to the Koran as authoritative guidelines in Muslim faith and law.

Many Muslims stress the similarities between Islam and the principal Abrahamic faiths in the United States. For example, Jewish and Islamic dietary laws resemble one another very closely. According to Islamic law, Muslims may not drink alcoholic beverages, eat pork, or gamble. Muslims honor Jesus as one of the prophets of the Bible but not as the son of God. Most who practice the faith are religious conservatives with a literalist view of the holy book of Muslims.

The five religious obligations of Muslims begin with the public witness, or *shahadah*, "I testify that there is no God but God; I testify that Muhammad is the Messenger of God." Saying this confession with conviction makes one a Muslim.

Short prayers, or *salah*, are recited by individuals five times daily at intervals from early morning to evening, each time after washing hands, arms, face, hair, and feet (although rubbing water lightly over socks is permissible). Facing east (toward Mecca), Muslims go through prescribed motions of standing, kneeling, and touching the floor with the forehead and palms. Congregational prayers at Friday noon are led by an *imam*, or spiritual leader.

Alms giving, or *zakat*, is the duty of sharing with the poor a small percentage of wealth beyond one's basic expenses.

Fasting, or *sawm*, is central during **Ramadan**, the ninth month on Islam's lunar calendar. Ramadan commemorates the prophet Muhammad receiving revelations from the angel Gabriel. Ramadan is a time to reflect on the meaning of Islam, to rejuvenate faith. Muslims abstain from food, drink, and sexual intercourse during the daylight hours. Nourishment is allowed only for the sick, the elderly, the pregnant, and the very young.

At least once in a Muslim's lifetime, a believer is expected to make a pilgrimage, or **hajj**, to Mecca. It is an elaborate series of rites requiring several days.

Muslims generally fall into either the Sunni or the Shiite branch. The **Sunni**, who account for 85% to 90% of the world's Muslims, believe that Muslim leadership in the early years passed to a series of caliphs, whereas the **Shiite** Muslims believe that leadership fell to the martyred Ali, Muhammad's cousin and son-in-law, and his descendants. Shiites tend to be more ecstatic in religious practice and have messianic

Stamp issued in 1979 honors pilgrims at Holy Ha'aba Mecca Mosque.

expectations of a future imam who will bring justice to the world. Sufism is an ascetic movement throughout Islam directed toward mysticism and a direct personal experience with God.

The *sunnah* are the traditions relating to the deeds and utterances of Muhammad. Together with the Koran, they are the basis of the *sharia*, or canonic law. The legal system is different from Western models. The sharia

> My Islam is a religion of tolerance and brotherhood.
>
> —Sai'd Al-Ashmawy,
> former chief justice,
> Egypt's Supreme Court
>
> Jews and Christians and whoever believes in God . . . and does what is right shall have nothing to fear or regret.
>
> Among his other signs are the creation of the heavens and the earth and the diversity of your tongues and colors. Surely there are signs in this for all mankind.
>
> —Koran

system relies far less on physical evidence than on the accused's statements and answers to questions posed by judges. Cleric-scholars using the Koran and the acts of Muhammad as their guide get to the truth through patient questioning. If they err, they must answer to Allah. Anecdotal evidence indicates that the crime rate is low by Western standards. The Koran and sunnah dictate specific penalties for some crimes, such as amputating a thief's hand. Contrary to popular belief, these are rarely carried out because the crimes are narrowly defined and proof is strict. For example, a shoplifter would not suffer amputation because shoplifting is not considered a theft as the goods were not locked up. Executions occur only if all heirs of the victim demand it. Judges often encourage the family to accept "blood money," traditionally the price of 100 camels, instead. Punishment is often mild by Western standards. Some trials fall short of international standards—even "divine law must be carried out by mortals."

Most cultural differences come from the religion's conservatism. Muslims preserve ethics and family values. There are strict prohibitions against alcohol, smoking, and premarital sex. To many Muslims, people in the United States don't care about families, abandon parents when old, and have an epidemic of AIDS, pornography, pregnant teenagers, abortions, and illegitimate babies. These aspects of U.S. culture are not desired by Muslims as they bring shame on the family. To Muslims, God and family are most important. The dividing line between the Arab and Western worlds is religion. Islam is a religion, a way of life, and the central force of Arab existence.

The prophet Muhammad achieved victory as a military commander and political ruler. The state has been the instrument of Islam and God was considered to be head of both the state and the religion. This is in sharp contrast to Western Christian countries, which separated church and state. Perhaps as a consequence only four of the Arab states have developed even nominal democracies (Lewis, 2002).

SAUDI ARABIA

Geography

Because of the importance of Saudi Arabia in the Arab world, we need to pay particular attention to this country. Saudi Arabia occupies nearly 90% of the Arabian peninsula and is the 12th largest country in the world—2,250,000 square kilometers (868,730 square miles), or one-fourth the size of the United States. As 98% of the land is desert, most cities are built on the coast and on oases. With an average of only 10 centimeters of rainfall a year, Saudi Arabia gets most of its water from underground aquifers filled with fossil water thousands of years old. This water—like oil—is a nonrenewable resource. Desalination provides only a small percentage of Saudi Arabia's water.

Discovery of Oil

In the 1940s, Saudi Arabia was mostly unknown to the rest of the world, and the rest of the world was unknown to most Saudis. Nomads outnumbered the settled. The economy was on a subsistence level. Illiteracy was high. In 1933, U.S. oil companies launched the California Arabian Standard Oil Company, which later became the Arabian-American Oil Co. (ARAMCO). With monies from the oil discovered in the late 1930s, Saudi Arabia developed at a pace unparalleled in history. With 25% to 30% of the world's proven oil reserves, Saudi Arabia became one of the strongest economies in the world, with oil as the source of its income. Saudi Arabia is wealthy, but is deeply in debt partly because of lower oil prices, government deficits, and rising unemployment as contributing factors. As a result, young Saudis are no longer guaranteed good salaries and prestigious jobs. In 1981, per capita income in Saudi Arabia was equal to that of the United States (about $28,000 in current dollars), but because of falling oil prices it is now about $6,800.

Ruling Saud Family and
Conservative Wahhabism

Saudi Arabia's ruling Saud family gained power in the 1920s by consolidating feudal tribes through an alliance with an ultraconservative brand of Islam

A shop closed during Muslim prayers is a typical sight in Saudi Arabia.

SOURCE: Tom Loos. Used by permission.

known as Wahhabism that frowned on smoking, drinking, and virtually any contact between unmarried members of the opposite sex. In this sense, Wahhabism can be compared to the Puritans. Even today, as guardian of the two holy Muslim mosques in Mecca and Medina, Saudi Arabia is the most conservative Islamic country in the world. Islam as practiced in Saudi Arabia remains today much as it was in the time of Muhammad.

Media

The government licenses all bookshops, printing presses, and public relations agencies to ensure that standards of taste are maintained. There are at least 10 daily newspapers and 9 weekly or monthly magazines published in Saudi Arabia. All are privately owned but subsidized in varying degrees by the government. Editors patrol themselves, deferring to the government's Ministry of Information in questionable cases.

Some advertisers have attempted to adapt to Arab cultural values, such as in the portrayal of women. European ads for the men's perfume Drakkar Noir by Guy Laroche showed a man's hand clutching the perfume bottle and a woman's hand seizing his bare forearm. In the Saudi version, the man's arm is clothed in a dark jacket sleeve and the woman is touching the man's hand only with her fingertips. Even so, some might find such ads objectionable in that they suggest sexual temptation (Nafeesi, 1986).

Satellite television brings in *The Sopranos, Ally McBeal, Sex and the City,* and other U.S. shows. Saudi Arabia is saturated with symbols of U.S. culture, but at the same time promotes hostility against U.S. foreign policy, values, and Judeo-Christian beliefs.

Matawain

Public morality committees, the **matawain** or the regional Societies for the Preservation of Virtue and the Prevention of Vice, ensure strict compliance with religious requirements. Salaried morals police patrol the public domain, making sure that businesses close at prayer times and that women are properly covered and observe the off-limit signs. There are no public worship services of any religion except Islam. There is no church, no temple of any kind, and no missionary work allowed.

In fact, the Koran is part of Saudi Arabia's constitution. The country bases its legitimacy on its commitment to Islam and the implementation of sharia, or Islamic law. Anything that is not allowed in Islam will not happen.

Contact With the United States

Just weeks before his death, President Franklin Roosevelt hosted King Saud aboard a U.S. ship and gave the aging king his wheelchair. They formed a relationship that has continued between the two countries. President Harry S. Truman signed the first security agreement with Saudi Arabia in 1947. For years, United States and Saudi peoples worked together, liked each other, but didn't know much about each other. For example, the ARAMCO compound in Dhahran is like a 1950s midwestern U.S. small town isolated from the rest of the country with well-sprinkled lawns, neat houses, U.S.-brand groceries in stores, and even U.S. electrical current—not Saudi.

The following full-page advertisement appeared in newspapers on September 13, 2002:

The President
The White House
Washington, DC 20500

Dear Mr. President:

On the eve of the first anniversary of the terrorist attacks against the American people, I take the opportunity to renew to you and the families of the victims and indeed the entire American nation, the sincere condolences and sympathy of the Saudi people and myself.

As long as I live, I shall never forget the horrible scenes of carnage, the raging fires, the smoke that covered the horizon, and the innocent people who jumped out of windows in their attempt to escape. On that fateful day, the whole world stood with the American people in unprecedented solidarity that made no distinction as to race, religion or language.

It was the perverted hope of the perpetrators of this heinous crime that they could bring humiliation to and terrorize the American nation. But the brave people of the United States of American, whose greatness lies in the strength of its brave sons and daughters in facing adversity, and which is enriched by their remarkable achievements, all of this will make them ever stronger than the designs of the evildoers. Instead of being terrorized by this catastrophe, they become more steadfast and determined.

The target of the terrorists who engineered this crime was humanity at large. They hoped that this outrageous act would incite and ignite bloody strife among different faiths and civilizations. But their evil was turned against them, for all humanity united to fight terrorism, and wise voices from all corners of the world arose to echo your declaration that terrorism has no religion or nationality, that it is pure evil, condemned and abhorred by all religions and cultures.

Mr. President, we in Saudi Arabia felt an especially great pain at the realization that a number of young Saudi citizens had been enticed and deluded and their reasoning subverted to the degree of denying the tolerance that their religion embraced, and turning their backs on their homeland, which has always stood for understanding and moderation. They allowed themselves to be used as a tool to do great damage to Islam, a religion they espoused, and to all Muslims. They also aimed at causing considerable harm to the historic and strong relationship between the American people and the people of Saudi Arabia. I would like to make it clear that true Muslims all over the world will never allow a minority of deviant extremists to speak in the name of Islam and distort its spirit of tolerance. Your friends in the Kingdom of Saudi Arabia denounced and condemned the September 11 attacks as strongly as did the American people. We, like you, are convinced that nothing can ever justify the shedding of innocent blood or the taking of lives and the terrorizing of people, regardless of whatever cause or motive. Therefore, we do not simply reiterate sincere and true condolences to the relatives of the victims, but assure all of our continued will and determination to do our utmost to combat this malignant evil and uproot it from our world.

The Kingdom of Saudi Arabia continues to stand solidly against terrorism. We shall act, independently as well as collectively, with the U.S.-led international coalition to wage a fierce and merciless war against the terrorists in order to eradicate this deadly disease that threatens all societies.

In conclusion, I would like to say to you, my dear friend, that God Almighty, in His wisdom, tests the faithful by allowing such calamities to happen. But He, in His mercy, also provides us with the will and determination, generated by faith, to enable us to transform such tragedies into great achievements, and crises that seem debilitating are transformed into opportunities for the advancement of humanities. I only hope that, with your cooperation and leadership, a new world will emerge out of the rubble of the World Trade Center: a world that is blessed by the virtues of freedom, peace, prosperity and harmony.

Sincerely,
Abdullah bin Abdulaziz al-Saud
Crown Prince, Deputy Prime Minister,
and Commander of the National Guard
Jeddah, 10 September 2002 AD
3 Rajab 1423 Hijra

Today, the United States is the world's largest oil consumer, and Saudi Arabia is the largest market for U.S. consumer products in the Middle East. Saudi Arabia has spent tens of billions of dollars on Western technology, including $270 billion on high-tech weapons since the 1991 Gulf War.

The 1991 war in the Persian Gulf (for which Saudi Arabia reimbursed the United States $55 billion) brought individuals from the two cultures into contact, and, as we have seen, neither will be the same in the future. A number of reform-minded Saudi businessmen, government officials, and academics used the 1991 war as an opportunity to advocate for expanded rights for women, a reliable court system, and an elected parliament. The Bush administration hoped that the 2003 war with Iraq would lead to more democratic changes in conservative regimes elsewhere in the Middle East. The conservatives have worked to make Islamic Saudi Arabia even more fundamentalist—particularly in the areas of economic policies (i.e., eliminating Western-oriented banks), the parts of the legal system not fully based on sharia law, censorship of foreign media with secular ideas, and a heavy dependence on the West in foreign and defense policies—particularly in light of the 2003 war with Iraq.

Although Saudi Arabia is a monarchy, an age-old practice of **majlis** provides any citizen access to the king and local governors. Also in Bedouin tradition are diwaniyahs, political meetings where men discuss community issues and debate politics. Perhaps in response to calls for change from both religious conservatives who resented the influx of Western forces during the Gulf War and liberals who saw the war as an impetus for opening the kingdom more to the West, early in 1992 King Fahd announced on national television a new administrative structure for the country. The king created a national consultative council that would review government policies and advise the Cabinet of Ministers, thus providing citizens a voice in government, and announced guarantees for personal liberties, such as freedom from unreasonable searches, for the first time in history. After King Fahd experienced a stroke in 1995, Prince Abdullah took over governing the country.

OMAN

In contrast to Saudi Arabia is its neighbor Oman, one of the most tolerant countries in the region. Oman is a small country about the same size as the state of New Mexico with 1.7 million Omanis and 500,000 foreign guest workers. For centuries, Oman had been a thriving seafaring nation. Its merchant ships sailed the waters between India and the east coast of Africa. It governed Zanzibar and the Kenyan seaports of Mombasa and Lamu and grew wealthy on spices, gold, ivory, and slaves. Its merchant ships could not compete with British and French steam vessels, and the country sank into bankruptcy and decay in the early 20th century. Sultan Said ibn Taimur inherited the nearly penniless state from his father. The country had only three elementary schools educating a maximum of 900 students and one hospital operated by missionaries. Modern conveniences such as eyeglasses and private cars were banned.

Travel was by foot, donkey, or camel. Disease was rampant and life spans short. The sultan sent his only son to Britain's Sandhurst Military Academy and later recalled him to keep him in seclusion with his mother and a teacher of the Koran.

Opposition to the sultan reached a peak with open rebellion and Said's only family conspiring with the British who had been handling Oman's external defense for decades. A coup on July 23, 1970, brought his son Kaboos ibn Said to power. Kaboos has reinvented Oman by encouraging modernization in education, commerce, technology, and democracy.

Like Saudi Arabia, oil made Oman a wealthy nation. Oman's oil production is 800,000 barrels a day, and it has 5.6 billion barrels in reserves. But, unlike Saudi Arabia, Oman has charted a different path.

Oman's oil reserves may last another 25 years. One goal has been to diversify the economy before the supplies are depleted. The objective is to replace 90% of the 500,000 foreign guest workers with Omani nationals by 2010. That requires an educated workforce. The sultan's pride is the Sultan Kaboos University established in 1985. The majority of its students are women. Four more universities are planned.

In 1970, the country had no electricity, three miles of paved roads, and 12 telephones. Today, Oman is a model of development with thousands of miles of highways. It is open to world communication, commerce, and tourism. It is building one of the largest container ports in the world to take advantage of its location on the world's main east-west shipping lines. The economy is now starting to move from government-dominated to private sector-led.

Oman is the only Persian Gulf country to have a Basic Law, or constitution, that guarantees inalienable rights to its citizens. In 1994, Oman became the first of the six Gulf Cooperation Council countries to allow women to vote and hold national office. Kaboos has retained the right to appoint members of Oman's Consultative Council from a pool of candidates approved by voters. In 1999, four women sat in its Consultative Council, which Kaboos is moving to transform into a full-fledged parliament. He has announced plans to allow direct elections to the Consultative Council. He has also announced plans to institute the region's first independent judiciary.

Oman has also become one of the region's most tolerant countries. The sultan himself has built churches and Hindu temples for Christian and Indian minorities in the overwhelmingly Muslim country. Kaboos was the first to appoint a female ambassador from an Arab Gulf country and the only Arab leader to support Egyptian President Anwar Sadat's 1979 peace treaty with Israel.

Kaboos married only briefly and has no children. According to the Basic Law, on his death his relatives will gather to appoint a successor.

DOMINANT CULTURAL PATTERNS

Muslims represent a growing social and political force that questions some of the West's dominant cultural patterns, particularly the following:

- The relationship between God and humankind

- The role of morality in human affairs

- The role of technology and modernization

- The nature of progress

Using the categories developed to describe dominant U.S. cultural patterns, a description of Arab cultural patterns provides a useful comparison.

Worldview

As referred to before, worldview is the outlook that a culture has concerning the nature of the universe, the nature of humankind, the relationship between humanity and the universe, and other philosophical issues defining humans' place in the cosmos.

In all aspects, Arab worldview is derived from Islam and expressed in its language. Islam draws no distinction between religion and the temporal aspects of life. According to Islam, everything in the world except humans is administered by God-made laws. The physical world has no choice but obedience to God. Humans alone possess the qualities of intelligence and choice. Humans can choose to submit to the Law of God and in so doing will be in harmony with all other elements of nature.

Islam holds that the world is totally real. It is incumbent upon every Muslim to seek knowledge in the broadest sense from the created universe, as it reveals knowledge and truth. Although Islam demands faith in God as the basis of knowledge and research, it encourages all methods of gaining knowledge, whether rational or experimental. This overwhelming quest for knowledge gave birth to, among other things, the modern sciences of mathematics, physics, chemistry, and medicine and triggered the Renaissance in Europe (Haiek, 1992).

Islam does not hinder private enterprise or condemn private possessions but does not tolerate selfish and greedy capitalism. This is an expression of the general philosophy of Islam of a moderate and middle but positive and effective course between the individual and the state—yet among the most egregious violators of human rights are the authoritarian regimes in the Muslim world, such as Saddam Hussein's Iraqi regime.

Activity Orientation

Earning a living through labor is not only a duty but also a virtue. Islam respects all kinds of work as long as there is no indecency or wrong involved. Whatever a person makes is one's private possession that no one else may claim. Islam encourages Muslims to work, to engage in free enterprise, and to earn and possess, but the "owner" is God and the human is the trustee. This means the Muslim has a responsibility to invest and spend wisely.

Just as Islam provides the values for work, it also guides other aspects of human activity. Islam encourages practicality. It does not encourage wishful thinking but does encourage one to accept and deal with the reality within one's reach.

Adherence to Islam conflicts with uncritical acceptance of progress and change. Islam is conservative because of its adherence to the Koran.

Time Orientation

Saudi accounting of time shows a strong relationship to the cosmos. Saudi Arabia adheres to the traditional *Hijrah* (or *Hegirian*) calendar, which is based on the cycles of the moon. A lunar month is the time between two new moons. The Hijrah year contains 12 months and so is 11 days shorter than the solar year. As a result, the months shift gradually from one season to another. Months in the Hijrah calendar have no relation to the seasons.

The first day of the first year of the Hijrah calendar corresponds to July 15, 622, the date on which Muhammad fled Mecca for Medina to escape persecution at the hands of the Quraish. The Western method of designating Islamic dates is A.H. (*anno Hegira*). August 2003 A.D. corresponds to Jumaada Thani 1424 A.H.

The traditional system of accounting time during the day is tied to the rising and setting of the sun. International communications, however, forced Saudi Arabia to adopt Greenwich mean time. Saudi use of time shows a difference as well. Edward Hall (1983) has provided a useful way of describing how cultures use time. One way is to do one thing at a time, which Hall labels **monochronic time;** this is characteristic of Northern Europe and the United States. These cultures tend to try to plan the order of their use of time.

Doing many things at once is called **polychronic time** and is characteristic of Latin America and the Middle East. Polychronic time stresses the involvement of people and completion of transactions rather than adherence to schedules. In polychronic cultures, nothing is firm; plans can be changed up to the last minute. Arab markets and stores appear to be in a state of mass confusion as customers all try to get the attention of a single clerk. Arab government offices may have large reception areas where groups of people are all conducting affairs at the same time.

As a polychronic culture, Arabs can interact with several people at once and still be immersed in each other's business. Polychronic managers can supervise a large number of people. By their actions, polychronic cultures demonstrate that they are oriented to people, human relationships, and family.

Human Nature Orientation

Muslims believe that every person is born free of sin. When a person reaches the age of maturity, the individual becomes accountable for deeds and intentions. Thus, human nature is more good than evil, and the probability of positive change is greater than the probability of failure. God created only humans endowed with intelligence and choice. The purpose of human life is to worship God by knowing, loving, and obeying him.

Relational Orientation

As we have seen, Arab culture is group oriented. Social lives are organized around the family and tribal line. Loyalties are to family, clan, tribe, and government in that order. Individuals subordinate personal needs to the family and the community.

Saudis live in large extended families, and devotion to the family is central. In contrast to Western culture, the concept of individuality is absent. There is a strong sense of identity with the family. Saudis see themselves in the context of family. Duty is not to oneself but to the group. Loyalty is first to the family. All family members suffer from the dishonorable act of any one of them. Honor is the collective property of the family.

Islam unifies humanity on the basis of equality. There are no bounds of race, country, or wealth. All are born equal and should have equal civil, political, and spiritual rights. In this sense, Islam is an international religion.

Central to the Arab culture's social organization is family and Islam. Generous hospitality is a manner of honor and a sacred duty.

A man is considered a descendant only of his father and his paternal grandfather. A man's honor resides in the number of sons he sires. A man belongs to his father's family. Decisions are made by the family patriarch—not by the individual.

Role of Women

Muslims would say that women in Arab cultures are equal to men. The prophet Muhammad revolutionized life for women in the 7th century by granting women access to the mosque, full participation in public affairs, and the right to inherit property. The rights and responsibilities of women are equal to those of men but not identical with them. In Arab cultures, equality and sameness are two quite different things. It is said that women are deprived in some ways but are compensated in other ways. Thus, Arab women are equal as independent human beings, equal in the pursuit of knowledge, and equal in the freedom of expression. An Arab woman who is a wife and mother is entitled to complete provision and total maintenance by her husband. She may work and own property herself.

A traditional Saudi woman does not go out alone. She speaks to no man other than her husband or blood kin. All public facilities are segregated by sex. Women who work outside the home work in capacities with other women exclusively. Saudi society is structured to keep a woman within strictly defined limits to protect her chastity.

Wearing the *abaya* and the veil is an old tradition to safeguard women from the actions of strange men. A woman is not permitted to expose any part of her body before strangers. Thus, the abaya and the veil represent honor, dignity, chastity, purity, and integrity.

The great majority of Saudi women are willing to accept this position in society in return for the guarantee of security that Arab traditions provide. Those who want change want it within the context of the Arab culture.

COMMUNICATION BARRIERS

In summer 1990, there were no Western journalists and only a few thousand U.S. military advisers in Saudi Arabia. The war in the Persian Gulf changed that. By February 1991, more than 700 journalists and half a million U.S. troops were stationed there. Many U.S. soldiers spent up to 20 classroom hours learning about Arabs and Arab culture before being sent to Saudi Arabia. U.S. soldiers and Saudis started to get to know each other as individuals.

Political Unrest

Several barriers unique to the United States and Arab countries impede effective intercultural communication. One is the continuing political unrest in the region.

Islam emphasizes community over individual rights, and because the Koran provides rules for governing society, the line between religion and politics is blurred. Eight of the world's most authoritarian monarchies are in Islamic countries. Four Arab states—Iraq, Libya, Sudan, and Iran—have at times been labeled "outlaw" states by the United States and other countries. And 15 of the 19 suspected hijackers in the September 11, 2001, attacks on the World Trade Center and the Pentagon were Saudis.

The effect of the 2003 war with Iraq is yet to be fully known. Initially, the televised images of the rapid U.S. thrust into Baghdad were seen as occupation—not liberation. In 1917, the British took Baghdad from the Ottoman Turks. The British general Frederick Stanley Maude told the citizens the British came not as conquerors but as liberators. The British stayed as colonialists until 1932. Some saw the United States acting to protect oil reserves and to create governments that would not threaten Israel.

Before and after the 1991 war in the Persian Gulf and the 2003 war with Iraq, the major issue between the United States and the Arab world was Israel. The U.S. recognized Israel as a country within minutes of its creation and has been its staunchest ally ever since.

Westernization Versus Cultural Norms

The conflict that Westernization provides is a lingering problem. The West has technological and organizational superiority. Petrodollars brought a modern infrastructure to Saudi Arabia. To operate that infrastructure, Saudi Arabia relies on foreign workers: Up to one-third of the residents and up to half of the workforce are foreigners with diverse religious and cultural backgrounds. Westernization and the presence of the foreign workforce have put a strain on family life, caused women to question women's role, and put corrupting pressures on the devout. Negative aspects of family life in U.S. culture such as divorce are not desired by Arabs. In the face of Westernization, Saudi Arabia remains committed to traditional values. That also poses a barrier to intercultural communication.

Stereotypes

However, the major barrier to intercultural communication between United States and Arab peoples appears to be the stereotypes each holds of the other. Shaheen (2001) contends that U.S. media has vilified Arab Muslims in the aftermath of the September 11 attacks.

Arabs tend to stereotype Western women as loose or immoral. Men in other cultures are stereotyped as well: the British as obnoxious, the Germans like a mechanized tank division, the French as impossible, and the Americans as cowboys—not all that different from how some in the United States stereotype the Arabs as Bedouins who roam the desert.

To counter Arab-language radio and television in the Middle East that U.S. officials say feeds public stereotypes against Israel and the United States, the United States funds Radio Sawa, which targets Arab youths under 30. *Sawa* means "together" in Arabic. Its message is that the West and the Arab world are not as estranged as it may appear.

FROM THE INTERCULTURAL PERSPECTIVE

Western and Arab cultures have much contact with each other, and misunderstandings occur between them. Intercultural communication barriers, especially stereotypes and insufficient knowledge of each other's cultures and languages, contribute to these continuing problems.

All the Arab countries have a common language and religion. They are the Arabic language and the Islamic faith. The major difference between Western and Arab cultures is religion. The Islamic faith controls the lives of its members (called Muslims) in all areas of life. These areas include spiritual beliefs, lifestyle, laws, and government.

Arab cultural patterns can be described by using the value orientation categories discussed in Chapter 9: worldview, activity orientation, time orientation, human nature orientation, and relational orientation. Arab cultural values are strongly influenced by the Islamic religion.

In Arab worldview, everything in the world follows God's law perfectly, except for human beings, who have the choice of whether or not to follow God's law. Arab activity orientation encourages work and practicality. Progress and change, however, are accepted carefully because technology should not go against the teachings of the Koran (Islamic holy text). One important aspect of Arab time orientation is the idea of polychronic time.

Unlike monochronic cultures, polychronic cultures do many things at one time. In Arab countries, it is common for people to conduct business with many different people at the same time. Muslims view humans as basically good. People are born free of sin and become responsible for their actions when they grow up. Arab relational orientation is based on the group, especially the family. People live in large extended families with a patriarch as family leader. What affects one member of the family affects the rest of the family. In Arab culture, a woman's honor is protected by following strict clothing guidelines and by not interacting with males except for her husband or family members. Although there are many restrictions on women, women are viewed as equals to men.

KEY TERMS

Arabs	matawain	Ramadan
gross domestic product (GDP)	monochronic time	Shiite
	Muhammad	Sunni
hajj	Muslim	
majlis	polychronic time	

CHAPTER 11

Women, Families, and Children

What You Can Learn From This Chapter

Various perspectives on the communication of women

How the status of women varies by culture

When scholars and researchers use the words *sex* and *gender* today, they refer to different concepts. The word **sex** is most used to refer to the biological features that distinguish men from women. The word gender is most often used to refer to the learned behaviors and attitudes associated with the words *feminine* and *masculine*. Traits that are considered feminine traits are attributes such as affection, compassion, nurturance, and emotionality. Traits that are considered masculine traits are typically attributes such as strength, assertiveness, competitiveness, and ambitiousness. These differences are consistent with cultures that divide family, work, and social interaction roles along sex-linked lines. **Sexism** is the term for limiting women to traditional women's roles and men to traditional men's roles.

The status of children, women, and families in diverse countries tells us much about the cultures of those countries. This chapter describes the status of children and women worldwide in diverse cultures and describes diverse perspectives on the communication of women.

PERSPECTIVES ON COMMUNICATION OF WOMEN

When you consider women and men as groups, you must first ask if such a grouping by biological sex is, in fact, real or constructed; that is, do the terms *women* and *men* actually reflect discrete and separate groups of people? At base, females and males are different because of two distinct chromosomes. Is that difference alone sufficient to create two separate groups, or have two groups been constructed by culture?

You know the importance of language in defining a culture. One important consideration, then, for saying there are separate groups—real or constructed—would be the use of a unique language code.

> Language use does have important consequences: How would you refer to a group of both sexes—"men and women" or "women and men"? Does the word order convey any message? Did you notice that this book uses "women and men"?

In certain languages, great differences exist between the sexes—so much so that speakers of other languages might think that the women and men in that culture were speaking totally different languages. In Zulu, for example, women and men use different words to refer to the same thing.

A thousand years ago in rural China, women devised a secret language called **Nushu**, or woman's writing, to use to communicate with other women in male-dominated China. The women in Hunan province took characters from **standard Chinese** and gave them a new value corresponding to phonetic sounds in the local dialect. At its height, most women in central China corresponded in the language. Nushu poems were common wedding gifts, and women often took Nushu books to the grave. Thousands of poems, songs, letters, and historical anecdotes were written in Nushu over the centuries. The language fell out of use when women were allowed to attend schools and learn written Chinese.

In Japanese, the words for "it's beautiful" are *kirei dawa* if the speaker is a woman and *kirei dana* if the speaker is a man; the words for "(I) want to eat" are *tabetai wa* if the speaker is a woman and *tabetai na* if the speaker is a man. For the most part, women and men use the same nouns, but, as in these examples, the final particle indicates female or male speech. In general, *wa* is used by females and *na* by males. The resulting difference is one of tone rather than of meaning. Japanese male language sounds "stronger, less refined, more direct." Some members of the U.S. military who were taught Japanese by Japanese women learned the female style. To Japanese men, the language sounded "feminine, weak, sensitive."

Within U.S. culture, Miller, Reynolds, and Cambra (1987) have demonstrated that Japanese-American and Chinese-American males use more intense language than female counterparts. And differences such as this are not restricted to the United States. The argument that women and men live in separate cultures is supported by other work done by anthropologists who have shown that women share some common communication behaviors across cultures. Women in completely different cultures are known to engage in ritual laments, spontaneously producing rhyming couplets that express pain, such as over the loss of a loved one. Men are more likely to use language to compete with one another by trading playful insults and put-downs.

The ability of the culture to mold our conception of what is natural or normal behavior for females and males is immense. Although female and male infants are born with similar potentials, parents and other socializing agencies impose different standards of behavior on the offspring in accordance with cultural guidelines. You learn as children what actions and attitudes are associated with your biological self. Along with different communication patterns are different normative expectations. Women clearly exhibit characteristic patterns of behavior that are sufficient to distinguish women from men.

Although there is considerable variation from country to country, the sexes do differ in clothing style, color and reading preferences, and life plans and career choices. Culture shapes the way you think of yourself and how you interact with others. Therefore, as a learned concept, the understanding of gender can vary from culture to culture.

Because feelings, thoughts, and actions are rigidly tied to cultural expectations of gender, all are denied the opportunity to freely express the full range of their humanity. Women are pressured to be submissive and dependent, regardless of individual personality traits, and men are pressured to be assertive, competitive, and in control, regardless of individual personality traits. That pressure is reflected in the language that parents use with children: Girls are more likely to hear twice as many diminutives—affectionate words like *kitty* or *dolly* in place of *cat* or *doll*—than are boys.

Years earlier, Carl Jung (1960) had spoken of masculinity and femininity as inherent in everyone, with both striving for recognition and integration within the functioning of each individual. Jung emphasized the need for all individuals to recognize and integrate within themselves those cross-sex characteristics that are inconsistent with dominant sex role traits. Androgyny, then, has decisive psychological advantages for both sexes. Women and men can then express both masculine and feminine behaviors.

STATUS OF WOMEN

More studies are available on the status of women, and these serve as the basis for our study of cultural influences.

Human Development Index

In 1990, the United Nations Development Programme (UNDP) first used the Human Development Index (HDI) as a measure of life expectancy at birth, educational attainment, and adjusted per capita income. These were selected as quantitative measures of leading a long life, being knowledgeable, and enjoying a decent standard of living. Table 11.1 shows the 20 countries with the highest scores on the HDI.

In its 1993 report, the UNDP calculated separate HDI scores for females for 33 countries from which comparable data were available. The report concluded that no country treated its women as well as it treated its men. In some cases, the gap was substantial. Japan had the world's highest HDI rating that year but fell to 17th on the female HDI scale. Sweden was fifth overall but first on the female version. Gender equality is not dependent on the income level of a country. Several developing countries outperform much richer countries in the opportunities afforded women.

The HDI masks the differences in human development for women and men. In its 1995 report, the UNDP focused even more sharply on the status of women by using two new measures: the Gender-Related Development Index (GDI) to reflect gender imbalances in basic health, education, and income for 130 countries from which comparable data were available and the Gender Empowerment Measure (GEM) to evaluate a country's progress in political and economic advancement of women. The GEM ranked 116 countries with comparable data on women's representation in parliaments, share of positions classified as managerial or professional, participation in the

Table 11.1   Twenty Highest-Scoring Countries on the
Human Development Index

1.   Canada
2.   Norway
3.   United States
4.   Australia
5.   Iceland
6.   Sweden
7.   Belgium
8.   The Netherlands
9.   Japan
10. United Kingdom
11. Finland
12. France
13. Switzerland
14. Germany
15. Denmark
16. Austria
17. Luxembourg
18. Ireland
19. Italy
20. New Zealand

SOURCE: United Nations Development Programme, *Human Development Report,* 2000.

active labor force, and share of national income. Table 11.2 shows the 20 countries rated highest on the GDI, and Table 11.3 shows the 20 countries rated highest on the GEM.

The GDI for every country remains lower than its HDI, implying that there continues to be gender inequality in every country. The closer a country's GDI is to its HDI the less gender disparity there is in the country. Countries with the greatest difference between their HDI and GDI ranks are Oman, Belize, Yemen, and Saudi Arabia.

Literacy and Education

Nearly two-thirds of the world's 862 million illiterate people are women. South Asia reduced its female illiteracy rate from 81% to 67% between 1970 and 1990. The Arab states more than doubled the reduction in women's illiteracy rate from 45% to 19% during the same period. More than one in four

Table 11.2   Twenty Highest-Scoring Countries on the
Gender-Related Development Index

1. Canada
2. Norway
3. United States
4. Australia
5. Iceland
6. Sweden
7. Belgium and Iceland
8. The Netherlands
9. Japan
10. United Kingdom
11. Finland
12. France
13. Switzerland
14. Germany
15. Denmark
16. Austria
17. Luxembourg
18. Ireland
19. Italy
20. New Zealand

SOURCE: United Nations Development Programme, *Human Development Report,* 2000.

women aged 15 to 24 are illiterate in at least 20 countries. Over 40% of African women (except in South Africa) are illiterate; 29% in South Asia (United Nations, 2000).

Women's access to education has increased dramatically. In developed regions of the world, enrollment in primary and secondary education is nearly universal. In South America, the Caribbean, and South Africa, more than 90 girls per 100 school-aged girls are enrolled. In Southeast Asia, western Asia, and northern Africa, the ratios are about 70 for girls and 80 for boys. In South Asia, the ratios are 64 for girls and 77 for boys. In **sub-Saharan Africa** (excluding South Africa) the ratios are 47 for girls and 59 for boys (United Nations, 2000).

In higher education, female enrollment was less than half the male rate in 1970. By 1990, it had reached 70%. More women than men are enrolled in higher education in 32 countries.

Table 11.3   Twenty Highest-Scoring Countries on the
Gender Empowerment Measure

1. Norway
2. Iceland
3. Sweden
4. Denmark
5. Finland
6. Germany
7. The Netherlands
8. Canada
9. New Zealand
10. Belgium
11. Australia
12. Austria
13. United States
14. Switzerland
15. United Kingdom
16. Bahamas
17. Barbados
18. Portugal
19. Spain
20. Venezuela

SOURCE: United Nations Development Programme, *Human Development Report*, 2000.

Life Expectancy

Life expectancy at birth worldwide is 65 years for females and 62 years for males. In countries where females are treated more equally, there are about 106 females for every 100 males. In sub-Saharan Africa, there are 102 females for every 100 males. This ratio is reversed in China and South and West Asia where there are only 94 females for every 100 males.

In industrial nations, maternal deaths are rare. Almost all births are attended by trained health personnel. But according to the World Health Organization, Bangladesh, India, and Pakistan account for 28% of the world's births and 46% of its maternal deaths. In developing countries, fewer than half the births, and in South Asia fewer than a third, are attended by any health personnel.

Table 11.4   Women's Wage as Percentage of Men's Wage, by Selected Countries

Country	Percentage
Tanzania	92.0
Vietnam	91.5
Australia	90.8
Sweden	89.0
Norway	86.0
Colombia	84.7
Turkey	84.5
Jordan	83.5
Denmark	82.6
France	81.0
Egypt	79.5
Poland	78.0
Brazil	76.0
Germany	75.8
United States	75.0
Singapore	71.1
Spain	70.0
United Kingdom	69.7
Canada	63.0
Philippines	60.8
Chile	60.5
China	59.4
Korea	53.5
Bangladesh	42.0

SOURCE: United Nations Development Programme, *Human Development Report,* 1995.

NOTE: World average = 74.9%.

Economics

Women represent over 40% of the global workforce. Outside agriculture, the average wage for women is about three-fourths of men's, ranging from 92% in Tanzania to 42% in Bangladesh (see Table 11.4). Canada ranked first on the overall HDI in 1995 but ninth on the GDI due to the lower participation of women in the labor force and lower average wage rates for women. In the United States in 2000, women earned 76.5% of what men earned—up from 59% in 1977. Women with 4 years of college earn roughly the same median salary as men with a high school education. These statistics need to be interpreted carefully. The 1963 federal Equal Pay Act outlawed gender-based wage discrimination and requires employers to pay women and men the same wages for the same work. The difference in earnings result from women being available to work fewer hours than men, on average, and from lower salaries paid in fields traditionally held by women.

The proportion of women in managerial and administrative positions worldwide is 14%, ranging from 28% in industrial countries to 3% in sub-Saharan Africa. In most of the Arab states and in South Asia, the proportion is less than 10%. In the United States and Canada, women make up 46% and 42% of management, respectively; however, women in management tend to be concentrated in functions such as labor relations and personnel.

The majority of women in the workforce perform manual labor that requires minimal skills. As economies move toward greater use of technology, women are often the first unemployed by the changes. Of the estimated 1.3 billion people living in poverty, more than 70% are women. In the United States in 1940, 40% of the poor were women; in 1980, it was 62%. Poverty has long been a women's issue. In the 1990s, two out of three poor adults were women; one in three female-headed families lived below the poverty line; one in two poor families was headed by a woman.

Violence

Women internationally are the victims of violence rooted in patriarchy and its underlying assumption of the subjugation of women. Many countries have no laws on violence against women. In much of Latin America, the law excuses the murder of a woman by her husband if she is caught in the act of adultery. In other countries, the laws offer limited protection. Domestic violence is treated as a private, family matter.

Female genital mutilation flourishes in many countries in the belief that it prevents promiscuity among women. It is performed on an estimated 2 million children each year in more than 30 countries, primarily throughout the central belt of Africa from Senegal to Somalia and by minority groups in the Middle East and Asia. There are no state or federal laws that ban the practice in the United States.

Women are victims of neglect of daughters, trafficking of girls into prostitution, rape, incest, wife battering, political torture, abuses of refugees, and the ravages of war. One-third of women in Barbados, Canada, the Netherlands, New Zealand, Norway, and the United States report sexual abuse during childhood or adolescence. As stated earlier, an estimated 1 million children, mostly girls in Asia, are forced into prostitution. Studies from Canada, New Zealand, the United Kingdom, and the United States show that one woman in six is raped in her lifetime. And studies from Chile, Mexico, Papua New Guinea, and the Republic of Korea indicate that two-thirds or more of married women have suffered domestic violence.

For example, during most of Korea's history, the wife stayed home and cared for the children and the husband's mother, who lived with them when she became a widow. The husband worked during the day and often spent evenings with his friends. At times, the husband came home after an evening of drinking, and the conflict with his wife over this often resulted in physical abuse that was so common it was not thought of as a problem, just an aspect of marriage. Only recently have Korean married couples recognized equality, shared responsibility, and mutual respect.

Political Participation

In the ancient Roman era, women were not considered citizens. By the 1860s, middle-class women in Great Britain were organizing for voting rights. John Stuart Mill, recently elected to the British Parliament, presented a women's petition for suffrage in 1866, initiating the first parliamentary debate on the subject. Later, in 1869, Mill published *On the Subjection of Women* in which he argued the feminist case in terms of liberal individualism. Particularly in Australia, New Zealand, and the United States, the women's suffrage movement gained strength from the temperance movement. New Zealand became the first country in the world to grant women the vote in 1893. A South Australia state followed the next year and Australia as a whole in 1902. Only in the 20th century did women gain the right to vote and to be elected to political office in almost all countries that have representative governments (see Table 11.5). Until 1918, the Texas Constitution excluded "idiots, imbeciles, aliens, the insane, and women" from voting. Today, women cannot vote in Kuwait; only men over 21 who have held Kuwaiti nationality for at least 20 years can vote.

Worldwide, women's representation in national parliaments is about 13.1%, ranging from 3.6% in the Arab states to 38.9% in the Nordic countries. In 50 countries, women constitute 5% or less of the parliament. These countries range from very poor to reasonably affluent. This would seem to indicate that

Table 11.5   Year in Selected Countries That Women Won the Right to Vote

Country	Year
Finland and Norway	1906-1907
Denmark	1915
Germany, Sweden, and the United Kingdom	1918
United States	1920
France	1944
Italy and Japan	1945
India	1950
Mexico	1953
Egypt	1956
Switzerland	1971
Yemen	1984

exclusion from politics is not as much a function of a country's level of development or the educational and income level of women as it is of social and cultural constraints.

Only six countries have more than one-third female representation:

> There is no occupation concerned with the management of social affairs which belongs either to women or to men, as such.
>
> —Plato, *The Republic*, circa 390 B.C.E.

Sweden, Denmark, Finland, Norway, the Netherlands, and Iceland (see Table 11.6). The leaders in female representation among developing nations are South Africa (30%), Argentina (28%), Cuba (28%), and China (21.8%).

Local representation surpasses national representation in about half of the countries. In 1995, 20.7% of all U.S. state legislators were women. The range of women legislators was 36% in Arizona to 8% in Alabama in 2001. In 2003, 73 women serve in the U.S. Congress (14 in the Senate and 59 in the House). The number of women in statewide elective executive posts is 79, and state legislatures include 22.3% women.

Representation will increase as more countries reserve seats for women. According to the United Nations Development Fund for Women (UNIFEM), 32 countries have some kind of female quota for local or national assemblies. Beginning in 1994, India reserved a third of all *panchayat* (local council) seats for women, and in Uganda, by law a third of local council seats must go to women. Other countries have a quota for candidates. Germany's Christian

Table 11.6   Percentage of Parliament Seats Held by Women as of January 2000

By Region	Percentage Both Houses Combined
Nordic countries	38.9
Americas	15.3
Asia	14.6
Pacific	14.1
Europe (excluding Nordic countries)	12.4
Sub-Saharan Africa	11.3
Arab states	3.4

By Country Rank	Lower or Single House	Upper House
1. Sweden	42.7	0
2. Denmark	37.4	0
3. Finland	37.0	0
4. Norway	36.4	0
5. The Netherlands	36.0	26.7
6. Iceland	34.9	0
7. Germany	30.9	59.8
8. South Africa	30.0	31.5[a]
9. New Zealand	29.2	0
10. Bosnia and Herzegovina	28.2	0
18. Australia	22.4	30.3
20. China	21.8	0
23. Canada	20.6	30.5
28. United Kingdom	18.4	0.6
29. Mexico	18.2	17.2
44. United States	13.3	9.0
65. India	9.0	8.6
94. Japan	4.6	17.1
100. Republic of Korea	3.7	0
Djibouti	0	0
Jordan	0	0
Kuwait	0	0
United Arab Emirates	0	0

SOURCE: Inter-Parliamentary Union, http://www.ipu.org/wmn-e/world.htm.

a. South Africa figures do not include the 36 rotating delegates appointed on an ad hoc basis.

Democratic Union (former Chancellor Helmut Kohl's party) reserved a third of party posts and election candidates for women beginning in 1995. And in Belgium, one gender cannot make up more than two-thirds of the candidates for the Chamber of Representatives and the Senate.

Worldwide, women's representation in cabinets was about 6.8% in 1996. Nearly 30% of governments worldwide had no women members, and many who did limited women's participation to areas such as social services and health. Leading countries include Finland (39%), Norway (35%), and the Netherlands and Seychelles (31% each). In 1995, Sweden formed the world's first gender-balanced cabinet: 50% of the ministers are women.

In 1997, 4 countries had a woman head of state, 10 had women United Nations ambassadors, and 17 had women speakers of parliament.

Laws

With limited participation in political decision making, women worldwide are not treated as equal to men in laws governing travel, marriage and divorce, acquisition of nationality, property management, employment seeking, and property inheritance, as the following examples show:

- In some Arab countries, a husband's consent is necessary for a wife to obtain a passport. Women cannot leave the country without the husband's permission in Iran.

- Married women are under the permanent guardianship of husbands and have no right to manage property in Botswana, Chile, Lesotho, Namibia, and Swaziland.

- Husbands can restrict a wife's employment outside the home in Bolivia, Guatemala, and Syria.

In 1979, the United Nations adopted the Convention on the Elimination of All Forms of Discrimination Against Women. Forty-one countries have not signed it; 139 have. Of those 139, 6 have signed without ratification (including the United States) and 43 have ratified it with reservations.

COMPARISON OF INDIVIDUAL COUNTRIES

It is no surprise that gender equality is not explained by a country's income level. Hofstede (1980) identified masculinity as one value dimension

Norwegian stamp honoring
International Women's Year.

across which cultures vary. The status of women is dependent on a culture's values.

Nordic Countries

The five countries of Denmark, Finland, Iceland, Norway, and Sweden have a shared political, economic, and cultural development. Danish, Faroese, Icelandic, Norwegian, and Swedish are all North Germanic languages. A Dane, a Norwegian, and a Swede can understand each other with varying degrees of difficulty, but none will fully understand Faroese or Icelandic without studying the language. Finnish, however, is a Finno-Ugric language related to Estonian and Hungarian. The term "Nordic countries" is used to refer exclusively to these countries.

Hofstede (1997) argues that the concentration of feminine cultures in northwestern Europe (Denmark, Finland, the Netherlands, Norway, and Sweden) derives from shared historical factors. During major portions of their history, values associated with femininity were functional. A culture based on sailing and trading would value maintaining good interpersonal relationships and caring for ships and merchandise. During the Viking period, women managed the villages while men were away on long trips. And later, the association of trading towns of the Hanseatic League required feminine values to maintain such an association.

The Nordic countries have a strong value for personal freedom. One of the expressions of this freedom is that in Finland, Norway, and Sweden all residents have free access to the forests, seas, and uncultivated land. The Nordic people were converted to Catholicism in the 10th to 12th centuries, but the Lutheran Reformation overcame most Catholic customs and memories in the 16th century. The Lutheran ideal of enabling everyone to read the Bible on his or her own encouraged strong education programs that with a strong work ethic contributed to decreasing social inequality.

A long tradition of egalitarianism and a strong women's movement contributed to Norway having one of the world's most gender-balanced political systems. Women's movements in Norway since the beginning of the 20th century have had a politics-first strategy. In 1981 (and again in 1986-1989 and 1990-1996), the head of Norway's Labour Party, Gro Harlem Brundtland, was Norway's first woman prime minister. In 2003, Finland became the first country in Europe to have women serving as prime minister and president at the same time.

While the demographic data do seem to support the Hofstede ranking of the Nordic countries, there is another interpretation. That interpretation is that the political and governmental structures are still dominated by men with patriarchal values who espouse equality as a rhetorical act in order to retain power. More than 80% of the electorate vote in national elections. Since the mid-1970s, political parties have instituted quotas for female representation. Women in political parties have used the slogan "women representing women."

It is not surprising that these countries have adopted gender equality and women's empowerment as national policies. Consultative rather than confrontational politics focus political competition on issues. The Nordic countries have legislated equal rights, inexpensive child care, free contraception and abortions, and parental leave policies. The women's movement now addresses the issues of wage differences, job segregation, and violence against women. Table 11.7 shows that the Nordic countries also rank high on foreign aid and honesty.

Mexico

For most of the 20th century, Mexican politics were dominated by what was called the "revolutionary family"—men who fought the Mexican Revolution and their offspring—and by groups of male politicians known as *camarillas*.

Women have become more prominent in recent years. In the 1980s, enrollment of women in the universities skyrocketed. Economic crises forced more women into the workforce. And while the government's response to the 1985 Mexico City earthquake was ineffectual, grassroots women's groups formed to deal with the emergency.

In government, the left-wing Democratic Revolution Party (PRD) in 1998 announced that women would make up half of its candidates for high offices by 2000. The dominant Institutional Revolutionary Party (PRI) set a quota of 30% for congressional candidates on the nationwide slate. Women in the legislature from different parties are working together to promote women's issues such as laws punishing violence within the family and sexual harassment. In 1998, Rosario Green was appointed Mexico's foreign minister, the highest-ranking woman ever in the nation's government. And by 2000, women made up more than 15% of the Mexican Congress, exceeding the percentage of women in the U.S. House. Newly elected Vicente Fox's inner cabinet

Table 11.7   Rankings of Countries by Foreign Aid and Corruption

Share of GNP Spent by Selected Nations on Foreign Aid in 1994	
Country	*Percentage*
Norway	1.05
Denmark	1.03
Sweden	.96
France	.64
Canada	.43
Germany	.34
United Kingdom	.31
Japan	.29
Italy	.27
United States	.15

Ranking of Least Corrupt Countries, as Perceived by Businesspeople

1. New Zealand
2. Denmark
3. Sweden
4. Finland
5. Canada
6. Norway
7. Singapore
8. Switzerland
9. The Netherlands
10. Austria

SOURCE: Organization for Economic Cooperation and Development, *U.S. News & World Report,* May 20, 1996, p. 29, and *Time,* June 10, 1996, p. 24.

included 3 women out of 19 appointees, and more than half of the cabinet of the Mexico City mayor were women.

China

The experience in China demonstrates that a country with a low per capita income can achieve human development levels similar to those countries with much higher per capita incomes when it makes a political commitment to do so. China is 10 GDI ranks above Saudi Arabia, even though its real per capita income is one-fifth as high.

In traditional Chinese culture, the family comes before the individual and boys are valued more than girls. In the family, the respect for age exists as does pride in sons. Women have lived by the Confucian ethic of serving fathers in their youth, husbands in marriage, and sons in old age. Before the Communist revolution, girls were subjected to feet-binding, and peasant girls were at risk of being kidnapped and sold into marriage.

Even though the improved status of women in China was state initiated, barriers such as Confucian traditions still remain (Wang, 1996). The very first law passed by the Chinese Communist Party abolished the holding of concubines and gave women the right to own property, choose husbands, sue for divorce, and use their own names. China's constitution states, "Women enjoy equal rights as men in all aspects, including politics, economy, culture, society and family life."

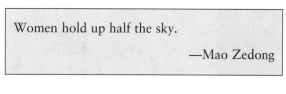

Women hold up half the sky.

—Mao Zedong

China's literacy rates for women more than doubled in the past 50 years to 77.1% in 2001. Enrollment in higher education increased tenfold. The average life expectancy of women in China climbed from 36 years in 1949 to 72 years in 1995, three years longer than the average life expectancy for men in China.

Between 1979 and 1988, women's employment grew nearly 5% a year, and by 1997 as many as 56% of Chinese women were in the labor force. While women in the countryside continue to have employment opportunities, in the later 1990s massive downsizing of money-losing state enterprises put millions of women out of work. Women made up 40% of the urban workforce but 60% of its laid-off workers. Chinese women hold 30% of official jobs, and more than a fifth of parliamentary deputies are women. That gives China the 4th highest female participation rate among developing countries and the 12th highest in the world.

Family planning has been well established in China since 1956. It was not until 1971, though, that a reduction in the **fertility rate** became a national priority. That year the third family planning campaign known as the *Wan, Xi, Shao* program was initiated. These terms represent the three slogans of the campaign: late marriage, longer intervals between children, and fewer children. The fertility rate fell from 5.4% in 1971 to 2.7% in 1979.

In 1979, the **one-child campaign** was introduced. The goals of the program were to eliminate all births above or equal to three per family and to encourage most families, particularly in urban areas, to have no more than one child.

This program was undertaken to hold China's population at 1.3 billion by the end of the 20th century. However, China's population is so large that even this slow rate of growth will increase the population to 1.6 billion by 2050. For example, even with the campaign in effect, in 1992, 24 million children were born, a figure only slightly less than the population of Canada. In most of China's major cities, a person from a single-child family who marries is allowed to have two children. As children born under the one-child policy in the past two decades come of age, by about 2005 nearly every couple will be eligible to have two children.

The Chinese government went to great lengths to ensure the success of the one-child policy. It was a familiar sight in China to see billboards advertising birth control and the one-child goals, yet enforcement became sporadic because of loopholes, corruption, and defiance. Families with unauthorized births paid a fee. It was also not unusual to hear of coercion, abortions, and sterilizations being used to enforce the one-child policy. Sonogram technology has contributed to abortions of female fetuses—a practice the government condemns. Still, the gap between male and female births continues to widen. In 1999, China had a ratio at birth of 100 girls to 117 boys.

The people of China have made a critical choice. As a family-oriented culture, it was not unusual for one couple to have as many as eight children. Now, with the one-child policy, large families are much less common. The children of today's children will have no brothers or sisters, no aunts, uncles, or cousins. The family will consist only of grandmothers, grandfathers, mother, father, and child. Implications for the society range from pampered overweight children dubbed "Little Emperors"—four grandparents to spoil one child—to the world's largest elderly population no longer being able to rely on a large family to provide care in old age.

Few Chinese can understand why the United States does not look more favorably on China's efforts to limit the growth of its huge population.

Japan

In pre-World War II Japan, education was completely segregated by gender. Women were effectively forbidden from voting or going to 4-year colleges. In 1925, Japan's fertility rate averaged 5.1 children per woman. The postwar constitution clearly stipulated equality under law and excludes discrimination on the basis of sex, but in the 1993 HDI report, Japan had the world's highest HDI rating but fell to 17th on the female HDI scale.

The role of women is changing in Japan. With high levels of education, health care, and income, Japanese women have more choices than ever before. Japanese women are postponing marriage. Japanese women's average age at first marriage is 27.0, and for Japanese men, 28.8 (per 2000 data). (In the United States, the average age in 1994 was 24.5.) Although the average age for men at their first marriage has been relatively steady since 1987, the average age for women has been climbing since 1992. Also, the fertility rate has plummeted to the lowest in Japanese history: 1.53 in 1991. As a result, without immigration, Japan's population will begin to decline by 2007. The decline in the marriage rate and the relatively older age at which couples now get married, on average, are considered to be two factors behind the downtrend in the birthrate.

The modern trend is away from traditional large multigenerational families and toward small families consisting of a husband and wife and one or two children. Some writers have described Japanese families today as like families in the United States in the 1950s—except the houses are much smaller. High-rise apartments are common. The average home in Tokyo is a four-room condo of less than 1,000 square feet. Within the home, women control the household income and family life. It is the wife who handles the money and makes all of the family's financial decisions. In a country where serving men had been the long-accepted female role, some continue to want the woman inside the house all the time to serve her husband's needs day and night.

> Japanese men have a saying: "To have the best of all worlds is to have an American house, eat Chinese food, and have a Japanese wife. To have the worst of all worlds is to have a Japanese house, eat British food, and have an American wife."

Women are increasingly active outside the home. A higher proportion of women than of men have voted in elections since 1980, but women constitute only about 10% of the Japanese legislature. Even though the national legislature and cabinet remain male dominated, women are a significant force in local government.

A 1986 equal employment opportunity law prevents discrimination against women in hiring. Some companies are using a two-track hiring system, which puts most female employees on career tracks to lower-paying positions. The traditional female role reappeared during Japan's economic slump in the mid-1990s when there was a scarcity of jobs. Women job applicants and existing female employees began to experience increased sexual harassment. Some accepted the harassment as normal in Japan's male-centered workplace.

Among Japanese holidays are the Festival for Children ages 3, 5, and 7, also called *Shichi-go-san*, and Adults' Day (or Coming of Age Day), also called *Seijin no hi*, for those turning 20 years old (right). All young people who turn 20 in that year are celebrated on Seijin no hi. Twenty is the age considered to be the beginning of adulthood. It is also the minimum legal age for voting, drinking, and smoking. Celebrations are held nationwide in every town with most of the people turning 20 participating in formal dresses. Seijin no hi is a national holiday.

SOURCE: Copyright © 1984 and 1986, Japan National Tourist Organization. Reprinted with permission.

Nonetheless, the most dramatic change in modern Japan is the changing role of women. Prescribed gender roles are breaking down. Japanese women are defining a unique interpretation of equality in gender relations in the home and in society. Along with changes affecting family structure, views on the proper relationship between women and men, student and teacher, employee and employer are all changing. In 2001, Crown Prince Naruhito and Princess Masako gave birth to their first child—a girl. This may become a catalyst for legal, cultural, and social change and accelerate the redefinition of women's roles. Also in 2001, Prime Minister Junichiro Koizumi appointed five women to his cabinet.

South Korea

Korea's version of Confucianism is a "neo-Confucian" set of values devised as a formal state ideology in 1932 by Yi Song Kye, the first king of the last Korean dynasty, imposed as a way to consolidate power. So deeply rooted and pervasive are these ethics that the average citizen does not think of them as Confucian.

South Korea's family law institutionalizes many elements of this traditional male-dominated family succession system. In many households, the eldest son is held in highest esteem to continue the lineage of an unbroken line of male-linked kin, perpetuate the family name, inherit the family property, and preside over ancestral rites. A bride is absorbed into her husband's household and is expected to adopt its ways in everything from laundry methods to cooking styles.

A Korean wife who does not produce a healthy son under Korean custom could be driven from the home and deprived of her status as a wife. Under the law, women are denied the right to become heads of household—a condition with implications for divorce, child custody, and communal property ownership. Most of the Confucian-based discrimination against women in the nation's laws has been eliminated in recent years.

India

Similar to China, India has a history of female infanticide, which explains why there are 35.5 million fewer females than males. Most Indian parents prefer to have boys because girls require a costly dowry at marriage. The advent of sex determination tests has led to widespread abortions of unwanted females. India has recently passed a law preventing doctors from telling parents the sex of the fetus, but still in 2000 there were 927 girls to 1,000 boys.

Yet India is one country with female quotas for a seat in parliament. India already had 50 years of a tradition of quotas for indigenous peoples, outcasts, and Indians of British descent in state and national parliaments. The idea of extending quotas to women was suggested by former Prime Minister Rajiv Gandhi, son of Indira Gandhi, India's only female leader. India's Parliament has not extended the female quota to higher offices.

Sub-Saharan Africa

African societies are largely patriarchal societies. Despite constitutional guarantees of female equality, Zimbabwe's Supreme Court issued a ruling in 1999 declaring that it is in "the nature of African society that women are not equal to men. Women should never be considered adults within the family, but only as a junior male or teenager." Women have fared better in countries where there was participation in campaigns against colonialism, White minority rule, or authoritarian regimes. South Africa's postapartheid Constitution, for example, bars discrimination based on gender, marital status, sexual orientation, and pregnancy.

In Uganda, one-third of local council seats must, by law, go to women. Uganda's quotas grew out of the National Resistance Army's (NRA) guerrilla war in the 1980s when women fought side by side with men. In recognition, each of the rebel councils includes a secretary for women's affairs. After the NRA victory, the new president applied the same policy to national

> In Kenya, women are taught that sex other than that to conceive children is to give pleasure to men.

politics. The women in Uganda's Parliament were successful in amending a land act to allow married women to share property ownership with husbands and in increasing women's access to education.

Saudi women and children.

SOURCE: Photo by Jodi Cobb © National Geographic Society. Reprinted with permission.

Arab States

In 7th-century pre-Islamic Arabia, girls were seen as having little value. Female infants could be buried alive. The Koran, which was revealed to the prophet Muhammad, revolutionized life for women. In the Koran, all are equal in God's eyes—women and men, slave and master, subject and ruler. Against the status quo of the time, Islam gave women rights in marriage, divorce, property ownership, business, and inheritance. Muhammad welcomed women in the mosque as members of the community of believers.

Muslims would say that women in Arab cultures are equal to men. The rights and responsibilities of women are equal to, but not identical with, those of men. In Arab cultures, equality and sameness are two quite different things. It is said that in some ways women are deprived but are compensated in other ways. Thus, the Arab woman is equal as an independent human being, equal in the pursuit of knowledge, and equal in the freedom of expression. She is the wife and mother and is entitled to complete provision and total maintenance by her husband. She may work and own property herself.

Actual practices have not met Islam's ideal. Many Muslims contend, then, that the repressive practices against women ascribed to Islam are based on patriarchal cultural traditions, social considerations, and contested interpretations of the Koran. Even though women's education has advanced in the Arab states, women face barriers in building and using their capabilities. Several Arab states rank markedly higher in terms of average levels of human development than in terms of gender equality.

In Arab cultures, a man is considered a descendant only of his father and his paternal grandfather. A man's honor resides in the number of sons he sires. A man belongs to his father's family. A divorced woman may keep her children until they are 7 years old, but then they go to the father's family. Decisions are made by the family patriarch—not by the individual.

Marriages in Saudi Arabia today may still be alliances between families. Islamic law gives the Saudi woman the right to approve or reject her family's choice.

Legally, a Muslim man can have four wives at once—if he can give each wife equal material goods and equal time—but a woman can marry only one man. Monogamy is the common practice today. "Strict disciplining" of women is openly encouraged. Divorce is discouraged, but marriage can be terminated by mutual consent, judicial ruling on the wife's request, or repudiation by the husband. He needs only to say, "I divorce you" in front of a witness. He does not need to give a reason. If the woman does not want the divorce, she can claim her rights in court according to Islamic law.

While not true of all Islamic countries, Saudi Arabia does enforce strict codes of behavior for women. Women are not allowed to register in hotels or leave the country without a male relative's or husband's written permission. Before 1999, women—including foreigners—were not permitted to drive cars. Since 1999, Saudi Arabian women who are married and over 35 years old have been allowed to drive cars during daylight hours, provided they have the husband's written permission. Even Saudi-trained scholars agree that the restriction on women driving is not grounded in the Koran but is a modern social consideration to prevent women and men from being together in unsafe or unexpected circumstances.

A traditional Saudi woman does not go out alone. She speaks to no man other than her husband or blood kin. All public facilities are segregated by sex. Women who work outside the home work in capacities in which the customers or clients are other women exclusively. Today's Saudi women may be teachers, computer technicians, social workers, laboratory technicians, physicists, engineers, bankers, or filmmakers, but most work in all-female facilities. Saudi society is structured to keep a woman within strictly defined limits to protect her chastity.

In Saudi Arabia, women must follow a rigid dress code. Observant Muslim women dress modestly and must be completely covered except for face and hands. Women walk the streets wearing a long black cloak called an **abaya** (also known by the Persian word *chador*). Most use veils to cover the face. Under the abaya, however, anything goes—from colorful cottons to blue jeans to haute couture.

The abaya and the veil represent an old tradition to safeguard women from advances by strange men. She is not permitted to expose her body before strangers—thus the abaya and the veil represent honor, dignity, chastity, purity, and integrity.

The majority of Saudi women are willing to accept women's position in society in return for the guarantee of security that Islamic traditions provide. Those who want change want it within the context of the Arab culture.

STATUS OF FAMILIES

The family unit—however defined—remains the organization in which the majority of human beings continue to exist. Family could mean any one of several groupings. The **nuclear family** is composed of one married pair and their unmarried offspring. Anthropologist George P. Murdock found that in 92 of the 192 societies he studied the extended family was predominant. The **extended family** is composed of two or more nuclear families joined by an extension of the parent-child relationship (Murdock, 1949).

French social historian Emmanuel Todd (1985) developed a schema of family types in an attempt to link a country's prevailing family structure with its political ideology, arguing that why a country has a particular form of government is that it is consistent with the prevailing family structure. Todd based his schema on the earlier work of 19th-century French political philosopher Le Play (1884). Le Play identified two criteria: (a) whether sons continued to live with their parents after marriage (community family) or set up independent homes (nuclear family) and (b) whether inheritance was shared among all sons or whether one son only inherited.

Todd added the criteria of marriage partner choice. **Exogamy** refers to the practice of marrying outside a defined group. **Endogamy** refers to the practice of marrying within a defined group. Todd focused on whether marriage between first cousins was accepted or not.

Using these criteria, Todd developed the following family types, which he related to the countries in which they were dominant:

- Exogamous community family in which equality of brothers is defined by rules of inheritance, married sons cohabit with their parents, and cousins do not marry. Spouses are selected by custom. Typical in China, Vietnam, Russia, Hungary, and northern India.

- Authoritarian family in which there is inequality of brothers as inheritance rules transfer patrimony to one of the sons, the married heir cohabits with his parents, and there is little or no marriage between the children of two brothers. Spouses are selected by parents. Typical in Japan, Korea, Germany, Austria, Sweden, Norway, Scotland, and Ireland.

- Egalitarian nuclear family in which equality of brothers is laid down by inheritance rules, married children do not cohabit with their parents, and there is no marriage between the children of brothers. Spouses are selected by the individual with a strong exogamous obligation. Typical in northern France, northern Italy, central and southern Spain, central Portugal, Greece, Poland, and Latin America.

- Absolute nuclear family in which there are no precise inheritance rules so there is frequent use of wills, married children do not cohabit with their parents, and there is no marriage between children of brothers. Spouses are selected by the individual with a strong exogamous obligation. Typical in Holland, Denmark, and the Anglo-Saxon world.

- Endogamous community family in which there is equality between brothers established by inheritance rules, married children cohabit with their parents, and there is frequent marriage between children of brothers. Spouses are selected by custom. Typical in the Arab world, Turkey, Iran, Afghanistan, and Pakistan.

- Asymmetrical community family in which equality between brothers is established by inheritance rules, married sons cohabit with their parents, and marriages between the children of brothers is prohibited, but there is a preference for marriages between the children of brothers and sisters. Spouses are selected by custom. Typical in southern India.

- Anomie family in which there is uncertainty about equality between brothers since inheritance rules are egalitarian in theory but flexible in practice, cohabitation of married children with parents rejected in theory but accepted in practice, and consanguine marriage possible and sometimes frequent. Spouses are selected by the individual with a weak exogamous obligation. Typical in Cambodia, Laos, Thailand, Indonesia, the Philippines, and South American Indian cultures.

Knighton (1999) demonstrated a correlation between Hofstede's individualism dimension and Todd's family types. Countries with predominantly absolute nuclear families and with authoritarian families tend to be individualistic; those with egalitarian nuclear families tend to be collectivist. Countries that have rules regarding equal partition of parental property among all offspring tend to be collectivist. Those countries that have rules prescribing unequal partition of inheritance and those that have historically allowed parents (usually fathers) to have full freedom in deciding who will inherit tend to be individualist.

Marriage

Cultures regulate how many spouses a person can have, which partner has more authority and dominance in the union, and from what group a person can choose. Buss (1989, 1994) reported a study of criteria for selecting marriage partners in 37 countries. Mutual love, kindness, emotional stability, intelligence, and health were universally desired, but others varied by cultural dimensions. Brides in collectivist countries want age differences at marriage to be larger and they want their husbands to be wealthy. Industriousness is a minor factor and chastity not at all. Bridegrooms in collectivist countries want age differences at marriage to be larger and put more stress on the bride being industrious, wealthy, and chaste. Grooms in high uncertainty avoidance and in masculine countries more highly value chastity. And in masculine countries, industriousness is deemed more important for women than for men; in feminine countries, it is equally important or unimportant.

Hofstede (1996) studied boyfriend and husband preferences of women in eight Asian cities. In the more masculine cultures, boyfriends should have more personality and more affection, intelligence, and sense of humor. Husbands should be more healthy, wealthy, and understanding. In the more feminine cultures, there was little or no difference between the preferred characteristics of boyfriends and husbands. Hofstede concludes then that in masculine countries love and family life may be seen as separated, whereas in feminine countries they are the same.

In Western countries, marriage as an institution has waned (see Table 11.8). More than a quarter of all children born in the United States, a third of those

Table 11.8   Divorce Rate per 100 Marriages

Country	1970	1990
Canada	18.6	38.3
Czechoslovakia	21.8	32.0
Denmark	25.1	44.0
England and Wales	16.2	41.7
France	12.0	31.5
Greece	5.0	12.0
Hungary	25.0	31.0
Italy	5.0	8.0
The Netherlands	11.0	28.1
Sweden	23.4	44.1
United States	42.3	54.8
(former) West Germany	12.2	29.2

SOURCE: Bruce, Lloyd, and Leonard (1995).

in France, and half of those in Sweden and Denmark are born outside marriage. The Population Council research found that between the early 1970s and mid-1980s the number of single-parent households rose worldwide. In the United States, the figure rose from 13% to 23.9%. In the United States, Australia, and Canada, more than half of all one-parent families are considered poor. In Great Britain and Germany, it is about one-third. In the industrialized world, only in the Nordic countries is the poverty rate below 10% for one-parent families.

Worldwide, with more women moving into the workforce, the parents' role in preparing children for adulthood is diminishing. A Population Council report (Bruce, Lloyd, & Leonard, 1995) found that in only 1 of 10 diverse nations—Indonesia—did both parents devote more than a combined average of 7.5 hours a week in direct child care. In parts of Africa where the extended family had an important role in children's socialization, the decline of the kinship system has left children without their traditional direction.

The Nordic countries with the greatest gender equity and the United States with strong individualism values may demonstrate that individual freedom and self-fulfillment affect the form and duration of the family. The authoritarian father rule has given way to a democratization in these cultures freeing women and children from domestic tyrannies. Of course, families held together by duty and social responsibility still exist, but the trends demonstrate that cultural values affect the composition, size, and role of families.

STATUS OF CHILDREN

The concept of "child" varies worldwide. Children have been directly involved in household economies for thousands of years. In agricultural societies, children were seen as assets as they worked in the fields while acquiring life and social skills. French historian Philippe Ariés (1962) described how the concept is now defined in Western cultures. As individuality, privacy, family, and home emerged in the 15th through 19th centuries, children were set apart from the everyday life of adults. Industralization limited children's economic role, and legislation restricted and later banned their paid labor altogether. The economic role was replaced with compulsory education. Children in Western cultures became dependents.

In 1989, the United Nations unanimously adopted the Convention on the Rights of the Child, the first human-rights treaty to be almost universally ratified. Only Somalia and the United States have not ratified it. The convention asserts that every child has a legal right to a name, a family, health, and education. It also aims to limit and regulate child labor.

A 1994 United Nations report concludes that more progress has been made in the past 50 years in providing health care and education to children than was made in the previous 2,000 years. Since World War II, deaths of children under 5 years of age have been halved. The percentage of rural families with access to safe drinking water has risen from less than 10% to 60%. Overall, between 70% and 80% of all children now have basic health and sanitation needs met. And despite the growth in population, the percentage of children in developing countries who receive at least some education has risen from less than half to more than 75%.

The other side of the picture is that some 12.2 million children younger than 5 die each year, most from preventable causes such as respiratory infections, diarrhea, measles, and malaria. India is home to more malnourished children than any other country, with some 75 million younger than age 5. Eighteen of the 20 worst-performing countries in terms of mortality among children younger than 5 are in Africa.

After declining for decades, child labor is on the increase. Child labor has become the major form of child abuse, with children forced to work in debt bondage or even in conditions of slavery—particularly as child prostitutes. Statistics on child labor are difficult to come by, but estimates are that 250 million children under age 15 work worldwide, about half of them full-time, and many under dangerous conditions for low or no wages. One-quarter of the world's child labor is said to be in India. In Bangladesh, 40% of the 700,000 garment workers are children; in Nepal, 160,000 children work in carpet mills

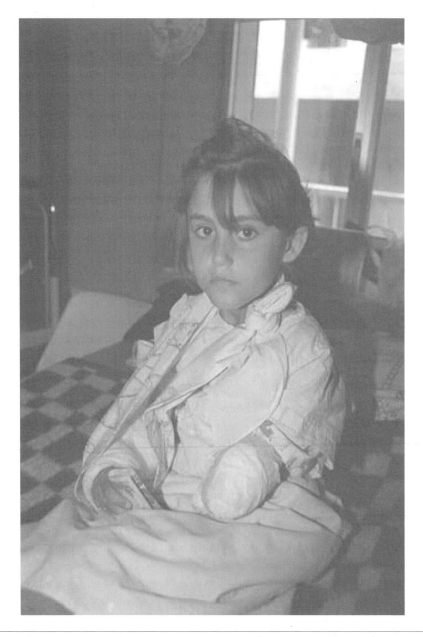

In the past decade, wars have killed more than 2 million children, injured between 4 and 5 million, orphaned more than a million, made 12 million homeless, and left 10 million severely traumatized. Many of these young victims have been the casualties of landmine explosions.

SOURCE: UN/DPI. Photo by J. Isaac. Used by permission.

under conditions little better than slavery (Pradhan, 1993); in Pakistan, children work in sporting goods companies making field hockey sticks, soccer balls, and volleyballs that are exported to the United States.

An estimated 1 million youngsters are prostitutes in Asia, particularly in Cambodia, China, India, the Philippines, Sri Lanka, Taiwan, and Thailand. Young rural women are recruited as prostitutes by procurers who often provide the girls' parents with new homes or money. Families in northern Thailand have started to celebrate the birth of a daughter, knowing that she can be sold to a brothel at age 10. Of the up to 1 million females working in urban Thai brothels, 25% are children. Some Asian governments are now prosecuting foreigners who have sex with female and male minors. The United Nations Children's Fund (also known as UNICEF) estimates that at least 100,000 homeless children in the United States are prostitutes.

The minimum age for recruitment of soldiers, as specified in the Convention on the Rights of the Child that has been signed by more than 160 countries, is 15. Girl and boy soldiers are most common in Africa. UNICEF issued a report in 1995 stating that at least 6,000 children under age 15 fought in Liberia's civil war and that 2 million children were killed in wars in the past decade. Millions more are disabled, made homeless, or orphaned. A 2001 report showed that as many as 300,000 children in 41 countries are actively fighting as soldiers.

FROM THE INTERCULTURAL PERSPECTIVE

Although the political and economic status of women is higher in some countries than in others, in all countries the status of women is lower than the status of men. It does not matter if a country is rich or poor; large differences between women's and men's status can occur in any country. Even though women and men do not have the same status, they are the most equal in the Nordic countries—Denmark, Finland, Norway, and Sweden—where women have a high rate of participation in government and their incomes are the closest to men's. In countries where there is a big difference in the economic status of women and men, there is often a noticeable lack of political participation and representation by women.

Girls and boys grow up in different worlds where they learn to communicate in different ways. For girls, language is for connection and intimacy. They play in small groups and share secrets. If a disagreement occurs while playing, girls typically stop the game and start a new one to avoid conflict. Boys, however, are taught that language is for getting and maintaining status and independence. They often play in larger groups and do team activities. When a disagreement occurs, boys typically stop the game and argue over the rules. In this way, they compete for status and the ability to control the activities of other boys. These two differing ideas of communication (language of connection or language of status) also are reflected in other aspects of women's and men's communication. For example, more women make suggestions, whereas more men give orders; more women use and accept touching more than most men do; and more women use conversation to create a feeling of connection, whereas most men give information. It is important to remember that these differences reflect only the average of all women and all men. In every culture, differences exist between women and men, and many of these differences are the result of cultural expectations and expected gender behavior. All people have similar potentials, but as we grow up we are taught gender roles that separate females from males and limit our potentials. For example, all people have the same potential for feeling emotions, but females are generally allowed to show a wider range of them. In modern times, the media have a strong influence on our images of women and men.

Key Terms

abaya
endogamy
exogamy
extended family
fertility rate

gender
nuclear family
Nushu
one-child campaign
sex

sexism
standard Chinese
sub-Saharan Africa

CHAPTER 12

Contact Between Cultures

What You Can Learn From This Chapter

How discursive imperialism contributed to colonialism

Diffusion and convergence processes

Communication strategy of adapting to the receiver in the diffusion process

Marketing of U.S. cultural icons

Fears underlying cultural hegemony

In this chapter, you'll examine what happens when people from diverse cultures interact with one another. First, you'll focus on diffusion, or the spread of practices from one culture to another. You'll identify the roles in the diffusion process and the characteristics of those most likely to use new practices first. You'll see through examples that key to successful diffusion is adapting the new practice to the receiving culture.

Then, in contrast, you'll look at the most successful of U.S. marketing abroad: the marketing of U.S. cultural icons such as Coca-Cola and McDonald's. In contrast to other products, icons are minimally changed for the receiving culture. Finally, you'll look at cultural hegemony, or the fear of the influence one culture can develop over another.

COLONIALISM

Cultures of humans have been coming into contact with one another for untold centuries. The nature of that contact probably varied widely. However, for the purpose of better understanding the relations among peoples and countries today, an examination of contact between cultures must begin with colonialism.

Hawaii

In chants, legends, and *mele* ("vocal music"), Hawaiians trace the origins of the culture to daring seafarers who discovered and colonized the islands. Sometime around 1000 A.D., isolated from further outside influence, a unique culture emerged. Hawaii's society was hereditary and composed of the *ali'i* ("ruling class"), *kahuna* ("priests" or "experts"), *maka'âinana* ("commoners"), and *kauwâ* ("slaves"). The society operated under a strict *kapu* ("restriction," "consequence," "separation," or "forbidden") system that dictated daily activity between the classes and between the people and nature and the gods. A culture of about 1 million people had developed a harmony with its isolated, island environment (Young, 1980).

Captain James Cook arrived in 1778. Edward Said (1978, 1981) describes the contact and subsequent linguistic construction of non-Western cultures as "Orientalism," a process of labeling the peoples of "underdeveloped" cultures as insignificant "others." Captain Cook and his men, for example, wrote of the Hawaiians as "savage or animal-like or heathen." While the Hawaiians were labeled as savages, the Europeans interpreted the Hawaiians' actions as deifying Captain Cook. The ship's journals state that "they [the Hawaiians] venerated [Cook] almost to adoration," looked upon Cook as "a kind of superior being," honored him "like a god," and "as far as related to the person of Captain Cook, they seemed close to adoration" (Obeyesekere, 1992). The Europeans labeled the Hawaiians not by any uniqueness but on the basis of what the Hawaiians were not (i.e., not civilized by European standards). Shome (1996) calls this **discursive imperialism** (also see Tanno & Jandt, 1994).

The dehumanization of the Hawaiians into "others" contributed to near destruction of the Hawaiian culture. A similar dehumanization occurred in Australia.

Australia

In a similar way, all that is known of the European contact with Australia's Aboriginals is from the written journals and history of the Europeans.

Eighteen years after Captain Cook first arrived off the eastern coast of Australia, Captain Arthur Phillip arrived with 11 ships and their cargo of prisoners who established the British settlement on the shores of Sydney Harbor in January 1788.

Captain Phillip's view of the colonists as "guests" of the indigenous inhabitants and edict prohibiting molesting or killing Aboriginals was not long lasting. The Europeans occupied coastal hunting grounds and disturbed sacred sites of local Aboriginals, not having learned of their existence, much less importance. There were no large-scale wars like those with American Indians and New Zealand Maori. The Aboriginals resisted with spears and stone weapons in encounters that would later be called "guerrilla warfare."

In the book *Ancient Society* published in 1877, the Australian Aboriginal was described as "the living representatives of that worldwide primeval culture from which all other cultures had evolved." The Aboriginal was labeled as not evolved, an oddity, or semi-human.

As the Europeans moved further into the continent with farming and cattle raising, the Aboriginal population was decimated. Arsenic was mixed with the flour or inserted into the carcasses of sheep given to the Aboriginals for food. Numerous instances of large-scale slaughter have been documented, including the entire Aboriginal population of Tasmania (Isaacs, 1980).

DIFFUSION MODEL

One result of contact between cultures is that through interaction one culture may learn and adopt certain practices of the other culture. Perhaps the most significant example of adopting new practices resulted from Columbus's sailings linking two separate worlds into one. The Old World brought horses, cows, sheep, chickens, honeybees, coffee, wheat, cabbage, lettuce, bananas, olives, tulips, and daisies. The New World provided turkeys, sugarcane, corn, sweet potatoes, tomatoes, pumpkins, pineapples, petunias, poinsettias, and the practice of daily baths—a practice abhorred by Europeans.

This is the process of **diffusion**. Everett Rogers (Rogers & Shoemarker, 1971) has studied the communication process by which innovations are spread to members of a social system. Since the early 1960s, communication researchers have investigated the agricultural, health, educational, and family planning innovations in developing nations. The communication model presented in Chapter 2 has been particularly robust in analyzing and planning innovation diffusion.

Roles

Opinion Leadership and Change Agents

Important roles in the diffusion process are opinion leadership and change agents. **Opinion leadership** is accomplished by individuals who are able to influence informally other individuals' attitudes or overt behavior in a desired way with relative frequency. A **change agent** is a person who influences innovation decisions in a direction deemed desirable by a change agency.

Adopters

The rate of adoption is the relative speed with which an innovation is adopted by members of a social system. Important to understanding the diffusion process are adoption categories or classifications of the members of a social system on the basis of innovativeness. In order of their adoption of a change they are innovators, early adopters, early majority, late majority, and laggards.

Box 12.1

WHAT IS TRULY AMERICAN?

The service of diffusion in enriching the content of individual cultures has been of the utmost importance. There is probably no culture extant today which owes more than 10 per cent of its total elements to inventions made by members of its own society. Because we live in a period of rapid invention we are apt to think of our own culture as largely self-created, but the role which diffusion has played in its growth may be brought home to us if we consider the beginning of the average man's day. The locations listed in the following paragraphs refer only to the origin points of various culture elements, not to regions from which we now obtain materials or objects through trade.

Our solid American citizen awakens in a bed built on a pattern which originated in the Near East but which was modified in Northern Europe before it was transmitted to America. He throws back covers made from cotton, domesticated in India, or linen, domesticated in the Near East, or wool from sheep, also domesticated in the Near East, or silk, the use of which was discovered in China. All of these materials have been spun and woven by processes invented by the Indians of the Eastern woodlands, and goes to the bathroom, whose fixtures are a mixture of European and American inventions, both of recent date. He takes off his pajamas, a garment invented in India, and washes with soap invented by the ancient Gauls. He then shaves, a masochistic rite which seems to have been derived from either Sumer or ancient Egypt.

Returning to the bedroom, he removes his clothes from a chair of southern European type and proceeds to dress. He puts on garments whose form originally derived from the skin clothing of the nomads of the Asiatic steppes, puts on shoes made from skins tanned by a process invented in ancient Egypt and cut to a pattern derived from the classical civilizations of the Mediterranean, and ties around his neck a strip of bright-colored cloth which is a vestigial survival of the shoulder shawls worn by the seventeenth-century Croatians. Before going out for breakfast he glances through the window, made of glass invented in Egypt, and if it is raining puts on overshoes made of rubber discovered by the Central American Indians and takes an umbrella, invented in southeastern Asia. Upon his head he puts a hat made of felt, a material invented in the Asiatic steppes.

On his way to breakfast he stops to buy a paper, paying for it with coins, an ancient Lydian invention. At the restaurant a whole new series of borrowed elements confronts him. His plate is made of a form of pottery invented in China. His knife is of steel, an alloy first made in southern India, his fork a medieval Italian invention, and his spoon a derivative of a Roman original. He begins breakfast with an orange from the eastern Mediterranean, a canteloupe from Persia, or perhaps a piece of African watermelon. With this he has coffee, an Abyssinian plant, with cream and sugar. Both the domestication of cows and the idea of milking them originated in the Near East, while sugar was first made in India. After his fruit and first coffee he goes on to waffles, cakes made by a Scandinavian technique from wheat domesticated in Asia Minor. Over these he pours maple syrup, invented by the Indians of the Eastern woodlands. As a side dish he may have the egg of a species of bird domesticated in Indo-China, or thin strips of the flesh of an animal domesticated in Eastern Asia which have been salted and smoked by a process developed in northern Europe.

When our friend has finished eating he settles back to smoke, an American Indian habit, consuming a plant domesticated in Brazil in either a pipe, derived from the Indians of Virginia, or a cigarette, derived from Mexico. If he is hardy enough he may even attempt a cigar, transmitted to us from the Antilles by way of Spain. While smoking he reads the news of the day, imprinted in characters invented by the ancient Semites upon a material invented in China by a process invented in Germany. As he absorbs the accounts of foreign troubles he will, if he is a good conservative citizen,

(Continued)

Box 12.1, *Continued*

thank a Hebrew deity in an Indo-European language that he is 100 per cent American.

The foregoing is merely a bit of antiquarian virtuosity made possible by the existence of unusually complete historic records for the Eurasiatic area. There are many other regions for which no such records exist, yet the cultures in these areas bear similar witness to the importance of diffusion in establishing their content. Fairly adequate techniques have been developed for tracing the spread of individual traits and even for establishing their origin points, and there can be no doubt that diffusion has occurred wherever two societies and cultures have been brought into contact.

SOURCE: Ralph Linton, *The Study of Man,* circa 1936, reprinted 1964, pp. 326-327. Reprinted by permission of Prentice Hall, Englewood Cliffs, New Jersey.

The diffusion process can also be observed within a culture as it adopts new technologies. Everett Rogers (1986), in his book *Communication Technology,* recounts the introduction and adoption of bank automated teller machines—ATMs.

For banks, ATM technology has many advantages: The machines seldom make mistakes, and they save on labor costs. Each ATM transaction costs banks 21 cents, whereas each transaction completed face-to-face with a human teller costs banks more than twice as much. With these advantages, it is not surprising that banks across the country installed some 70,000 ATMs in the late 1970s and early 1980s at a cost of some $1 billion.

By 1985, only about one in three customers used them. The innovators, early adopters, and some of the early majority were users. As this 33% use seemed to be fairly stable, bankers began to speak of "smashing the wall"; that is, bankers began to try incentives to increase the percentage of customers using the ATM—or converting the late majority and laggards.

Who are the innovators? Studies of **adaptation potential,** or an individual's possible success in adapting to a new culture, give us hints of likely innovators. Age and educational background are good predictors as innovators tend to be younger and better educated. Another characteristic of innovators is familiarity with the new technology or belief through previous contact, interpersonal contacts, and mass media. Personality factors, such as gregariousness, tolerance for ambiguity, risk taking, and open-mindedness, and other related factors are also good predictors of cultural adaptation and likely characteristics of innovators.

Change Agent Ethics

One final aspect of the diffusion process is **change agent ethics**. You might ask yourself the "pill question." If you had a pill that could cure cancer, would you give it to a society? It would cure cancer, but the result would be the loss of jobs in health care. It might also cause people to live longer, thus putting a strain on the resources of that society. In response to that strain, that society may move to mandatory deaths of its citizens at age 70. Would you want that to happen?

What are the consequences of providing birth control information and technology to a developing country? What might be the consequences on family size? The role of women? Support for the elderly? It is this fear of the consequences of culture contact that is the reason why products are rejected.

Case Study: Quality Circles

In the following case study, you will see an example of the diffusion of management concepts from the United States to Japan and then from Japan back to the United States.

Post-World War II Japan had its industry destroyed. Japanese products of the time were popularly known as "junk"—they might last a day or two. "Made in Japan" meant the same thing as cheap and shoddy merchandise. General Douglas MacArthur asked Washington to send someone to help conduct a national census and assess Japan's ability to rebuild. Dr. W. Edward Deming (1900-1993), a relatively unknown statistician for the U.S. government, was sent.

Beginning in 1948, he gave lectures for the Union of Japanese Scientists and Engineers (JUSE), eventually lecturing to representatives of virtually every major Japanese corporation. Deming's message was that quality is the result of consistency, efficiency, and continual improvement. Deming believed that workers are intrinsically motivated to do well but that efforts are thwarted by incompetent, narrow-minded management. Deming stressed achieving uniform results during production rather than through inspection at the end of the production line. Deming's message was empowering workers with quality control decisions, monitoring the results statistically, and systematic cooperation with suppliers and buyers. In 1951, the JUSE honored his services by establishing the Deming Award for Quality. His portrait in Toyota headquarters is larger than that of the company's founder.

Later, Dr. Joseph Juran lectured in Japan on extending quality from just manufacturing to the entire process from product design to product delivery to the customer. By 1956, there was a weekly radio series on quality, and in 1960, the government declared November "National Quality Month."

From Deming's and Juran's work, Japan developed by 1962 the concept of the **quality circle**—a group of from 3 to 10 employees who meet on the job to discuss and solve quality problems (Ingle, 1982). This and other efforts had by the 1970s resulted in top-quality cameras, electronics, motorcycles, television sets, and radios.

Why did the quality circle as a concept succeed so well in Japan? The most important reason, as you've seen, is that the concept of working together in groups to benefit organization matched with the Japanese cultural value placed on group affiliation or homogeneity.

But the story is not over. In the 1960s, the United States was beginning to lose its lead in manufacturing. In the late 1960s, Dr. Juran published stories describing Japanese quality circles. Companies such as Lockheed and Honeywell started similar pilot programs. By 1973, Lockheed's programs were receiving wide publicity and wide imitation. Although many Fortune 500 companies began using quality circles, the programs did not have the same impact they had in Japan. Quality circles did not fit in well with the dominant U.S. value of individualism.

In the first part of this example, General MacArthur provided the opinion leadership and Dr. Deming was the change agent. In the second part of the example, Dr. Juran provided the opinion leadership for the United States. In the second part, quality circles coming to the United States, the innovator was a corporation: Lockheed was the innovator in using Japanese quality circles in the United States.

CONVERGENCE MODEL

There has been much criticism of the diffusion model, including its heavy identification with mass media channels. The model has been modified to treat communication as a process of convergence among members of interpersonal networks (Rogers & Kincaid, 1981).

In the **convergence** model, communication is defined as a process in which information is shared by two or more individuals who converge over time toward a greater degree of mutual agreement. Whereas the diffusion model focuses on what one individual does to another, the convergence model focuses on the relationship between those who share information. Thus, the level of analysis shifts from the individual to the dyad or on the macrolevel to groups and cultures.

Democracy in Bolivia and Botswana

In many ways, democracy can be considered an innovation. Democracy can be presented as it exists in the West. But one of the strengths of democracy has been its adaptability to local situations: Two millennia ago, democracy empowered only educated, upper-class White males; by the 20th century, diverse societies had adapted democracy. As such, the spread of democracy is an example of the convergence model.

Bolivia had a sophisticated culture that flourished 6 centuries B.C.E. However, in a 162-year period in the 19th and 20th centuries, Bolivia had 189 regimes. Today, the population is 65% indigenous.

The developing democracy in Bolivia is a blend of traditional ways with Western practices. Centuries ago, Bolivia's Aymara Indians elected a chief authority to oversee agriculture, religious rites, and clan coordination in clan-based groups called *ayllus*. Today, the ayllus elect local governments to run everything from schools to development projects. Other Indian groups do the same thing through family- or community-based groups.

In Botswana, Africa's most stable country, tribal traditions have blended with Western democratic practices. The traditional village councils, or *kgotla*, permitted everyone to speak as issues were discussed and consensus evolved. The village chiefs then pronounced decisions as made by the kgotla. Botswana's parliament preserves this tradition.

Its House of Chiefs has an advisory role on all legislation and resembles Great Britain's House of Lords. The government ignores the chiefs' advice "at its peril."

In both Bolivia and Botswana, the innovation of democracy merged or converged with local tradition. Its acceptance and success are more likely.

ADAPTING THE MESSAGE

As you've seen, key to the diffusion and convergence processes across cultures is adaptation of the message to the receiving culture. The key is to adapt to the local culture, localize thinking, localize the product, and localize the marketing strategy.

De Mooij (1998) has reviewed research and been able to relate advertising styles to Hofstede's dimensions: Japanese advertising reflects Confucian and collectivistic values. Concepts of face and harmony relate to an indirect communication style. It is said that the goal of Japanese advertising is to win the trust and respect of the consumer. Advertising is serene, mood creating, and subtle with much symbolism. Dependency, nature, and respect for elders can be seen.

Taiwan advertising generally links the product to the consumer's traditional Chinese values, such as family relations and respect for authority. The advertising is indirect and promises an ideal that may be reached through the use of the product. Spanish advertising is less direct than the advertising style of northern European countries because Spain's culture is more collectivistic. People are depicted in family and other groups. Feminine aspects of the culture are seen in the softer approaches and relatively low use of celebrity endorsements. The use of art, color, and beauty are related to a strong uncertainty avoidance.

U.S. advertising reflects assertiveness, the direct approach, and competitiveness, which de Mooij relates to a configuration of masculinity and individualism. Overstatement and hyperbole are typical, as are direct comparisons.

Two examples of message adaptation are the marketing of baby food worldwide and missionary work in New Guinea.

Marketing Gerber Baby Foods Worldwide

Gerber Products first entered Australia in 1959, Japan in 1960, and the Philippines in 1972 under the assumption that the world would like and buy what was popularly used in the United States. The company discovered that each country not only likes different foods but also has different baby-feeding practices. Gerber then established advisory committees in those countries to determine what products would be acceptable. Out of that came "lamb stock stew" for Australia, "rice with young sardines" for Japan, and "strained mango" for the Philippines.

In Japan and South Korea, there are pressures on mothers to make meals for the family from scratch. Here Gerber positions itself by marketing its products as part of a "scientifically based" feeding plan. The food containers are labeled as "lessons" to demonstrate that Gerber provides something that the mothers cannot make for babies.

Religious Missionary Work in New Guinea

Before reading how missionaries took Christianity to the peoples of New Guinea, understand that missionaries look for what is called a **redemptive analogy**, or something in the culture that can be compared to the gospel and hence makes the unknown knowable to the culture (Richardson, 1974).

One missionary came upon the practice of peace making between two villages. A man from each village handed over to the other village one of each village's babies to live among the other people. The people in New Guinea called these children *tarop tim*, or "peace child." According to the tradition, everyone in the village must then touch the peace child as a symbol of accepting the peace. As long as the children were alive, no fighting was allowed to occur between the villages.

The missionary built his message around the concept of the peace child. He explained how God gave his "peace child" to the world. In the local culture, fighting could begin again if the children died, but God's peace child is eternal because he rose from the dead and is still alive.

CULTURAL IMPERIALISM

The cultural imperialist approach to communication recognizes that mass media is not value free—the media also carry important cultural values (Nordenstreng & Schiller, 1979; Schiller, 1976). Countries with media able to capture and dominate international markets in this theory serve the originating country's intentions. The single largest export industry for the United States is not aircraft. It is entertainment. Hollywood films grossed more than $30 billion worldwide in 1997. Hollywood gets 50% of its revenues overseas (United Nations Development Programme, 1999). Schiller (1976) points to the unrestricted flow of media from the United States having the effect of surreptitiously affecting other people's goals and aspirations. It was just that concern that led Canada to require that radio stations devote at least 30% of their programming to Canadian music.

One country in particular is symbolic in its concerns over cultural invasion. By 1757, the British had control over parts of India, and by 1857 virtually controlled the entire country. The British presence with its East India Company was a combination of political and commercial interests. India is one country that has on occasion responded to cultural invasion with protests and opposition from activists and politicians.

Coca-Cola was forced to leave India in 1977 after pressures from socialists who labeled the soft drink a new form of colonialism pushing the American culture. Coke returned to India in 1993. Kentucky Fried Chicken faced opposition to serving poultry with hormones and chemicals. Other U.S. companies that have met resistance in India are Pepsi, DuPont, Cargill, and Enron.

China was one of Coca-Cola's first overseas markets when bottling plants were established in Shanghai and Tianjin in 1927. Forced to leave in 1949 by

Mecca-Cola, a new soft drink and part of anti-American sentiment around the world.

China's Communist Party as a symbol of U.S. imperialism, Coke returned in 1979. There have been new movements in China to limit the growing sales of U.S.-made Coke and Pepsi to protect local beverages.

Barbie dolls are considered anti-Islamic and importing them into Iran is prohibited. Barbie's makeup and "indecent" clothes are considered Western cultural influences. An Iranian government-sponsored project designed Sara and Dara dolls. Sara wears long, flowing clothes and wraps. Her companion, Dara, is her brother, who comes with the long coat and turban of an Islamic cleric. Some Arabs and other Muslims boycott U.S. products over the U.S. backing of Israel. Sales of the Iranian soft drink Zam Zam Cola, with its name taken from a holy spring in Saudi Arabia, increased in 2002. Another, Mecca-Cola, sold in Europe, is marketed as a protest to U.S. foreign policy.

In Taiwan, some are talking about a "new colonialism" and one newspaper carried the headline, "Be Careful! Your Kids Are Becoming Japanese." Japanese television reaches 75% of Taiwanese households on cable. Japanese comic books and trendy fashion magazines such as *Non-No* and *Check* are popular among teens, as are Japanese merchandise and pop singers. Teens say that Japanese popular culture is easy to relate to because the cultures are similar. Older people remember Japan's 50-year rule of Taiwan and have called for a boycott of Japanese products to preserve Chinese heritage.

The counterargument to cultural imperialism is that there are no surveys showing that people are becoming more alike. While media flow globally, people receive and use the messages differently. Global marketing may symbolize the lifestyles that people aspire to, but there is evidence that local cultures have taken on a renewed significance as political movements promote local cultures and local identities. Finally, there is evidence that cultures do not only flow in one direction. Salsa music originated in the Caribbean but is now known worldwide, as are Ethiopian and Thai cuisines.

> I do not want my house to be walled in on all sides and my windows stuffed. I want the cultures of all the lands to be blown about my house as freely as possible. But I refuse to be blown off my feet by any.
>
> —Mohandas (Mahatma) Gandhi, quoted in United Nations Development Programme, *Human Development Report*, 1999

CULTURAL ICONS

In his book *Mediamerica*, Edward Jay Whetmore (1987) writes of icons and artifacts as aspects of popular culture. An **icon** is a special symbol that tends to be idolized in a culture (Disney's Mickey Mouse is a good example); an **artifact** is an object less widely recognized. Icons of U.S. culture are so popular for the very reason that they represent U.S. culture.

Other cultures, as well, have representative icons. For example, English gardens, golf, English tea, Winnie the Pooh, Burberry, Laura Ashley, and the Body Shop represent British culture to many. Kangaroos, koalas, and boomerangs represent Australia to many.

A global brand carries the same brand name or logo worldwide. Its values and positioning are identical in all countries, and it has brand loyalty in all countries in which it is marketed. Marlboro is an example. It is positioned worldwide as an urban premium brand appealing to the desire for freedom and open physical space symbolized by the "Marlboro man" and "Marlboro Country." Global brands may be modified to meet local consumer needs and competitive requirements. For example, both Coca-Cola and Pepsi-Cola increase the sweetness in the Middle East where consumers prefer a sweeter drink. Other examples of global brands are Braun, Budweiser, Canon, Cartier, Club Med, Disney, IBM, KFC, Kodak, Levi's, McDonald's, Mercedes, Mitsubishi, Philips, and Sony. The majority of global brands are of U.S. origin and to many represent the U.S. lifestyle and culture (de Mooij, 1998).

Marketing Cultural Icons

In marketing the culture itself, adapting to the receiving culture is not an issue. In fact, adapting would defeat the purpose.

U.S. cultural icons are most important in motion pictures, travel and recreation, and franchising. For example, the owner/manufacturer of a popular U.S. icon may franchise the use of that icon in other markets to local companies. The owner receives payments for its use.

Coca-Cola and Pepsi

Without doubt, the most widely recognized U.S. icon worldwide is Coca-Cola. The company has marketed internationally since 1900. Today, Coke sells 1 billion servings daily in nearly 200 countries. Although U.S. residents drink 524 million servings daily, 80% of the company's operating income comes from outside the United States.

Beginning in 1992, Coke began its first global marketing campaign—six commercials broadcast at the same time all over the world. So it's not all that surprising that Coca-Cola wanted Chinese characters that "sounded like" its name in English. That's what it was selling.

The first U.S. factory to open in Vietnam since the United States restored diplomatic relations in 1995 was Coke. Coke is seen as a status symbol. The Vietnamese pay 10% more for Coke than for a Vietnamese cola.

Pepsi is second to Coke worldwide except in Pakistan, parts of the Middle East, and in Quebec where Pepsi leads 2 to 1. Pepsi had been using U.S. ads translated into French in Quebec. Then its advertising agency started using a comedian with caricatures drawn from stereotypical *Quebecois* characters, such as a bizarre ice hockey player who could not pronounce *Pepsi* correctly. Sales soared.

McDonald's

The McDonald brothers operated a hamburger stand in San Bernardino, California, that offered a limited menu and used "assembly-line" procedures for cooking and serving food.

Ray Kroc first visited it in 1954 and in the following year, in partnership with the McDonald brothers, opened the first restaurant (Ritzer, 1993). By 1998, McDonald's had about 25,000 restaurants in more than 110 countries. In a 1986 survey, 96% of the schoolchildren surveyed were able to identify Ronald McDonald—second only to Santa Claus in name recognition.

Coca-Cola markets an international T-shirt showing the various spellings of its name. Note that the trademark ribbon, part of Coke's logo, is always present.

SOURCE: Coca-Cola is a registered trademark of the Coca-Cola Company. Permission for use granted by the Company.

In each country, it faces the challenge of adapting its menu to local tastes without weakening its appeal as a U.S. icon.

When McDonald's opened its first restaurant in Singapore in 1982, it quickly became the largest-selling McDonald's in the world. In early 1990, McDonald's opened its first restaurant in Moscow. One journalist described it as the "ultimate icon of Americana." Russians were unaccustomed to eating finger food, and Russian workers were unaccustomed to smiling and looking customers directly in the eye. McDonald's knew it was selling U.S. popular culture and kept much of the product the same. In 1992, McDonald's opened its largest restaurant at that time in Beijing with 700 seats, 29 cash registers,

McDonald's placemat in German.

SOURCE: Permission for use granted by McDonald's.

and nearly 1,000 employees. On its first day of business, it served about 40,000 customers (Ritzer, 1993).

In 1996, McDonald's opened in New Delhi, India, but without all-beef patties because 80% of the population are Hindu, a religion whose followers don't eat beef. The menu features the Maharaja Mac—"two all-mutton patties, special sauce, lettuce, cheese, pickles, onions on a sesame-seed bun." The restaurant opened with a traditional Hindu ceremony.

In Jerusalem, McDonald's has nonkosher and kosher restaurants. As Jewish law forbids the cooking, serving, or eating of meat and milk products together, the kosher restaurants do not have cheeseburgers, milkshakes, or ice cream. The restaurants also close on Saturdays to observe the religious injunction against working on the Sabbath.

McDonald's placemat in Malay.

SOURCE: Permission for use granted by McDonald's.

McDonald's in Great Britain, France, Germany, and Brazil serve beer and wine. The McDonald's in Brazil has "happy hours" with salsa bands. McDonald's found that adaptations to local tastes can go too far: The McPloughman's sandwich, a version of the British pub staple featuring bread, cheese, and pickle, was not popular nor was the forced "Thank you, please call again."

By 1992, McDonald's had 882 outlets in Japan. These offer soup and fried rice to cater to Japanese eating habits, but the golden arches are there. McDonald's competitor in Japan is Japanese-owned MOS (Mountain, Ocean, Sea). Ironically, the MOS burger is based on the one made at Tommy's, a famous Los Angeles hamburger franchise.

What "message" representing the United States does McDonald's communicate to the world? Ritzer (1993) identified the principles of the fast-food

McDonald's now stresses its ties to local economies. The Kiwiburger™ packaging features New Zealand icons.

SOURCE: Permission for use granted by McDonald's.

restaurant that are coming to dominate more and more sectors worldwide. He calls this the "McDonaldization of society."

- *Efficiency*. The McDonald's fast-food model offers an efficient method of satisfying many needs.

- *Quantification*. Time is quantified in terms of how quickly one is served, and quantity ("bigger is better") becomes more important than quality.

- *Predictability*. The food McDonald's serves in Baltimore is essentially identical to the food it serves in Houston. It offers no surprises.

- *Control*. Employees are trained to do a very limited number of things, and customers as well are controlled through limited options.

Kentucky Fried Chicken

Kentucky Fried Chicken (KFC) was a leader in the international market. Today, it has more than 10,000 restaurants in 78 countries, including some 1,000 outlets in Japan. Original Recipe™ is sold in every KFC restaurant

Japanese fast food courtesy of the KFC Colonel.

SOURCE: Tokyo Friends.

around the world. The KFCs in Japan adapt to the Japanese palate by making the cole slaw a little less sweet than the U.S. version of the popular side dish. The Colonel still smiles at every purchase.

In 1987, KFC opened the first Western fast-food restaurant in China in Beijing's Tiananmen Square. KFC meals became a political statement at the prodemocracy demonstrations there. Since then, some 500 restaurants have been built in 120 cities. The target is 5,000 restaurants within two decades. As a result, KFC is the most recognizable international icon of any kind in China.

Budweiser

Anheuser-Busch launched Budweiser beer in China in summer 1995. More than 800 breweries compete for the Chinese market. Other international competitors coming into China are San Miguel of the Philippines, Fosters Brewing Group of Australia, and Denmark's Carlsberg and Heineken. Anheuser-Busch's successful international strategy has been to form partnerships with leading local brewers around the world through joint ventures or licensing agreements. The local partners know the local market and the local distribution system.

Budweiser is known for having the same taste worldwide. In focus groups conducted in China, it became clear that the Chinese knew nothing about the name Budweiser. So Anheuser-Busch will market Budweiser with the U.S. value of personal independence, the freedom to do what you want to do, along with popular sports and the outdoors.

Other Icons

Other U.S. icons with worldwide recognition are Kodak, Disney, IBM, and Pepsi-Cola. In Sweden, "ukla" sweatshirts are a sought-after product. Who makes the "ukla" brand? UCLA, of course. Tex-Mex food offered by the U.S. restaurant chain Chi-Chi's has become popular. (Its menu explains how to make fajitas, and servers explain that bread is not served.) And 2001 marked the 20th anniversary of MTV now seen, with its Western images of cars, clothes, and relationships, from Senegal to Russia and that claims to be the largest television network in the world.

What's in a brand name? A look at Table 12.1 shows which ones are readily known worldwide and which are important to those living on the West Coast in the United States.

Remember, what is being sold is the U.S. cultural icon, so only minor adaptations are made. For example, in Thailand, Pizza Hut puts pineapple on its pizza. KFC offers "hot and spicy" chicken, Burger King promotes chicken sandwiches, and Hard Rock Cafe's waiters don't sit with customers when taking orders (the Thai don't sit with servants). Hard Rock has kept the word *cafe* even though it means "brothel" in Thailand.

Another U.S. product being marketed internationally today as a cultural icon is cigarettes. According to the World Health Organization, 25 years ago the industrialized West led the world in smoking; today, poor countries lead the list. Cigarette advertising in developing countries shows glamorous scenes of life in the United States. Smoking is advertised as sophisticated and cosmopolitan to match the way many of its audience see the United States.

Marlboro is among the most advertised foreign products in China. The "Marlboro man" can be seen on billboards in China even though the government has banned cigarette advertising. In Hong Kong, the Marlboro man is

Table 12.1   Ten Most Powerful Brand Names, 1990

Worldwide

1. Coca-Cola
2. Sony
3. Mercedes-Benz
4. Kodak
5. Disney
6. Nestlé
7. Toyota
8. McDonald's
9. IBM (International Business Machines)
10. Pepsi-Cola

U.S. West Coast

1. Disney
2. Campbell's
3. Levis
4. Coca-Cola
5. Black & Decker
6. Kodak
7. Pepsi-Cola
8. NBC (National Broadcasting Corporation)
9. Crest
10. GE (General Electric)

SOURCE: Landor Image Power Survey in the *Los Angeles Times,* September 13, 1990, p. D2. Copyright © 1990, Los Angeles Times. Adapted with permission.

presented as a clean-cut man of property who lives in a big ranch house and rides a white horse—a symbol of good luck. U.S. cigarettes have associated themselves with a social and political message that says freedom, modernity, and luxury. The unofficial cigarette of protest at Tiananmen Square was Marlboro. In Russia, cigarettes are advertised with images of U.S. good life: L&M cigarettes were superimposed on a photo of the Golden Gate Bridge with the slogan "Date with America."

Marketing has led to the development of a global pop culture. Coca-Cola is sold in more countries than the United Nations has members and it is claimed that "Coke" is the second most universally understood term in English after "okay." Levi's jeans are sold in more than 70 countries. German game shows and a Brazilian soap opera are popular on Cameroon television. International

Table 12.2   Top U.S. International Restaurant Chains, Ranked by 1998
               International Sales

International Chain	Total Units	Percentage of Units Outside the United States	International Sales ($1,000s)
McDonald's	12,328	49.7	17,856,000
KFC (Kentucky Fried Chicken)	5,291	50.8	4,207,000
Pizza Hut	3,814	31	2,250,000
Burger King	2,316	22.7	2,237,000
Tim Horton's[a]	1,567	94	835,000
Wendy's	657	12.3	700,000
Domino's Pizza	1,730	27.8	700,000
Subway	2,006	14.8	530,000
Dairy Queen	792	13.5	400,000
Hard Rock Cafe	59	62.8	390,000

SOURCE: *Restaurant Business,* November 1, 1999.

a. Coffee and baked goods. Founded in Canada and named after Toronto Maple Leaf hockey player. Merged with Wendy's in 1995.

students from Kenya are relieved to discover that KFC is available in the United States too (see Table 12.2 for top U.S. international restaurant chains). And Wal-Mart stores in Mexico display signs stating "Proudly Mexican."

CULTURAL HEGEMONY

Some nations, like the United States, are major exporters of their own cultures. Although some societies are excellent markets for U.S. icons, other societies may resist adopting these ideas because they fear the changes that may accompany the new ideas. Some societies may perceive the increasing popularity of those icons as a form of cultural **hegemony,** or the fear of the predominant influence that one culture can develop over another.

It is believed that what is being transmitted are the values of the culture. The receiving culture can unconsciously, or perhaps uncritically, absorb the values. Cultural dependency is the belief that a receiving culture becomes accustomed to cars from Japan or movies and TV from Great Britain or the United States and that it is natural that they come from there, thus discouraging local businesses.

The introduction or rejection of an innovation has consequences for a society. As was indicated earlier, all the parts of a culture are interrelated. One change can have repercussions in other areas. Not all of those consequences can be anticipated.

It is important to recognize that the adoption—or rejection—of any innovation has consequences for the society. Introducing axes to the indigenous Australian tribes by missionaries (the change agents) resulted in an improved standard of living for the tribes but also contributed to the breakdown of the family structure, the rise of prostitution, and "misuse" of the axes themselves. Axes made hunting possible, which required men to live apart from their families, and axes could be used to kill humans as well as animals.

Examples

Disneyland Paris

The first Disneyland outside the United States opened in 1983 in Tokyo totally owned by Japanese companies. Disney's $4.4 billion Euro Disney opened outside Paris in April 1992. Some European intellectuals labeled the park a "cultural Chernobyl." Some were concerned how the park would affect French culture.

Disney made an attempt to "Europeanize" its attractions and products and downplayed the U.S. culture. Souvenir shops carried sweatshirts with small, discreet Disney logos. Rather than only fast-food restaurants, Euro Disney offered table-service restaurants. Disney's objective was to attract people from all over Europe and thus hired multilingual workers from all over Europe.

The French have had little experience with theme parks. The French often dedicate Sunday—and only Sunday—to family outings. Most French do not snack and insist on eating at 12:30. This could create enormous and hostile bottlenecks at park restaurants. And French employees have an aversion to providing the smiles and friendly greetings so expected at any amusement park.

Food, merchandise, and hotel business was weak: Europeans brought bag lunches and left early—not spending money at the park's gourmet restaurants and showcase hotels. Some European investors complained about a rigid, myopic U.S. management style.

At one point the park was losing $1 million a day, forcing Disney to bring in a Saudi prince as a major investor and rename the park Disneyland Paris.

Disney had discounted its own value as a U.S. icon, which is just what the French wanted to experience. Frontierland was just as popular as Discoveryland. French visitors to the park didn't want a leisurely, sit-down lunch; they wanted fast food. European visitors to the park didn't want discreet sweatshirts; they wanted sweatshirts with huge letters and big pictures of Mickey Mouse. After these changes, the park made its first small profit in the fiscal year ending in 1995. It has now become the most popular tourist attraction in France.

Box 12.2

A VOICE AGAINST DISNEYFICATION

A vote against pink-castellated Disneyfication, Lesley Garner in London is disappointed with a world where plaster fish, puppets and mechanical elephants are preferred to the real thing.

There were the prettiest advertisements in British papers recently showing a fantastical castle with blue turrets set against a deep pink sky.

"Imagine . . . " it said. "Imagine what it would be like if Disneyland was right here in Europe . . . Just a dream?"

Not just a dream: just an irresistible offer to become a shareholder in Euro-Disneyland.

Anyone who has been to Disneyland knows that the place is less a dream machine than a device for extracting money.

Even the sanest people leave in Minnie Mouse T-shirts or wearing hats with Goofy ears.

The boredom of snaking in those endless queues can only be alleviated with candy and popcorn and ice cream. And the mistaken idea that the rides are free—the cost of entry for three of us more than two years ago [1987] was $90 ($60 even at today's [1989] rates)—leads to crazed behaviour.

Hysterically sobbing children are forced on to rides as night falls because parents are determined to wrest every drop of pleasure from their outlay.

For a future shareholder this suggests profits as glittering as Tinkerbell's trail.

For a moment I was tempted. Then reason took over.

Not only do I find the place sinister, I think the very concept of Disneyland is a threat to civilisation as we in Europe know it. Forget the pink turreted castles and the power of the word "imagine."

Disneyland is not about imagination and adventure at all. It is about control.

I learnt this when I went straight to the world of Disney from Boston. In Boston we had marvelled at the stunning column of glass in the New England Aquarium that enclosed a coral reef.

The reef swarms with hundreds of spectacular fish. As we stood pressed against the glass, sharks and rays seemed to whirl about our heads in hungry perpetual motion.

In Disneyland there is a ride called something like 20 Thousand Leagues Under the Sea. You go in a submarine beneath the aquamarine waters of a clear coral-reefed lagoon. Fresh from our experience in Boston, we looked down at the red and golden coral in the blue water and queued eagerly for another glimpse of tropical magic.

What we got was sinking disappointment. We found ourselves face to face with a plaster fish on a piece of wire.

Now the creators of Disneyland may declare this was not a rip-off because they never pretend anything in Disneyland is real. Indeed, as far as I can see, they go to enormous lengths to see that it is not.

Fake pirates yo-ho-ho at you in Pirates of the Caribbean (apparently Michael Jackson's favourite ride). Fake elephants squirt water over themselves in the lakes.

Nevertheless, presented with a plaster fish hovering on a length of wire, I defy anyone not to feel that they have been had. Avoidance of reality in Disneyland is as whole-hearted as the pursuit of the Holy Grail.

It is a bastion of the family outing, and, on the days I was there, much appreciated by nuns. There is much to admire. There is no litter, no alcohol, no unpleasantness.

Americans who go to Disneyland escape from the squalor of motorised urban living.

Their towns are approached by miles of motels, petrol stations and fast-food joints.

In Disneyland they find Main Street, just as grandpa knew it, except that cute shops sell Mickey Mouse T-shirts and the Disneyland parade, with its maddening tune, regularly stomps along it, followed by cheery sweepers to clean up.

No dirt is allowed on a Disneyland street. Peter Pan may have said that to die would be an awfully big adventure but for terminally ill American children the adventure is a known quantity. In the last stages of their illness they get taken to Disneyland. It is the nearest place to Paradise that America knows.

Only a sour person could object to this, you might say, but in Europe we still have some of the real magic that Disneyland can only caricature.

There is something totalitarian about the unrelenting imposition of this vision. The plaster fish, the puppets, the mechanical elephants are preferred to the real thing because they can be controlled. So can the people. The crowd control in Disneyland is awesome. Visitors are so snaked about that they never comprehend the real despairing length of their queue.

The writer Bill Bryson, in his very funny new book *The Lost Continent*, encountered the same queuing phenomenon in colonial Williamsburg. "I don't think I had ever

(Continued)

Box 12.2, *Continued*

seen quite so many people failing to enjoy themselves," he wrote. "The glacial lines put me in mind of Disney World, which was not inappropriate since Williamsburg is really a sort of Disney World of American history."

What Bryson also observed was the lobotomising effect of this unreal experience, the process I call Disneyfication. Disneyfication leads in America—and why not in Europe—to small, preserved ghettos of cloying cuteness while the rest of the world goes mad. What does it matter what becomes of our world as long as there is Disneyland?

Bryson hit it on the nail when he said: "You would think the millions of people who come to Williamsburg every year would say to each other, 'Gosh, Bobbi, this place is beautiful. Let's go home to Smallville and plant lots of trees and preserve fine old buildings.' But in fact that never occurs to them. They just go back and build more parking lots and Pizza Huts." So I am not sending for a Euro-Disneyland "mini prospectus."

I am voting against the ghettoisation of magic and for keeping imagination in the real world, where it belongs.

German Reunification

One outcome of World War II was a divided Germany. For nearly 50 years the two Germanys lived apart. Nowhere was the division more obvious than in Berlin where the 100-mile-long concrete and barbed wire wall erected in 1961 divided the city. Although almost no physical trace of the wall remains, there is still a wall of cultural differences.

West Germany worked an economic miracle and became the world's third strongest economy. The contrast could even be seen in automobiles: The West Germans had the Mercedes Benz; the East Germans had the Trabant, with its two-stroke, 26-horsepower motor and resin and cotton matting body. West Germans believed that East Germans lived under a neo-Stalinism that stifled personal initiative, scorned self-promotion, and suppressed individual thinking.

Then in late 1989, the wall fell with shouts of *"Wir sind ein Volk!"* ("We are one people!"). East and West Germans danced together atop the Berlin

East and West Germans came together on the Berlin Wall at Brandenburg Gate, November 9, 1989.

SOURCE: German Information Center.

Wall. Hugs, waves, and honking horns were shown on television across the world. October 3 is now celebrated as German Unity Day. After unification, Germans learned that, indeed, two separate cultures had developed. Chancellor Kohl admitted, "We have drifted much further apart than we thought," or as a floor leader for the Social Democrats said, "One nation, two different worlds." One-third of those polled in both parts of Germany almost 10 years after reunification said that "in essence we will always be two separate countries" (Dornberg, 1999). Unification caused a collision between the individualistic, confident, open, upfront West Germans and the introverted, passive, loyal, and withdrawn East Germans.

West Germans complained about higher taxes. However, East Germans' lives have undergone complete change. Guaranteed jobs and low, fixed rents were gone. Schools and curricula were reorganized. The banking, health, and

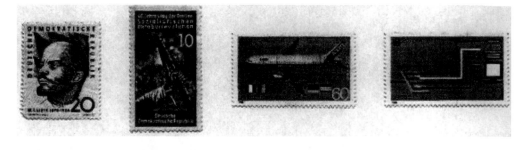

Stamps from East Germany (left) honor the 90th anniversary of Lenin's birth and the storming of the Winter Palace. Stamps from West Germany (right) honor transport and communication.

legal systems all had to be transformed. Roads, the telephone system, and buildings had to be repaired and modernized. Everything changed (Schneider, 1991).

After unification, East German women argued that reunification had taken away rights. The women found it harder to get a job, child care, a divorce, an abortion, or birth control. East German divorce required one court appearance. Under West German law, a couple had to be separated a year for an uncontested divorce; a contested divorce required a 3-year waiting period. East Germany had free child care, birth control, and abortions in early pregnancy. Under West German law, abortions were forbidden except in unusual circumstances such as rape. In 1995, the laws were reconciled by compromise: Abortion is officially illegal, but women who receive counseling will be allowed to have an abortion up to the 13th week of pregnancy.

Because of the housing shortage in East Germany, extended families tended to live together in one flat (apartment). West Germans lived as separate nuclear family households. Because of this and the proliferation of nursing homes for elderly people in West Germany, many East Germans felt that the West Germans had lost any sense of family obligations.

During the period of separation, the German language in the East and West began to diverge. Each had developed different words for some things such as "grocery bag." West Germans had adopted many English words such as "leasing," "cash," and "surfboard." In the East, the government had modified the language along socialist lines, so East Germans used words meaning "year-end winged figure" for "Christmas angel," "waving element" (*Winkelement*) for "flag" (*Fahne*) because the people were expected to wave them at parades, *Kader* in place of the West German *Personalchef* ("personnel chief"), and *der antifaschistische Schutzwall* ("antifascist protective wall") for the Berlin Wall.

New words developed after unification: For example, *Ossie* and *Wessie* differentiate eastern from western Germans. New newspapers and magazines developed in the East and supported a separate *Ossie* identity. East Germans carried "how to" articles on obtaining work, on self-salesmanship, and on fighting depression. The book *Wendewut* about a middle-aged East German woman's problems in adjusting to her changed life became a bestseller in the East sector but was largely unnoticed in the West.

Stereotypes arose: The term **Ossie** means naive, confused, inexperienced; **Wessie** means slick, arrogant, know-it-all. Politicians use the pronouns "we" and "they" and refer to the East sector as "over there." West Germans refer to the former East Germans as "silly *Ossis*," and East Germans refer to former West Germans as "Besserwessie" or "know-it-alls."

There is now a contrast in nonverbals: Westerners characterize Easterners as provincial and incomprehensible and as people who avoid direct eye contact. Easterners characterize Western acquaintances as aggressive people whose direct eye contact is irritating. Values are different: Easterners are more likely to place a higher value on group solidarity rather than individual achievement, to reject the importance of money in relationships, and to value friendship over competition and passivity over assertiveness.

Differences in decision making can be seen in Parliament. Western members attack ideas; new Eastern members ask if it is permitted to ask a question.

The irony of unification is that it has produced an Eastern identity that decades of Communist propaganda failed to achieve: *Die Mauer ist weg, aber es gibt eine neue Mauer in den Köpfen.* (The wall is gone, but there is a new wall in people's heads.) Products made in the East sector are experiencing a revival as a way to assert a separate identity. F6, a cigarette brand left over from Communist days, is the leading cigarette in the East. T-shirts there have the phrase "I Want My Wall Back." The invisible wall that now exists will take generations to fall because the redevelopment of a homogeneous society takes time. One of the forces contributing to that redevelopment began as the Berlin Wall was coming down: Coca-Cola immediately began trucking its drinks into what had been East Germany and as soon as possible bought all four soft-drink bottling plants there.

Another divided country watches German reunification. Korea has been divided for more than 50 years. Koreans on both sides of the demilitarized zone (DMZ) share ethnicity and language but now share little else. Perhaps one-seventh of the population have relatives on the opposite side with whom they have had no letters or telephone calls. The economic disparity is far greater than what existed between East and West Germany. West Germans were about 4 times richer than East Germans; the income disparity between

South and North Koreans is about 16 to 1. The annual sales of just one Korean conglomerate, Daewoo, exceed the entire gross domestic product of North Korea. The collapse of the Soviet Union and droughts, floods, and tidal waves since 1995 have severely weakened North Korea's economy and created widespread malnutrition. In 2000, reconciliation talks began and resulted in some limited family reunions. Later tensions resulted from growing demands for reunification.

FROM THE INTERCULTURAL PERSPECTIVE

When cultures have contact with each other they often learn new ideas and practices from each other. There are two models of how ideas travel from one culture to another: the diffusion model and the convergence model.

Diffusion happens when a culture learns or adopts a new idea or practice. There are two important roles that help a new idea or practice to diffuse into a culture. The first role is opinion leadership. Opinion leadership is held by individuals who can influence other people. These people help change people's behavior and attitudes about the innovation (new idea). The other role is change agent. Change agents have influence over innovation decisions; that is, they help decide whether or not to use a new idea. When a new idea or practice is adopted, some people begin to use it very quickly, whereas others are slow to change. People who use the new idea can be divided into groups depending on how quickly they decided to use the idea. They are innovators, early adopters, early majority, late majority, and laggards. Innovators are often young, well-educated, risk takers, open-minded, and already familiar with the change.

The diffusion process can be seen in the development of quality circles in Japan. The idea of quality circles (a technique for quality control in manufacturing) was developed by a man from the United States. Japanese manufacturing companies borrowed the ideas and successfully adapted the process to Japanese culture. U.S. businesses saw how successful Japan was in using quality circles and decided to use quality circles, too. However, because U.S. businesses did not try to change the practice to fit the U.S. culture, quality circles did not succeed very well (even though quality circles were originally a U.S. idea). It is important, therefore, for the change message (innovation) to be adapted to the new culture.

The convergence model describes a process of sharing information. Over time, individuals from the different cultures come to a greater level of agreement with each other. An example of this is how the idea of democracy was adapted to traditional customs in Bolivia and Botswana.

Although an important part of diffusion is adapting an idea to a new culture, there are times when this is not desirable. For example, in marketing cultural icons (symbols of a culture like "Mickey Mouse" or "Coke") to other cultures it is not desirable to change the idea. What is actually being sold is a "piece" of culture.

When contact occurs between cultures, change can occur in any part of the cultures. This is why many countries do not want too much contact with other cultures. They fear cultural hegemony or the influence that other cultures may have on their own culture. To avoid hegemony, many cultures do things like limiting the kinds and amounts of products from other countries. For example, India did not allow Coke to be sold in its country from 1977 to 1993.

KEY TERMS

adaptation potential	diffusion	Ossie
artifact	discursive imperialism	quality circle
change agent	hegemony	redemptive analogy
change agent ethics	icon	Wessie
convergence	opinion leadership	

PART IV

Cultures Within Cultures

CHAPTER 13

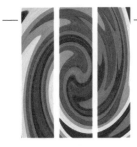

Immigration and Acculturation

What You Can Learn From This Chapter

The effects of culture shock

Patterns of immigration

Predictors of acculturation potential

How modern media and transportation systems have affected immigrant groups today in contrast to earlier immigrant groups

---

A *tourist* visits a country for a short period of time for such goals as relaxation and self-enlightenment. A **sojourner** lives in a country for a limited period of time, from as little as 6 months to as long as 5 years, with a specific and goal-oriented purpose, such as education. The word **expatriate** is more often used to refer to a noncitizen worker who lives in a country for an indeterminate length of time. Many people labeled "immigrants" in the United States and Europe are in fact sojourners or expatriates whose intent is to work but not to become full-fledged members of the culture. Both tourists and sojourners fully expect to return home (Furnham, 1987). Most immigrants are willing and eager to become members of the new culture and fully expect to remain in the new country.

In this chapter, you'll look at who the immigrants to the United States were and are today. You'll discover how modern media and transportation systems have significantly changed immigration and acculturation from what immigrants of a century ago experienced.

CULTURE SHOCK

Whether an individual enters a host culture as a sojourner or as an immigrant, **culture shock** is the first likely response (Furnham & Bochner, 1986). Making a call on a public telephone or using public transportation where the systems are different can present challenges. Unless you are prepared to function in the new culture, the situation can be highly stressful. Refer back to the intercultural barrier identified in Chapter 4 as anxiety. This form of stress and anxiety is called culture shock. Studies show that from 30% to 60% of expatriates suffer serious culture shock, whereas about 20% have no difficulty and enjoy the challenge.

The phrase was popularized by anthropologist Kalvero Oberg (1960) to describe the feelings of disorientation and anxiety that many people experience for a period of time while living in a foreign country. It results from an awareness that one's basic assumptions about life and one's familiar ways of behaving are no longer appropriate or functional.

Stages of Culture Shock

Adler (1975), Pedersen (1995), and others have described culture shock as a five-stage process.

The first stage of initial contact, sometimes called the "honeymoon stage" or initial euphoria, is where everything is new and exciting. The person is basically a tourist with her or his basic identity rooted in the home culture.

The second stage involves disintegration of familiar cues and irritation and hostility with the differences experienced in the new culture. For example, an international student in a U.S. grocery may be asked, "Paper or plastic?" The student knows what paper is and what plastic is, but doesn't understand the question. The student can experience feelings of inadequacy and can withdraw or become isolated.

The third stage involves a reintegration of new cues and an increased ability to function in the new culture. Perhaps surprisingly, though, the emotions experienced at this stage are typically anger and resentment toward the new culture for "being different."

Learning how to use a new currency is a cultural adaptation skill. Shown here: Cambodian riel.

In the fourth stage, gradual adjustment continues toward gradual autonomy and seeing "good" and "bad" elements in both the home and new cultures. The individual becomes more comfortable in the new culture as more things are predictable. There are fewer feelings of isolation and people feel more in control and more comfortable.

The final, fifth stage is described as reciprocal interdependence where the person has achieved **biculturalism** by becoming able to cope comfortably in both the home and new cultures. Full adjustment can take years.

Reverse Culture Shock

However, if a person has adjusted exceptionally well to the host culture, **reverse culture shock** may occur upon return to the home country. This type of culture shock may cause greater distress and confusion than the original had. In reverse culture shock, the home culture is compared adversely to the admired aspects of the new culture.

Symptoms

The symptoms of culture shock are pervasive and vary in intensity, duration, and severity among individuals. Individuals can experience both physical and psychological symptoms.

Physical symptoms are overconcern about cleanliness of food, bedding, and dishes; extreme stress on health and safety; fear of physical contact with anyone in the new country; great concern over minor pains and skin eruptions; craving "home cooking"; use of alcohol and drugs; and a decline in work quality.

Psychological symptoms are insomnia, fatigue, isolation and loneliness, disorientation, frustration, criticism of the new country, nervousness, self-doubt, irritability, depression, anger, and emotional and intellectual withdrawal.

The effects of culture shock on intercultural communication are obvious: The immigrant's—or visitor's—intercultural communication becomes less effective. For example, frustrations with the new culture may be interpreted by intercultural receivers as hostility toward them. Intercultural communication receivers need to be sensitive to the difficulties of culture shock that an individual may be experiencing.

Third-Culture Kids

The term *third culture* has been used by some to refer to a lifestyle shared by individuals acting in missionary, diplomatic, and business roles attempting to relate their home and sojourn cultures. Ruth Hill Useem (Useem & Downie, 1976) first coined the term *third-culture kids* to refer to children in expatriate families who reside outside of their home culture for years at a time. Other terms that have been used are global nomads, transnationals, and internationally mobile children (Gerner, Perry, Moselle, & Archbold, 1992). Eakin (1998) and Useem (1999) (cited in Kidd & Lankenau, n.d.) argue that these people integrate elements of their home culture and their various cultures of residence into a third, different and distinct culture and may experience cultural marginality because of no longer feeling comfortable in any specific culture.

While most research has been with children from the United States, studies have shown that third-culture kids have a high level of interest in travel and learning languages and feel accepting of cultures and diversity (Gerner et al., 1992). Iwama (1990) found third-culture kids to be more self-confident, flexible, active, and curious and to have greater bilingual ability.

Does biculturalism as represented by third-culture kids represent a way to transcend nationalism and ethnocentrism and a way to create diverse communities (Willis, 1994)? There are suggestions of difficulties: Third-culture kids may have difficulty in maintaining relationships and in direct problem solving (Smith, 1991).

IMMIGRATION

Today, about 185 million people live outside their countries of birth, up from 104 million in 1985 and 84 million in 1975. The actual total is much higher. People migrate for a variety of reasons—from fleeing

Soon after arriving in the United States from Peru, I cried almost every day. I was so tense I heard without hearing, and this made me feel foolish. I also escaped into sleeping more than twelve hours at a time and dreamed of my life, family, and friends in Lima. After three months of isolating myself in the house and speaking to no one, I ventured out. I then began to criticize everything about this new culture: values, customs, climate, and its people. During this time I began to idealize my own homeland. I also began to have severe headaches. Finally I consulted a doctor, but she only gave me a lot of drugs to relieve the pain. Neither my doctor nor my teachers ever mentioned the two magic words that could have changed my life drastically during those times: culture shock! When I learned about this I began to see things from a new point of view and was better able to accept myself and my feelings.

I now realize most of the Americans I met in Lima before I came to the U.S. were also in one of the stages of culture shock. They demonstrated a somewhat hostile attitude toward Peru, making crude jokes and fun of the people and culture around them. Peruvians sensed this hostility and usually moved from an initially friendly attitude to a defensive, aggressive attitude or to avoidance as in my case. The Americans mostly stayed within the safe cultural familiarity of the embassy compound. Many seemed to feel that the difficulties they were experiencing in Peru were specially created by Peruvians to create discomfort for "gringos." In other words, they displaced their problem of adjustment and blamed everything on Peru for being an underdeveloped culture.

—R. Bimrose, July 1981, quoted in
Handbook of Intercultural Training
(Landis & Brislin, 1983, p. 30)

from war or persecution to better economic opportunity, from political conflict to labor surpluses.

Judge Learned Hand (1944) could have been speaking of all immigrants when he said,

> Some of us have chosen America as the land of our adoption; the rest have come from those who did the same. For this reason we have some right to consider ourselves a picked group, a group of those who had the courage to break from the past and brave the dangers and loneliness of a strange land. What was the object that nerved us, or those who went before us, to this choice? We sought liberty; freedom from oppression, freedom from want, freedom to be ourselves. (p. 26)

Judge Learned Hand omitted an important group—slaves—brought involuntarily to the United States, which you'll study in more detail in Chapter 18.

The following examples demonstrate how the immigrant acculturation experience proceeds.

Migration From Japan to Brazil and Peru

Brazil is home to the largest Japanese community outside Japan. Some 1.5 million people of Japanese origin now live in Brazil. Most arrived in Brazil to work on coffee plantations. Some have built up large agricultural concerns. Similarly, Japanese who migrated to Peru went as contract laborers. The Japanese in Peru have gone through periods of prejudice to assimilation as an immigrant's son became a popular president of the country.

Japanese migration to Peru began in 1899 when contract workers began to arrive to work on large haciendas. By 1923, when contract labor was stopped, some 18,000 Japanese lived in Peru. Relatives of previous immigrants continued to arrive.

Many of the Japanese settled in Lima and other cities and opened small businesses. Before World War II, two incidents greatly affected the Japanese immigrants: A popular book by a Peruvian journalist contended that the Inca Empire founder had been a Japanese fisherman. This led to speculation that Japan would try to lead Peru's Indian majority in an uprising against the White government. Then, rumors spread that caches of weapons had been found on property owned by Japanese immigrants. So after Pearl Harbor, the government closed Japanese schools and social organizations, seized business properties, and deported more than 1,700 *nikkei*, or people of Japanese descent, to relocation camps in the United States. Some were deported to Japan in exchange for U.S. civilian prisoners held in Japanese-controlled territories.

Today, the nikkei population is estimated as anywhere from 50,000 to 100,000, a small percentage of Peru's 24 million residents. Like Indians and Blacks, the nikkei experience racial prejudice from Peru's White upper class, but the nikkei are assimilating. Half of the Japanese-Peruvians are of mixed origin, and most do not speak Japanese. A 1989 census found that over 90% of Japanese-Peruvians are Roman Catholic, with fewer than 3% Buddhist. At least 40% maintain no contact with nikkei social organizations.

Migration to Argentina

Like the United States, Argentina, with a population of about 33 million, is a nation of immigrants. One group arrived in 1865 from mining towns in Wales seeking to escape English rule and establish a Welsh state. They were welcomed by an Argentine government eager for growth. The Welsh built self-contained farming and sheep ranching communities in Patagonia on the eastern slopes of the Andes. Their town councils were notably democratic, allowing women to vote.

The immigrants remained nationalistic. The great-grandchildren of the original immigrants are Argentine, yet their language and customs are in some ways more traditional than modern-day Wales. Exchange students study in Wales, and the regional government invites teachers from Wales to keep the language and culture alive.

Late into the 19th century, Argentina was still only sparsely populated, largely with descendants of Spanish settlers and only the remnants of indigenous groups. A strong agricultural economy brought immigrants from southern and eastern Europe—primarily Italy and Spain. Argentina became a blend of Italian and Spanish. Writer Abel Posse, in *The Dogs of Paradise* (1989), for example, describes Christopher Columbus as a typical Argentine—"an Italian who learned Spanish." By 1914, more than a third of Argentina's population was foreign born.

Argentina has been described as the "most European" of the Americas. The third largest ethnic group is made up of Jews from Russia, followed by Arabs.

Argentina continues to be a magnet for immigrants, a land of promise. However, the "Latinamericanization" of new immigrants has raised concerns. The new immigrants are more likely to be racially mixed and darker skinned. And competition for jobs has become an issue. To deal with the increasing illegal immigration, Argentina is attempting to control its borders.

Migration From the United States to Brazil

Following the Civil War in the latter half of the 19th century, thousands of people from all over the South migrated to Mexico, Cuba, and Brazil. Ellsworths, Lees, McKnights, Stegalls, and Yancys were part of an estimated 10,000 to 40,000 Confederates who emigrated, many to Brazil, where the government promised cheap land in the hope that the immigrants would establish Brazil as a cotton-producing country where slavery was still legal.

The immigrants settled in several parts of Brazil: in an area located 500 miles from the mouth of the Amazon River which became the city of Santarem, in Rio Doce near the coast, and in settlements called Juquia, New Texas, Villa Americana, and Xiririca in southern Brazil near São Paulo. Only Villa Americana prospered.

Some failed and moved to the cities or returned to the United States. Others were successful and made fortunes in cotton and watermelons. The immigrants brought baseball, peaches, pecans, and various strains of rice to Brazil.

The immigrants remained in cloistered communities and established schools, churches, and cemeteries because the Roman Catholic Church in Brazil would not allow the Protestant Confederates to be buried with Catholics. Even 80 years later, many spoke English exclusively in homes. But with time, more and more of the descendants moved to the cities and assimilated into the Brazilian culture.

Today, the descendants of the Confederates are attempting to recover this heritage through picnics and celebrations wearing antebellum gowns and Civil War uniforms, flying the Confederate flag, and sharing old photographs and stories, speaking Portuguese in a Southern drawl.

The experience of the Confederates in Brazil is not unlike the experiences of immigrants in the United States.

Immigration to the United States

Perhaps the least understood immigration into the Americas was the first one. The migration experiences of the groups now known as American Indians are lost in history, so this chapter begins with immigration to Colonial America.

Colonial Policies on Immigration

In Colonial America, three principal responses to immigration developed. Massachusetts wanted settlers who were "religiously pure." Virginia and Maryland recruited immigrants for cheap labor but did not allow full participation in government. Pennsylvania welcomed all European settlers on equal terms and as equal participants in the colony. Later, the Pennsylvania model largely prevailed in the new nation, which in its first 100 years encouraged immigration.

U.S. Policies on Immigration

Congress has total and complete authority over immigration. The president is limited to policies on refugees. Congress defines a **refugee** as a noncitizen outside the United States who is unable or unwilling to return to the country of nationality because of persecution or a well-founded fear of persecution and an **asylee** as a noncitizen inside the United States who is unable or unwilling to return to the country of nationality because of persecution or a well-founded fear of persecution.

In 1798, Congress passed the Act Concerning Aliens, which gave the president power to deport all immigrants deemed dangerous to national security.

Beginning in 1875, the first federal laws limiting immigration were enacted to bar convicts and prostitutes. Over the years, other laws excluded those having "physical, mental, and moral defects," those who advocated "subversive doctrines," and those who had "economic disqualifications" or were illiterate (Carliner, 1977; Carliner, Guttentag, Helton, & Henderson, 1990).

> Uncontrolled immigration threatens to deconstruct the nation we grew up in . . . Balkanization beckons.
>
> —Patrick J. Buchanan,
> *The Death of the West* (2002)
>
> Once I thought to write a history of the immigrants in America. Then, I discovered that the immigrants were American history.
>
> —Oscar Handlin,
> Pulitzer Prize-winning historian

Beginning in 1921, the U.S. Congress established country quotas based on the origins of the existing U.S. population to prevent major changes in the country's racial and ethnic makeup. These laws had the effect of favoring immigration from northern and western Europe. In 1965, country quotas were replaced with hemisphere quotas.

The Immigration Act of 1990 raised the annual immigration level from 540,000 to 700,000 in 1992 through 1994, thereafter dropping it to an annual minimum of 675,000. The new law also cuts back on provisions under which potential immigrants have been denied entry in the past on grounds of ideology or sexual orientation and allows more immigrants to qualify for permanent residency by virtue of investment capital and professional skills rather

DRAWINGBOARD / CONRAD

SOURCE: By political cartoonist Conrad, which appeared August 21, 1996, in the *Los Angeles Times*. Copyright © 1996, Los Angeles Times. Reprinted by permission.

than family ties. Current immigration policy favors foreigners with immediate relatives in the United States. This benefits the relatives of the more recent immigrants—Asians and Latin Americans. To diversify the flow of immigrants, Congress created a permanent immigration "lottery" that will provide from

40,000 to 55,000 visas to residents of mostly European countries.

One consequence of the September 11, 2001, attack on the United States is that immigration law has achieved new visibility and a much greater sense of national importance in the minds of legislators, the Bush administration, the media, and the public. This attention has already resulted in changes in immigration law and practice in the post-September 11 era. Many more changes are likely in the future.

Illegal immigrants who enter the United States come from all over the world. In 1997, the U.S. Immigration and Naturalization Service (now the Bureau of Citizenship and Immigration Services [BCIS], a part of the U.S. Department of Homeland Security) put the number of illegal immigrants at 5 million—half being in California. Half of these arrive with temporary visas, typically at airports. The remainder enter without valid documents, usually across the U.S.-Mexico border. About half of the total originate from Mexico. Today, the children of illegal immigrants have the same right to attend school as do U.S. citizens and permanent residents based on the 1982 Supreme Court ruling on *Plyler v. Doe*. Voters in Texas and California challenge this practice in the belief that recent immigration unfairly burdens the states' economies.

Ways in Which Foreign-Born Persons May Legally Be in the United States

Temporary visas are issued for a wide range of time spans. A transit visa may be good for as little as two days for a traveler stopping here en route to another country. There are also tourist and student visas. Work visas are often issued for several years at a time, and almost all of them are renewable.

Immigrant visas are popularly known as "green cards," even though the color of the card has been changed to pink. They are the most prized possession, allowing immigrants to reside permanently in the United States. "Green card" status makes immigrants eligible for full citizenship in 5 years. Most green cards issued each year go to family members who have relatives already living here.

Citizenship gives the immigrant additional rights, including the right to vote, hold some public offices, and obtain federal government jobs. The Fourteenth Amendment to the Constitution states that all persons born in the United States and subject to its jurisdiction are citizens. (One exception to this is children born to diplomats.) Immigrants who become citizens receive priority in petitioning the government to issue green cards to their relatives.

SOURCE: Compiled from the *Los Angeles Times*, October 1, 1991, p. H4, and *Time*, October 14, 1991, p. 26.

Contributing Countries Prior to 1800

Prior to 1800, the number of immigrants from Europe to the New World was between 4 million and 5 million. In comparison, the largest migration was

You've probably heard some of these lines from this poem mounted on the pedestal of the Statue of Liberty. Are there any that change the meaning of the commonly known ones?

The New Colossus

Not like the brazen
giant of Greek fame,

With conquering limbs
astride from land to land;

Here at our sea-washed,
sunset gates shall stand

A mighty woman with a
torch, whose flame

Is the imprisoned lightning,
and her name

Mother of Exiles. From her
beacon hand

Glows world-wide welcome;
her mild eyes command

The air-bridged harbor
that twin cities frame.

"Keep, ancient lands, your
storied pomp!" cries she

With silent lips. "Give me
your tired, your poor,

Your huddled masses yearning
to breathe free,

The wretched refuse of
your teeming shore,

Send these, the homeless,
tempest-tost to me,

I lift my lamp beside the

golden door!"

SOURCE: Poem written in 1883 by Emma Lazarus, a Sephardic Jew.

the movement of slaves from Africa mainly to the New World. It is estimated that 12 million people were transported as slaves, with 10 million actually surviving the trip. This group was largely held in a state of separation and segregation.

Contributing Countries

Since the beginning of the 19th century, as many as 70 million people have immigrated to the Western Hemisphere. Between 1846 and 1932, 53 million people migrated, all but 2 million from Europe and more than three-quarters of that number from five areas: the British Isles, Italy, Austria-Hungary, Germany, and Spain. The United States received 60% of those.

Ellis Island processed its first immigrant in 1892 and its last in 1954. More than half of the immigrants entering the United States between 1892 and 1924 passed through its gates. In its peak year, 1907, 1 million immigrants were processed. The center handled 17 million newcomers from more than 90 countries. Of the total, 2.5 million were from Italy, 2.2 million from Austria-Hungary, 1.9 million from Russia, and 633,000 from Germany.

Today, 40% of the country's population—more than 100 million—can trace a heritage to a family member who passed through the immigration processing station on Ellis Island a

Table 13.1   Immigration to the United States

Decade	Number Immigrated	Major Contributing Countries
1820s	152,000	Ireland, Great Britain, France
1830s	599,000	Ireland, Germany, Great Britain
1840s	1,713,000	Ireland, Germany, Great Britain
1850s	2,598,000	Germany, Ireland, Great Britain
1860s	2,315,000	Germany, Great Britain, Ireland
1870s	2,812,000	Germany, Great Britain, Ireland
1880s	5,247,000	Germany, Great Britain, Ireland
1890s	3,688,000	Italy, Austria-Hungary, Russia, Germany
1900s	8,795,000	Austria-Hungary, Italy, Russia
1910s	5,736,000	Italy, Russia, Austria-Hungary
1920s	4,107,000	Italy, Germany, Great Britain
1930s	528,000	Germany, Italy, Great Britain
1940s	1,035,000	Germany, Great Britain, Italy
1950s	2,515,000	Germany, Canada, Mexico, Italy
1960s	3,321,700	Mexico, Canada, Cuba
1970s	4,493,300	Mexico, Philippines, Cuba, Korea
1980s	8,500,000 [a]	Mexico, Philippines, Vietnam, China
1990s	10,000,000 [b]	Mexico, Philippines, China, Vietnam
2000s	10,000,000 [c]	Not yet known

SOURCE: U.S. Bureau of the Census, *Statistical Abstract of the United States,* various editions, and *Los Angeles Times,* May 5, 1991, p. M3. Copyright © 1991, Los Angeles Times. Adapted with permission.

a. Not including 2.3 million under the 1986 amnesty law.
b. Estimate by Gene McNary, commissioner of the Immigration and Naturalization Service.
c. Estimate by Center for Immigration Studies, Washington, D.C.

half mile from the Statue of Liberty. In 1990, the facility was restored as a museum.

As you study the history of immigration presented in Table 13.1, identify the years of least and most number of immigrants. What happened in those years that affected immigration? Identify the decades of significant shifts in the major contributing countries. What impacts did those shifts have on the United States?

Each major wave of immigrants experienced discrimination. In the 1850s, the Germans and Irish who were fleeing economic destitution were largely viewed as a "lower class of people." In the 1880s and 1890s, eastern and southern European immigrants were viewed with suspicion because of darker skin and the religion of Catholicism. The Irish were blamed for bringing

Immigrant recollections:

Bismarck united Germany and in 1871 our father was on Germany's side against Napoleon II of France. He was in the reserves, and saw no fighting. He disliked militarism and the ungodly life of most soldiers. Therefore he moved to America before his oldest son, John, would be registered for service.

I am quite sure the ship's name was "Werra." We sailed on the Rhine River to the City of Köln (Cologne), then by rail to Bremen; on the "Werra" to New York; and by rail to New Braunfels, Comal County, Texas, March 9, 1885. I remember red hot pipes (too hot to sit on) on board ship; also the immigrants standing on deck singing:

"Noah's Arche schwankte/Lang of grauser Fluth,

Wie das Schiff auch wankte/Ihm sank nicht der Muth."

—Phillip Herbold, German immigrant

In 1880, encouraged by the success of the Swiss settlers in Texas, a group of capitalists in Basel, Switzerland, organized a land company called the Basle Land Gesellschaft. The company provided the finances for the founding of a Swiss colony on the Guadalupe River approximately three miles south from Seguin. Around 1880, ten families left Switzerland and settled on the company's land. Each one was provided with sixty acres of land, a log cabin, a horse, a cow, chickens, hogs, and two hundred dollars per year to take care of the family needs.

Samuel Prabst was the first administrator of the colony. He was succeeded by Fredrick Wilhelm Naumann, who was given four hundred acres of land for his service. After a few years the colony failed and many of the original settlers moved to other parts of the state leaving only a few of the first settlers.

—Texas Institute of Cultures, San Antonio

cholera, the Italians for bringing polio, the Chinese for carrying bubonic plague, the Jews for spreading tuberculosis, and the Haitians for bringing AIDS (Kraut, 1994). However, over the course of generations, immigrant groups successfully moved from segregation to assimilation.

Studies of immigration in the 1990s have shown that the educational level of immigrants has increased. In 1960, about one-third of all new immigrants had less than 8 years of education. In the 1990s, that dropped to one-quarter. The immigrants of the 1990s did not draw on welfare any more than others. The percentage of foreign-born on welfare is presently 6.6%. Refugees are guaranteed welfare by federal law. Taking out that group, 5.1% of nonrefugee working-age immigrants receive welfare, compared to 5.3% of working-age native born. The study from the National Research Council showed that, overall, immigrants were a net economic gain for the country but that the six states with the highest concentration of immigrants were experiencing pressures as taxes go mostly to the federal government.

Distribution Within the United States

The 1980s marked the second largest immigration decade in U.S. history. Those who immigrated in the

> We find ourselves threatened by hordes of Yankee emigrants. What are we to do?
>
> —Manuel Micheltorena, Mexican governor of California, 1846

1980s are especially visible because 80% are concentrated in six states and primarily in urban areas (see Table 13.2). Special attention needs to be focused on California. The United States receives nearly as many immigrants as all other countries put together. Half of that is to California, which in terms of the pressures of immigration likens it to New York in the early 1900s. In 1970, the percentage of minority students in California public schools was 27.3%; by 1980, it was 42.9%. In 1998, California became the nation's first "majority-minority" state with less than 50% White population. If current trends continue, by 2020 California's population will be 40% Hispanic, 39% White, 14% Asian-American, and 7% African-American.

There are now 50 ethnic groups with sizable populations in the United States. Florida's Dade County School District, the country's fourth largest, enrolls students from 123 countries. In New York City, 1 in 4 children under 10 years of age has non-English-speaking immigrant parents. During the 1991-1992 school year, minorities became the majority in Texas public schools. In the San Antonio School District, 81% of its students were Hispanic, 12% were African-American, and 7% were White and other ethnic groups.

PREDICTORS OF ACCULTURATION

No immigrant, as long as livelihood needs are to be met in a new country, can escape acculturation. Individuals do differ, however, as to what degree they become acculturated. Young Yun Kim (1986, 1988) has identified background characteristics that are accurate predictors of an immigrant's success in acculturation.

Similarity of Culture

The similarity of the original culture to the new host culture is one of the most important factors in successful acculturation. For example, an immigrant from Canada to the United States finds acculturation easier than a Vietnamese immigrant from Southeast Asia will. There can be differences

Table 13.2   Percentage of U.S. Foreign-Born Population, by State, 1997

California	24.9
New York	19.6
Hawaii	18.1
Florida	16.4
New Jersey	15.4
Arizona	14.4
Texas	11.3

SOURCE: U.S. Census Bureau, *Profile of the Foreign-Born Population in the United States,* 1997.

NOTE: 31 states have less than 5% foreign born. These include most states in the Midwest and the South.

among immigrants from the same country—depending on, for example, whether they grew up in a cosmopolitan urban center or in a rural area where there existed relatively less outside influence.

Personal Characteristics and Experiences

Younger immigrants adapt more easily than older ones. Educational background also plays a part, and a person's personality (risk taking or being gregarious and curious or not, for example) can determine how readily they will desire to blend in with a new culture. Finally, previous travel, contact with overseas friends or family, and mass media influence also come into play.

Effect of Media and Transportation Advances

It is useful to compare the immigration peaks of the early 1900s with today's. The European immigration of the early 1900s brought millions of people who at the time seemed just as alien to many native-born U.S. citizens as Salvadorans or Koreans do today. However, there are some important—and critical—differences in the intercultural communication context: Media and transportation advances contribute to the difference.

The immigrants of the 1900s left homes permanently, with little hope of returning even for a visit, and thus lost much of the original culture in assimilation. The immigrants of the 1900s had little contact with friends and families left behind. Letters and messages brought by friends were slow. Immigrants in the United States did find newspapers and periodicals printed entirely or in part in languages other than English. These not only helped immigrants maintain contacts with other immigrants but also adjust to life in the United States. The non-English press was weakened by restrictive legislation in the 1920s and by a drop in the number of new immigrants. At the same time, members of the second generation were not interested in newspapers in the languages of their parents (Govorchin, 1961). According to the 1940 U.S. Census there were 8,354,700 people in the United States whose native language was a language other than English. At that time, there were about 1,000 newspapers and periodicals printed entirely or in part in languages other than English (Chyz, 1945). In 1942, there were nearly 1,000 radio stations in the United States, 200 of which broadcast in some 26 languages. In fact, though, the media contributed to assimilation. Today, there are some 200 ethnic newspapers and magazines in New York. San Jose, California, has dozens of Vietnamese publications.

Today's immigrants can easily return for visits. Today's immigrants can watch television programs from home countries and be in easy telephone contact. There is not as great a pressure to assimilate. It is quite possible to maintain original cultural identity and participate in a meaningful way in the larger society (see Box 13.1).

Box 13.1

GERMANS' REMINDER OF HOME LIVES ON

Germans first arrived in large numbers in the 1720s, settling in Pennsylvania. A second and larger wave arrived between the 1830s and 1930s, with most going to the Midwest and the Upper Plains states. Today, about 23% of the U.S. population list German ancestry first on census forms. The German-born population was a record high 30% in 1890.

Immigrant farmers from the fertile lowlands of northern Germany—conquerors of Ohio's Great Black Swamp—turned Henry County into what some believe is a mirror image of their "fatherland."

Walter Delventhal, who recently shepherded the organization of the Low German Club through Napoleon and Henry County officials, said the majority of the German people in Henry County came from the Visselhovede area, a small community in the northern German lowlands generally between Bremen and Hamburg.

And the majority of people in Henry County are of German descent.

A sampling of ancestry of Henry County residents, taken from 1990 Census reports, showed that 18,832 residents claimed to be of German ancestry.

(Continued)

Box 13.1, *Continued*

The second-largest group, by ancestry, were the English, with a total of 1,518.

. . .

Earlier this month, the county commissioners and Napoleon Mayor Don Strange signed an agreement establishing a sister city-county relationship with Visselhovede. They hope the relationship will encourage Henry County residents to seek their roots in Germany.

Mr. Delventhal and his wife, Lucia, have returned to their hometown of Visselhovede three times, in 1972, 1983, and 1984.

"It's just like going home," he said with a smile. "They talk just like we do."

The Delventhals still speak "Low German" at home as their first language. Their children can understand it but do not speak it.

The phrase "Low German" refers to the flat lowlands of northern Germany. The language is different from "High German," which is spoken in the southern highlands, including the Black Forest.

The Delventhals attend St. John Lutheran Church in Freedom Township, which until the 1960s had both German and English services.

Germans traditionally had strong ties with their churches, and that continued when they came to the United States.

"What happened was that one family moved from Visselhovede or Walsrode, a village to the south, then wrote back to their relatives talking about how good things are in their new home," he explained. Soon, their relatives wanted to come too.

Speeding the exodus was the German tradition that the oldest son always inherits the family farm.

That left a lot of other family members disgruntled and anxious to move to the new world, he said.

Russell Patterson, a Napoleon druggist and grandson of a German immigrant, said his grandfather, Wilhelm Frederick Franz Bernicke, paid $30 for steerage passage to the United States.

Like others, he arrived on the East Coast in 1893 to find that all of the farmland already was owned, so he used his money for a train ride west. He ultimately landed in Henry County.

Hamler, once the hunting grounds of the Ottawa, Shawnee, Seneca, and Miami Indians, today is best known for its summer festival, when upwards of 25,000 or more polka lovers descend on the town.

SOURCE: William Ferguson, "Germans' Reminder of Home Lives On," *The Blade*, May 25, 1997, pp. A11-A12. Used with permission.

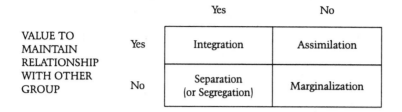

Figure 13.1   Dimensions of acculturation include original cultural identity and relationships with other groups.

CATEGORIES OF ACCULTURATION

Acculturation, or **cultural adaptation**, refers to an immigrant's learning and adopting the norms and values of the new host culture. Unlike a temporary visitor, the immigrant must find a new source of livelihood and build a new life. This adapting to a new host culture is called acculturation. Berry, Kim, and Boski (1987) have described acculturation in relation to two dimensions: the value placed on maintaining one's original cultural identity and the value given to maintaining relationships with other groups in one's new culture.

As shown in Figure 13.1, **assimilation** results from giving up one's original cultural identity and moving into full participation in the new culture. The person identifies with the country and not an ethnic group. Assimilation is a long-term and sometimes multigenerational process. True **integration** is maintaining important parts of one's original culture as well as becoming an integral part of the new culture. Integration ensures a continuity of culture. The words *biculturalism* and *pluralism* have also been used to describe integration. The person feels as loyal to the country as to any ethnic group. Integration is supported by the dual-nationality trend, which allows expatriates from immigrant-sending nations to retain rights as nationals while taking on citizenship status in the United States or elsewhere. In a seeming paradox, new U.S. citizens must formally renounce allegiances to foreign governments as part of the naturalization process, but U.S. law still permits citizens to possess other nationalities.

Separation and **segregation** refer to maintaining one's original culture and not participating in the new culture. To some, segregation connotes a judgment of superiority and inferiority and prejudice and hatred between groups. Others

Czech immigrants founded dozens of communities in Texas, making the language the third most-spoken in the state. Annual fests renew ties to the culture with music and kolaches.

SOURCE: Photo courtesy Fort Bend County Czech Alliance.

use the term *insularity* to connote separation only. The person has a strong sense of ethnic identity.

Marginalization refers to losing one's cultural identity and not having any psychological contact with the larger society. The person has feelings of "not belonging anywhere."

Keep these terms in mind as you read the following chapters that describe various cultures within U.S. culture.

Melting Pot Concept

The phrase most often used to describe the assimilation of the early immigrants into the United States is "melting pot," which comes from Israel

Zangwill's popular 1908 play *The Melting Pot.* The **melting pot** of old included English, German, Irish, French, and Italian immigrants and encouraged ethnic uniformity. Patriotic significance was placed on learning English and becoming "American." You seldom think of those of English, German, Irish, French, and Italian descent as "ethnic groups" because throughout the generations these groups have become assimilated into a somewhat "homogenized" society. There are, for example, more than 50 million people of German heritage in the United States, yet that culture is not particularly evident today.

Automaker Henry Ford established for his company the "English Melting Pot School." The graduation ceremony featured the automaker's foreign-born employees, dressed in Old World costumes and carrying signs noting their birthplace, marching into a large, kettle-shaped prop labeled "Melting Pot." Moments later, the same people would emerge dressed in neat business suits and waving small U.S. flags.

Even in that era there were concerns about immigration. In the time between 1870 and 1920, approximately 15% of the U.S. population was foreign born (see Table 13.3). President Theodore Roosevelt (1901-1909) urged "native Americans" (he didn't mean indigenous peoples) to have more children to combat the disintegration of racial purity that he said was threatening the American way of life. Charles Davenport, a leader of the Eugenics Movement, argued for protecting racial purity from eastern and southern European immigration. His lobby helped pass the Immigration Act of 1924, which is one of the most restrictive and discriminatory immigration statutes ever enacted in the United States.

CITIZENSHIP POLICIES

Germany

Germany had the industrialized world's most liberal political asylum law (O'Connor, 1991). After World War II, Germany wrote into its constitution a guarantee to shelter all persecuted people. In the first year after unification, about 250,000 foreigners sought asylum—most in the Eastern sector and most not political exiles but economic refugees hoping for a better life. That number doubled the next year. The hearing process for refugees could take up to 3 years, and less than 5% were finally granted permanent asylum. During that waiting period the refugees were given full access to Germany's generous welfare system that provided free housing, electricity, medical care, schooling for children, and stipends of up to approximately

Table 13.3   Profile of the U.S. Foreign-Born Population

Time Period	Number (in millions)	% of Population
1850	2.2	9.7
1860	4.1	13.2
1870	5.6	14.4
1880	6.7	13.3
1890	9.2	14.8
1900	10.3	13.6
1910	13.5	14.7
1920	13.9	13.2
1930	14.2	11.6
1940	11.6	8.8
1950	10.3	6.9
1960	9.7	5.4
1970	9.6	4.7
1980	14.1	6.2
1990	19.8	7.9
1997	25.8	9.7
2000	28.4	10.4

Countries of Birth of the U.S. Foreign-Born Population, 1997	Number (in thousands)
Mexico	7,017
Philippines	1,132
China	1,107
Cuba	913
Vietnam	770
India	748
Soviet Union	734
Dominican Republic	632
El Salvador	607
United Kingdom	606
Korea	591
Germany	578
Canada	542

SOURCE: U.S. Census Bureau, *Profile of the Foreign-Born Population in the United States,* 1997.

$10,000 a year. These benefits often far exceeded what refugees could make at home—and exceeded what many Germans, particularly Easterners, made.

Chancellor Helmut Kohl labeled the asylum issue second in importance only to monetary stability. In 1992, Germany announced plans to repatriate thousands of Romanians (most being denied asylum of this group are Roma), and in 1993, the German Parliament voted to end the constitutional right of foreigners to seek asylum. Only those foreigners who arrive by air from dangerous homelands and who hold proper travel documents may now file for refugee status.

In addition, the German constitution gives automatic right of abode to ethnic Germans scattered throughout Eastern Europe and the former Soviet Union. As a result, more than 1.5 million immigrants from the former Soviet Union, most with little or no German language proficiency, received citizenship over the past decade based on their forebears having settled along the Volga River as much as 300 years ago.

Postwar immigration brought the percentage of non-ethnic German to about 5% of Germany's population. Germany did not strive to be a melting pot. Hundreds of thousands of Turks, for example, fluent in German whose families have lived in Germany for two or three generations, were not eligible for citizenship. People of non-ethnic German heritage who have lived in Germany for some time are called *auslander*, which translates as outlander or foreigner. Immigrants came and were accepted as laborers in Germany's booming economy. Most expected to return home. By 1999, there were 7.3 million foreign nationals among Germany's 84 million residents. Approximately half had lived in Germany at least 10 years, 30% at least 20 years, and at least 1.5 million were born in Germany.

Social movements beginning in the late 1960s encouraged immigrants to become more involved in public life. But without voting rights or a voice in social affairs immigrants experienced antiforeigner sentiments particularly in regions with high unemployment. Attacks on these foreigners and on those seeking asylum led to renewed charges of German **xenophobia**, or fear of strangers or foreigners, and of extreme nationalism. The violence, however, has been concentrated almost exclusively among the small-fringe skinhead youth group, and thousands of Germans have protested the violence against foreigners.

There were three ways of becoming a citizen of Germany: by birth, by naturalization, and for ethnic Germans from Eastern Europe and the Soviet successor states, by claim under the "Right of Return." Traditionally, Germany granted citizenship on the basis of descent, the principle of *jus sanguinis* or of defining citizenship by inheritance. Effective in 2000, a new nationality law came into effect that grants citizenship by place of birth, the principle of *jus soli*, in an attempt to ensure social and domestic peace.

The German government estimated that half of the foreigners living in Germany became eligible for citizenship under the new law. All children born in Germany now automatically receive citizenship if at least one of their parents lived in Germany for at least 8 years. Children of foreign parents born in Germany are now entitled to dual citizenship until age 23 when they must then choose one or the other. To receive German citizenship, they must be loyal to Germany and its people and have a good command of the German language. The new citizenship law also facilitates the naturalization of foreign nationals who have lived in Germany for many years.

Israel

Proclaimed on May 14, 1948, Israel was a relatively poor, besieged nation in need of building the country's population. Citizenship may be acquired by birth, residence, naturalization, and the Law of Return. The Proclamation of the Establishment of the State of Israel stated, "The State of Israel will be open for Jewish immigration and the ingathering of the exiles; it will foster the development of the country for all its inhabitants; it will be based on freedom, justice, and peace as envisaged by the prophets of Israel; it will ensure complete equality of social and political rights to all its inhabitants irrespective of religion, race or sex." A fundamental aspiration of the State of Israel is *aliyah*, literally ascending, the Hebrew word for immigration into Israel. The Law of Return enacted in 1950 granted anyone with a Jewish mother or who had converted to Judaism the right to come to Israel as an *oleh* (a Jew immigrating to Israel) and become a citizen. By 1951, the number of immigrants more than doubled what the Jewish population of the country had been in 1948. The government devoted much effort to absorbing the immigrants through residence construction, job creation, Hebrew language instruction, and educational expansion to meet the needs of children from diverse cultural backgrounds. (See Table 13.4 for immigration into Israel by year.)

Since 1970, the right to immigrate under the Law of Return was extended to include the child and the grandchild of a Jew, the spouse of a child of a Jew, and spouse of the grandchild of a Jew. The purpose of the change was to ensure the unity of families where intermarriage had occurred even though the Halakha, or Jewish religious law, specifies that only those born to a Jewish mother and those who have converted are Jews. Since the establishment of Israel, more than 2.5 million people have immigrated, the largest numbers

Table 13.4   Immigration Into Israel, by Year

1948-1951 (4-year total)	688,000
1952-1959 (8-year total)	272,000
1960-1969 (10-year total)	374,000
1970-1979 (10-year total)	346,000
1980-1989 (10-year total)	154,000
1990-1991 (2-year total; Soviet immigration)	375,000
1992-1999 (8-year total)	582,000
2000-2002 (3-year total)	140,000

SOURCE: The State of Israel.

from "countries of distress," places where Jews are unwelcome, harassed, or persecuted.

Today, Israel is a prosperous nation with at least no immediate threats from its neighbors. Israel's population today is about 6 million, which includes about 1 million Israeli Arabs. Soviet Jews were permitted to leave the Soviet Union in large numbers in the late 1980s. The collapse of the Soviet Union in late 1991 brought more Soviet immigrants. Some of these have a spouse, father, or grandparent who is Jewish but are not Jews themselves under Jewish religious law. Some Israelis fear that the country is become a preferred destination for non-Jews from the former Soviet Union and other economically depressed areas who immigrated only for economic reasons and who have no desire to become Jewish. Some have proposed limiting immigration. The issue is no less than the character of Israel as a Jewish state.

Japan

Unlike the United States, immigration was not a concern until recently. Between 1976 and 1983, the total inflow of documented immigrant workers into Japan was between 20,000 and 30,000 a year. The numbers began to increase in 1984 and reached 95,000 in 1990. Undocumented immigrant workers based on violations of the Immigration Act were only 1,889 in 1982, but grew to 36,264 in 1990. Estimates of the number of undocumented workers in 1991 ranged from 200,000 to 500,000.

In 2000, a new immigration law went into effect. Under the new law, illegal immigrants can no longer avoid the possibility of being fined or

After Japan attacked Pearl Harbor, President Franklin D. Roosevelt signed Executive Order 9066, which led to the forced evacuation of about 120,000 people of Japanese descent from the West Coast and their relocation to 10 internment centers. (Approximately two-thirds of those relocated were U.S. citizens.) Internees lost their houses and farms, their livelihoods, and their freedom. Japanese-Americans remained loyal to the United States. In fact, the 422nd Regimental Combat Team, which included Japanese-American volunteers from these camps, is the most highly decorated unit in U.S. military history. Notice how the camp newspaper stresses loyalty to the United States. In 1988, the U.S. government apologized for the internment and paid each camp survivor $20,000 as reparations. In 1998, President Bill Clinton apologized for the internment of more than 2,200 people of Japanese ancestry from 13 Latin American countries and pledged payments of $5,000 each.

imprisoned after being in Japan for 3 years. And once deported, illegal immigrants are banned from returning for 5 years. However, as in the United States and Germany, the number of undocumented workers is increasing.

FROM THE INTERCULTURAL PERSPECTIVE

International travel is becoming more and more common. Some people may stay in a country for a short time; others may stay longer or even permanently. If a person lives in a new culture for some time (typically a few months or more), that individual usually experiences culture shock. Culture shock is used to describe feelings of anxiety and disorientation that come from living in a new culture. Over time, people learn how to live in and adapt to the norms and values of the new culture. This process is called acculturation. There are several things that affect how well a person may acculturate. When a person's home culture is similar to the new culture, it is easier to adjust to the new culture. Generally, younger and better-educated people adjust more quickly to a new culture. Also, a person's personality can affect acculturation. Outgoing, curious, and talkative people are often very successful at acculturating. People who have had contact with the culture before, such as through travel, on television, or in movies, also may acculturate better.

The United States is literally a country of immigrants because for more than 100 years immigration has been encouraged. This policy came from the Pennsylvania colony's tradition of allowing open immigration. Most people came voluntarily, mostly looking for economic opportunity. However, the largest group of people who came before 1800 did not immigrate by choice. It is estimated that 12 million people were taken to the Americas as slaves. Only about 10 million survived the conditions on the ships.

The years between 1880 and 1919 represent a major period of immigration to the United States. This period of time has been called the "melting pot" era because so many people came to the United States and became citizens. The word that describes this "melting pot" concept is assimilation. When people assimilate into a new culture, they leave their old culture behind. They identify with the new culture, learn the culture's language, and try to participate as a member of the new culture as much as possible.

After every large wave of immigration to the United States, the group of new immigrants experienced discrimination. In the past, there was strong pressure to assimilate, and this discrimination may have added to it. However, most of the pressure to assimilate must have come from travel and communication difficulties. It was very difficult to travel between continents, and the mail system was very slow. More recent immigrants to the United States do not feel as much pressure to assimilate. Modern transportation and media allow people to continue to have contact with their old culture. For example, they can visit their home countries, watch television programs in their native languages, and talk on the telephone with friends and family back home.

KEY TERMS

acculturation	expatriate	reverse culture shock
assimilation	integration	segregation
asylee	marginalization	separation
biculturalism	melting pot	sojourner
cultural adaptation	oleh	xenophobia
culture shock	refugee	

CHAPTER 14

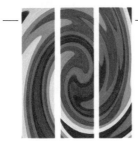

Forces Against Assimilation

What You Can Learn From This Chapter

The status of indigenous languages and cultures

The marginalization of some members of the Hmong culture

How the voluntary separation of the Amish supports cultural values that contrast to dominant U.S. cultural values

History of Asian immigration into the United States

Communication factors acting to maintain Asian-American groups' cultural identity today

Y ou read in Chapter 1 about the controversy over the use of the words *subculture* and *co-culture* and the reasons why this text uses the phrase "cultures within cultures." Cultures within cultures are most often based on economic or social class, ethnicity, race, or geographic region. Cultures within cultures usually encompass a relatively large number of people and represent the accumulation of generations of human striving. Awareness of cultures within cultures is a critical intercultural communication skill.

The focus of Chapter 13 was on patterns of immigration into the United States and other countries. In this chapter, you will read about several cultures within cultures created by immigration. First, though, the special case of indigenous cultures that experienced cultural domination is examined. Then, you'll look at two new immigrant groups, some of whom exist in marginalization. You'll look at the Amish as a culture, with strongly defined and communicated values, which has long resisted acculturation through voluntary separation. Finally, you'll review the history of Asian immigration into the United States.

The major objective of this chapter, though, is to begin to look at specialized communication media and segmented marketing as forces against assimilation. As you saw in Chapter 13, modern transportation and communication technology have modified immigrants' pressures to acculturate. In contrast to a century ago, specialized communication media and segmented marketing can have the effect of strengthening a culture's identity and lessening the pressures it feels to acculturate.

When you think of cultures within cultures, you probably think of immigrant groups. Scholars first used the word **diaspora** to refer to the experiences of Jews and, later, Armenians who were both forcibly exiled from homelands. More recently, scholars have expanded that definition to include all groups that move from one part of the world to another even if that migration was of free choice. Diaspora, of course, can have the effect of creating cultures within cultures in the country into which peoples move, as is the case with the Iu Mien and the Hmong who left the villages of Laos for life in the United States.

INDIGENOUS CULTURES

Indigenous cultures merit special consideration. The state of indigenous cultures after contact with colonizers can be traced through a historical study of the state of indigenous languages. In Canada, after the 1812 war, British colonists no longer required indigenous peoples as allies, explorers, or traders. Instead, they came to be seen as obstacles to Canadian settlement. From the early 19th century on, Canada rejected extermination for its "Indian problem" but pursued a policy of absorbing the peoples by undermining the cultural distinctiveness of aboriginal society and subjecting the indigenes to the rules and values of Euro-Canadian culture. In the United States, Congress passed the Indian Removal Act in 1820 to force American Indians west of the Mississippi River. Later, as colonists moved westward, the U.S. government sent many tribes to reservations and passed legislation intended to integrate American Indians into the rest of U.S. society. Only English-speaking teachers were

Chief Joseph of the Nez Percé nation.

employed to assimilate indigenous children into the dominant culture (Baron, 1990; Piatt, 1990).

Similar methods were widely used all over the world in an effort to assimilate indigenous peoples. In Taiwan, aboriginal tribes were dispossessed, forced to adopt Chinese names, and punished for speaking their languages. In Paraguay, the government banned Guaran from schools and required teachers to use only Spanish. The Sami people in Norway were prevented from renting or buying state-owned land by a 1902 law that required use of the Norwegian language in everyday life. In Australia, under a government policy that ran from 1910 until 1971, as many as 10% of all Aboriginal children were taken from their families to speed the process of assimilation. In countries all over the world, it was expected that the indigenous cultures and languages would eventually disappear naturally or by absorption into the population of an emerging national culture (Cobo, 1987).

Beginning in the second half of the 20th century, the situation began to shift. In the 1950s, Mexico was the scene of serious discussions and by the middle of the 1960s, the policy had changed to early literacy in one's native language and teaching Spanish as a second language (Stavenhagen, 1990). In Norway, Sami was allowed back as a language of instruction in schools in 1959. In 1969 and 1990, the right of indigenous children to be instructed in the indigenous language was legally formalized. Now, Norway, Finland, and Sweden have elected Sami consultative "parliaments." In 1975, Peru made Quechua an official language. In Paraguay now, teaching in Guaran and Spanish is mandatory. An executive decree issued in 1992 amended the constitution to include a provision protecting the development of indigenous languages, cultures, uses, customs, resources, and social organizations. Finally, in New Zealand, numerous court decisions confirmed that the Maori language is protected under the Treaty of Waitangi as a *te reo Maori*, a valued Maori treasure. Thus, in 1987, Maori was made an official language.

Without question, early laws had as an objective the assimilation of indigenous peoples into national cultures as quickly as possible and at any human cost. The trend today is decidedly different. Indigenous peoples are encouraged or forced to learn a national official language but also are allowed to, and in some cases assisted in, developing and promoting indigenous languages and cultures.

The United Nations Declaration on the Rights of Indigenous Peoples unequivocally suggests that indigenous peoples should occupy a privileged political and legal position. Indigenous peoples should have the right to autonomous governing and legal structures and institutions, including some power of taxation and control over resources and the right to use indigenous languages. In the cases where assimilation policies approached cultural genocide, such as in Australia and North America, the language of the declaration suggests that the governments could be obligated to assist in correcting past injustices and practices.

MARGINALIZATION: THE HMONG

The Hmong are among recent immigrants who have been called the most ill-prepared people ever to immigrate to the United States. The extent of differences to dominant U.S. cultural patterns places these immigrants in a state of marginalization and raises the question of whether this group will maintain a separate identity in the United States or will someday assimilate into the dominant culture.

Tran Minh Tung (1990) described the groups within the Cambodian, Laotian, Hmong, and Vietnamese refugee cultures most at risk for marginalization:

- *Newcomers*. Those who went through relocation camps experienced fear and humiliation in dehumanizing conditions resulting in passivity, dependency, and learned helplessness. The first year of relocation to the United States can be a disappointment compared to what dreams had been. Newcomers see opportunities but also experience fear, uncertainty, and unhappiness.

- *Refugee teenagers*. While the majority of refugee teenagers are well adjusted and do well in school, a significant number become involved in gang criminal behavior. Loss of traditional values and lack of support and guidance from parents themselves experiencing stress may be contributing factors.

- *Elderly refugees*. Minimal or nonexistent English-language skills result in social isolation. Family structure changes as children and grandchildren begin to take places in the new culture and become strangers. The U.S. urban environment and value placed on individualism reduce the need for interdependence traditionally provided by the family.

- *Rural refugees*. Often less sophisticated than urban counterparts, rural refugees do not fare well in a capitalistic society, although the children progress economically and socially.

The majority of young refugee adults have jobs, homes, and cordial, even if brief and infrequent, relations with U.S. colleagues and neighbors. Most of the refugees' social interactions occur within a small circle of relatives and friends in the numerous Little Saigons that have sprung up in several urban areas and re-create some feeling of home.

History

The **Hmong** (pronounced MONG and literally meaning "free men"), also known as Montagnards (Geddes, 1976), are an ancient Asian hill tribe that has resisted assimilation for millennia. A people long persecuted, the Hmong written language was destroyed centuries ago. The Hmong are thought to have originated in the Russian steppes and to have been pushed out of China in the early 1800s for refusing to discard unique ways. The Hmong kept migrating south to the highlands of northern Laos. As mercenaries for the Central Intelligence Agency (CIA) in the 1960s and 1970s, the Hmong fought the Communists in Laos. More than 40,000 died in that war. After the U.S. withdrawal from Vietnam, Hmong villages in Laos were attacked by the Laotians and Vietnamese. Many Hmong fled to refugee camps in Thailand.

Hmong refugees migrated to Australia, Canada, France, the United States, and other parts of the world. Hmong immigration to the United States started in the late 1970s. Today, more than 200,000 Hmong reside in the United States, primarily in California, Minnesota, and Wisconsin. The San Joaquin Valley in central California has become home to some 88,000 Hmong; some 32,000 reside in St. Paul, Minnesota; and 15% of the population of the small town of Wausau is now Hmong.

Cultural Patterns

Hmong culture is evident in the United States: grocery stores with familiar food, radio programs with familiar music and community news, Lao family centers and festivals, and traditional farming and funeral practices.

The Hmong continue religious practices that blend ancestor worship, animal sacrifice, and shaman healing. The killing of chickens, pigs, and an occasional dog inside the home of the ill is practiced by shamans to placate evil spirits. Rites for the dead stretch some 72 hours and mix mourning, feasting, and woodwind music. The Hmong believe that any metal in and around the body prevents passage to the other life. Hence gold and silver tooth fillings are removed. Instead of metal coffins, the Hmong use handmade oak Orthodox Jewish caskets. Red twine is strung from the casket to a cow outside the funeral chapel. The cow is sacrificed, and the meat is then cooked and brought back to the chapel where it is eaten in honor of the deceased. Hmong religious practices are misunderstood and a source of prejudice in the United States.

Hmong practices of early marriage age for females and fertility rates of 9.5 children per mother are continued by many. Between 50% and 70% of Hmong females are married before the age of 17—many at the age of 12, even though these marriages are not recognized by the state. The Hmong tribal tradition of "marriage by capture" is considered an acceptable form of elopement.

Traditionally, the girl feigns resistance as the male takes his intended to his family's home. There the father performs a 30-second ceremony using a live chicken. The bride's parents are then notified, and the payment due from the bride's family is negotiated. In Fresno, California, a Hmong immigrant kidnapped and raped a Hmong woman. His defense for abuse was to claim that marriage by capture is a form of courtship in his native Laos. His cultural defense served to reduce the criminal charges against him to false imprisonment.

Ill-prepared for life in the United States and with few marketable skills, the Hmong have the highest welfare dependency rate of any refugee group in the United States. Some Hmong youths are acculturating. Teenagers wear popular California sweat pants and sneakers. Many Hmong children are achievers in the school system and have been high school valedictorians. Some adults are adapting to the U.S. culture, but most older adults continue to exist in a state of marginalization—the homeland lost and the U.S. culture hostile and strange.

SEPARATION: THE AMISH

The Amish immigrated to the United States as a religious community. Religion provides a complete defining cultural identity for the Amish, who have voluntarily chosen to live apart from the dominant culture and resist acculturation. That separation extends to not voting.

History

The Amish and Mennonites grew out of the **Anabaptist** movement that developed in Switzerland during the 1500s. The Mennonites took their name from the Dutch reformer Menno Simons and adhered to pacifism and a strict separation of church and state. The Amish were named after the leader Jacob Ammann, a Swiss Mennonite bishop. In the late 17th century, the Amish broke away from the Mennonites, who had begun taking a more liberal view over the policy of shunning the excommunicated. As Anabaptists, the Amish believe in adult baptism and living apart from the world, preferring a simple, agrarian lifestyle. The Amish migrated from Switzerland in the 1720s to Pennsylvania to be welcomed by William Penn and to find an abundance of land for farms and freedom to worship. About 5,000 Amish lived in the United States in 1900. Today, the Amish number about 130,000 in North America and are concentrated in Lancaster County and other parts of Pennsylvania and in parts of Ohio, Indiana, Kansas, Mexico, and Ontario, Canada. Two and a half centuries later, the Amish remain basically the same (Aurand, 1938; Hostetler, 1980; Kraybill, 1989).

Values

Religion

Gelassenheit is a common German word in Amish life. Translated it means submission. The Amish believe in complete submission to God and do not separate religion and life. The Amish home serves as the church. Every moment in Amish life is a religious one. The **Ordnung** contains the church rules and outlines the values of the community. Humility, obedience, simplicity, sharing, and community cooperation are valued. The Amish do not pay or accept Social Security; elderly Amish remain in the family's home.

Pride is a sin in the Amish community. Pride is the evil face of individualism that is believed to be the death of the community and of the family. This value is even reflected in clothing. Hooks and eyes replace buttons. Shirt pockets are prohibited as they can become a place to display fancy things and hence are prideful. Indeed, the Amish are often referred to as "plain people" because of dress and lifestyle.

Controlled Use of Technology

The Amish do not condone technology unless it is clearly beneficial to the community by making it possible to continue as a community (Kraybill, 1989). The most conservative and strict, the **Old Order Amish**, avoid any use of electricity and automobiles. **New Order Amish** use telephones and powered farm equipment but use batteries and generators rather than public electricity. The **Beachy Amish**, named after the leader Moses Beachy, divided from the more conservative Amish in 1927 and use both automobiles and electricity.

Automobiles threaten the family, so horses and carriages are used and symbolize as well the tradition of a slower pace and a closeness to nature. Some Amish have adopted automatic milking machines and refrigeration because that continues to make the family farm possible. Telephones and answering machines are not permitted in homes, but Amish may be found phoning inside wooden shanties (an outhouse-type version of the phone booth) across the road from an Amish home. Telephones in the home could lead to a change in values.

Internet pioneer Howard Rheingold (1999) visited the Amish to observe telephone use. He found that the Amish do not fear technology as such but, rather, fear the ideas that technology is always beneficial, that individuality is a precious value, and that the goal of life is to get ahead. Rheingold asked, "If we decided that community came first, how would we use our tools differently?" (p. 163).

Gender Roles and Family

During what is called "time out" or *rumschpringes,* teenage Amish boys are given quite a bit of freedom to investigate the outside world before deciding whether to rejoin the church for the rest of their lives. Young men may obtain driver's licenses, travel to large cities, and adopt contemporary clothing. Occasional instances of drug possession have even been reported. To marry an Amish woman, though, a man must join the church and choose the Amish way of life. Amish society is male dominated. Women are respected and run the household, but the men have the final say. The Amish have large families: Seven children is about average.

Education

The Amish have received a unique status in the educational system of the United States. The practical skills of everyday life—spelling, English, German, mathematics, geography, and health—are taught in small private schools. Parents are involved in the curriculum, instruction, and administration of the schools. Religion is not taught in the schools as it is believed to be too important to be taught there instead of in the family and church. After the eighth grade, Amish children may continue education at home on the farm to learn the practical skills of providing for family and community. Further education is discouraged as it instills feelings of superiority that would lead to placing the needs of the self over those of the community (see Box 14.1).

Box 14.1

SUMMARY IN THE *YODER* CASE

Imagine you were the attorney for one side and then for the other. What arguments would you present?

STATE OF WISCONSIN, Petitioner,

v

JONAS YODER et al.

Argued December 8, 1971. Decided May 15, 1972

SUMMARY

The defendants, who were members of the Amish faith, refused to send their children, aged 14 and 15, to public school after the children had completed the eighth grade. In Green County Court, Wisconsin, the defendants were convicted for violating Wisconsin's compulsory school attendance law requiring children to attend school until the age of 16. The Wisconsin Circuit Court affirmed the convictions, but the Wisconsin Superior Court, sustaining the defendants' claims that their First Amendment right to free exercise of religion had been violated, reversed the convictions.

On certiorari, the United States Supreme Court affirmed. In an opinion by BURGER, Ch. J., expressing the views of six members of the court, it was held (1) that secondary schooling, by exposing Amish children to worldly influences in terms of attitudes, goals, and values, contrary to sincere religious beliefs, and by substantially interfering with the religious development of the Amish child and his integration into the way of life of the Amish faith community at the crucial adolescent state of development, contravened the basic religious tenets and practice of the Amish faith, both as to the parent and the child; (2) that since accommodating the religious objections of the Amish by forgoing one, or at most two, additional years of compulsory education would not impair the physical or mental health of the child, nor result in an inability to be self-supporting, or to discharge the duties and responsibilities of citizenship, or in any other way materially detract from the welfare of society, the state's interest in its system of compulsory education was not so compelling that the established religious practices of the Amish had to give way; and (3) that since it was the parents who were subject to prosecution for failing to cause their children to attend school, and since the record did not indicate that the parents' preventing their children from attending school was against the children's expressed desires, it was the parents' right of the exercise of religion, not the

(Continued)

Box 14.1, *Continued*

children's right, which had to determine Wisconsin's power to impose criminal penalties on the parents.

STEWART, J., joined by BRENNAN, J., concurring, joined in the court's opinion and stated that the case in no way involved any questions regarding the right of the children of Amish parents to attend public high schools, or any other institutions of learning, if they wished to do so.

WHITE, J., joined by BRENNAN and STEWART, JJ., concurring, joined in the court's opinion on the grounds that it could not be said that the state's interest in requiring 2 more years of compulsory education in the ninth and tenth grades outweighed the importance of the concededly sincere Amish religious practice to the survival of that sect.

SOURCE: *U.S. Supreme Court Reports*, 32 L. Ed. 2nd, pp. 15-16. Copyright © 1972 by Lawyers Cooperative Publishing, a division of Thomson Legal Publishing Inc. Reprinted with permission.

What makes it possible for the Amish to remain a distinct culture separate from the culture around them?

SOURCE: Brian Mowers. Used by permission.

Work

Work is important to Amish life. Work is preferred over idleness, which is believed to breed laziness, a trait of the outside world. Work also becomes a way to bring generations together on the farm: Grandparents, parents, and children all work together. Also, work can bring the community together in projects such as barn raisings. Now, a major source of income for the Amish is handicrafts, such as quilts, rugs, furniture, and other household products. Amish handicrafts, prized for their design and workmanship, are sold to the "English" world. The Amish refer to anyone not Amish as English.

Change

The most important characteristic of the Amish in contrast to the dominant culture is the way change is handled. Change does not come easy to the Amish. Many considerations must be examined before a change is adopted in the community. Tobacco-growing Amish participated in growing genetically engineered tobacco. This change permits the farming culture to continue.

Any change that decreases the amount of family or community solidarity, increases visibility, promotes individualism, or threatens the values of the Amish in any way is rejected. If a change will better the life of the community without threatening the Amish society as a whole, it may be gradually adopted into Amish life. The Amish try to control the technology.

The tradition of the Amish is farming—and the farms are profitable. Cultivating and nurturing the land is an important Amish value. But increasing population and land prices force change. Some Amish have emigrated to other areas to continue farming. Others have taken nonfarm employment to make it possible to remain near family and community.

In comparing Amish cultural patterns to dominant U.S. cultural patterns, major attention must be given to how the Amish control change. Each change is evaluated in terms of how it will affect the culture. A major factor in maintaining control of change was the dominant culture's allowing the Amish an educational system.

In the 1972 landmark Supreme Court ruling in *State of Wisconsin v. Jonas Yoder et al.* (see Box 14.1), Justice Burger wrote, "There can be no assumption that today's majority is right and the Amish and others like them are wrong. A way of life that is odd or even erratic but interferes with no rights or interests of others is not to be condemned because it is different." No matter how much the world changes, the Amish will strive to preserve the serenity of Amish culture.

Diversity Among the Amish

An Amish settlement refers to a geographic area. Within each settlement, there are one or more affiliations of people who share a set of theological rules and practices. Each affiliation makes its own decisions in meetings of members who, by consensus, develop their own set of rules. Each affiliation is made up of church districts or groups of 25 to 35 families.

Each affiliation reacts to change from the same Amish religious value context but with seemingly contradictory results. Thus, the Dover affiliation prohibits the use of milking machines while others do not. The Lancaster affiliation permits the use of plows with two blades, while the Dover affiliation permits only the single-blade walking plow.

FROM SEPARATION TO INTEGRATION: ASIAN-AMERICAN CULTURES

Asian Immigration to the United States

As discussed in Chapter 5, the category Asian-American includes individuals from diverse Asian cultures including people who trace their ancestry to Cambodia, China, India, Japan, Korea, Laos, Pakistan, the Philippines, Thailand, Vietnam, and Pacific Island nations. What the U.S. Census Bureau labels "Asian-American" had a population of about 1.5 million in 1970. At that time, Japanese-Americans were the largest Asian-American group in the United States.

In 2000, the Asian-American population was counted at about 11.9 million, or about 4% of the U.S. population. By ancestry, the largest groups are Chinese, 25.4%; Filipino, 19.3%; Asian Indian, 17.6%, Vietnamese, 11.7%, and Japanese 8.3% After some five generations in the United States, Japanese are highly assimilated, marrying members of other ethnic groups at a rate of 50% to 70%. Asian-Americans constitute the majority in Hawaii. The highest concentration on the mainland—in San Francisco—is over 35%. Asian-American populations are also concentrated in New York, Texas, and Illinois.

Just 10 metropolitan areas, led by Los Angeles, New York, and San Francisco, are home to over 60% of all Asian-Americans.

In contrast to the immigrants arriving at Ellis Island from Europe, immigrants from Asia were more likely to be treated as sojourners or as separates. The first Chinese immigrants arrived in San Francisco in the 1840s and provided labor for Gold Rush mining and for building the transcontinental railroad completed in 1869. The Naturalization Act of 1870 excluded Chinese from citizenship and prohibited wives of Chinese laborers from entering the United States. Later, in 1910, the Naturalization Act of 1870 was expanded to exclude all Asians from citizenship. In response to China being a World War II ally, Congress repealed the ban of Chinese immigration and naturalization in 1943. Filipinos and Asian Indians were made eligible for naturalization in 1946 and Japanese in 1952.

"Ellis Island of the West" was Angel Island in San Francisco Bay. An immigration station was built

The Chinese Exclusion Act was enacted by the U.S. Congress on May 6, 1882. It was revised in 1888 and remained in effect until 1943 when it was repealed as a gesture of friendship to China during World War II:

Whereas, in the opinion of the Government of the United States the coming of Chinese laborers to this country endangers the good order of certain localities within the territory thereof: Therefore,

Be it enacted by the Senate and House of Representatives of the United States of America in Congress assembled, That from and after the expiration of ninety days next after the passage of this act, the coming of Chinese laborers to the United States be, and the same is hereby, suspended; and during such suspension it shall not be lawful for any Chinese laborer to come, or having so come after the expiration of said ninety days, to remain within the United States. . . .

Section 14. That hereafter no State court or court of the United States shall admit Chinese to citizenship.

there in anticipation of large numbers of European immigrants entering the United States by way of the newly opened Panama Canal. World War I put an end to that immigration. Instead, the Angel Island facility served as a detention center for the majority of the approximately 175,000 Chinese who immigrated between 1910 and 1940. Immigrants passed through Ellis Island in hours or days; the Chinese faced detention of days, weeks, and even years.

Many Japanese were brought to this country to work in undesirable agricultural jobs. At the turn of the 20th century, Japanese men earned 78 cents a day, women 55 cents. The Japanese shared the status "aliens ineligible to citizenship" with other Asians.

Between 1952 and 1965, the U.S. government did not encourage any immigration. The new immigration law of 1965 abolished national origin quotas and substituted hemispheric quotas, which allowed more Asians to immigrate. The end of the Vietnam War brought more immigration from Southeast Asia, and the establishment of normal diplomatic relations with China brought more immigration from that country.

Communication Barriers

Communication barriers and racial tension can exist among groups within diverse cultures. One example has been African-American and Korean-American conflict. Today, about 85% of the Korean-American population are immigrants. Some African-Americans have viewed Korean-Americans in business as exploiters. The idea of a neighborhood business with no community commitment was unacceptable. Some Korean-Americans experiencing difficulty with English use words and phrases such as "Go" or "Come back later," which can be viewed as aggressive to customers expecting phrases like "Please come back later." Since the 1992 riots in Los Angeles, Korean-American immigrants have received acculturation and U.S. business practices training to avoid the behaviors that have often been misinterpreted by those unfamiliar with Korean culture. Groups such as the Korean American Management Association advise shopkeepers to greet customers as visiting relatives rather than ignoring customers.

Inappropriate smiles in the Korean culture are interpreted as shallow and thoughtless, so Korean-Americans accustomed to reserving smiles and small talk for friends and families are encouraged to smile and shake hands firmly.

An African-American entering a small store expects eye contact and some small talk. If the Korean-American storekeeper, reluctant to develop friendship with a stranger, doesn't engage in those behaviors, the African-American customer may think the store owner is disrespectful or rude. The Korean-American storekeeper, however, raised in a highly structured Confucian culture that stresses formality, sees the outgoing style of the African-American as inappropriate and threatening.

Acculturation also involves learning U.S. values such as the presumption of innocence until proven guilty. In Korea, a person caught shoplifting can be "roughed up" by anyone. Korean-American shopkeepers now learn that that same behavior could result in charges of battery and assault.

Box 14.2

CULTURAL GAP PAINFUL FOR VIETNAMESE

Misunderstandings about folk medicine practiced by Vietnamese refugees have led to charges of child abuse and at least one suicide, an article in the *Western Journal of Medicine* reports.

The practice of *cao gio*—rubbing coins with hot balm oil on the chest and back of a sick person—led to the jailing of one father, who subsequently committed suicide, writes Maj. Duong Nguyen, a U.S. Army doctor.

Such confusion, he writes, is one example of the differences between U.S. and Vietnamese cultures that make Western medical care difficult for the 580,000 Indochinese refugees in the United States.

Among the examples Nguyen cites:

- The Vietnamese have only a few family names, with Nguyen [pronounced NWEN] being the most common. This causes medical records confusion.

- Vietnamese are considered 1 year old at birth and gain a year every lunar new year, or Tet. A child could be 2 years old by Vietnamese counting, yet less than a month old by U.S. counting.

- Because of the importance of the family, medical decisions are rarely left to the patient. "In most cases, the relatives, more than the patients, are the ones to be convinced before the patient can start or continue a therapeutic program," one psychiatrist says.

- A diet heavy in salt is mistakenly believed to be good for pregnant women. Many Vietnamese believe that eating tiger bones, cooked to a gelatinous product, will make them strong.

Understanding of the cultural differences, Nguyen writes, could help prevent "further unfortunate incidences such as the child-abuse accusations and subsequent suicides."

Asian-American Cultures

Some important values have been maintained in Asian-American families. The U.S. Census data show that Asian-American children are more likely to be raised in families with two parents present than are children in any other census grouping. This higher rate of two-parent families may be attributed in part to the traditional family-oriented Asian cultures from which Asian-Americans come.

That and other traditional values are supported in the specialized media and segmented marketing that has arisen to support Asian-American communities despite significant differences between the diverse Asian cultures.

Media

Print. In the New York metropolitan area alone, there are five Chinese-language daily newspapers and four weeklies. Dozens of Chinese-language magazines—most imported from Hong Kong, Taiwan, and mainland China—are easily available. Chinese bookstores carry a wide selection of Chinese publications (Lum, 1991). In southern California, there are at least 15 Vietnamese-language newspapers, more than 12 Chinese newspapers, and 3 Japanese papers.

Local radio and television stations. Electronic mass media provide Asian-Americans with a forum for community issues. Two Chinese-language radio stations serve the metropolitan New York area. Their programming includes news, drama, music, language lessons, and social services, such as immigrant law and tax advice. Six television companies serve the metropolitan New York area (Lum, 1991). In Los Angeles, there are at least nine Chinese-language television companies and six radio stations. Three stations broadcast in Korean to an estimated audience of 600,000, and there is one full-time Vietnamese radio station. Many offer English lessons and immigration information.

> *liang hao san huai, mhan chiu su*
>
> [three balls and two strikes, full count]
>
> *Oakland yun dong jia dvei ying leh zhe chang chiv.*
>
> [The Oakland A's have won the game.]
>
> —KCNS-TV, San Jose, California
> —Mandarin broadcast of
> Oakland-Minnesota game,
> June 12, 1993

Satellite and cable television. The Chinese Communication Channel (CCC), a division of North America

YOLK is a popular-culture magazine for young Asian-Americans. According to the managing editor, the magazine's name stands for skin color. The magazine features stories for young-adult, English-speaking Asian-Americans.

Television Corporation (NATV), was the first to use satellite transmission to Chinese-speaking viewers all over North America. Its programs can be received only on cable and through a miniature satellite dish and special receiver that sell for less than $500. This dish gained popularity in Taiwan during the 1988 Olympics as it enabled viewers to receive Japanese television coverage from Seoul. Viewers can hear programs in Cantonese, Mandarin, and Taiwanese. Besides news, NATV carries programming from Hong Kong and Taiwan. People living in the eastern region of the United States can receive NHK-Japan. Other programming available by satellite includes Chinese Television Network (CTN) in Mandarin, the Asia Network (TAN) in Korean, and the Filipino Channel.

The Internet. The Internet has become a meeting place for worldwide communities. One example is Vietspace, a Web site that features Vietnamese newspapers, wire reports from Vietnam, live radio broadcasts, archived television shows, and chat. The site has featured film clips from Vietnamese filmmakers, songs by musician Pham Duy, works by prominent Vietnamese painters, new literature from contemporary magazines, and illustrated children's stories. Vietspace unites Vietnamese separated across the United States and the world.

Marketing

One aspect of specialized media is segmented marketing. Even though each separate Asian-American ethnic group is a separate ethnic market with diverse languages and cultures, market researchers have concluded that Asian-American consumers value quality above price and convenience more so than the general population does. The median household income of Asian-Americans in 1997 was $45,249—more than $6,000 higher than White households—so advertisers' efforts have been directed at instilling brand loyalty.

Cultural awareness in advertising. In advertising to the general population, Metropolitan Life Insurance Company of New York runs ads featuring the comic strip character Snoopy saying, "Get Met; it pays," but in its campaign directed at Chinese-Americans and Korean-Americans, the company stresses its prestige as well as Asian values such as financial security and family responsibility. Instead of showing Snoopy, it shows several massive office buildings owned by Metropolitan Life. AT&T first ran Asian-language print ads in the mid-1980s; its first TV ads in Asian languages appeared in 1990. AT&T customers are urged to call home during "Moon Festival" celebration—a Chinese holiday similar to Thanksgiving. Bank of America used print ads in 1987, TV spots in 1992, and is moving toward printing deposit slips and credit card applications in Asian languages.

Adaptation of business practices. United Bank, F.S.B., concentrates chiefly on the Asian-American community. All of its press releases and ads are bilingual, and most of its employees are bilingual with some fluent in multiple dialects. Its automated teller machines (ATMs) display bilingual messages. As the weekend is a more common time for Asians to transact business, the bank is open on Saturdays and Sundays. Chinese holidays are observed. At branch openings, traditional lion dancers perform to chase away evil spirits and bring prosperity. The bank is now the largest minority-owned savings institution in the nation. Later, Bank of America followed with Chinese-language ATMs in California. Brokerage firm Merrill Lynch & Co. attempts to create a "commercial comfort zone" with artwork depicting goldfish and bamboo, a symbol of peace and upward mobility, and making sure the number 8, a symbol of prosperity, appears in every account number.

All varieties of businesses are adapting their product or service and their marketing to the needs of diverse cultures. Ethnic supermarkets feature dried fungus, preserved bean curd, and slices of boiled octopus. Even funeral customs from around the world are now found and advertised in the United States. The National Association of Colleges of Mortuary Science is preparing a textbook on world funeral customs: Korean families decline to schedule funerals on even-numbered days, which are considered unlucky. Vietnamese immigrants burn incense. Muslims prepare the dead by gently washing the body as an act of devotion that takes families into the traditionally off-limits preparation rooms. Asian extended families crowd viewing rooms that were designed with smaller nuclear families in mind.

FROM THE INTERCULTURAL PERSPECTIVE

You may remember that the United States used to be called a "melting pot." This was because people who immigrated to the United States left their old languages and cultures behind and assimilated into the dominant culture. However, assimilation is not the only thing that may happen when people immigrate to a new country. Remember that cultures may exist within cultures. People may become marginalized, experience separation, or integrate. Marginalized people lose their identity and connection with their old culture but do not have meaningful interaction with the new culture. Immigrants may also live separately from the dominant culture and maintain their own cultural identity. This may be voluntary or involuntary. Immigrants who integrate into the dominant society learn the language and values of the dominant culture but also maintain their old language and culture. In this way, they can interact well with both cultures.

An example of marginalized people can be seen in the experience of Hmong refugees. Because of war, they were isolated from their home culture. Since they did not speak English, they were also isolated from the U.S. culture.

The Amish people are an example of how a culture can live in separation from the dominant society. The Amish live in farming communities and maintain cultural values that are quite different from dominant U.S. cultural values. One of the biggest differences is that the Amish limit their use of technology and accept change slowly.

Historically, Asian immigrants to the United States experienced separation. A well-known example of this kind of treatment was the internment of Japanese-Americans during World War II. Recently, however, Asian-Americans have experienced more integration. Two areas that have helped Asian-Americans have stronger cultural identities are specialized media and segmented marketing. Specialized media include Asian-American magazines, newspapers, radio, and television. Segmented marketing is done by businesses that want to sell their products to Asian-Americans. These businesses use their knowledge of Asian cultures and languages to help them advertise and do business in Asian-American communities.

Key Terms

Anabaptist	Gelassenheit	Old Order Amish
Beachy Amish	Hmong	Ordnung
diaspora	New Order Amish	

CHAPTER 15

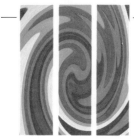

Forces to Conform to One Cultural Identity

What You Can Learn From This Chapter

Communication factors acting to maintain Hispanic groups' cultural identity today

Intercultural communication opportunities and challenges presented by strong cultural identity

In earlier chapters, you read about naming or labeling and the consequences of categorization that result. You read about words arbitrarily used to designate race and about the consequences of dehumanized words facilitating prejudice and racism. You read about how the term Asian-American can be misleading and a barrier to intercultural communication. The label not only affects how a group is perceived by others but also how members of the group perceive self. There is a tendency in the United States to group many people together under one label. A major objective of this chapter is to look in more detail at the effects of this labeling on the peoples being labeled and on the people doing the labeling.

This chapter first identifies the labels currently in use to label diverse groups and then identifies the specialized media and segmented marketing that serve to strengthen a cultural identity. A major point in this chapter is that what is labeled the Hispanic culture in the United States is vast, dispersed, heterogeneous, multilingual, and multiclass with Mexican, Puerto Rican, Cuban, and Central American origins yet bound by the shared Spanish language and culture.

HISTORICAL PERSPECTIVE

It is estimated that by the 15th century 40 million or more peoples lived in the Americas. These peoples varied greatly in physical appearance and culture. Different civilizations dominated at different times. Perhaps the most complex of these were the Mayas, with a reliable agricultural base, a polytheistic religion, and a developing mathematics, astronomy, and other sciences. As the Mayan culture declined, others arose including the Aztecs, who through military organization and trade administered a large territory of some 10 million peoples. The Aztecs' special strength was synthesizing and using cultural elements from many conquered peoples. Its great city Tenochtitlán (Mexico City today) had a population of 100,000—four or five times that of contemporary London, Madrid, or Paris (Meier & Ribera, 1993).

The Aztecs were soon to meet the Spaniards, a people with a similar history of cultural synthesis. The Celts from south-central Europe merged with earlier inhabitants on the Iberian peninsula to form the Celto-Iberians. The following years brought influence from the Phoenicians, Greeks, Carthaginians, Romans, Jews, Germanics, Norsemen, and Arab Muslims. Each group contributed to the developing culture, but perhaps none did more than the Romans, who imposed their government, their religion Christianity, and their language. The Romans named the peninsula Hispania.

Spanish influence in the Americas was largely one of cultural blending rather than of cultural extinction as occurred on the North American East Coast. Although the Spanish imposed government, religion, and technology, the basic Mesoamerican culture remained. The result was a new culture that in the latter two-thirds of the 16th century expanded northward.

At the height of its influence in the late 18th century, Spain claimed most of the current U.S. South and the entire West. Spaniards introduced cattle, sheep, horses, grasses, and firearms. The U.S. ideas of community property and monetary system are derived from the Spaniards. Spanish and Mexican influence can also be found in U.S. art, architecture, literature, music, language, law, ranching, and food. Many U.S. city names reflect Spain's influence: for example, San Francisco, Santa Barbara, Los Angeles, San Diego, Tucson, Santa Fe, San Antonio, Pensacola, and St. Augustine.

As the United States expanded its borders westward, settlers came into contact with established communities of the Southwest. The Louisiana Purchase of 1803 annexed the northern Mexican areas of Texas, New Mexico, Arizona, and California. The Mexican War and the Peace Treaty of Guadalupe-Hidalgo in 1848 added more territory and a large Spanish-speaking population. In the treaty, the United States guaranteed protection for the language, religion, property rights, and "all rights of citizens of the United States" to Mexicans who continued to reside in the seized lands (McWilliams, 1990). Over the years, their descendants have been joined by Spanish-speaking immigrants from Latin America and Puerto Rico.

Immigration from Mexico has largely been tied to labor needs in Mexico and the United States. Late-19th-century immigrants worked in Southwest agriculture, in building railroads, and in mining. Immigration accelerated in the 1920s following the economic tumult of the Mexican Revolution.

The Depression era brought public outcry against illegal immigrants. Many illegal as well as legal immigrants and U.S. citizens were picked up for deportation. The changing labor market brought on by World War II saw the birth of the *bracero* program, a guest worker initiative for agriculture that lasted until the 1960s.

By 1960, fewer than 600,000 Mexican-born people resided in the

Mexicans have been the target of prejudice and racism. Arguing against the 1848 Peace Treaty of Guadalupe-Hidalgo, Senator John C. Calhoun of South Carolina said on the Senate floor:

We have never dreamt of incorporating into our Union any but the Caucasian race—the free white race. To incorporate Mexico, would be the very first instance of the kind of incorporating an Indian race; for more than half of the Mexicans are Indians, and the other is composed chiefly of mixed tribes. I protest against such a union as that! Ours, sir, is the Government of a white race. The greatest misfortunes of Spanish America are to be traced to the fatal error of placing these colored races on an equality with the white race. That error destroyed the social arrangement which formed the basis of society.... Are we to overlook this fact? Are we to associate with ourselves as equals, companions, and fellow-citizens, the Indians and mixed race of Mexico? Sir, I should consider such a thing as fatal to our institutions.

United States. By 1980, that number had grown to more than 2 million and increased 50% from 1990 to 1996. This migration is the largest sustained mass migration of one group to the United States, far eclipsing earlier migrations of Irish and Italians. More than 7 million Mexican-born people now reside in the United States.

The U.S. Hispanic population is regionally concentrated according to national origin and exhibits differences (Szalay & Inn, 1987). Over 75% of the U.S. Mexican-origin population resides in the Southwest and the Pacific region, and over time is dispersing beyond the border states to virtually every region of the country. Over 60% of the U.S. Puerto Rican population is found in New York, with another sizable population living in Chicago. The Cuban population is primarily concentrated in Florida, but there is also a large Cuban population in New York. The Central and South American population in the United States is dispersed geographically, with most centered in large urban centers such as New York, San Francisco, Los Angeles, Chicago, and Miami.

HISPANIC CULTURES

Terminology

Tanno (1994) and Mirandé and Tanno (1993) have called attention to the meaning and importance of ethnic labels. For example, "Spanish-speaking," "Spanish-surnamed," "Spanish-origin," "Hispanic," "Chicano," "Latino," and "Mexican-American" have all been used interchangeably to refer to that culture in the United States whose members originally came from a Spanish-speaking country. Antonio Guernica (1982) offers these distinctions:

- **Spanish-speaking** refers to the population with the ability to speak and comprehend the Spanish language—whether as a primary or secondary language. This term encompasses non-Hispanics as well as Hispanics.

- **Spanish-surnamed** refers to the population segment whose last name has been identified as Spanish by the U.S. Census Bureau.

- **Spanish origin** refers to that segment of the population who came from a Spanish-speaking country or whose ancestors came from a Spanish-speaking country. This term does not indicate that the person is Spanish-speaking or personally identifies with Hispanic cultures.

- **Hispanic** came into common use as a result of the 1980 Census to identify various U.S. Spanish-speakers' shared roots to Spain. It refers to that population segment with the capability of speaking and comprehending the Spanish language, whose ancestry is based in a Spanish-speaking country, and who identify with Hispanic cultures. The term has been rejected by some because its use was imposed by the government.

- **Chicano** most often refers to that segment of the population born in the United States whose ancestors came from Mexico. The label Chicano has a political meaning and is often used to represent a nationalist or separatist identity and a commitment to disassimilation (Sedano, 1980).

- **Latino** most often refers to Spanish-speaking individuals who came from, or whose ancestors came from, anywhere in Latin America. The term is more commonly used in the U.S. Southwest.

In 1993, Mexico issued new currency (adopting a new monetary unit called the nuevo peso [N$] or new peso) with a value equivalent to 1,000 pesos—the result of hyperinflation in the early 1980s that drove the peso's value from 12 per U.S. dollar to 3,000 per dollar.

- **Mexican-American**, a term similar to Irish-American, indicates a person from a specific country of origin in the assimilation process (Hurstfield, 1978).

- **Tejano** is a term in widespread use in Texas to refer to people born in Texas of Mexican ancestry.

As Tanno (1994) argues, none of these terms is accurate and yet all are. An individual could identify with one or more of these at different times in his or her life and be enriched by the opportunities each provides.

Is there one label by which to identify a distinct culture? Any single label that includes Spaniards, Cubans, Mexican-Americans, Latinos, and Puerto Ricans groups together peoples with very diverse history and culture. A Black Cuban, a Uruguayan Jew, a multiracial Peruvian, and a multiracial Puerto Rican all living in New York City share a heritage of language and culture that originated in Spain, hence it is accurate to say they are all Hispanic. Important differences, however, can be lost; for example, Cinco de Mayo is a Mexican holiday—not a Hispanic holiday. This text uses the terms Hispanic and Hispanic cultures to identify groups of diverse peoples as a survey has shown that that term, at least at this time, is preferred by the diverse group of peoples to whom it has been applied (see Table 15.1). The forces of media and marketing, among others, support a single identifying label even though some studies

Table 15.1   Hispanic Self-Identification Preferences

As part of a review of which race and ethnic categories to use in its job statistics, the U.S. Labor Department asked people nationwide in approximately 60,000 households how they prefer to be identified.

Hispanic	57.9%
Of Spanish origin	12.3%
Latino	11.7%
Some other term	7.9%
No preference	10.2%

SOURCE: U.S. Labor Department, reported in *U.S. News & World Report,* November 20, 1995, p. 28.

continue to show rejection of the term. It is not clear, however, if the term or the forced labeling is being rejected (de la Garza, 1992).

The major consequences of labeling is categorization, the act of setting the peoples labeled as separate and apart. Gonzalez (1990) has identified in labeling the themes of inclusion and separation. Inclusion is desire for belonging on the basis of one's worth; separation is the fragmentation of not belonging, of being, for example, Mexican-American, not Mexican, not American, but somehow both. These themes can be seen in the complex feelings about language use and media and in feelings about ethnic identity and assimilation.

We all identify with multiple groups. Consider, for example, what it means to be Texan. When one chooses to, Texans can be quite different from others in the United States—different in vocabulary, pronunciation, clothing, manner, and so on. Yet, at the same time, Texans are patriotic. To be a Texan, then, is simply a unique way of being a part of the U.S. culture. In a similar way today, choosing to identify oneself as Hispanic can be a unique way of being a part of the U.S. culture.

Values

In 1996, the Tómas Rivera Center released "Hispanic Perspectives," a survey of Hispanic public attitudes in Texas, California, New York, and Florida. The majority supported affirmative action programs and thought Hispanic communities had benefited from these programs. Almost 70% of Hispanics in Texas believed that each had an equal chance as an Anglo in getting a job for which both were qualified. In the other states, there was a simple majority agreement. The majority in all four states believed that most people receiving public aid do so because of not wanting to work. The majority, except for those in California, supported the issuance of government ID cards to all legal residents and citizens. And the majority agreed that illegal immigrants who pay taxes should receive government services.

Just from these few results, you could not say that Hispanics were conservative or liberal or that Hispanics in Texas held the same views as Hispanics in California.

Hispanic Americans

A Proud Heritage USA 20

What does exist behind this diversity are many shared values. Studies using 50 years of census data (Hayes-Bautista, 1992) show that, compared to Whites, African-Americans, and Asians, Hispanics have consistently had the highest labor force participation, the least use of welfare programs, and the highest rate of family formation. Compared to Whites and African-Americans, Hispanics have a longer life expectancy; less cancer, heart disease, and respiratory disease; the fewest low-birth-weight babies; the lowest infant mortality; and the fewest babies damaged by drugs. Such behaviors are related to strong shared cultural values—an explicit moral structure, a Roman Catholic tradition, and social integration that binds individuals and families together into a larger community.

Often referred to as family oriented (Sabogal, Marín, Otero-Sabogal, Marín, & Perez-Stable, 1987) compared to Anglo-Americans, Hispanics rely on extended families for emotional support and feel more anxiety when separated from families (Griffith & Villavicencio, 1985; Levine & Padilla, 1979).

There also exists a growing shared appreciation for the art, music, dance, cuisine, literature, and other elements of an international Hispanic culture. Traditions that had been put aside are now gaining new followers. The Mexican tradition of *Dia de los Muertos*, the Day of the Dead, which combines Aztec and Catholic beliefs, has become a popular day to remember departed family members and reclaim a cultural tradition.

For Nobel Prize-winning Mexican writer Octavio Paz, the coexistence with death is one of the cultural distinctions between Mexico and the United States:

The word "death" is not pronounced in New York, in Paris, in London, because it burns the lips. The Mexican, in contrast, is familiar with death, jokes about it, caresses it, sleeps with it, celebrates it.

Life extended into death, and vice versa. Death was not the natural end of life, but one phase of an infinite cycle. Life, death and resurrection were stages of a cosmic process.

—Octavio Paz, *The Labyrinth of Solitude* (1961)

Demographics

The Hispanic population in the United States has often been the subject of general-circulation media. The October 16, 1978, *Time* magazine cover story was "Hispanic Americans: Soon the Biggest Majority." *Newsweek* and *U.S. News & World Report* carried similar stories. In 1980, CBS-TV newscaster Walter Cronkite anchored a series of reports on the U.S. Hispanic population. Generally, these reports have taken the same approach as one would in writing about a foreign country and often present a stereotype of poverty.

As of January 1, 1980, the Hispanic population of the United States was estimated as 14,974,800. That figure placed the United States as the fifth largest Hispanic nation in the world. Unofficial estimates, however, ranged from 14 million to 25 million, depending on how the population was operationally defined and if it included projections of the undocumented population.

The 2000 Census counted 35.3 million people of Hispanic origin or 13% of the U.S. population. While there is debate over the counting, Hispanics may now equal or exceed the number of African-Americans.

The Hispanic population is growing five times faster than other groups in the United States. Based on growth rates that considered a higher fertility rate for Hispanic women, the U.S. Census Bureau estimated that by 2005 the Hispanic population would grow to 36 million to become the nation's largest ethnic group, that by 2020 the Hispanic population would grow to 53 million, representing 1 in 6 persons in the United States, and that by 2050 Hispanics would constitute 24.5% of the total population. It is important to note that this projection came from an ideology of segregation, that is, that the boundaries of a population labeled Hispanic are firm. In fact, not only do many people reject the label, the projections do not account for intermarriage. For example, an estimated 40% of U.S. Hispanics of Puerto Rican ancestry are married to non-Hispanics.

It is often reported that, nationwide, Hispanic families are nearly three times more likely to be poor than non-Hispanic families. In 1970, the overwhelming majority of Hispanics were born in the United States. This group earns wages comparable to others with similar education and skills and is nearly as likely to finish high school as non-Hispanics. Over the past three decades, large numbers of Spanish-speaking immigrants have entered the United States. In the 1980s alone, at least 3 million immigrants came from Latin America. Now, about 40% of the Hispanic population are immigrants, and another almost 30% are children of immigrants.

The stereotype of poverty ignores how recent immigration has skewed the statistics on education and income. This group has yet to participate fully in the country's educational and economic systems. Hispanic immigrants are succeeding at about the same rates as immigrants of a century ago. The wages of second-generation Mexican-Americans are nearly identical to those of non-Hispanic Whites of similar education.

Spanish-Language Use

The 1996 report "Toward a Latino Urban Policy Agenda" released by Latino Urban Policy Agenda shows that 93% of Hispanics born in the United States speak English well and that 66.1% of Colombian immigrants, 61.1% of Cuban immigrants, and 51.3% of Mexican immigrants speak English well.

The Hispanic culture has two distinct characteristics: Spanish language and identification with all Hispanic cultures. Spanish has spread across the world for 500 years but has maintained an amazing coherence of grammar and vocabulary.

Nonetheless, the presence of Spanish and the interface of Spanish and English languages is producing **Spanglish** (or Tex-Mex or Cubonics)—a practice called **code-switching** by linguists to refer to changing from one language to another for a single word, phrase, clause, or entire sentence (Eastman, 1992; Lipski, 1985). Spanglish used by Hispanics reflects both a knowledge of Spanish and an awareness of the U.S. culture. A teenage girl, for example, may admonish her mother by saying, "No seas tan old-fashioned!"

Usually, the simpler word from either language is used. For example, "income tax" is used for *impuesto sobre la renta* and *"ir al* supermarket" replaces a longer explanation for leaving. Code-switching goes both ways: In areas with a high concentration of Hispanics, Spanish words are used by those with no knowledge of Spanish. Examples are *gracias, bueno, amigo,* and *por favor.* Other words move into more general mainstream use through popular literature and music. Spanglish is appearing on the WB network's show *Mucha Lucha!* and Hallmark greeting cards.

Immigrants of the 1960s and 1970s who experienced discrimination believed that the children would do better speaking unaccented English. These immigrants, like immigrants from other eras, did not speak Spanish with their children. One indictor of an increasing cultural identity is a growing number of people learning the Spanish of immigrant parents and grandparents.

CULTURAL IDENTITY AND MEDIA

Even though many Spanish-origin individuals can neither read nor understand spoken Spanish, Hispanic cultures in the United States have a rich

The U.S. Army slogan "An Army of One" became "Yo Soy el Army" (I Am the Army) rather than "Un Ejército de Uno."

media—Spanish-language magazines, newspapers, radio, and television. Hispanic media, like other forms of minority media, provide a forum where minority issues can be freely discussed (Downing, 1990). It is these media that help continue the culture.

Print

In Mexico, well-read people patronize "libraries," which are bookstores, or pay a fee to take books from a lending library. It is frequently hypothesized that Hispanics in the United States have a reading tradition. Hispanic print media often appear in both Spanish and English to serve that portion of the culture who cannot read Spanish.

Only four other countries in the world buy more Spanish-language books than the United States. More than half of the books that Mexico exports are sent to the United States.

The number of national Hispanic-oriented publications has grown from more than 700 in 1990 to more than 1,200 in 2000. More than 80% of these are in Spanish. Combined circulation is approximately 33 million. Traditionally, the most successful Spanish-language magazines in national distribution have been geared toward the Hispanic woman. *Vanidades* entered the U.S. market in 1961, making it the first Spanish-language women's magazine available nationally. Since then, the number of magazines has grown and diversified, although those for women retain prominence. The New York-based *Latina*, a bilingual quarterly for women, started publication in 1996 as did *People en Español* and *Newsweek en Español*. Other new magazines include *Moderna* and *Latina Style* (fashion, fitness, finances, and travel), *Frontera* (music and entertainment), *Generation Ñ* (Cuban culture), and *POZ en Español* (HIV community).

Examples of popular magazines published in Spanish-language editions.

VANIDADES

Estados Unidos

JUVENTUD INMEDIATA PARA TU PIEL

Leonardo DiCaprio
"De mí han dicho tantas mentiras"

MARIA TERESA Y ENRIQUE DE LUXEMBURGO
Los nuevos soberanos en entrevista exclusiva

Lucía Méndez
la diva mexicana
nos habla de su cirugía
y lipoescultura

Audrey Hepburn
gana un Oscar siendo una actriz inexperta
(LA NOVELA DE SU VIDA)

"ME LO CUENTA TODO"
POR CORIN TELLADO

2.95 Dólares

0 9776349 0 06

MODA
La colección de Versace: un éxito para Donatella

EXCLUSIVAS

People EN ESPAÑOL

JORGE
RAMOS
SU PASADO
NUDISTA

LA
LUCHA DE
SALMA
HAYEK

LAS PAREJAS DEL MOMENTO

» Y LOS QUE NIEGAN LO QUE DICEN LAS FOTOS

JULIO SABALA Y ANA BÁRBARA

JACQUELINE BRACAMONTES Y VALENTINO LANÚS

ENRIQUE IGLESIAS Y ANNA KOURNIKOVA

U.S. $2.79 / CAN. $3.99

MEXICO $25.00

DISPLAY UNTIL 12/8
EXHIBA HASTA EL 8 DE DICIEMBRE

0   70989 10229   3

1 2>

DICIEMBRE DEL 2002

MURILO BENICIO Y GIOVANNA
ANTONELLI DE *EL CLON*

There are approximately 14 Spanish-language daily newspapers in the United States. *La Opinión,* published in Los Angeles, is the largest Spanish-language daily in the United States. It emphasizes coverage of Mexican-American personalities and events, features on specifically Mexican-interest topics, and news of Mexico itself—particularly U.S.-Mexico relations.

Besides the dailies, there are hundreds of Spanish-language weeklies and biweeklies that tend to emphasize news of local interest, such as community affairs and upcoming events in the local Hispanic community.

Radio

While Spanish-language newspapers have been largely owned by members of the immigrant community, radio stations that broadcast in Spanish were at first owned by majority culture entrepreneurs (Rodriguez, 1999). In 2002, the number of Spanish-language radio stations was 692, almost double what it had been 10 years earlier. The growth of Spanish-language radio can be seen in Los Angeles, the largest and fastest-growing Spanish radio market in the United States. Forty years ago, there was one full-time Spanish-language station. Ten years ago, there were six. In 1997, 17 of the market's 82 radio stations were full-time Spanish-language stations. Two of the 17 are consistently in the top 10 highest-rated stations. Both San Antonio and Los Angeles have had Spanish-language stations rated first in Arbitron's ratings.

Local independent radio stations are being replaced with national network affiliates. The top Spanish-language radio broadcaster in the United States, the Hispanic Broadcasting Corporation, which owned 40 Spanish-language stations in 11 of the top 15 Hispanic markets, was acquired by Univision in 2003. Rather than national programming, it provides regionally based programming.

Historically, radio has been an important medium in Spanish-speaking communities as more people can speak Spanish than can read it. Spanish-language stations serve as a primary source of news and information for much of the audience. Music, however, constitutes the bulk of the programming day, although a few stations in New York, Miami, and Los Angeles-Orange County have all-talk formats.

Spanish-language radio programming has been said to create a strong emotional tie to the Hispanic culture as Hispanics have higher-than-average station loyalty. Spanish-language radio stations frequently have close community involvement. A broadcast announcement of a family without housing or food because of fire or flood brings quick and generous responses.

Some stations have experimented with a bilingual format that attempts to bridge the two cultures by speaking both languages. These stations mix diverse musical styles with news and public affairs segments that focus on such issues as immigration, economic opportunities, and the problems in growing up in two cultures. The bilingual announcers switch often and effortlessly from Spanish to English and back again—sometimes in midsentence. This is code-switching in action. The changes are brief enough that a speaker of one language only never feels lost, and the context provided by the language one knows encourages learning the new language (Downing, 1990).

Music

With language use goes music. Spanish-language business in the United States tripled in sales from 1991 to 1995 and continues to grow based on the popularity of Luis Miguel, José José, Gloria Estefan, Jon Secada, Ricky Martin, Jennifer Lopez, and Spanish-language recordings by Boyz II Men and Madonna. Spanish-language music groups are gaining widespread appeal. The Web page of the Spanish rock lovers' magazine *Retila* gets 10,000 hits a week.

Recognizing that U.S. families are keeping traditional languages such as Spanish alive in homes, in 1995 Disney began releasing Spanish-language and bilingual products the same time as the English material. Disney released *Pocahontas*, for example, with a Spanish-language sound track. Spanish-language sound tracks have also been made available for such films as *The Lion King* and *The Little Mermaid*.

Television

In 1961, Mexican mogul Emilio Azcarraga Vidaurreta bought KCOR-TV in San Antonio, the nation's first Spanish-language TV station. SIN—Spanish International Network—grew in one decade to nine stations and experimented with cable outlets, microwave and satellite interconnections, and repeater television stations (Rodriguez, 1999).

By early 1982, there were 12 Spanish-language television stations in the United States. Ten of them were SIN affiliates. SIN's programming was also carried by more than 100 cable systems and translators (low-power repeater stations). Hallmark Cards bought SIN in 1987, renaming it **Univision**, and then in 1992 announced its sale to an investment group linked with the huge Mexican media conglomerate Grupo Televisa and Venezuela's leading network

Venevision, making it the dominant force in Spanish-language broadcasting in the United States and the fifth largest U.S. prime-time network. Univision grew to command 80% of the U.S. Spanish-language market and some 92% share of prime time audience that watches TV in Spanish.

The second Spanish-language network, **Telemundo**, was created by Saul Steinberg and based in Miami. In 2001, NBC purchased Telemundo for $2.7 billion

To demonstrate to advertisers that people were watching Spanish-language television, Nielsen Media Research, with financing by Univision, began to develop a national Hispanic television rating service to help Spanish-language television compete for advertising revenue. One consequence of these efforts is the reinforcement of the label Hispanic to refer to a single co-culture (Rodriguez, 1999).

Univision and Telemundo now compete with cable stations. Galavision and TeleFutura are Univision's cable Spanish-language networks. Others include Gems, a channel geared to women; H-TV, a music channel; CBS-Telenoticias, a news channel; and Fox Sports Americas, a sports channel. The satellite system DirecTV Para Todos provides more than 20 Spanish-language channels. Traditional networks are competing as well: CBS now broadcasts *60 Minutes* nationally with Spanish closed-captioning. In 1993, CNN launched CNN International, with live Spanish newscasts aired periodically throughout the day, and HBO launched HBO en Español. Other national Spanish-language cable channels are MTV Latino and CNBC's all-Spanish channel.

In Los Angeles, Univision's Spanish-language KMEX/34 regularly wins news ratings over English-language stations. In Miami, Univision's WLTV in 1998 was the first Spanish-language station to get top ratings in both news and prime time. Spanish-language programming produced in the United States is, however, basically limited to local news programs, talk shows, and public affairs presentations. Imported programming offers *novelas* (which, unlike U.S. "soaps," usually come to a conclusion within a few months), news shows, movies, magazine-style shows, children's shows, talk shows, and variety. Among its offerings, Telemundo airs a Spanish rock video program produced by MTV. From 1989 through 2001, Univision presented *Cristina*, the No. 1 rated television show on Spanish-language TV, with more than 2.6 million U.S. viewers and more than 100 million viewers worldwide in 18 countries compared to *Oprah*'s 30 million worldwide. Its host has been compared to Oprah Winfrey ("*Oprah con salsa*") because she delves into a variety of subjects previously considered taboo for Spanish-language television. In 1992, Cuban-born Cristina Saralegui was the first Spanish-language talk-show host to "cross over" to non-Spanish stations with a syndicated talk show.

In 1995, Televisa began coproduction with the Children's Television Workshop of *Plaza Sesamo*—with a bird that looks like Big Bird, except this one is a green parrot and has friends with names like Pancho and Lola, and the children learn to count *uno, dos, tres* and name colors *rojo, blanco, y azul.*

In 1997, Univision introduced *Despierta América* ("Wake Up America"), a weekday morning program with a mix of news, weather, interviews, and topical segments. And by 2000, nearly half of Univision's programming originated in the United States, with the bulk of the remaining programming from Mexico. In the 2003 war with Iraq—with its record number of Hispanic participants—Spanish-language media exhibited their close ties with the Spanish-speaking population by offering comfort and connections to families of servicemembers. Their war coverage tended to be cast in more personal terms, while English-language coverage tended to have a greater focus on military tactics and politics. On station KMEX, the war was branded "*La Guerra de Todos*" ("Everybody's War")—a reference to the Hispanic involvement.

The Nielsen study of Hispanic television viewing (Rodriguez, 1999) showed that Hispanics watch very different TV shows than the general public does. Adults prefer Univision and Telemundo to the English-language network shows 3 to 1. Of English-language shows, only 1 in 4 of the top 10 shows preferred by the general public rated in the top 10 for Hispanics. The study showed that Spanish language was the most important factor in reaching the Hispanic audience. It is no surprise, then, that the major English-language networks began to program for Hispanics: Showtime offered *Resurrection Blvd.*, ABC offered *George Lopez*, and PBS offered *American Family*.

CULTURAL IDENTITY AND MARKETING

Undisputable evidence of a culture's existence are the attempts made to sell services and products to individuals in that culture by appealing to the values of that culture. The existence of this advertising also serves to continue and strengthen the culture.

Early studies of the Hispanic market, for example, revealed an important trait: intense brand loyalty—40% more than the general population.

In 1985, marketing companies placed the national Hispanic market at between $50 billion and $76 billion annually and predicted growth at 6.5 times that of the rest of the population. By 1998, Hispanic buying power (after-tax income) was placed at between $300 billion and $380 billion. By 2002, it was $580.5 billion—more than the total for the entire state of Texas. According to *Hispanic Business Magazine*, total Hispanic advertising reached $1.7 billion in

1998. Some 50 companies spent at least $1 million each on advertising to Hispanic consumers in 1988. By 1995, McDonald's had spent $12 million in Spanish-language advertising. With 55% of Hispanics within 15 minutes of a Kmart, in 2002 it began publishing its weekly advertising circular in Spanish.

One study by Strategy Research Corporation for Laredo National Bank showed that in 1997, 48% of Hispanics in five major U.S. cities preferred Spanish for advertising.

Many attempts at marketing in Spanish revealed translation errors. According to *Advertising Age*, one cigarette company advertising "low tar" cigarettes used a phrase that translated to "low asphalt." An old Braniff Airlines ad that invited Spanish speakers to settle back *en* (in) luxuriant *cuero* (leather) seats inadvertently said passengers could fly without clothes (*encuero*). A Miller Lite slogan told readers that the beer was "Filling, and less delicious." And a Coors beer slogan "Get loose with Coors" became "Get the runs with Coors." As one restaurant chain learned, *nieve* means "ice cream" to some Mexican-Americans but "cocaine" to many Cuban-Americans.

Advertisers discovered that marketing to the Hispanic community involves not only language and images that mean something to the buyer but also cultural traditions and values. And the larger advertisers have learned that the Hispanic culture is not one culture but many, with diverse experiences all of which are changing and evolving. For example, advertisers now recognize a "boomerang effect" or "retro-acculturation": Hispanic teens who are attracted to general market media but who return to their roots when they marry to ensure that the children retain a sense of heritage.

Budweiser was early to advertise in Spanish. In a 1979 print and television campaign, Budweiser advertised to three regional subgroups: In California, Texas, and the Southwest, advertisements aimed at Spanish-speakers of Mexican heritage featured cowboys and cactus; in the Northeast, advertisements aimed at Puerto Ricans featured cityscapes and salsa music; and in Florida, advertisements aimed at Cubans featured palm trees, cigars, and bananas. Each advertisement featured differently accented Spanish and national-origin-appropriate music. Other early advertisers, such as Procter & Gamble, Colgate Palmolive, and Coca-Cola, used a similar strategy (Rodriguez, 1999). Miller Brewing, Chevron, Nike, and Ford have all had Spanish-language ads with English subtitles on English-language television stations.

A truly national advertising campaign would need to be based on some shared culture. Coca-Cola was the first major corporation to systematize segmenting Hispanics in advertising. Coke directs its ads not to the consumer but to the Hispanic *community*, showing sensitivity toward such issues as

One in the five-check series painted by San Francisco artist Carmen Lomas Garza for Bank of America.

SOURCE: Reprinted with permission of Bank of America.

job training and education. For the 1992 quincentenary celebration of Columbus's landing in America, Coke planned advertising recognizing Hispanic contributions to U.S. culture and featuring prominent Hispanic-Americans, such as actress Rita Moreno.

To communicate an interest in the community, both Coke and Pepsi sponsor ethnic festivals and concert tours and place special promotional displays in neighborhood stores. Pepsi sponsored the U.S. tour of Santo Domingo native Guerra and his group 4.40. Pepsi also designed a Hispanic version of its "Gotta Have It" ad campaign, featuring Guerra, tennis star Gabriela Sabatini, and comedian Paul Rodriguez.

Budweiser and Bud Light beers sponsor Cinco de Mayo celebrations—U.S.-Mexican fiestas in honor of the 1862 Mexican victory over the French. In 1988, Budweiser began awarding about $1.5 million annually in college scholarships to Hispanic students. Because of these efforts, Anheuser-Busch has more than doubled the Hispanic market share of its nearest competitor.

Appealing to similar values, Bank of America offers bilingual automated teller machines, envelopes, and checks. The check series, called *Im genes Familiares* ("Family Images"), portrays five Hispanic family scenes. The checks have "pay to the order of" and "dollars" in both English and Spanish. The message the bank wants to make is that it respects the Hispanic culture and wants to do business with Hispanics.

SOURCE: Bridgestone.

Carl's Jr. simply wanted to translate its popular television ads into Spanish, but when it took its account to one of a growing number of Hispanic advertising agencies, the agency explained that the humor in the English-language ads directed at young males would confuse mothers in Hispanic households, who typically decide where families eat. The agency produced a series of highly successful ads for Carl's Jr. featuring Hispanic actors performing traditional dances.

In 2001, Mattel introduced its first Hispanic-targeted brunette Barbie in the gown of the quinceanera, the traditional Mexican celebration marking a young girl's 15th birthday.

In 1989, Ford Motor Company introduced a Spanish-language version of its buying guide "Car and Truck Buying Made Easier." Ford advertised its availability in cities with large Hispanic populations. Multilingual advertising is not new, of course. However, now it seems that all types of businesses have discovered that "money talks, but it speaks many languages." Not everyone approves of the growing trend. One English-as-the-official-language organization is campaigning against multilingual customer service, arguing that it perpetuates linguistic divisiveness and separation.

Spanish-Language Internet

As late as the mid-1990s, the Spanish-language Internet was small. The growth of portals and Web sites catering to U.S. Hispanics has been recent but fast. In 1998 and 1999, U.S. Hispanic households were acquiring computers at a faster rate than the national average. Internet service providers AT&T and Prodigy launched Spanish-language services. Yahoo has been available in Spanish since 1998 and Lycos since 1999. In 2000, Univision launched its own Spanish-language Internet portal with online shopping and chat as well as its own newscasts and updates of its popular novelas. Univision.com soon became the leading Spanish-language Web site. Along with these generalized sites are those with a specific agenda, such as the politically driven "pages" of U.S. presidential candidates Republican George W. Bush and Democrat Al Gore designed to convince Spanish speakers to vote for one over the other in the November 2000 election. Later as president, George W. Bush became the first president to deliver a version of his weekly radio address from the Oval Office entirely in Spanish. And in 2002, Texas Democratic gubernatorial candidates Tony Sanchez and Dan Morales conducted their first debate in Spanish.

> I'm for making a cantonal system. The massive waves of Latinos sweeping across the border are quite correctly taking what they call "the occupied lands"—Southern California, Arizona, New Mexico, Texas. They're reoccupying it, and have no particular interest in the Anglo culture.
>
> My theory is that, essentially, the thing is never going to integrate anymore. . . .
>
> We're going to end up with, if we're lucky, something like Switzerland with sort of Spanish cantons. . . . I like the diversity of it.
>
> —Gore Vidal, novelist and grandson of Senator Thomas Gore

SOURCE: *Los Angeles Times*, December 15, 1991, p. M3. Copyright © 1991, Los Angeles Times. Reprinted with permission.

FROM THE INTERCULTURAL PERSPECTIVE

Categories are useful for helping people define and understand things. Often, people place themselves in a category, and from that category they gain identity. But sometimes people are placed in categories or are forced to choose one they would not choose for themselves. This has been the experience of many

Hispanic people in the United States. When Hispanics apply for a job or fill out official forms such as the U.S. census form (the census counts and categorizes all the people living in the United States), they often must indicate their ethnic identity. The choices provided are very limited, and so Hispanic people often must report an ethnic identity that they really do not identify with.

Some people in the United States do not realize that the Hispanic culture includes people from many different countries and ethnic backgrounds. For example, many immigrants are actually American Indian (ethnic background) but come from Mexico (country of origin). Also, people who identify with being Hispanic may or may not speak Spanish. A mistake often made is assuming that people can speak Spanish just because they have Spanish-sounding last names.

Recently, a lot of attention has been given to the number of Hispanic immigrants coming into the United States and the effect that this influx may have on the country. However, Hispanic people and culture are not new to the United States, for Hispanic people lived in the southwestern region of North America even before it was a part of the United States. Hispanic culture is already a large part of the culture of this region of the United States.

In the past in the United States, there was a lot of pressure for people to assimilate into the dominant culture. Today, however, the pressure is not as strong. Two areas that help Hispanic people maintain a cultural identity in the United States are specialized media and segmented marketing. Specialized media include Hispanic magazines, newspapers, radio, and television. These media generally use the Spanish language and focus on things that are important to the Hispanic community. And sites on the Internet in Spanish connect Hispanic people to the global Hispanic community. Advertising also helps continue and strengthen the culture.

Key Terms

Chicano	Mexican-American	Spanish-surnamed
code-switching	Spanglish	Tejano
Hispanic	Spanish origin	Telemundo
Latino	Spanish-speaking	Univision

CHAPTER 16

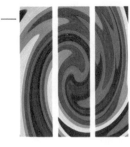

Reclaiming a Culture

I n the preceding two chapters, you read about cultures in the United States that were established by immigration. One culture—African-American—has had a completely different history and experience. No other immigrant group was held as slaves. No other immigrant group had the same restrictive laws limiting rights.

In an article titled "Black, Negro, or Afro-American? The Differences Are Critical!" Fairchild (1985) analyzed the significance of race names. Each label has different historical and emotional connotations. Since that article was written, the label *African-American*, analogous to labels such as *Polish-American*, has become commonly used to refer to people of African descent living in the Americas. However, just as many Whites feel no kinship to the land of their ancestors, some African-Americans feel no kinship to Africa. Again we see the importance of the name, the label. This text uses the term *African-American* but be reminded that group names are likely to keep changing as ethnic groups

Table 16.1   African-American Self-Identification Preference

As part of a review of which race and ethnic categories to use in its job statistics, the U.S. Labor Department asked people nationwide in approximately 60,000 households how they prefer to be identified.

Black	44.2%
African-American	28.1%
Afro-American	12.1%
Negro	3.3%
Colored	1.1%
Some other term	2.2%
No preference	9.1%

SOURCE: U.S. Labor Department, reported in *U.S. News & World Report,* November 20, 1995, p. 28.

redefine identity (see Table 16.1). This text uses the term *Black* to refer to people of African heritage who aren't Americans (e.g., Africans in South Africa) or when another source has used that term.

The ancestors of most of today's African-Americans lived on the northwestern coast of Africa. It was a region of diverse cultures with some 250 different languages, all subgroups of Sudanic, Bantu, and Hamitic.

AFRICAN WORLDVIEW

Although there are many cultures and languages in Africa, Daniel and Smitherman (1976) have identified a shared African worldview:

- *Unity between spiritual and material aspects of existence.* In traditional African worldview, God, humans, and nature are united with God as the head of the hierarchy followed by lesser deities, humans, other forms of life, and things. Humans, in the middle of the hierarchy, are composed of both a spiritual and material self. The African world is alive with Gods, spirits, the recent dead, humans, animals, plants, and objects. Human nature is to move on to the spiritual world.

- *Centrality of religion.* Religion is the pervasive, dominating force in the life of humans. There is no dichotomy between sacred and secular life. African people do not exist without religion; religion plays an active role in every aspect of life.

- *Harmony in nature and the universe.* In African worldview, the laws governing the universe and the self are one and the same. One should strive to live in harmony with the universe, to become a microcosm of the universe. All things are complementary, not opposites: Day and night, good and bad, life and death, beginning and end are synergic in nature and produce a rhythm such as the beat of the heart.

- *African society patterned after natural rhythms.* African people pattern social interactions and communities after the presumed existence of natural rhythms. Neither "I" nor "we" have meaning apart from the other. What happens to one affects the entire community, and what happens to the community affects all as individuals.

- *Time as participation in events.* Time is defined in terms of participation in experienced events rather than as fixed points. Everything takes place in cycles or spirals. Time is rhythmical and cyclical rather than linear. The future is perceived as the past recurring in a different form.

AFRICAN-AMERICANS

U.S. Census Bureau 2000 data put 34.7 million people, or 12.3% of the population, as of African descent. The African-American population is both rural and urban. Most of the 99 African-American-majority counties are in the rural South; among the states, Mississippi has the highest percentage of African-Americans. Three urban areas have more African-Americans than does all of Mississippi—New York, Chicago, and Los Angeles.

African-American culture, while having its roots in Africa, was constructed in the United States but apart from the dominant culture. It is important to recognize that African-Americans have a diverse ethnic heritage. Most African-Americans are a mixture of African, European, and American Indian heritage.

African-Americans and West Indians share the history of the slave trade. African slaves brought to the Caribbean islands primarily under British rule during the 17th and 18th centuries were freed in 1833 and later developed independent island nations. That experience is nothing like the experience of African-Americans who experienced segregation in the United States.

To understand the relationship and communication between African-Americans and the White culture in the United States, we need to study that relationship as it has evolved over time. The four time periods suggested—slavery, segregation, integration, and culture within a culture—are not mutually

| (a) | (b) | (c) | (d) |

(a) Jean Baptiste Point du Sable (1745?-1818), fur trader who established a trading post that became the basis for modern-day Chicago

(b) James Welden Johnson (1871-1938), teacher, lyricist, U.S. consul in Venezuela, author, and organizer and field secretary of the NAACP

(c) Jan E. Matzeliger (1852-1889), inventor of lasting machine used in the manufacturing of shoes

(d) Ida B. Wells (1862-1931), educator, journalist, and anti-lynching campaigner

exclusive but are intended to highlight that evolution. Each of these periods is discussed in turn.

Slavery

Slavery has a long history. Athens and Rome were slave states. The African slave trade, too, has a long history. It may have been first conducted by Arabs in collaboration with warring African tribal states centuries before European White traders appeared on the continent at the end of the 15th century and still continues in the form of chattel slavery. In the United States, slaves were owned by Whites, although a few Blacks also owned African slaves.

Jackie Robinson (1919-1972), first African-American to play baseball in the major leagues

To focus on slavery and its effect on cultural differences in the Americas, let's begin by comparing and contrasting African-Americans and Irish-Americans. As you saw in Chapter 13, Irish immigration to the United States occurred predominantly from the 1820s through the 1880s. Although famine or the threat of war or the promise of a better life may have been the motivation, Irish immigrants freely chose to come to the United States.

Africans were brought as slaves to the Americas because Europeans wanted to sweeten their coffee and tea. Before Columbus, Europeans obtained sugar from apothecaries to make medicine taste better. Sugar was a luxury. Columbus carried a few pieces of sugar to the Caribbean, and by the middle of the 16th century, tropical forests had been converted to vast cane-growing plantations cared for at first by the indigenous people. As the indigenous people perished, Africans were brought in as slaves. Portuguese and later British ships carried textiles, guns and gunpowder, whiskey, and other manufactured wares to Africa in exchange for slaves, who were then taken to the West Indies and traded for sugar.

Scholars estimate that over the period of four centuries 12 million Africans were enslaved and shipped to the Americas. Two million may have perished en route. Of the 10 million who survived the trip, many died on the plantations. It is estimated that each ton of sugar cost the life of one worker.

The first slaves to arrive in what would become the United States were 20 indentured servants sent to Jamestown, Virginia, in 1619. For the next 250 years, slavery was sanctioned.

In 1783, a Massachusetts court awarded freedom to a slave who claimed that right under the preamble of the state constitution that declared all men free and equal. That same year, Massachusetts prohibited slavery. Connecticut, New Jersey, and Rhode Island followed suit the next year.

The slave-based plantation system spread to the Carolinas and Georgia for the production of rice, indigo, and cotton, and additional large numbers of slaves were imported to do the labor. It is estimated that in 1860, of the more than 1.5 million families in the South, 385,000 owned the nearly 4 million slaves, and of these only 25,000 owned 2 million.

In 1998, U.S. President Bill Clinton visited Slave House on Senegal's Goree Island, the transit point for millions of manacled Africans en route to slavery in the New World, and made the following statement:

In 1776, when our nation was founded on the promise of freedom as God's right to all human beings, a new building was dedicated here on Goree Island to the selling of human beings in bondage to America. Goree Island is, therefore, as much a part of our history as a part of African history.

Loss of Culture

Did the Africans brought as slaves to the United States at first strive as a group to maintain the original culture as did the Hmong and the Irish? One critical fact prevented that: Slave owners attempted to strip slaves of African languages and cultures and beliefs and values. Marriages were not recognized. Groups and families were broken up, so languages were lost. Slaves were

Some states adopted a poll tax as a requirement for voting. The tax disenfranchised many African-Americans.

forced to speak English, to worship in certain ways, and to conform to English law.

Communication Under Slavery

Cal Logue (1981) describes communication under slavery: Slave owners created a climate of fear through punishment. They maintained slaves in a state of ignorance, restricted oral communication, and required slaves to behave in a submissive manner. Slaves could adopt defensive responses of accommodation and aggressive responses through concealment and deception, such as using common words with special meanings known only to other slaves and expressing ideas through singing. Popular oral folktales helped maintain hopes for a better life by describing how small, seemingly weak animals, such as Brer Rabbit, defeated larger beasts and how slaves ingeniously outwitted the White masters. Stories of escaped slaves, known as **maroons**, who established independent societies in Brazil (Palmares survived nearly 100 years in the Amazon) and in Jamaica and Haiti also circulated.

So, whereas Irish-Americans voluntarily gave up the Irish culture during acculturation into the United States culture, slaves were stripped of African culture. Then, did African slaves start a new culture? It is a mistake to assume that an African-American culture started in the Carolinas or Georgia. Even though slavery stripped slaves of much of African culture, remnants of the culture remained.

Segregation

Creation of Separate Cultural Identity

Following the Civil War, a substantial number of African-Americans were elected mayors, sheriffs, and legislators. As a White backlash emerged, the Ku Klux Klan became more powerful, and racist legislation known as "Jim Crow" laws, such as the poll tax, forced African-Americans into second-class citizenship in the South. Legal racial separation or segregation existed for almost the next 100 years. By 1901, there were no African-American members of Congress from the South. (It wasn't until 1967 that Andrew Young of Georgia was elected to the House of Representatives.)

The early 20th century saw many African-Americans leave the South for urban areas. In 1910, three-fourths of the nearly 10 million African-Americans lived in rural areas and nine-tenths lived in the South. The years 1910 to 1920 saw nearly 1.5 million African-Americans immigrate from the South to urban areas. By 1950, three-fourths lived in cities and slightly more than half lived outside the South.

In 1896, the Supreme Court decision in *Plessey v. Ferguson* established the "separate but equal" concept. Segregation excluded African-Americans from White neighborhoods, schools, and other organizations. Segregation not only minimized the association between African-Americans and Whites but also defined what communication there was in clearly defined subordinate-superior roles. Segregation, then, prevented acculturation and hence contributed to the forming of a separate cultural identity.

Two contradictory consequences of segregation were accepting the White culture as the standard to strive for and continuing the efforts to regain African culture. Some African-Americans affected the manners, dress, and behavior of Whites. In a classic study, Clark and Clark (1947) asked African-American children to choose between two Black and two White dolls. Two-thirds of the children preferred White dolls.

Accepting the White culture as the standard to strive for was scathingly attacked by African-American sociologist E. Franklin Frazier in his 1957 book *Black Bourgeoisie*. More recently, writer Alice Walker (1983, 1992) has spoken about colorism, or the prejudicial or preferential treatment of same-race people based on skin color. For example, Whites may give preferential treatment in the workplace to light-complected African-Americans and African-Americans may prefer light-complected spouses. As recently as 2002, Maddox and Gray have shown that both Blacks and Whites are more likely to associate positive traits to light-skinned Blacks and negative traits to dark-skinned Blacks.

For many African-Americans, though, regaining an African culture became an important part of taking back what slavery took away.

In the 1930s, the concept of **negritude**, an assertion of the importance of the African heritage, was advanced by such French-educated Black intellectuals as Léopold Senghor and Aimé Césaire. Others who advocated an Afrocentric perspective were David Walker, an abolitionist and Black nationalist of the early 1800s; W. E. B. Du Bois, the scholar, writer, and father of Pan-Africanism; and Carter G. Woodson, cofounder of the Association for the Study of Negro Life and History.

More recently, the concept of Afrocentricity has been explored by Molefi Asante (1987, 1988). **Afrocentricity** is a way of interpreting the history, culture, and behavior of Blacks around the world in terms of dispersion or extension of African history and culture in the context of where it is found. For example, African-American culture can best be understood as a manifestation of African culture in the context of the United States.

From an Afrocentric perspective, the African-American experience has been described by African-Americans:

W. E. B. Du Bois promoted the cause for equality. He helped found the National Association for the Advancement of Colored People (NAACP).

> One ever feels his two-ness—an American, a Negro; two souls, two thoughts, two unreconciled strivings; two warring ideals in one dark body. . . . The history of the American Negro is the history of this strife—this longing to attain self-conscious manhood, to merge his double self into a better and truer self. . . . He would not Africanize America, for America has too much to teach the world and Africa. He would not bleach his Negro soul in a flood of white Americanism, for he knows that Negro blood has a message for the world. He simply wishes to make it possible for a man to be both a Negro and an American, without being cursed and spit upon.
>
> —W. E. B. Du Bois, *The Souls of Black Folk* (1903/1965, p. 215)

- 85% are "fairly religious" or "very religious" (Taylor & Chatters, 1991).

- African-Americans rely on family, friends, neighbors, voluntary associations, and religious figures (Hatchett & Jackson, 1993; Milburn & Bowman, 1991).

- African-Americans share a collective identity, outlook, and collectively defined interests and rely on the beliefs and behavior of other African-Americans for a frame of reference (Cooper & Denner, 1998; Crocker & Major, 1989; Frable, 1997).

Communication Style

Asante (1987, 1988) explains that much of communication in Africa is through the spoken word and characterized by a strong collective mentality where the group is more important than the individual and by an African quest for harmony or compatibility that is at the root of traditional African philosophy.

Jahn (1961) observed that in pan-African culture, everything in the universe exists for a purpose or a specific function. All living creatures have a reason for existence. Mankind (*mantu*) is one of four fundamental elements with things (*kintu*), place and time (*hantu*), and modality (*kuntu*). Mantu is distinguished from the other three elements by the possession of the magical power of the word, or **nommo**. Words mean power; words represent the life force of being.

Asante writes of the West African concept of *nommo* to illustrate the African concept of the generative and productive power of the spoken word. For example, the Dogon people of Mali believe that until an infant's name is spoken there is no life in the child.

Asante used this communication pattern as an example to explain Afrocentricity. Why did Marcus Garvey, Martin Luther King, Jr., Jesse Jackson, and other African-American preachers in the United States evoke spoken responses and interchanges from their congregations? This communication practice of punctuating a speaker's statements with expressions from listeners is identified as **call-response**.

Afrocentrists argue that call-response is the African concept of nommo, or the power of the generative word. In contrast to the Afrocentrists are those who argue that the African-American identity was forged primarily in America rather than in Africa. From this approach, for example, call-response is explained by others, such as Jack Daniel and Geneva Smitherman (1976), as emphasizing the more immediate influence of the African-American church in sustaining the culture and the communication practices of African-Americans.

> White Americans have never fully understood—but what the Negro can never forget—is that White society is deeply implicated in the ghetto. White institutions created it, White institutions maintain it, and White society condones it.
>
> —Report of the *National Advisory Commission on Civil Disorders*, Kerner Commission, 1969, pp. 1-2

Integration

Integration brought on a time of equal access to cultural institutions of neighborhoods, schools, and other organizations. Integration in the armed forces in World War II was followed by court-ordered removal of residential restrictive covenants that restricted sales of property to individuals based on race. That was followed by court-ordered integration of public schools in 1954, but complete legal equality has existed for only the past 35 years.

It has been observed that in a period of integration following a period of segregation the communication between the groups becomes preoccupied with the issues of housing, education, and suffrage and narrowly focuses on "race relations."

Effect on Communication

The conditions of slavery, the years of segregation, and African cultural roots contributed to a unique communication style. Anita Foeman and Gary Pressley (1987) identified five elements of African-American communication style:

- *Assertiveness*—drawing attention to the speaker's positive qualities or sense of individual power in a bold and un-self-conscious manner

- *Forthrightness*—straightforward, direct approach to problem solving

- *Ethical awareness*—beliefs in an overall balance of good and evil and in fairness and accountability resulting from the strong tradition in the church

- *Group identification*—a sense of community and collective responsibility

- *Language*—verbal inventiveness or linguistic adroitness and call-response in which the role of the listener becomes active

These elements are reflected in literature, music, and art. The old Negro spirituals were among the first American songs created. The use of call-response, clapping and stamping, and offbeat rhythm provides further evidence of Afrocentricity, for all are traceable to West African sources.

Much was written in the 1990s about **Black English,** or **Ebonics** (a combination of the words *ebony* and *phonics*). Some content evolved from West African languages and slave traders who used a form of pidgin English to communicate with African slaves who were neither allowed to speak their own languages nor to learn English. It survived among African-Americans who remained isolated racially and economically in poor African-American communities. Others contend that Black English is a creation of the second half of the 20th century.

Black English shares a vocabulary with mainstream English but is governed by distinct grammatical usages and differences in pronunciation. For example, West African sentence structure includes a construct known as topic and comment, as does Black English.

In "My sister, she smart," "My sister" is the topic and "she smart" the comment. One example of pronunciation differences is the word *ask*, which was pronounced *axe* until sometime between the 15th and 17th centuries when the *ks* sound slowly changed to the *sk* sound. The upper class adopted the change; slaves and poor Whites typically did not.

Black English, or Ebonics, has been the inspiration for poetry, spirituals, jazz, blues, rap, and other art forms, but it has also been dismissed as ghetto slang or ungrammatical English and a symbol of poor education.

In 1996, the Oakland, California, school board announced its decision to recognize Ebonics as a primary language for many of its African-American students so that it could provide teacher training in Ebonics and help African-American students who use Ebonics to master standard English. Reactions to media reports that the school board was recognizing Ebonics as a primary language were strongly negative from Whites and African-Americans including Jessie Jackson, Maya Angelou, NAACP President Kweisi Mfume, and U.S. Education Secretary Richard Riley.

Ebonics represents a troubling legacy of separation. Although Black English is not formally taught in schools, it survives, so it must serve an important function. Some argue that Black English is more commonly used by adolescents who become less likely to use it as adults (Abrahams, 1976). Formally educated African-Americans who use both standard English and Black English depending on the social context, known as code-switching, are part of two cultures. Some explain that Black English is a unique language of a culture and should be as respected as any other language is because it continues to provide a cultural identification. From the perspective of the Sapir-Whorf hypothesis, then, Black English presents its speakers with a unique, shared, and exclusive perspective on reality (Weber, 1985).

Successes

It has been argued that the simultaneous occurrence of the civil rights activism and national prosperity of the 1960s resulted in the most radical restructuring of society in the country's history.

In the 1940s, the majority of Whites opposed integrated schools. In 1942, only 32% of Whites supported integration, according to polls. The 1954 Supreme Court decision in *Brown v. Board of Education of Topeka, Kansas*, led to the 1964 Civil Rights Act, the 1965 Voting Rights Act, the 1968 Fair Housing Act, and the Supreme Court ruling striking down state laws outlawing interracial marriages.

By the 1980s, nearly all Whites supported some degree of school desegregation. By 1985, that percentage was 93%. This represents one of the most massive shifts in public opinion known. There are far more integrated neighborhoods today, and African-Americans and Whites are more likely to have friends of the other race than they did a decade ago. The number of elected African-American officials has risen from 300 in 1965 to more than 7,300 today.

Challenges

However, when looked at from an economic perspective, a far different picture emerges. African-Americans differ greatly in economic success. In the late 1990s, about 22% of African-American families had incomes below the poverty line and nearly a quarter of all African-Americans had incomes greater than $50,000 (Thernstrom & Thernstrom, 1997). Averaged as a group, African Americans trail Whites in life expectancy, education, and financial stability.

Polls continue to show that some Whites generalize the effects of poverty to all African-Americans *except those personally known*: One poll found that 56% of Whites believe that African-Americans are less intelligent, and 78% believe African-Americans are more likely than Whites to prefer living on welfare. Some Whites associate all African-Americans with crime, drugs, homelessness, and AIDS.

This misperception may explain why many Whites, whose real incomes have been stagnant over the past generation, believe the government should not intervene to enforce equal rights in housing and hiring. Political advertising has played to these feelings. A 1988 television ad by Republican Senator Jesse Helms of North Carolina showed the hand of a White job applicant crumpling a rejection slip he received because of an employer's affirmative action hiring plan.

To demonstrate how economic statistics could also be used negatively about Whites, consider the following: African-Americans live an average of 6 fewer years than Whites; therefore, Whites benefit more from Social Security than do African-Americans. In fact, Whites receive more per capita from Social Security than do African-Americans. It could be said then that White retirees benefit from African-American workers.

Has the African-American fully acculturated into a jointly shared U.S. culture? To explain the success and acceptance of many African-Americans and the contradictory negative attitudes, some have argued that negative attitudes held against African-Americans are really attitudes held against the poor. This would replace thinking along racial lines with thinking along economic lines.

Let's go back to our comparison with Irish-Americans to look at acculturation. Many Irish immigrants initially clung to the home culture, and many experienced discrimination. Signs in stores, for example, at one time read, "No Irish." However, over time, acculturation became so complete that it is unlikely that a fourth-generation Irish-American child on a school playground would identify as Irish-American or be identified that way by others. The African-American child on the school playground continues to be identified as Black. As was discussed in Chapter 5, that identification is evidence of racism. Reports of hate crimes against African-Americans have increased. African-Americans continue to experience bias in restaurants, stores, housing, workplaces, and schools and on the street. In 1991, for example, African-Americans at a Denny's restaurant in San Jose, California, were required to pay a cover charge and pay in advance for food. No White customers were asked to do so.

In an insightful study conducted in summer 1981, Gale Schroeder Auletta and John Hammerback (1985) reviewed television shows that had African-American and White characters. They characterized the relational communication between the characters as demonstrating dependence, independence, or interdependence based on the quality and extent of the relationship. Relationships between characters of the same race were more likely to be interdependent, but relationships between African-American and White characters were more likely to be independent. A later study of the 1987 season (Stroman, Merritt, & Matabane, 1989) found that African-American characters were most likely to appear in situation comedies set in an urban area in the Northeast. Although the characters in 1987 improved in status, competence, and appearance, they continued to be depicted in separate African-American settings.

Culture Within a Culture

It is a mistake to assume that races are cultures, yet generally all African-Americans are treated as a nondominant culture first. In many ways, it can be argued that integration and acculturation simply were not allowed to work. A 1993 study by the National School Boards Association reports that 66% of

African-American children attend schools with mostly minority students. The *Brown* decision could not have foreseen the deterioration of cities and White migration to suburbs (Massey & Denton, 1993).

Andrew Hacker wrote in a 1989 *New York Review* article,

> Recent studies show that black Americans spend more of their lives in segregated neighborhoods and schools than even recent immigrants do. . . . At the same time the distinctive forms of English that have emerged among black Americans during the history of segregation seem less suited to preparing students to pass scholastic aptitude and other academic tests . . . and the fact of continuing segregation makes it much harder for blacks to become, in effect, bicultural and bilingual. (p. 65)

In many ways, then, African-Americans may be evolving into a culture where there is legally enforced integration of institutions but voluntary segregation based on cultural identity. U.S. culture has been significantly shaped by African-Americans. Its respect for diversity was fought for and paid for by African-Americans. The concept of culture within a culture may be most accurate because it seems the original identity cannot or will not be permitted to be lost.

Contrasting Views of Martin Luther King, Jr., and Malcolm X

In the early years of the 20th century, the viewpoints of W. E. B. Du Bois and Booker T. Washington were in contrast: Du Bois called for civil rights to be gained through the political and legal transformation of society; Washington argued for group development through vocational education. John Lucaites and Celeste Condit (1990) have shown that the arguments for African-American as a culture within a culture continue to be reflected in the contrasting integrationist-separationist viewpoints of Martin Luther King, Jr., and Malcolm X. Dr. King, who was awarded the Nobel Peace Prize in 1964, argued for social and political reform to create a sameness between the two groups such that one becomes indistinguishable from the other. Malcolm X (born Malcolm Little—a surname given to one of his ancestors by a slave master) adopted the X to symbolize the loss of his original African name and a rejection of the slave name.

Thousands of African-Americans were drawn to Elijah Muhammad's Nation of Islam in the 1950s and 1960s. As the leading spokesman of the Nation of Islam, Malcolm X argued for a revolutionary creed of an economic and political base independent of the larger society, each as a clearly separate entity with its own identity and each similarly powerful. Some have argued that it was the Black nationalist thinking presented by Malcolm X that served as a threat to U.S. Whites and so gave King's movement the leverage needed to achieve its gains.

Malcolm X was influenced by Marcus Garvey, who in the early 1900s called for ethnic consciousness and for communal self-help. Garvey, and later Malcolm X, enabled African-Americans to use African-American standards. His speeches stressed self-improvement. In the final year of his life, Malcolm X took a pilgrimage to Mecca. Seeing Muslims of all races, his message changed to brotherhood of all human beings.

Today, only a small minority of African-American Muslims are members of the Nation of Islam now headed by Louis Farrakhan. Following the example of Elijah Muhammad's son, Imam W. Deen Mohammed, most have affiliated with other groups in the mainstream of Islam (Smith, 2000). It has been estimated that between 4 million and 7 million people practice Islam in the United States—40% or more of whom are African-American.

Effect on Communication

Communication breakdowns between African-Americans and Whites based on cultural differences have been demonstrated by St. Martin (1976). She prepared videotapes showing a female source communicating a variety of nonverbal messages, such as sadness, anger, surprise, and fear. She then studied how African-Americans, Hispanics, Malaysians, and White Americans decoded the messages and found that the greatest difference was between African-Americans and White Americans. Miller (1982) demonstrated a difference in "best friend" choice criteria: African-Americans emphasized argumentativeness, dramatic qualities in communicative style, and physical attraction, whereas the White Americans in his sample emphasized dominance and task attractions.

Kochman's (1981, 1986) studies of African-American and White American conflict styles were based primarily on inner-city African-Americans and middle-class White Americans. According to Kochman, the "Black mode" of conflict style is animated, interpersonal, and confrontational and the "White mode" dispassionate, impersonal, and nonchallenging. Kochman observed that African-Americans tend to use more emotionally expressive and involving modes of conflict management and White Americans tend to be more emotionally self-restrained and attempt to understate and diffuse unpleasant situations. Ting-Toomey (1986) reported that gender has a significant effect.

Although she found that Whites use more compromising conflict resolution strategies, she also found that Black and White males tended to prefer avoidance strategies to deal with relational conflict and that Black females tended to be more verbose and emotionally expressive than White females. Booth-Butterfield and Jordan (1989) found that Black women were more nonverbally expressive as well and interrupted each other more than White women did.

The characteristics of effective co-cultural communication between African-Americans and Whites have been carefully described in a series of studies headed by Michael Hecht (Hecht, Ribeau, & Alberts, 1989; Hecht, Ribeau, & Collier, 1992). The researchers identified seven issues that African-Americans perceived as salient in satisfying and dissatisfying interethnic communication. If the Miller (1982) study is accurate, Hecht et al.'s (1989) list resembles more the White Americans' choice criteria for best friends:

- *Negative stereotyping*—the presence of direct racial stereotyping or indirect stereotyping, such as talking about topics that were believed to be "African-American topics" such as sports or music

- *Acceptance*—a feeling that the other accepts, confirms, and respects one's opinions

- *Emotional expressiveness*—either verbally or nonverbally communicating feelings

- *Authenticity*—open disclosure or genuineness versus evasiveness

- *Understanding*—feeling that meaning was successfully conveyed

- *Goal attainment*—achieving objectives or obtaining desired ends from communication effort

- *Powerlessness*—feelings of being controlled, manipulated, and trapped versus feelings of having some control or influence over the conversation

Note that the issue of power is embedded in many of these issues—that is, satisfying interethnic communication requires a sharing of power and control by the communicators.

Shipler (1997) wrote that some African-Americans can move between Black and White worlds, having established a bicultural equilibrium between African-American identity and mainstream assimilation. But, he notes, many cannot and on leaving the "all-black comfort of family, neighborhood, and culture into the alien landscape of mostly white America" find life lonely in a world where "whites, mostly, hire and fire and make the rules and determine the styles of interaction" (p. 54). Shipler wrote that living in this White world entails a balancing act that "tears at black souls" (p. 54). There is no interest in transcending race if it means assimilating into a White world.

AFRICAN-AMERICAN IDENTITY AND MEDIA AND MARKETING

Throughout United States society today, we find growing evidence of culture-within-a-culture acceptance.

Media

The various entertainment media show evidence of a developing culture.

Comic Strips

Early comic strips showed African-Americans primarily in demeaning stereotypes. In the late 1960s and early 1970s, African-Americans Franklin and Lt. Flap joined the strips *Peanuts* and *Beetle Bailey*, respectively. In the early 1990s, newspapers turned to African-American comic strips *Curtis*, *Jump Start*, and *Herb & Jamaal*, all of which show life with a distinctive African-American sensibility.

Radio

In 1986, there were 94 AM and 56 FM African-American radio stations. Programming was urban contemporary (i.e., disco and rap), Black, adult contemporary (i.e., well-established and familiar popular music), and gospel. The National Black Network (NBN) had 94 affiliated stations (Downing, 1990).

Radio One is the largest U.S. broadcasting company serving African-American audiences. Early in 2000, Radio One became the owner of 48 stations in 19 cities. Its stations serve primarily African-American listeners in top urban markets and specialize in rap, R&B, hip-hop, and other urban music genres.

Television

African-Americans and Whites have distinctly different television viewing habits. During the 1985-1986 television season, 15 of the 20 shows most popular among African-Americans were also top shows among all viewers. But by the 1991-1992 season, for the first time in broadcast history, the top 10 shows for African-Americans were completely different from the top 10 for all viewers combined. For example, Fox's *In Living Color* was No. 4 in African-American homes and No. 68 overall, and NBC's *Fresh Prince of Bel Air* was No. 2 in African-American homes and No. 40 overall. In the 1995-1996 season, the only show that appeared on the Top 20 list in African-American homes and in White homes was *ABC Monday Night Football*. In 1999, in African-American homes the WB Network's *Steve Harvey Show* was the top-ranked series but was No. 127 with White viewers. No. 2, WB's *The Jamie Foxx Show* was No. 120 in White homes. In White homes, *ER* was No. 1 but was No. 15 in African-American homes, and *Friends* was No. 2 but ranked No. 88 among African-American viewers.

Black Entertainment Television Cable Network (BET) is part of BET Holdings, a media company targeting African-American consumers. BET reaches about 55 million households and features news and entertainment geared toward African-American viewers. In early 2000, BET announced a new Internet portal aimed at increasing Internet usage among African-Americans.

Marketing

As might be expected, then, as you've seen was the case for Hispanic cultures, media and marketing segment African-Americans directly under the assumption of shared values and norms.

Recently, some of that marketing has come under scrutiny: Makers of tobacco, beer, and liquor products have been charged with segmenting minorities who, it is charged, suffer a disproportionate number of health problems and financial hardships from the use of the products. R. J. Reynolds planned to market the cigarette Uptown to African-Americans, but protests stopped the project. The G. Heileman Brewing Company's plan to market Powermaster, a high-alcohol malt liquor, to African-Americans was also protested.

Businesses have discovered that African-Americans have both a unique vocabulary and different food tastes. Stove Top Stuffing found its sales improved among African-Americans when it used the word "dressing," which is more likely to be used by African-Americans. Sales at Kentucky Fried Chicken improved in African-American neighborhoods when KFC switched to African-themed uniforms and soul food.

Armstrong (1999) analyzed the logic of Nike's advertising messages, their grammar, and their overall style for elements of African-American culture. She

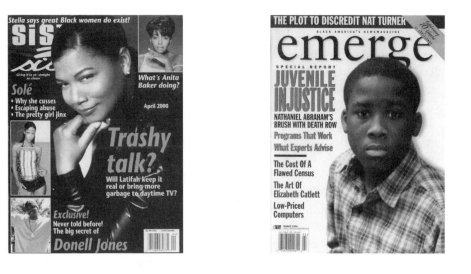

Examples of popular magazines among African-Americans.

found that the logic or premise of Nike advertising went far beyond functional product attributes to endorse and celebrate nuances, emotions, and interactions that occur within the African-American culture. The "Just Do It" message shows people overcoming social ills with the support of and through interactions with family and community. She found that people in the commercials spoke in slang, jive-talking, and with codes and jargon to "express themselves." Nonverbals including handshakes, hugs, high fives, and body gestures conveyed a consistent message. Background music was often rhythm and blues. The overall style of the advertising most often presented professional African-American male athletes and spokespeople portrayed in such a manner that reduced their celebrity status and made them believable people as opposed to privileged characters. Perhaps Nike's effectiveness in constructing its advertising with African-American cultural messages contributed to African-Americans' patronage of its products. While Nike has been criticized for being exploitative of the African-Americans, it has chosen to communicate with African-American consumers in commercials by focusing on human interaction and emotion with an inherent cultural message accompanied by a peripheral product endorsement.

Schools

There are currently about 350 Afrocentric schools nationwide educating approximately 50,000 youths. These schools aim for greater self-esteem and higher test scores through separate education.

Holidays

In 1966, Maulana Karenga founded the nonreligious African-American holiday **Kwanzaa** (Swahili for "first fruits") as a celebration of African culture and collective and community values. Today, some 18 million observe Kwanzaa. In 1992, Hallmark brought out its first Kwanzaa greeting cards, which are now a common sight in stores.

Kwanzaa is celebrated from December 26 through January 1 and highlights seven basic principles for families to live by. A candle is lit each day for each of the seven principles of unity, self-determination, collective work and responsibility, cooperative economics, purpose, creativity, and faith. Observers gather each evening to light one candle and discuss how the principle of the day affects life. Karenga describes the holiday as a reaffirmation of African culture and a recentering as Africans.

In 1997, the U.S. Postal Service released a stamp honoring Kwanzaa. The image was taken from the 1994 book *The Gifts of Kwanzaa* by Synthia St. James.

FROM THE INTERCULTURAL PERSPECTIVE

What's in a name? Certainly, we have seen that words have the power to influence our perceptions of reality. Names and labels are important because they help define our identities. African-Americans are one group whose label has changed over time. In the past, people used the words *Negroes* and *Blacks*. Now many people use the word *African-American*. These labels reflect the history and experience of African-Americans in the United States. African-Americans experienced slavery, segregation (separation from the dominant culture), integration (an end of separation and forced interaction with the dominant culture), and being a culture within a culture.

> You want to integrate me into your anonymity
>
> because it is my right
>
> you think
>
> to be like you.
>
> I want your right to be like yourself.
>
> —Opening lines of poem "Black Narcissus"
> by Gerald W. Barrax, in *The Poetry of
> Black America* (Adoff, 1973, p. 223)

African worldview includes the beliefs that the spiritual world and the physical world are one and that religion is a central part of life. African worldview also includes beliefs that nature and the universe exist in harmony, that society should follow natural patterns, and that time is cyclical. Afrocentrism is the belief that the history, culture, and behavior of Blacks around the world are an extension of African history and culture. An Afrocentrist might see a communication style (which emphasizes verbal ability) and strong involvement in churches and communities as coming from African culture. African-American culture in the United States has grown from the efforts of African-Americans to reclaim the culture that was lost during slavery. Things that support African-American cultural identity are media and marketing, special schools, and holidays such as Kwanzaa.

KEY TERMS

Afrocentricity	Ebonics	negritude
Black English	Kwanzaa	nommo
call-response	maroons	

CHAPTER 17

Identity and Subgroups

In Chapter 1, you read that subgroups pose similar communication problems as cultures and are characterized by a limited focus. Subgroups usually do not involve the same large number of people as cultures and are not necessarily thought of as accumulating values and patterns of behavior over generations in the same way as cultures. Existing within cultures, subgroups do provide members with relatively complete values and patterns of behavior.

In this chapter, you'll study the importance of language in communicating a subgroup identity and study the examples provided by the working class, Hell's Angels, British punk, corporations, and gay men and lesbians. These were chosen because they illustrate the unique intercultural communication challenges presented by all types of subgroups. Remember that each of us is a member of various subgroups throughout our lives. As you read this chapter, examine the ways your subgroups support an identity.

ARGOT

You've learned the importance of the study of a culture's language as a way to knowing that culture. The equivalent in learning about a subgroup is studying its specialized language, its vocabulary.

Specialized Vocabulary

According to the Sapir-Whorf hypothesis, language provides the conceptual categories that influence how its speakers' perceptions are encoded and stored. That same concept is true for subgroups but on the level of vocabulary. The specialized vocabulary identifies the subgroup and establishes the group's boundaries. The specialized vocabulary of subgroups, **argot** (pronounced AR-go), has been variously called jargon, cant, and slang.

Jargon has been used to refer to the technical language of a professional subgroup, such as doctors and lawyers. Jargon is the vocabulary that communicates the distinctions and specific meanings these professionals need to reference.

Cant has been used to refer to the specialized vocabulary of any nonprofessional subgroup, such as truck drivers.

Slang has been used to refer to the specialized vocabulary of "stigmatized" subgroups, such as gangs, drug dealers, and prostitutes, as well as to the specialized vocabulary of teenagers.

As argot is becoming the more commonly recognized term, it is used in this chapter to refer to the specialized vocabulary of subgroups regardless of how these subgroups are thought of by the dominant culture.

Argot and Subgroup Identity

The study of argot originated with the work of David Maurer (1981) in the 1930s. Before his work, observations of nonstandard language were limited to the study of regional dialects. Maurer, who had studied Sapir's work, was the first to gather, analyze, and present the speech of subgroups. He was also the first to observe that argots were not primarily secret communications used to deceive outsiders but, rather, were an important aspect of group identity.

In Maurer's studies of professional crime, he showed that individual criminals were not abnormalities but fully integrated and well-adjusted members of a subgroup. Professional crime is much more than individual lawbreaking; it is actually a way of life within certain subgroups. Crime is not a mere facet of the life of some groups but is an entire way of life. Maurer's studies demonstrate that membership in the subgroup provides an identity and that the key to developing and understanding that identity is its language.

Argot and Subgroup Boundaries

Besides developing an identity, a subgroup's argot defines the boundaries of the subgroup. Because its argot can change rapidly, to be a member of the subgroup, you have to know the vocabulary. If you don't know the vocabulary, you're obviously not a member. Correct use of the argot, then, establishes the subgroup's boundary.

Gang slang, for example, serves several important functions. A special language can contribute to feeling special, to developing a group identity. Besides argot, there may be unique nonverbal symbols such as handshakes or clothing styles. The language and clothes say, "I'm somebody." Use of the argot and nonverbal codes establishes the boundaries of the gang.

A particular gang slang may appear in another part of the country when gang members move. It may die unnoticed when a gang dies out. Some argot may be absorbed into more mainstream language. For example, four-twenty was once an obscure San Francisco Bay area term for marijuana. Later it began to show up nationally in advertising—420 Pale Ale, 420 Tours, and Highway 420 Radio.

Argot and Meaning

Argot also has specific, unambiguous meaning for a subgroup. Air traffic controllers and seafaring radio operators have an argot that has specific, unambiguous meaning. Various scientific disciplines have developed specialized argot to express nuances of meaning precisely. That preciseness of meaning is clear only to the subgroup's members.

The medical professions have developed an argot for preciseness of meaning to avoid misunderstandings that can hurt a patient's health. A limited vocabulary has been devised to ensure that each word has a precise, unambiguous meaning.

SUBGROUP MEDIA AND VALUES

Besides argot, media use and values contribute to defining subgroup identity and boundaries. Media distributed only to members can vary widely from graffiti to newsletters, but the subgroup's argot and pictorial images will be used. To get an idea of the media of subgroups, simply visit a large newsstand. You'll find specialty magazines that appeal to a wide variety of subgroup interests.

Most important, however, are common values or worldview shared by members of the subgroup. For many subgroups, that common value may be a reaction to society's disapproval—that is, "because we're outcasts, we're together"—but for other subgroups, the shared values may grow to provide a member with a relatively complete set of guiding values and patterns of behavior.

EXAMPLES OF SUBGROUPS

Just like cultures, ethnographic and cultural approaches can be applied to subgroups. There are many reports of observations of subgroups that range in method from "insider" to participant observer. Insider reports can be most interesting and valuable; some have been written for self-justification or profit. **Participant observer** reports are based on the researcher's orderly and scientific study of a subgroup by actually becoming accepted as a member. In one sense, these reports can be viewed as self-reports of the acculturation process of learning the culture of the subgroup. There are several fascinating reports of this kind available that provide insight into the argot, nonverbal symbols, media, and values.

The Working Class

In Chapter 1, social class was given as one basis for a subculture. Most scholars agree that working-class values include a high value placed on loyalty to one's community even at the cost of self-advancement, a lack of a sense of entitlement of privilege, and a shared resentment of perceived arrogance in wealthier classes (Denning, 1997; Roediger, 1999). And as you read in Chapter 1, working-class parents emphasize different values in child rearing than do middle-class parents.

While social class is more properly considered a subculture, studies by Gerry Philipsen (1975, 1976, 1989, 1992) of blue-collar, low-income Whites on the near south side of Chicago in the early 1970s is the best example of a study that focuses on the communication behavior of the group. Philipsen showed that to know how to present oneself as a man in this community, one needed to know the community's culture. In some situations, speech was appropriate in male role enactment, but in others it was not. To use speech where it was not appropriate cast doubts on the speaker's manliness. If the relationship was symmetrical—that is, matched on age, sex, ethnicity, occupation, and location of resident—then speech was appropriate. However, if the relationship was asymmetrical—that is, if a man was with his wife, child, or boss, was an outsider, or was of different ethnicity—then speech was not appropriate.

Hell's Angels

One of the more interesting examples is given by journalist Hunter Thompson (1966). Thompson, a political reporter for *Rolling Stone* magazine, "ran" with the Hell's Angels motorcycle gang for a year and established considerable trust with many of this subgroup's members. The first Hell's Angels chapter was established in 1948 in Fontana, California, by World War II veterans. In the mid 1960s, from 500 to 1,000 motorcyclists belonged to such clubs as the Gypsy Jokers, Nightriders, Comancheros, Presidents, Satan's Slaves, and the outlaw elite, the Hell's Angels, which is part of that supposed 1% of motorcyclists that the American Motorcycle Association refuses to claim as members.

Thompson's contact was Frenchy, a 29-year-old part owner of a San Francisco-based transmission repair garage called the Box Shop. Thompson describes his conversation with Frenchy in a local Angels bar:

Frenchy ignored me long enough to make things uncomfortable, then nodded a faint smile and rapped a shot toward one of the corner pockets. I bought a glass of beer and watched.

When the pool game ended, Frenchy sat down at the bar, and asked what I wanted to know. We talked for more than an hour, but his style of conversation made me nervous. He would pause now and then, letting a question hang, and fix me with a sad little smile . . . an allusion to some private joke that he was sure I understood. The atmosphere was heavy with hostility, like smoke in an airless room, and for a while I assumed it was all focused on me—which most of it was when I made my initial appearance but the focus dissolved very quickly. The sense of menace remained; it is part of the atmosphere the Hell's Angels breathe. . . . Their world is so rife with hostility that they don't even recognize it. They are deliberately hard on most strangers, but they get bad reactions even when they try to be friendly. I have seen them try to amuse an outsider by telling stories which they consider very funny—but which generate fear and queasiness in a listener whose sense of humor has a different kind of filter.

Some of the outlaws understand this communications gap, but most are puzzled and insulted to hear that "normal people" consider them horrible.

That was in early spring of 1965. By the middle of summer I had become so involved in the outlaw scene that I was no longer sure whether I was doing research on the Hell's Angels or being slowly absorbed by them. I found myself spending two or three days each week in Angel bars, in their homes, and on runs and parties. In the beginning I kept them out of my own world, but after several months my friends grew accustomed to finding Hell's Angels in my apartment at any hour of the day or night. (pp. 64-66)

After Thompson's favorable article on motorcycles appeared in *The Nation* magazine, the Angels became more accepting of him. Thompson, however, failed in adapting to all of this subgroup's norms in two ways: First, he bought a BSA bike—even though an Angel's bylaw requires that an Angel ride only a customized Harley 74; second, he fouled up an Angel's "game" of kissing as "a guaranteed square-jolter":

One night after I'd known the Angels for many months I walked into the Hyde Inn in San Francisco and joined a cluster at the bar. While I was reaching in my pocket for some beer money I was nearly knocked off my feet by a flying body that wrapped itself around me before I could see who it was. Everything went black, and my first thought was that they'd finally turned on me and it was all over: then I felt the hairy kiss and heard the laughter. Ronnie, the Oakland secretary, seemed offended that I hadn't caught him in mid-air, as he'd expected, and returned the kiss heartily. It was a serious social error. (pp. 253-254)

Thompson believed the Angels to be like any other subgroup.

The "all for one" concept was taken so seriously by the "Frisco Angels" that it was written into the club charter as Bylaw Number 10: "When an Angel punches a non-Angel, all other Angels will participate." Thompson quotes Tiny as saying, "Why can't people let us alone, anyway? All we want to do is get together now and then and have some fun—just like the Masons, or any other group" (p. 30).

Denounced in the U.S. Senate by George Murphy (whom Thompson described as "the former tap dancer"), the Angels eventually "stomped" Thompson on Labor Day 1966 when four or five Angels seemed to feel that he was taking advantage of the relationship.

Over the past 50 years, the Angels have grown to an estimated 2,000 members in more than 200 chapters worldwide. They deliver toys to sick and disadvantaged children and contribute to charities. Law enforcement officials contend the Angels are involved in extortion and international drug trafficking.

British Punk

A now-classic cultural studies analysis of a subgroup is Dick Hebdige's (1979) study of British punk youth culture. He described the use of random, mass-produced objects such as dog collars, safety pins, and school uniforms as a parody of consumerism.

Hebdige dates the origin of punk in the music press to the summer of 1976 as an alliance of diverse and superficial incompatible music traditions reproduced on the visual level in a clothing style. He interprets punk culture, in part, as a British White working-class "translation" of Black ethnicity and, in part, as the intentional self-construction of "Otherness," which challenged, on a symbolic level, class and gender stereotypes.

Hebdige shows how subgroups develop a style through the intentional use of clothing, dance, argot, and music. Punks repositioned and recontextualized commodities by subverting the conventional uses and inventing new ones. It is how commodities are used in the subgroup that marks the subgroup off from the dominant culture. Lavatory chains became jewelry; school uniforms were covered with graffiti; sexual fetish clothing became street clothes; dance became robotic. What appeared as chaos was actually orderly.

Hebdige acknowledges that not all punks were aware of the signification upon which the subgroup was based. The original or first wave of self-conscious innovators were aware and committed. The later "plastic punks" participated in the subgroup as a distraction from home, school, and work. Hebdige shows that the subgroup declined when punk's visual and verbal vocabulary became reassigned by the dominant culture as mass-produced commodities (clothing and music) and relabeled (boys wearing lipstick became "just kids dressing up" and girls in rubber dresses became "daughters just like ours").

Corporate Cultures

One popular business buzzword of the 1980s was **corporate culture**. It has been defined as "the way we do things around here," or the set of values, goals, and priorities encouraged through the policies and procedures of the organization. Companies can act like cultures and present the same communication challenges (Deal & Kennedy, 1982; Pacanowsky & O'Donnell-Trujillo, 1982; Putnam & Pacanowsky, 1983; Sypher, 1985).

In Chapter 1, you read that Hofstede (1994) classified the elements of culture as symbols, heroes, rituals, and values. Organizations can have their own symbols: their own argot, their own dress codes, and status symbols rec-

ognized by insiders only. Organizational heroes are those people, dead or alive, who serve as models of the Ideal Employee or the Ideal Manager for behavior within the organization. Founders of organizations sometimes become mythical heroes later on, and incredible deeds are ascribed to them: Thomas Watson, Jr., at IBM, Ray Kroc at McDonald's, Walt Disney at Disney Productions, and so on. Rituals in organizations are celebrations and also the many activities common to the organization, for example, meetings, memos, who may speak to whom, who can be late for meetings.

In Chapter 1, you read of cultures having myths. Corporate rituals can take the form of myths within organizations. Ruth Smith and Eric Eisenberg (1987) have shown, for example, how "drama" and "family" are important myths at Disneyland.

Finally, organizations can have their own values. Hofstede makes it clear that we enter work organizations as adults with most of our values firmly entrenched, but we do become socialized to the practices of the work environment. For many organizations, the value systems were established by the personality of the leader: These were value-shaping leaders with visions to excite thousands of employees.

> When several workers at Disneyland's Jungle Cruise lost their jobs for telling their own jokes with contemporary references instead of following the company's official script, Disneyland issued a brief statement:
>
> Our philosophy is that Disneyland is very much a theatrical house or stage, which means we view our park as having both onstage and backstage presence. We entertain our guests with quality family entertainment and put on performances every day. Our goal is to deliver a consistent quality show daily.
>
> —Quoted in the *Los Angeles Times*,
> October 13, 1997, p. A3

IBM's Thomas J. Watson, Jr. (1963) wrote an entire book about values. He observed,

> Consider any great organization—one that has lasted over the years—I think you will find that it owes its resiliency not to its form of organization or administrative skills, but to the power of what we call beliefs and the appeal these beliefs have for its people. This then is my thesis: I firmly believe that any organization, in order to survive and achieve success, must have a sound set of beliefs on which it premises all its policies and actions. (p. 5)

Corporations' values are often reflected in their advertising: Delta Airlines is known for team spirit, Blue Bell (Wrangler Jeans) for quality, and IBM for customer service.

But does having clearly defined and communicated values affect the profitability of a business? The book *In Search of Excellence* (Peters, 1982) argues that the better-performing companies all have a well-defined set of values. The poorly performing companies either have no explicit values or only quantified ones, such as "percentage increase over last year." The book makes it clear that a well-defined set of values motivates and serves to direct the behavior of thousands of employees.

Corporate culture became a major factor in recent corporate mergers. Exxon, an otherwise low-profile company known for the Valdez oil spill, merged with Mobil, known for sponsoring *Masterpiece Theatre* and for full-page ads expressing views on various issues. Daimler-Benz and Chrysler formed a post-merger integration team to deal with issues as far-ranging as language, clothing, clashing values (quality vs. efficiency), labor-management relations, spending priorities, and even the German *vesper*, or employee beer break. And Time-Warner's suited executives have merged with AOL's more casual dress style. (AOL, or America Online, is the largest U.S.-based Internet-access subscriber service.)

Case Study: Southwest Airlines

Herb Kelleher, an attorney in a San Antonio, Texas, law firm, developed the idea for Southwest Airlines in 1966. The meeting at which the idea was born is now part of the company's mythology, as the story is told and retold like a legend. The plan penciled on a cocktail napkin was to establish the airline as an intrastate carrier between the cities of Dallas, Houston, and San Antonio. It overcame overwhelming resistance from the major interstate carriers, but it was probably that resistance itself that helped shape the character of the company as reflecting efficiency, sound business decisions, and fun.

The Southwest corporate culture was developed by the gregarious, self-deprecating, chain-smoking, whiskey-drinking Kelleher who appears as Elvis at Southwest parties. The Southwest strong corporate culture "Keepin' the Southwest spirit!" is carefully reinforced in its hiring policy. Southwest rejects over 90% of job applicants to find those it describes as "wacky and terminally zealous."

Kelleher has the adulation of his workforce. Some say Kelleher used "an element of cultism"; others say he created an extended family or virtual community. Everybody hugs.

Photos of employees are everywhere. A 100-member employee "Culture Committee" devised all sorts of celebrations and incentives to keep the Southwest spirit alive.

Southwest has grown into the country's fifth largest airline. It has the youngest fleet, the best safety record, and awards for customer service. Continually profitable, Southwest was cited by a 1993 government study as the principal force behind fundamental changes in the airline transport business.

Box 17.1

SOUTHWEST'S CULTURE

Here's a riddle: You're in a room in Dallas with 135 people who've flown from as far away as Los Angeles, Orlando, Albany, Cleveland, Baltimore/Washington, and Seattle to hear a woman with bright blue eyes and a long, white ponytail talk about the "Golden Rule," servant leadership, and treating each other like family. You've seen an Elvis impersonator, and you've been blindfolded and led around by a stranger to demonstrate the importance of trust. Where are you?

At a Southwest Airlines Corporate Culture Committee meeting!

The woman with the long, white ponytail is Colleen Barrett, the "matriarch" of Southwest's Culture, and the airline's President and Chief Operating Officer. To some, she is the lesser known "sidekick" to Southwest's legendary Chairman Herb Kelleher. But, to those interested in the "heart and soul" of the Company, she has always been well-known. In 1990, in order to protect and maintain the Southwest Spirit, family values, and fun atmosphere that were created when Southwest was small and its future uncertain, she gathered 15 people and formed the first "official" Culture Committee.

Since then, the Corporate Culture Committee has grown to more than 100 Employees who serve on teams all across the country. Committee members donate their time to help with at least three Company events each year. Members might assemble goody boxes for our "Christmas Spirit" Team, pack snacks for the flight crews working Christmas Day, or cook burgers at a reservations center or maintenance base. After serving on the Corporate Culture Committee, members "graduate" to join the Alumni Committee, now more than 300 members strong. These volunteers visit and assist at two Company events each year. They also may choose to help show appreciation to Southwest's flight crews by preparing breakfast for crews who begin checking in for their early-morning flights.

Another committee, the Local Culture Committee, ensures the well-being of the Corporate Culture of Southwest Airlines in each Southwest city and works to represent the local interests of Employees. Volunteers raise funds for Employee events and donations to charities of local importance, and organize cookouts, potlucks, and costume days.

Working hard, having fun, and doing what it takes to keep the faith, Southwest's Culture Committee Members are committed to "creating, enriching, and enhancing" Southwest's Spirit and Culture—no easy feat since the Company boasts 35,000-plus Employees and service in 59 airports nationwide!

SOURCE: Judy Hearne, Southwest Airlines *Spirit*, October 2002, p. 139. Reprinted with permission.

LABELING SUBGROUPS AS "OTHERS"

Sexual orientation is not an ethnicity or nationality. Its definition as a subgroup comes from labeling applied to it by others based on behavioral components.

Hofstede (1998) reports that the masculinity cultural dimension is negatively related to the acceptance of homosexuality. Those cultures with a high acceptance of masculinity tend to be less accepting of homosexuality. The World Values Survey contained the question "To what extent can homosexuality be justified?" Table 17.1 shows the results from 14 countries. The percentage who answered "never" ranged from 22% in the Netherlands to 73%

Table 17.1   Rejection of Homosexuality in the 1981-1982 World Values Survey, by
Country

Country	Percentage Agreeing With the Statement "Can Never Be Justified"	Hofstede Masculinity Rank
Mexico	73	6
United States	65	15
South Africa	64	13.5
Italy	63	4.5
Ireland	59	7.5
Spain	56	37.5
Japan	52	1
Belgium	51	22
Canada	51	24
France	47	35.5
Great Britain	43	9.5
Germany	42	9.5
Denmark	34	50
The Netherlands	22	51

SOURCE: Inglehart (1990), Halman (1991), and Hofstede (1997).

in Mexico. Ross (1989) surveyed 600 gay men in Australia, Finland, Ireland, and Sweden. Ross reported that young gay men had more problems accepting a gay sexual orientation in Ireland and Australia, less in Finland, and least in Sweden. Ross ranks these societies in homophobia in the same order. It is also the order of these countries on the masculinity dimension. Homosexuality tends to be perceived as a threat in masculine cultures (Bolton, 1994) and considered a fact of life in feminine cultures. As the United States ranks high in both masculinity and in homophobia, the development of categorization and labeling of lesbians and gay men can be easily studied.

Throughout this text, you've read about the consequences of categorization and labeling of others, particularly of how a dehumanized label applied to a group can be associated with discrimination and violence directed toward that group. Subgroups subject to such labeling have their power, equality, and identity taken away from them.

Lesbians and gay men in the United States have been chosen as an example of subgroups and labeling because the process has been of critical importance to the subgroup itself and has been more carefully studied both by members of the subgroup and by nongay researchers.

Labeling

How did sexual behavior and sexual orientation become the basis of a subgroup? Did the subgroup exist before the label, or did the label, in some sense, create the subgroup? The development of labels discussed below intentionally refers only to gay men, as lesbians were largely ignored, and is limited to the United States (D'Emilio, 1992; Miller, 1995). Homosexual behavior is worldwide, but the notion of subgroup categories such as gay or straight is notably absent in many cultures. In Russia, for example, there is no equivalent for the word *gay*, and interestingly, sexual orientation is less of an either-or proposition and so people feel little need to announce a public identity.

In a 1998 essay, Gabriel Rotello framed the issue similar to one of immigration as one of assimilationists versus the radicals. Assimilationists argue that lesbians and gay men should be "just like everybody else"; radicals argue that gay men and lesbians should maintain a separate culture. Rotello contends that cultural separation occurs only when society stigmatizes a group. As long as society in some way stigmatizes gay men and lesbians, a separate culture will exist. Or as Harris (1997) wrote, if gay men and lesbians become too mainstream, what it means to be gay will be lost.

Kinsey long ago explained sexuality as a continuum. On the heterosexual-to-homosexual scale of 0 to 6 that he devised, only 50% of males can be classified as exclusively nongay and 4% exclusively gay. That recognizes that about 45% of men are bisexual. Kinsey's use of the term **homosexual** refers only to one's sexual activity. It says nothing about how one feels about self and that activity. A person could engage in occasional homosexual acts and yet identify as a heterosexual "no different from anyone else."

Meyer's (1995) review found that the term *homosexual* did not even exist until 1869. When the term was first used, it referred to those who today would be labeled as transgender.

During the first half of the 20th century, homosexual behavior became a concern of psychiatrists who, from a "mental illness" paradigm, labeled, treated, and institutionalized homosexuals (Harry & DeVall, 1978).

Evelyn Hooker's (1957, 1965) pioneering work first challenged this view. She examined the incidence of psychopathology in comparable nonclinical populations of heterosexuals and homosexuals and demonstrated that there was no difference between the pathologies of heterosexual and homosexual men, showing that homosexuals were not inherently abnormal. Her research was followed by other research conducted by psychologists and sociologists that resulted in the American Psychiatric Association deleting the entry "Homosexuality" from its *Diagnostic and Statistical Manual of Mental Disorders*.

Religious and politically conservative groups continue to advocate "reparative therapy" and other techniques intended to change sexual orientation, even though the American Psychological Association, the National Education Association, and other health and mental health professional groups have taken stands that there is no support for the idea that homosexuality is abnormal or mentally unhealthy.

The mental illness label was replaced with another label. Chesebro (1980) has described how the 1950s and 1960s research by psychologists and sociologists operated from a theme of "homosexual as degenerate" and described homosexuals as a deviant sexual underworld. The dominant culture's media picked up that theme in, for example, a 1964 *Life* magazine article that wrote of the "sad and often sordid world" of homosexuals and the 1962 movie *The Children's Hour* in which Shirley MacLaine played a self-loathing lesbian.

Pejorative labels such as "dyke," "faggot," and "queer" were used to identify individuals and the subgroup and individuals as "not heterosexual." The subgroup was labeled by what it was not. These labels when applied by the group with power can impose a negative self-image on individuals.

Claiming and Redefining the Label

A symbolic turning point in gay male and lesbian identity was the June 28, 1969, riot at Stonewall, a gay bar located in New York's Greenwich Village, in which patrons fought back against the police raiding the bar. Previous to that event, people at a gay bar might have tried to hide or otherwise escape police recognition. After that event, with the birth of the gay liberation movement as an active political force, it became "OK to be gay" (Katz, 1976). Each year, Stonewall is commemorated with parades in cities across the country. The 1987 March on Washington for Lesbian and Gay Rights had 650,000 in attendance and was the largest march on the nation's capital in history. Some say that the fact that it received so little publicity is an example of continuing discrimination by the media.

The gay movement removed the stigma of the labels by taking back those symbols and giving them a positive meaning. The words *dyke* and *faggot* now became symbols of gay pride. In a like manner, the word **lesbian** changed from a medical word to a label of pride. Queer Nation, a spin-off of ACT-UP (AIDS Coalition to Unleash Power) used the chant "We're here, we're queer, we're fabulous—get used to it." This self-labeling had a clear political utility (Epstein, 1990) in efforts to gain legal protections (Miller, 1998; Smith & Windes, 1997).

In the same way that word symbols are given positive meanings, nonverbal symbols facilitate group identification. For example, the pink triangle had its origin in Hitler's concentration camps where homosexuals were so identified. (Lesbians—and other women—were not judged to have any decision-making power or sovereignty and so were forced to wear black triangles, which labeled them "antisocials.") The rainbow flag, which had its first use in gay parades in San Francisco, is often seen now to identify the gay community.

The label **gay** was internally generated and accepted to refer in a positive way to individuals who form primary emotional attachments to members of the same sex and who value one another. One can be gay and not be sexual. Being gay means sharing certain beliefs and values with others. The same things later happened in other cultures such as in Germany with the word *schwul* and in Sweden with the word *boeg*.

How does one become gay? There is no simple answer. Almost all of us are born of nongay and nonlesbian parents, yet research suggests that genetics plays a role as do changes in the mother's immune response during pregnancy. Homosexuality is not a casual choice. You see primarily nonlesbian and non-gay relationships in families and in the media. Lacking readily available role models and information, each gay man and lesbian must find a place in the world and in the process find one another. Finding others like yourself leads you to know that you are not alone in the world.

Much has been written about the communication process of **coming out**, and there is now an annual national "Coming Out Day." Communication scholar Larry Gross (1993) wrote, "The preponderance of lesbian and gay political rhetoric, both within the community and externally, reflects an essentialist position, insisting that one doesn't 'choose' to be gay, but 'recognizes and accepts' that one is so" (p. 113). Before Stonewall, coming out was a great risk that you took as it could affect your career and family relationship. Today, coming out is a positive act of self-expression and identity. You might feel different from others, but with publicly disclosing the reason comes an acceptance of the label homosexual or gay. Now everyone knows, and some will treat you differently. That different treatment confirms your personal identification as a gay person.

Knowing that you will always be treated differently is both dangerous and self-affirming. Being known as gay opens you to stereotypical responses from other people. Remember, a stereotype causes us to assume that a widely held belief is true when it may not be and that a widely held belief is true of any one individual, and it leads us to interpret an individual's behavior through the perceptual screen of the stereotype. On the positive side, it makes other openly identified gay people more available to you as support as a subgroup.

That is why coming out is critical for all gay persons. One-on-one relationships with nongays are the best means of reducing prejudice. Antigay feelings are much lower among people who know gay people personally. Keeping silent—even to one's self—is to imply that one should feel ashamed.

Rejecting All Labels

Non-White, non-middle-class lesbians and gay men (Lorde, 1984) and people of sexualities of all kinds began to challenge the idea of a single gay/lesbian identity. The label—both externally applied and later redefined—categorized a group only on the basis of one dimension of sexual orientation. Identity politics imposed "a unitary identity upon gay men, lesbians, and bisexuals [that] is alienating to those who do not fit into the mold constructed by the leaders of the movement" (Slagle, 1995, p. 86).

What is known as queer theory challenges the idea of a single identity and rejects the categorization of heterosexuality and homosexuality. Queer theory argues that identities are multiple (sexual orientation and race and class and gender and so forth). Accepting such a label, even as an indicator of pride, can be restrictive in defining self (Fuss, 1991; Warner, 1993).

SUBGROUP INDICATORS

You read earlier in this chapter that argot, values, media, and segmented marketing are all indicators of a subgroup.

Argot

One characteristic of the gay subgroup is that its members share an argot. In 1976, Joseph J. Hayes described "gayspeak" as the language one acquires when entering the gay community. He identified three settings in which gayspeak is important: secret or threatening situations (that is, in the presence of people who are not gay), social settings (that is, in the presence of other gays), and radical gay activist settings.

Although not all lesbians and gay men recognize gayspeak, its acceptance by some suggests a dual persona, that is, using one language in the gay community and another language in the gay subgroup community.

Qantas ad announcing its sponsorship of the Sydney 2002 Gay Games.

Media and Marketing

Gay men and lesbians have supported extensive specialized media. Lesbian literature has been more prominent than other forms of lesbian media and has reflected a feminist perspective. Gay male literature of the 1960s and 1970s by such authors as James Baldwin, Truman Capote, Gore Vidal, and Tennessee Williams generally depicted gay men as social outsiders. Post-Stonewall writers, such as Andrew Holleran, Armistead Maupin, and Edmund White, created positive characters functioning within a gay community.

Local newspapers across the country focused on community events and contributed to a shared identity as did national magazines. Early gay male magazines did battle with the post office over issues of pornography. *ONE* magazine, for example, which was started in 1951, was seized by the post office as pornographic. The Supreme Court ruled in 1958 that the magazine served the needs of the gay community and was therefore not pornographic.

Gay male magazines in the post-Stonewall era focused on human rights issues. The magazines reported stories of repression and gay men's reaction in the gay liberation movement. They supported responsibility, caring for and supporting one another, and maintaining identity in the face of AIDS in a largely indifferent society. It was the gay press—not the popular press or the medical community—that brought AIDS to the attention of gay men, and as a consequence, the spread of AIDS declined in the gay community while growing dramatically in other segments of society (Fejes & Petrich, 1993).

Today, paid circulation among gay magazines such as *The Advocate*, *Out*, and *Genre* tops 250,000, and the magazines are written by and for lesbians as much as by and for gay men. Articles about travel, profiles, and lifestyle are popular as are interviews and articles on politics. *The Advocate*, for example, interviewed President Bill Clinton.

Specialized print media have long existed for the gay community and serve to reinforce its existence just as they do with other cultures and subgroups. By 1995, 46 radio stations across the country carried gay programming as did cable-access television. After the ratings success of Showtime's "Queer as Folk," plans for a gay cable channel were announced by MTV and Showtime. Market research has told advertisers that 6% to 10% of the U.S. market is gay. An often quoted statistic from *Business Week* is that gay individuals control 19% of the spendable income in the United States. Lesbians earn less than men, so the spending power is concentrated among gay men. These conclusions reflect readership of national gay magazines but do not apply to all lesbians and gay men. More recent surveys showed gays to be better educated, with 60% of those in the gay market holding a college degree, but less affluent than

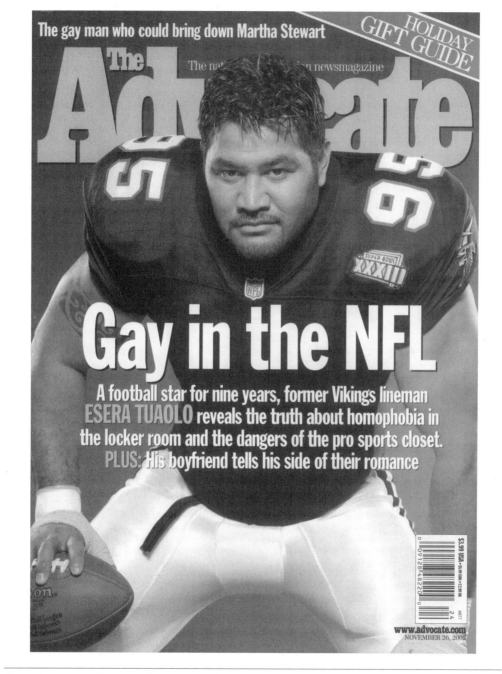

Examples of popular magazines among the gay community.

SOURCE: Reprinted from *The Advocate*, November 26, 2002. Copyright © 2002 by Liberation Publications, Inc.

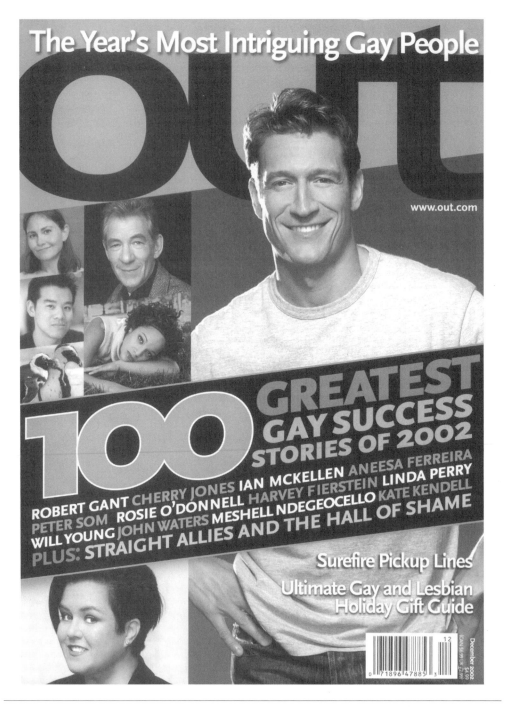

Out cover is reprinted with permission of the publisher.

SUBCULTURES OF GAYDOM

The Gay & Lesbian Review
WORLDWIDE

MARCH-APRIL, 2002 (Volume IX, Number 2) $4.95 USA | $7.00 Canada

On the Fringe

Carol LeMasters
Leatherdykes

Joseph DeMarco
Strippers' World

Marta Donayre
Binational Couples

Steve Anable
Leaving the Radical Faeries

Melinda Kanner
Toward a Semiotics of Butch

Rob Maitra
The Young and the Homeless

Andy Warhol
A new biography by Wayne Koestenbaum

HEFLING 2

The Gay & Lesbian Review cover is reprinted with permission of the publisher.

Live Responsibly
Threesome
My Man, My Beer, My Miller Time®.
Miller Lite
MORE THAN FRIENDS

The best relationships are the ones you never outgrow.

The same is true when it comes to your financial life. That's why at Bank of America, you'll find everything you need to manage your money, from your first bank account through retirement. And it's why we'll work with you to find the right accounts and services now and as your financial goals change. To get the most from your banking relationship, call us at 1.800.900.9000 or visit us at bankofamerica.com.

Bank of America.

Bank of America, N.A. Member FDIC. ©2001 Bank of America Corporation. 991616
SPN-43-4P-09751150-AD

Segmented marketing can reinforce subgroup identity, as shown in these ads for Miller Lite and Bank of America.

the general population. Seagrams's research of the psychographics of gay publication readers identified gay men as "fashion conscious and trend setting." Market research has also shown that gay men and lesbians are very brand loyal to companies that advertise first in the gay press.

Gay magazines draw advertising from car companies such as Saab and Saturn, from the travel industry such as Virgin Atlantic and American Express, from liquor companies such as Absolut vodka and Tanqueray gin, and from mainstream companies such as AT&T and MCI; Chase Bank, Chemical Bank, and Citibank; Evian and Perrier; Flowers Direct and Geffen records; and Quality Paperback Books and Viking/Penguin Press.

General circulation magazines run "gay-vague" advertising as well as advertising using homosexuality as a means to draw attention. Seagrams once marketed Boodles gin with a bar mirror that featured "Six Famous Men of History" etched on it: Oscar Wilde, Lawrence of Arabia, Walt Whitman, Edgar Allen Poe, Ludwig van Beethoven, and Edgar Degas. Probably, most nonlesbians and nongay men did not recognize the six as homosexual, but the gay community did.

The cutting-edge fashion industry has used sexuality in advertising. The Italian fashion house Dolce & Gabbana used ads in 1999 that featured diverse types of couples and included two women and two young men.

In 1994, furniture retailer Ikea aired a television ad showing two clearly identifiable gay men shopping for a dining room table. The couple's actions and dialogue clearly demonstrated a commitment to each other. This was the first time that gays were openly portrayed in mainstream television advertising. Later, in 1998, Virgin Cola ran the first television commercial with a gay kiss. Gay-vague advertising has been used on television as well. Volkswagen's "Da, Da, Da" commercial featured two young men who pick up and then discard a chair they find on the curbside. Gay viewers see the pair as a couple, while nongay viewers see the pair as just roommates.

PREJUDICE AGAINST SUBGROUPS

Can you identify members of a subgroup by appearance, behavior, language, or in any other way? Many people continue to stereotype gay men and lesbians. The stereotypes revolve around effeminacy, weakness, and passivity—all true for some but not for others. Stated simply, the gay subgroup encompasses as great a variety of appearance and behavior as does the nongay segment of the population. For example, some gay individuals dress a certain way—most don't. Some act a certain way—most don't. Some center leisure time around bars—most don't. The gay subgroup cuts across all segments of the population.

There are gay Republicans and Democrats, wealthy and poor gay people, rural and urban gays, gay Whites and people of color, and so forth. Lesbians and gay men differ little from nonlesbians and nongay men in terms of occupation, social class, age, race, and so on. The difference that matters is that gay individuals value primary emotional attachments to those of the same sex. But from that one difference has come prejudice and hatred. This irrational fear of gay men and lesbians is called **homophobia** (Pharr, 1988). It is related to heterosexism, the assumption that the world is and must be heterosexual, and patriarchy, the enforced belief in heterosexual male dominance and control.

Homophobia

Internationally, South Africa is the only nation whose constitution specifically protects lesbians and gays from discrimination by both the government and individuals. Canada extended civil rights protection to gays and lesbians in 1996.

Homophobia is a learned attitude. Many historical studies have shown that homosexuals were not feared or despised in the past. Some point to the 20th-century psychiatrists who created the paradigm of thinking of various forms of sexualities as diseases as resulting in negative stereotypes. Historian George Chauncey (1985) argues that the Cold War era of fear created the unfounded negative stereotype of homosexuals as subversive security risks.

In 1969, the year of the Stonewall riot, there were no policies, laws, or ordinances prohibiting discrimination against lesbians and gay men. In fact in 1967, the New York State Liquor Authority forbade bars to serve homosexuals, 49 states had laws banning sodomy, and there were no hate crime laws.

Media portrayal of gay men and lesbians contributed to stereotyping. The Motion Picture Production Code of 1930 banned all mention of homosexuality in U.S. films for more than 30 years. Russo (1987) has shown how the portrayal of lesbians and gay men in film has, until recently, been derisive and as victims.

The early 1990s saw a nationwide rise in hate crimes against gay individuals, which has been attributed in part to increased visibility and activism in the gay community. These hate crimes include harassment, vandalism, assault, and police abuse: Lesbian and gay high school students are the target of bullying, teasing, and violence. At California State University, Northridge, flyers offered free baseball bats for a "gay bashing and clubbing night." In North Fort Meyers, Florida, two men confessed to murdering a gay man by strangling him and pouring drain cleaner down his throat. In Burlington, Vermont, another man beat a gay man, leaving him brain-damaged and partially blind. The 1990 Hate Crimes Statistics Act requires federal authorities to monitor crimes based on sexual orientation, race, religion, and ethnicity. It is also the first federal law to contain a sexual orientation provision.

In 1992, 53% of Colorado's voters passed Amendment 2, which would have prohibited the state from ever passing a nondiscrimination law and voided existing local ones. In 1996, the Supreme Court ruled that the measure was unconstitutional on the grounds that it violated gay men's and lesbians' rights to equal protection under the law.

Discrimination continues in employment. Only 11 states have laws that prohibit job discrimination against lesbians and gay men. Many major U.S.

corporations, such as Harley-Davidson, IBM, Kodak, Time-Warner, and 3M, have policies banning discrimination based on sexual orientation. Gay activists argue that discrimination based on sexual orientation is still widespread. In 1991, Cracker Barrel Old Country Stores, a firm based in Lebanon, Tennessee, that runs restaurants along many Southeast interstates, fired several employees for being gay. The restaurant chain defended its actions by citing "traditional American values" and declared that it "is perceived to be inconsistent with those of our customer base to continue to employ individuals in our operating units whose sexual preferences fail to demonstrate normal heterosexual values which have been the foundation of families in our society." The restaurant chain later discontinued its practice, although gay activists say the rule still exists.

Problems that gay men and lesbians have faced in the workplace include being refused positions based on the perception of being gay, receiving anonymous harassing phone calls and letters, and not being promoted or retained when sexual orientation becomes known. Most discrimination against gays in employment in the 1990s was disguised. Employers who wanted to terminate a gay employee first found other reasons to disguise the termination. In early 2000, the Pentagon released a study of 72,000 troops. The results showed that 37% have witnessed or been targets of gay harassment. More than 80% reported hearing offensive speech, derogatory names, or jokes at least once over the past year, and more than 85% believed that antigay comments are tolerated at military installations or aboard ships.

Gay persons have experienced discrimination even in churches. In 1990, three Lutheran ministers were suspended for being "practicing homosexuals," a phrase that has developed a unique meaning. Most lesbians and gay men understand it to mean that you can be accepted if you don't "act gay," that is, if you don't come out, but to gays and lesbians, coming out is an important part of self-acceptance. Their congregations refused to rescind the ordinations, and the ministers were later expelled from the church.

Laws banning sodomy remain in 25 states. In 1992, Republican presidential candidate Patrick Buchanan used a homophobic television advertisement in his campaign. And in 1996, presidential candidate Robert Dole solicited funds from gay organizations and received a donation from the conservative Republican gay Log Cabin Club. When the donation was revealed in the press, Senator Dole publicly returned it.

Marriage or Partnership?

Gay friendships are often difficult for nongay members of society to understand. Gay friendships can often be stronger than traditional family relationships.

The title of Weston's (1991) book, *Families We Choose*, itself reflects that gay families are created in adult life and can include friends, current and past lovers, adopted children, children from previous heterosexual relationships, and children conceived through alternative insemination. Understood thus in families in relation to symbols, like home, that carry kinship, lesbians and gay men appear more accurately and completely rather than as caricatures.

A popular stereotype of gay men is as urban, single, sexually promiscuous, and not in stable relationships. In fact, well over 50% of the gay male and lesbian population live in long-term, committed, coupled relationships (McWhirter & Mattison, 1984), millions of lesbians and gay men are parents of children ("Developments," 1989), and the research on gay fathers and lesbian mothers with children has shown a striking absence of pathological behavior (Green & Bozett, 1991). Many lesbian and gay couples feel a commitment to each other and want to be married.

Mary Anne Fitzpatrick (1988) identified four types of relationships in her studies of heterosexual marriages: Traditionals, Independents, Separates, and Mixed. Traditionals hold conventional ideological values about relationships, demonstrate interdependence through sharing time and space, and describe their communication as nonassertive but engage in rather than avoid marital conflicts. Independents espouse nonconventional values about relationships (e.g., relationships should not constrain individual freedom), exhibit a high degree of sharing and companionship but maintain separate space (e.g., bathrooms and offices), and engage in rather than avoid conflict. Separates are conventional in their views on marital and family issues, yet at the same time uphold the value of individual freedom over relational maintenance, have less companionship and sharing, and avoid open marital conflicts. The Mixed couple type defines marital life differently according to ideology, interdependence, and communication.

Later research applying this model to gay couples (Fitzpatrick, Jandt, Myrick, & Edgar, 1994) suggests that they are less likely to be Independents. The overwhelming majority (83%) have a lifelong commitment to a relationship: 70% of gay men and 80% of lesbians have always been monogamous. Data from surveys of nonlesbian and nongay couples indicate that approximately 50% of those couples have not always been monogamous; hence, same-sex couples appear more likely to hold conventional attitudes about relationships.

In 1969, the year of the Stonewall riot, gay relationships were not recognized in any form. Despite the U.S. Supreme Court's statement that marriage is one of the "basic civil rights of men," no state law permits same-sex couples to marry. This denies couples social recognition of a relationship—the very thing that has so often been the root of discrimination and hate crimes. Gay couples also report experiencing discrimination in the areas of traditional "family" rights (i.e., hospital visitation, adoption, and employment benefits). One argument for same-sex marriages holds that the institution of marriage enhances the stability, respectability, and emotional depth of a relationship.

A September 14, 1992, *Newsweek* poll of a sample of registered voters in the United States revealed the following attitudes held about the rights of gay spouses: 70% approved of inheritance rights, 67% approved of health insurance, and 58% approved of Social Security benefits, but 61% disapproved of adoption rights. The majority of those polled (58%) disapproved of legally sanctioned gay marriages, and 45% felt that gay rights are a threat to the American family and its values.

Historian John Boswell (1980, 1994) has uncovered long-suppressed church documents sanctifying same-sex marriages. According to Boswell, intolerance of same-sex relationships was not an essential feature of early Christianity but became so only after nearly 1,200 years of church history. A growing number of European countries have registered partnership laws. Denmark's was the first in 1989, followed by Norway in 1993, Sweden in 1995, Iceland and Hungary in 1996, and France in 1999. The Netherlands became the first country to offer complete marriage rights to same-sex couples in 2001, and Belgium followed in early 2003.

In 1990, three same-sex couples in Hawaii challenged the state's proscription of same-sex marriage. In 1993, the Hawaii Supreme Court ruled that prohibiting one individual from marrying another on account of his or her gender violates the state constitution's guarantee of equal protection under the law unless the state could prove that it had some compelling, legitimate reason to ban same-sex marriage. After extensive testimony from psychologists and sociologists, the First Circuit Court found in 1996 that the state had failed to prove that same-sex marriages would harm anybody. In 1997, the Hawaii legislature approved a beneficiaries law in reaction to the same-sex marriage case. Hawaii will provide same-sex couples with a state certificate of "reciprocal beneficiaries" that will qualify the couples for about 60 benefits and privileges involving inheritance, insurance coverage, joint property, and victims' rights previously available only to married couples. In reaction, the state constitution was amended in 1998 to ban gay marriages.

The Vermont state supreme court ruled in 1999 that gay and lesbian couples deserve the same protections and privileges that nongay married couples receive under state law and ordered the state legislature to change the law to provide those benefits. Vermont's legislature passed a bill creating civil unions, which give same-sex couples the same rights and obligations that civil marriage does. The new law may be challenged.

In 35 states, preemptive laws were passed saying that the states would not recognize same-sex marriages if legalized in any other state. The U.S. Congress passed the Defense of Marriage Act, which banned federal recognition of same-sex marriages.

During the 1996 presidential campaign, eight Republican candidates pledged to sign a "Marriage Protection Resolution." Patrick Buchanan said, "And we can't put [gay marriage] into law in any country that we continue to call 'God's country.'"

At the same time state legislatures were denying gay couples legally sanctioned marriages, businesses were recognizing domestic partnerships based on the Equal Protection Clause of the Fourteenth Amendment; that is, same-sex couples should enjoy the same social and legal benefits as wedded heterosexual couples. A growing number of cities including New Orleans, San Francisco, and New York City began providing registrations for domestic partnerships, and Madison (Wisconsin), New York City, and San Francisco began providing nonbinding or symbolic civil wedding ceremonies for domestic partners. By 2002, the *New York Times* began publishing announcements of same-sex commitment ceremonies.

Corporate United States has become the unlikely leader for lesbian and gay equality. Hundreds of municipalities, academic institutions, and businesses including Apple Computer, Inc., American Airlines, Disney, Eastman Kodak Co., Hewlett-Packard, HBO, Intel Corp., Levi Strauss, Lotus Development Corporation, MCA/Universal, Microsoft, Nike, and Xerox grant employees some domestic partnership benefits. Nearly one-quarter of employers nationwide with more than 5,000 workers provide health benefits to nontraditional partners, often nongay as well as gay.

Discussion of inferiority versus equality and mainstream versus distinctiveness continues in the United States. James Chesebro (1980) has demonstrated these in the rhetoric of social science, and Jeffrey Nelson (1985) has shown how these questions are visualized in films such as *Victor/Victoria, Making Love, Personal Best, Deathtrap,* and *Partners.* These are the same questions that apply to every culture and subgroup in multicultural America.

FROM THE INTERCULTURAL PERSPECTIVE

Recall that language affects and is affected by culture. Every language is unique. It reflects how its speakers see reality and, in turn, controls how its speakers perceive and talk about reality. You may also remember that cultures and subcultures have their own languages; however, subgroups, too, may have their own special way of communicating. This is called *argot* (pronounced AR-go), which is a special vocabulary. In the past, this kind of special vocabulary had names like *jargon*, *cant*, and *slang*. However, argot is a term that includes these meanings and does not have the negative meanings that some of the other words have. Argot has two functions. First, it helps members of a subgroup create a feeling of identity with the subgroup. Second, it helps members know who is in their group and who is not.

Subgroups often have their own argot. Members of subgroups may communicate with each other through special media like magazines and newspapers. However, the most important element of a subgroup is that it provides its members with a set of values and norms for behavior. Recall that people may be members of many subgroups throughout their lives. Often, they are members of different subgroups at the same time.

The term *corporate culture* refers to how organizations behave like little cultures. One definition of corporate culture is "the way we do things around here." This shows that corporations provide their members with norms that control behavior. Often, organizations have their own argot and have the values of the organization's founder. Walt Disney Productions and Microsoft are two examples of corporations that have a special culture.

In the United States, homosexual people are a unique subgroup based on sexual orientation. Gays (homosexual men) and lesbians (homosexual women) show an awareness of subgroup identity. This identity is becoming stronger partly through the effects of segmented marketing and specialized media. Within the gay community, *coming out* (being openly gay) is seen as a very important part of a gay person's identity. This has positive and negative aspects. On one hand, being openly gay allows a person to receive emotional support from other gay individuals. On the other hand, an openly gay individual may become a victim of discrimination and violence (*gay bashing*). Being afraid of and hating homosexual people is called *homophobia*.

KEY TERMS

argot	gay	lesbian
cant	homophobia	participant observer
coming out	homosexual	slang
corporate culture	jargon	

CHAPTER 18

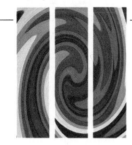

Multiculturalism

What You Can Learn From This Chapter

Development of cultural pluralism and multiculturalism in Mexico, Russia, Australia, and the United States

Components of White culture in the United States

Whether the United States can be a multicultural society

H omogeneous cultures are relatively rare in the world today. The ethnic homogeneity of Italy, Japan, Norway, and a few other countries was established centuries ago. Nationality based on descent is true for Israel, the only modern nation to grant the right to citizenship based on "blood." The 1990s saw ethnicity being proclaimed as the proper foundation for nations in the Balkans and in parts of the former Soviet Union.

More than 95% of the world's countries are ethnically heterogeneous. In this chapter, we'll look at how various countries have dealt with ethnic diversity. According to some estimates, there are close to 5,000 diverse ethnic groups in the world (Stavenhagen, 1986). In Chapter 7 you read that France values universalism and integration. Former Prime Minister Edouard Balladur said, "You have to understand that French civilization is a civilization of uniformity, while the Anglo-Saxon one is based on diversity." Many countries deal with ethnic diversity—Argentina, Brazil, Canada, and Zimbabwe, to name a few—but the United States has dealt with a greater range of diversity for a longer period of time than comparable countries have.

In this chapter, we'll briefly look at experiences in Mexico, Russia, and Australia and then at the United States in more detail. This chapter presents different views on multiculturalism and presents material by Edith Folb to help you decide which group in the United States dominates the culture and how that domination affects intercultural communication within the society.

Discussions of multiculturalism often use the word *minority*. Technically, of course, the word minority is used to describe numerical designations. A group might be a minority, then, if it has a small number of people than a majority group with a larger number. In the United States, the word *majority* has political associations as in the "majority rules," a term used so commonly in the United States that the two words have almost become synonymous. According to the *Oxford English Dictionary*, the term minority was first used to describe ethnic groups in 1921. Since that time, advantage has been associated with the majority and disadvantage has been associated with the minority.

MEXICO

All Mexicans are considered equal under the country's constitution, yet while the heroes of Mexico's Aztec past are honored in monuments, the living descendants of the Aztec are not allowed to eat in some of the country's finest restaurants. Sixty percent of Indians older than 12 are unemployed.

From the Spanish founding of Mexico, social class has been determined by racial purity (i.e., those born in Spain at the top and full-blooded Indians on the bottom). After centuries of intermarriage, almost all Mexicans are part Indian. The holiday Columbus Day in the United States is celebrated in Mexico as *Dia de la Raza* (Day of the Race). It commemorates the birth of the mestizo race, people of mixed European and indigenous ancestry who control today's Mexico.

Mexico's indigenous peoples have been denied rights for centuries. The Zapatista rose up in the southern state of Chiapas in 1994 to protest the repression of Indians across the country.

Mexico's army fought to contain the guerrilla movement. In 1996, the government of Mexico signed an agreement to amend the state's and nation's constitutions to guarantee respect for Indian languages and culture. This agreement marks the first time that the original peoples of Mexico have been recognized as equals.

RUSSIA

After centuries of conquests, annexations, and expulsions, post-Communist Russia is made up of more than 100 nationalities totaling 148 million people spread across 11 time zones and twice the territory of the United States. The range is from the nearly extinct Karelians near the border with Finland to the Turkic-speaking Yakuts of the Far East and from the Islamic peoples of the Caucasus territories to the Chukchis of the far northeast. Aleksandr I. Solzhenitsyn, the Russian author and nationalist conscience, has warned that if current low birth rate and short average life span continue, Russians will become a minority in the country. Russians currently make up 80% of the federation's population but have had decades of a declining birth rate and a rising mortality rate.

Resurgent ethnic awareness and the 1993 constitution's recognition of each people's right to "self-determination" have created nationalist movements across the country. Whereas the United States is a federation of states, Russia has become a federation of ethnicities. Minorities are demanding increased political and economic independence and are asserting local values.

The Russian Federation is made up of 89 republics and provinces. Agreements with Moscow range from total subjugation to virtual independence enjoyed by influential regions such as Tatarstan and Yakutia. Tatarstan is an important oil-producing region with important aviation industries. The population is 51% Tatar and 49% ethnic Russians. Flags flying from government buildings in the capital city Kazan are the red and green colors of ancient Tataria. Tatarstan trade offices in Turkey, Australia, and other countries are referred to as "embassies." And the local government has withheld federal tax payments to compensate Tatarstan industries for debts owed by Moscow.

The Central Asia nations of Kazakhstan, Kyrgyzstan, Tajikistan, Turkmenistan, and Uzbekistan were united under Genghis Khan and Tamerlane in the region known as Turkestan that stretched from Turkey to China. Stalin divided the region into the current states in 1924. Since the collapse of the Soviet Union, 54 million people are searching for a new identity. Pre-Soviet heroes, languages, and Islamic traditions are being revived. Ethnic languages and English are gaining favor, even though Russian remains the lingua franca. Arabic script is replacing Cyrillic. Islamic holidays are now shown on calendars, and the Koran is openly sold.

Chechnya's resentment of its annexation by Russia has persisted since the 1800s. During World War II, Stalin shipped the Chechens to Kazakhstan where they were forced to remain until the 1950s. With the breakup of the Soviet Union, Chechnya declared independence and fought a war with

Moscow from 1994 to 1996, which resulted in the republic winning de facto independence while nominally remaining part of Russia. Russia's President Vladimir Putin continues the fighting with the Muslim separatists.

Chechnya has sustained a staggering death toll in its attempt to break away. Its fate may discourage other secession-minded ethnic groups.

AUSTRALIA

Australia had a hardline ideology of assimilation for immigrants. The first act of the Australian Commonwealth in 1901 was to pass an immigration law banning non-Europeans from immigrating to the continent. The policy, known as "White Australia," was not fully abandoned until 1973.

Australia then moved to a policy of cultural diversity that was more accepting of immigrant cultures, races, and ethnicities to the limit of not threatening national unity or the security of society.

In the 1991 Census, of the identified population of 18 million, the Aboriginals and Torres Strait Islanders numbered fewer than 300,000 people. Asian immigrants now account for about 5% of the population. One-third of Sydney's 3.7 million people were born overseas, and Chinese is now the second most commonly used language.

Australia's multiculturalism encouraged individuals to assert cultural differences and asserted the equality of power and respect between groups. The terminology of *ethnicity* and *ethnic groups* became part of national political discourse.

Ethnicity and ethnic group were defined in cultural terms (i.e., language and values). From this perspective, inequities were addressed as language skills or attitudinal. For example, funds were budgeted for English-language instruction. Even so, there was the expectation that immigrants or their children would eventually assimilate. A factor that was not addressed was the existence of some well-defined groups that continued to exist as status-devalued groups.

One consequence of this perspective was the development of what was labeled "identity politics"—that is, where the discourse is focused on the rights of groups. For example, a number of the Australian states have adopted strict laws against making derogatory remarks or discriminating in jobs and housing.

Two factors have challenged these assumptions. One is that, rather than assimilating, second- and third-generation immigrants through intermarriage have more of a symbolic ethnic identity with no compelling sense of identification or group loyalty. Second, changing the immigration policy has resulted in increasing numbers of Asians entering the country and increasing importance placed on racial rather than cultural differentiation. Other critics of Australia's cultural pluralism point out that it focuses on material and social needs only and leaves largely intact the political control of the country by traditional groups (Jayasuriya, 1990).

A right-wing third political party, the One Nation Party, was formed in 1997 in part to address concerns of immigration. The word *multiculturalism* was seen as a threat to the Anglo, White Australian way of life. In the 1998 election, the party won nearly 10% of the national vote.

UNITED STATES

Immigration has made the United States home to many ethnic groups. U.S. citizenship is easy to acquire, hard to lose, and imposes few duties. Pressures to assimilate are more economic than legal.

The United States proclaims the Latin phrase *E Pluribus Unum* ("from many, one") on its coins to symbolize the desire that the many will see themselves as one. This appreciation for diversity, originally derived from incorporating 13 colonies into a single nation, has come to represent the country's social and religious heterogeneity.

This idea of the United States as a nation of people of many backgrounds has been a popular cultural myth. Many wrote of the diversity of the country's creation. Ralph Waldo Emerson (1909-1914) wrote of a "new race" drawing "the energy of Irish, Germans, Swedes, Poles, and Cossacks, and all the European tribes—of the Africans, and the Polynesians." Herman Melville (1849/1976) wrote, "On this Western Hemisphere all tribes and peoples are forming into one federated whole." More recently, former British Prime Minister Margaret Thatcher said of the United States that "no other nation has so successfully combined people of different races and nations within a single culture."

It is clear that the diversity of the country's creation is recognized, but can the unity of the product be assumed? As a country of immigrants, is the United States a nation defined by ethnic and racial community, or does it have a culture of its own? Is the United States a culture in which most native-born members of minority groups, White and people of color, see themselves primarily as U.S. citizens rather than as members of a minority group?

Persistent Labeling Practices

Let's trace Mrs. Thatcher's observation through various years of census practices.

Racial classifications in the United States predate independence to enforce distinctions between free citizens and slaves. These laws evolved into miscegenation laws designed to preserve the "purity of the White race" by making interracial sex a crime. Sixteen states banned interracial marriages until 1967 when the Supreme Court struck down such laws.

The first U.S. census was supervised by Thomas Jefferson in 1790. People were counted as free Whites, slaves, or "others," which included American Indians and free Blacks. In the 1790 Census, those of English ancestry accounted for about 50% of the population and African-Americans for about 20%.

By the early 1800s, people who were one-quarter Black (i.e., had one Black grandparent) were counted by the census as mulatto. Later, that became the "one-drop rule," a racist device to ensure that slaveholders' multiracial children remained slaves. The U.S. Census Bureau estimates that at least 75% of all African-Americans today are multiracial.

In 1911, a congressional commission developed the "Dictionary of Races of People" with 45 non-White racial subgroups. After opposition, the government discarded that category system. Yet other categories were used. After the Mexican-American War in 1848, the census counted people with Spanish surnames as White. By 1930, a separate "Mexican" category was created. By 1940, it was eliminated. Since 1980, Hispanic has been treated as an ethnicity apart from race as a separate question.

The census categories in use today were drafted to help agencies enforce civil rights laws. People have been asked to choose one racial classification from White, Black, American Indian or Alaska native, Asian or Pacific Islander, and "other." In a separate question, people were asked whether they were of Hispanic origin. In the 1980 Census, the Census Bureau for the first time asked U.S. residents to volunteer their ethnic origin. Ten percent did not answer. Of the remaining 90%, 83% identified with an ethnic group. Only 6% refused ethnic labeling by using the term "American." The "mix" of people in the United States has remained amazingly similar over the many years of immigration. The top four ancestry groups determined by the 1980 Census were, as far as one can tell from surnames, the same top four in the 1790 Census. In the 1990 Census, 58 million claimed German ancestry, followed by 38 million Irish, 32 million English, and 23 million African-American.

In the 1990 Census, Whites made up 80.3% of the population, African-Americans 12.1%, Hispanics 9%, Asian-Americans 2.9%, and American Indians 0.8%. In the 2000 Census, White (non-Hispanic) made up 69.1%, Black (including Hispanic) 12.4%, Hispanic (only Hispanic-White and Hispanic-other) 11.3%, Asian/Hawaiian/Pacific Islander (including Hispanic)

3.8%, and American Indian 0.9%. Also, the 2000 Census showed that German decreased to 43 million (15%), Irish or Celtic decreased to 30 million (11%), and English decreased to 24 million (9%), while people identifying themselves as American increased to 20 million. An increasing number of people are identifying themselves as "American."

Interracial Marriage

One night in Virginia in 1958, a sheriff barged into the bedroom of Richard Loving and his pregnant wife Mildred and told the couple they had violated Virginia's 1924 Racial Integrity Act, which provided that Whites could marry only other Whites and that Blacks could marry only other Blacks, American Indians, Hispanics, and Asians. The Lovings, who had gotten married in Washington, pleaded guilty and received a one-year suspended sentence on the condition they leave Virginia for 25 years. The Supreme Court in its 1967 decision on *Loving v. Virginia* declared state laws prohibiting interracial marriage unconstitutional and void.

Interracial marriages of all types have increased from 150,000 in 1960 when interracial marriage was still illegal in much of the South, to 310,000 in 1970, to 1.5 million in 1990, to more than 1 in 50 marriages today (see Table 18.1). Throughout the last century, more than half of Asian-Americans' and American Indians' marriages have been interracial.

> The United States "is the only country in the world that has ever had laws prohibiting intermarriage. Contrary to the prevailing attitude in the U.S., interracial marriages are generally accepted, both legally and socially, around the world."
>
> —Albert I. Gordon, *Intermarriage* (1964, p. 220)

Table 18.1   Interracial Marriages (in percentages)

Of ages 25-34	1940/1950	1990
African-American men	2	8
African-American women	1	4
White men	1	4
White women	1	3

SOURCE: Census data.

Person 6

Housing information helps your community plan for police and fire protection.

1 **What is this person's name?** *Print the name of Person 6 from page 2.*

Last Name

First Name   MI

2 **How is this person related to Person 1?** *Mark ☒ ONE box.*
- ☐ Husband/wife
- ☐ Natural-born son/daughter
- ☐ Adopted son/daughter
- ☐ Stepson/stepdaughter
- ☐ Brother/sister
- ☐ Father/mother
- ☐ Grandchild
- ☐ Parent-in-law
- ☐ Son-in-law/daughter-in-law
- ☐ Other relative — *Print exact relationship.*

If NOT RELATED to Person 1:
- ☐ Roomer, boarder
- ☐ Housemate, roommate
- ☐ Unmarried partner
- ☐ Foster child
- ☐ Other nonrelative

3 **What is this person's sex?** *Mark ☒ ONE box.*
- ☐ Male
- ☐ Female

4 **What is this person's age and what is this person's date of birth?**

Age on April 1, 2000

Print numbers in boxes.
Month   Day   Year of birth

NOTE: Please answer BOTH Questions 5 and 6.

5 **Is this person Spanish/Hispanic/Latino?** *Mark ☒ the "No" box if not Spanish/Hispanic/Latino.*
- ☐ **No,** not Spanish/Hispanic/Latino
- ☐ Yes, Mexican, Mexican Am., Chicano
- ☐ Yes, Puerto Rican
- ☐ Yes, Cuban
- ☐ Yes, other Spanish/Hispanic/Latino — *Print group.*

6 **What is this person's race? Mark ☒ one or more races** to indicate what this person considers himself/herself to be.
- ☐ White
- ☐ Black, African Am., or Negro
- ☐ American Indian or Alaska Native — *Print name of enrolled or principal tribe.*

- ☐ Asian Indian
- ☐ Chinese
- ☐ Filipino
- ☐ Japanese
- ☐ Korean
- ☐ Vietnamese
- ☐ Other Asian — *Print race.*
- ☐ Native Hawaiian
- ☐ Guamanian or Chamorro
- ☐ Samoan
- ☐ Other Pacific Islander — *Print race.*

- ☐ Some other race — *Print race.*

7 **What is this person's marital status?**
- ☐ Now married
- ☐ Widowed
- ☐ Divorced
- ☐ Separated
- ☐ Never married

2073

Form D-2

33

The Multiracial Label

Interracial marriages are not a new event: Beethoven, Alexandre Dumas, and Aleksandr Pushkin were all multiracial. An estimated 1 to 2 million

Person 6 (continued)

8 **a. At any time since February 1, 2000, has this person attended regular school or college?** *Include only nursery school or preschool, kindergarten, elementary school, and schooling which leads to a high school diploma or a college degree.*

☐ No, has not attended since February 1 → *Skip to 9*
☐ Yes, public school, public college
☐ Yes, private school, private college

b. What grade or level was this person attending? *Mark ☒ ONE box.*

☐ Nursery school, preschool
☐ Kindergarten
☐ Grade 1 to grade 4
☐ Grade 5 to grade 8
☐ Grade 9 to grade 12
☐ College undergraduate years (freshman to senior)
☐ Graduate or professional school *(for example: medical, dental, or law school)*

9 **What is the highest degree or level of school this person has COMPLETED?** *Mark ☒ ONE box. If currently enrolled, mark the previous grade or highest degree received.*

☐ No schooling completed
☐ Nursery school to 4th grade
☐ 5th grade or 6th grade
☐ 7th grade or 8th grade
☐ 9th grade
☐ 10th grade
☐ 11th grade
☐ 12th grade, **NO DIPLOMA**
☐ **HIGH SCHOOL GRADUATE** — high school DIPLOMA or the equivalent *(for example: GED)*
☐ Some college credit, but less than 1 year
☐ 1 or more years of college, no degree
☐ Associate degree *(for example: AA, AS)*
☐ Bachelor's degree *(for example: BA, AB, BS)*
☐ Master's degree *(for example: MA, MS, MEng, MEd, MSW, MBA)*
☐ Professional degree *(for example: MD, DDS, DVM, LLB, JD)*
☐ Doctorate degree *(for example: PhD, EdD)*

10 **What is this person's ancestry or ethnic origin?**

(For example: Italian, Jamaican, African Am., Cambodian, Cape Verdean, Norwegian, Dominican, French Canadian, Haitian, Korean, Lebanese, Polish, Nigerian, Mexican, Taiwanese, Ukrainian, and so on.)

11 **a. Does this person speak a language other than English at home?**

☐ Yes
☐ No → *Skip to 12*

b. What is this language?

(For example: Korean, Italian, Spanish, Vietnamese)

c. How well does this person speak English?

☐ Very well
☐ Well
☐ Not well
☐ Not at all

12 **Where was this person born?**

☐ In the United States — *Print name of state.*

☐ Outside the United States — *Print name of foreign country, or Puerto Rico, Guam, etc.*

13 **Is this person a CITIZEN of the United States?**

☐ Yes, born in the United States → *Skip to 15a*
☐ Yes, born in Puerto Rico, Guam, the U.S. Virgin Islands, or Northern Marianas
☐ Yes, born abroad of American parent or parents
☐ Yes, a U.S. citizen by naturalization
☐ No, not a citizen of the United States

14 **When did this person come to live in the United States?** *Print numbers in boxes.*
Year

15 **a. Did this person live in this house or apartment 5 years ago (on April 1, 1995)?**

☐ Person is under 5 years old → *Skip to 33*
☐ Yes, this house → *Skip to 16*
☐ No, outside the United States — *Print name of foreign country, or Puerto Rico, Guam, etc., below; then skip to 16.*

☐ No, different house in the United States

Form D-2
34

Portion of the year 2000 U.S. Census Bureau forms.

children have been born to interracial couples of all types since about 1970. Yet this is a very minor trend in comparison to the forces establishing a permanent co-cultural identity. Remember, though, not to make the mistake

Table 18.2   Multiracial Self-Identification Preferences

As part of a review of which race and ethnic categories to use in its job statistics, the U.S. Labor Department asked people nationwide in approximately 60,000 households how they prefer to be identified.

Multiracial	28.4%
Mixed race	16.0%
More than one race	6.0%
Biracial	5.7%
Mestizo or Mestiza	2.3%
Some other term	13.9%
No preference	27.8%

SOURCE: U.S. Labor Department, reported in *U.S. News & World Report*, November 20, 1995, p. 28.

of assuming that race and culture are the same. Peoples of various ethnic backgrounds may share the values of the culture.

Demands for a multiracial category for the 2000 Census were rejected. A multiracial category would, for example, include a person with one Black parent and one Cherokee parent with a person with one Korean parent and one White parent, thus negating the "sameness" necessary for an identity and a category. Instead, people were able to choose more than one racial classification (see Table 18.2). U.S. business recognizes the demographic shift in the population. In 1921, the image of Betty Crocker was created to be a female symbol for baking products. The image has slowly changed several times over the years. The multiethnic 1996 version is younger with a tan complexion.

In 1997, professional golfer Tiger Woods was asked on the *Oprah Winfrey Show* if it bothered him to be called an African-American. He replied, "It does. Growing up, I came up with this name: I'm a 'Cablinasian,'" which he explained reflects his Caucasian, Black, American Indian, Thai, and Chinese ancestry.

From Melting Pot to Symphony and Stew

A century ago, there may have been a greater consensus as to cultural norms, religion, and what it meant to be a "true American." The traditional melting pot assimilation theory held that ethnic identity largely disappeared in one or two generations after arriving in the United States.

The melting pot metaphor was rejected as early as 1915 by philosopher Horace Kallen (1915, 1924/1970), who set forth the idea of cultural pluralism to describe the United States. He employed the metaphor of a symphony orchestra. Each instrument was an immigrant group who together with other immigrant groups created harmonious music. Kallen's opponents included John Dewey (Westbrook, 1991), who warned that cultural pluralism supported rigid segregation lines between groups.

Kallen's cultural pluralism predates today's debate over **multiculturalism**. Hollinger (1995) has described the issue as a two-sided confrontation between those who advocate a uniform culture grounded in Western civilization and those who promote diversity. Some use the word to refer to ethnic preservation, the drive to recover and preserve cultural and subgroup identification. This view raises the issue whether all cultures should receive equal attention in the schools. Others use the word to refer to globalism, the awareness of the interdependence of the world's peoples. Opponents to this view argue that an emphasis on differences between people actually impedes the goal of human equality.

Today, there may no longer be a consensus as to the cultural norms, religion, and behavior that define a U.S. culture. More recent immigrants experience less pressure to immediately

---

Two Views on Multiculturalism in Education

Multicultural education should not be the primary goal of education even though it promotes tolerance and provides an informed perspective.

. . . The acculturative responsibility of the schools is primary and fundamental. To teach the ways of one's own community has always been and still remains the essence of the education of our children, who enter neither a narrow tribal culture nor a transcendent world culture, but a national literate culture.

—E. D. Hirsch, *Cultural Literacy* (1987, p. 18)

Multiculturalism does not simply mean other races and nationalities but virtually every conceivable human grouping that separates from the norm, develops a separate identity as well as its normative identity. Indeed each person is of many cultures simultaneously. One has a sexual identity; a racial identity; a religious identity; a class/work identity; a school identity; an identity from the friends one keeps; a family identity; several geographic identities: neighborhood, city, state, country, hemisphere, etc. Human tendency to be relatively unconscious of other cultures is dysfunctional in our society as well as in any association, and it is clear that much hostility is created by ignorance of other cultures and the failure to recognize their existence.

—Executive Committee, Association of College Unions–International, July 1987

learn fluent English and otherwise become Americanized than did earlier immigrants.

The number of people in the United States whose usual language or first language is other than English rose from 28 million in 1976 to 34.7 million in 1990. That number was projected to reach 39.5 million by 2001. Those for whom Spanish is the usual or first language have risen from 10.6 million (38% of the total) in 1976 to a projected 18.2 million (46%) by 2001.

U.S. residents today increasingly recognize their own immigrant roots. Acculturation is defined more in terms of integration than assimilation. Today's immigrants find a much more ethnically diversified country. In some areas, people of similar ethnic origin reside together in large communities. People in the United States today can maintain some original cultural identity and values and participate meaningfully in the larger society. Some argue that the melting pot myth was never true. Today, you are more likely to hear the **salad or stew analogy** to suggest that the elements maintain their own taste or identity but exist together to create the whole.

One U.S. state, Texas, has been taking steps toward multiculturalism, as outlined in a 1991 editorial by Jesse Trevino, an editor of the *Austin American-Statesman* (see Box 18.1). What suggestions for the United States are contained in his editorial?

Box 18.1

**TEXAS IS POINTING THE WAY
TO OUR MULTICULTURAL FUTURE**

The New York education establishment—much like many other sectors of society—is grappling with the question of how to deal with the new Multicultural Age. The huge influx of immigrants from all parts of the world is having a significant impact on U.S. society, and the immediate worry is that the many cultures present in America threaten it.

But the committee responsible for recommending how to address multiculturalism in New York schools concluded [in 1991] that a multicultural approach can coexist with the process generally called assimilation.

The question is, can today's immigrants become Americans, while still retaining important parts of the original home culture?

The new Multicultural Age bothers the country. It is having real trouble with multiculturalism—especially as America comes under economic assault. The loss of jobs to foreign competitors does not endear newcomers to this land. Nor do unscrupulous politicians who use race in campaigns, like George Bush did in 1988 and evidently plans to do again in 1992, help matters.

In Texas, the multicultural challenge revolves largely around the Latino question, although growing communities of Vietnamese and other Asians also flourish.

Despite its large size, the Latino population is under the influence of a very strong assimilating and acculturating process. The majority of Texans probably do not understand how strong it really is. It is not uncommon for Mexican-American first-graders in San Antonio to know little more than a few words of Spanish.

But that does not mean those first-graders will not feel very Hispanic in the future. Language, the crucible of a culture, remains important but no longer critical in the expansion of a culture. Texas proves it.

In many ways, Texas points the way on multiculturalism without having intended to do so. Despite the heavy assault on that large part of the Texas soul that is described as Hispanic, the Mexican-Spanish culture survived—but not without changing both the state and itself.

Texas will never be as Spanish as it once was. But, by the same token, Texas has no option on multiculturalism. It and large parts of the United States are prisoners of geography. Even if the state's Mexican-American population wanted desperately to assimilate, it could not. Geography and history prevent it. So does the non-Hispanic population that keeps attempting to group diverse peoples under the label Hispanic.

Mexico is a huge counterweight to the assimilative process that Mexican-Americans would no doubt undergo if the two countries were separated by miles of ocean. Even the first-graders who may know little Spanish in the early years will be cognizant of Mexican roots. No Latino can escape it.

Mexico's influence, in fact, will increase, not wane, as time passes, for this country is forging links with it that extend beyond the depth of its past relations.

Mexico has become an object of desire for American business, which I might remind the reader is the institution that more than any other in this country has done the most to identify and reinforce the Hispanic culture by infusing American's airwaves with Hispanic-oriented advertising and Hispanic foods, tastes and music.

This new-found interest in Mexico and the Hispanic Hemisphere will only make the first-grader in San Antonio aware of his roots and culture more quickly. And older Mexican-Americans, who became aware of ancestry either through families or, more cruelly, through the separation that many experienced while growing up in Texas, will not ever become less-colorized versions of "being an American." Geography forbids it.

It may well be that the definition of what constitutes an American will change. But it will not be the dark future some Texans expect: the phantom Quebec will remain

(Continued)

Box 18.1, *Continued*

that, a ghost. Why? For the same reasons that the Spanish culture was never eradicated: Powerful forces have taken Mexican-Americans under the American tent. It would take an extraordinary effort to walk out from under the heavy canopy of the American culture.

And so, multiculturalism has gone much further down the road in states like Texas and California than in other places. Other states are wrestling with a question that Texas has slowly provided an answer to for 500 years.

Certain institutions—such as the state's colleges and universities—have yet to adapt to the multicultural demands that geography imposes on them. But they, like government, must slowly bend to what is a fact of life in this state: Like its history, the state's future is multicultural, with a heavy emphasis on that part which is Spanish.

What New York is doing now—officially declaring that multiculturalism can be a part of New York's life while at the same time its immigrants can become thoroughly American—is not new. Texas, without fanfare, proves that the future is multicultural.

SOURCE: Jesse Trevino, "Texas Is Pointing the Way to Our Multicultural Future," San Antonio *Light,* June 30, 1991, p. D3. Copyright © by San Antonio Light. Reprinted with permission.

The question that cultural pluralism and later multiculturalism raised is whether the United States is a "canopy" under which many cultures continue to exist, or is it a cultural entity itself?

Gary B. Nash, former president of the Organization of American Historians, is a principal author of a series of popular multicultural textbooks. These school textbooks all devote extensive attention to the contributions of various ethnic groups. Yet Nash has been critical of ethnocentric interpretations of U.S. history. Nash (1992) argues that there are core values, shared by all groups, that are the democratic values stated in the nation's founding documents that endow the same rights on all individuals of whatever group identification. One's response to Nash is to ask if all individuals do in fact have the same rights.

Multiculturalism and Power

Edith Folb (1994) argues that in most societies there is a hierarchy of status and power. Nondominant groups are those who have not historically or traditionally had continued access to or influence on or within the dominant culture's institutions. These include people of color, women, gays, the physically challenged, and the aged, among others.

The power elite need not be the majority. The power elite are individuals who have influence within the culture's social, political, legal, economic, and religious institutions. The power elite control both the material resources and goods of the country and the means and manner of production and distribution. These dominant groups operate as power elites to maintain positions of power.

Folb argues that in the United States the economic power is largely held by youthful (at least in appearance), able-bodied, heterosexual White males and those of the other gender or sexual orientation or diverse ethnicity who subscribe to the values of heterosexual White males.

The privileged status of British and Western ancestry is one of the most widely recognized themes in U.S. history. Every U.S. president, except for the Dutch Martin Van Buren, has been of either German, Irish, or English ancestry.

The debate over multiculturalism in the United States is often stated in terms of whose values will be imposed. It is often stated in terms of how U.S. history should be conceived and is often accompanied with charges and counter-charges of "Eurocentrism" and "ethnic separatism." Some argue that multi-culturalism has not meant the integration of diverse cultures but an acceptance by the dominant White Western male ethnic category of the "exotic" foods, dress, and rituals of cultural minorities.

Description of White Culture

Katz and Ivey (1977) contend that Whites in the United States tend not to recognize the existence of the dominant White culture (see Table 1.3 in Chapter 1). Peggy McIntosh (1994) uses a comparison to being right-handed. Pick up a pair of scissors, grasp a door handle, sit at a student's desk. They are all designed for right-handed people. Yet right-handed people do not tend to recognize how the world favors right-handedness.

White culture resulted from a synthesis of ideas, values, and beliefs inherited from European ethnic groups in the United States. As the dominant culture in the United States, White culture is the foundation of social norms and organizations (see Table 18.3).

McIntosh (1994) has written about **White privilege**, which describes how a dominant culture empowers some:

As a white person, I have realized I had been taught about racism as something which puts others at a disadvantage, but had been taught not to see

Table 18.3   Components of White Culture: Values and Beliefs

Rugged individualism
Individual is primary unit
Individual has primary responsibility
Independence and autonomy highly
  valued and rewarded
Individual can control environment

Competition
Winning is everything
Win/lose dichotomy

Action orientation
Must master and control nature
Must always do something about a
  situation
Pragmatic/utilitarian view of life

Decision making
Majority rule when Whites have power
Hierarchical
Pyramid structure

Communication
Standard English
Written tradition
Direct eye contact
Limited physical contact
Controlled emotions

Time
Adherence to rigid time schedule
Time viewed as a commodity

Holidays
Based on Christian religion
Based on White history and male
  leaders

History
Based on European immigrants'
  experiences in United States
Romanticize war

Protestant work ethic
Working hard brings success

Progress and future orientation
Plan for the future
Delayed gratification
Value continued improvement and
  progress

Emphasis on scientific method
Objective, rational, linear thinking
Cause-and-effect relationships
Quantitative emphasis
Dualistic thinking

Status and power
Measured by economic possessions
Credentials, titles, and positions
Believe "own" system
Believe better than other systems
Owning goods, space, property

Family structure
Nuclear family the ideal social unit
Man the breadwinner and head of the
  household
Woman the homemaker and
  subordinate to the husband
Patriarchal structure

Aesthetics
Music and art based on European
  cultures
Women's beauty based on blonde,
  blue-eyed, thin, young
Men's attractiveness based on athletic
  ability, power, economic status

Religion
Belief in Christianity
No tolerance for deviation from single
  God concept

SOURCE: Katz (1985, p. 618).

one of its corollary aspects, white privilege, which puts me at an advantage. I think whites are carefully taught not to recognize white privilege, as males are taught not to recognize male privilege. So I have begun in an untutored way to ask what it is like to have white privilege. I have come to see white privilege as an invisible package of unearned assets which I can count on cashing in on each and every day, but about which I was "meant" to remain oblivious. White privilege is like an invisible weightless knapsack of special provisions, maps, passports, code books, visas, clothes, tools and blank checks. (p. 12)

Examples of White privilege include the following:

- If I make any grammatical or spelling errors, no one will attribute my mistakes to my race or my ethnic group.

- If I have a responsible job, no one thinks that I got it because of "quotas."

- No one assumes that when I give my opinion on something that I am speaking on behalf of my own race.

- I can go into a supermarket and find the staple foods that fit with my cultural traditions or go into a hairdresser's shop and find someone who can cut my hair.

Postethnic United States

You read earlier that John Dewey criticized cultural pluralism as encouraging people to identify themselves as a member of one group, and experience in the United States shows that that group is most often an ethnic group. If a person is born a woman in Texas of immigrant parents from Mexico who becomes an attorney, a Republican, and a Baptist who lives in Minneapolis, who is she? In the United States, she will most likely be identified as Hispanic.

A postethnic perspective recognizes that each of us, like the Minneapolis attorney, lives in many diverse groups and so is not confined to only one group. Angela Davis (1992) used the image of "a rope attached to an anchor": While we may be anchored in one community, our "ropes" should be long enough to permit us "to move into other communities."

A postethnic perspective does not assume that "everyone is the same." Rather, it recognizes our interdependent future and "stretches" the boundaries of "we."

Hollinger (1995) describes a postethnic perspective as a challenge to the "right" of our grandparents to establish our primary identity. **Postethnicity**

> He drew a circle that shut me out—
>
> Heretic, rebel, a thing to flout.
>
> But Love and I had the wit to win:
>
> We drew a circle that took him in!
>
> —Edwin Markham, "The Outwitted," in
> *The Shoes of Happiness and*
> *Other Poems* (1915)

"prefers voluntary to prescribed affiliations, appreciates multiple identities, pushes for communities of wide scope, recognizes the constructed character of ethno-racial groups, and accepts the formation of new groups as a part of the normal life of a democratic society" (p. 116). Postethnicity recognizes that groups based on affiliations are as substantive and authentic as groups based on blood and history.

In one sense, postethnicity is an idealistic attempt to redefine groups rigidly based on ethnicity into groups based on voluntary interests. However, if viewed from the perspective of dominant U.S. cultural values—particularly individualism—postethnicity is a reaffirmation of the individual's right to define herself or himself by individual interest and not by heritage. Postethnicity in the United States may be an extension of extreme individualism.

It is important to recognize the criticism of postethnicity: that it is idealistic to assume that others will not continue to label some people as members of a group and communicate with them as members of that group and not as individuals.

COMMUNICATION CHALLENGES

Some practical intercultural communication problems are presented by immigration and multiculturalism.

Culture Shock

First, there is *culture shock* and, with it, the effects of language skills. If the person seems relatively noncommunicative, for example, the problem may be difficulty with the new language. Be sensitive to the individual's need for clarification of directions and other communications.

Don't simply ask, "Do you understand?" at the end of a direction or comment. Any person anxious to please you will say, "Yes," regardless of whether or not the message is completely clear. Instead, explain at the start that you understand the difficulties of learning a new language and that you encourage the individual to ask questions whenever something is unclear.

A woman in Los Angeles could not make herself understood to health care workers who assumed she was Spanish-speaking and spoke to her only in Spanish. In fact, she spoke Q'anjob'al, a Mayan language of her native Guatemala.

Assessing Degree of Acculturation

The key to more effective communication with the "new immigrant" is to understand how acculturated the person is. If the individual is far into the acculturation process, there will be few, if any, communication or social problems resulting from the person's ethnic background. Such problems may arise, however, for the newly immigrated individual just starting the acculturation process.

At a large Los Angeles bank where people from many ethnic groups were employed, an Asian immigrant, who was fired for just cause, asked permission to return to the bank to apologize personally to every other employee of her ethnic background. It was her belief that she had failed her group. Her values placed much emphasis on a responsibility to group membership but also illustrated a sense of security within that group that she did not feel with other members of the organization.

At this same bank, managers began to notice that on coffee and lunch breaks workers from the same ethnic background consistently sat together. The managers recognized that it was over those breaks and lunches that employees discussed their jobs and the organization. Moreover, management recognized that such social separation did nothing to enhance a holistic identity for the company—it may have, in fact, served to segregate the efforts of what should be a team organization. Management soon decided that it was in the company's interest to actively stimulate acculturation for immigrant workers.

Besides suggesting continued education, the manager can encourage the new worker to spend time with other workers in an effort to become more involved. Likewise, the manager might remind the company's "old-timers" of the importance of socializing with the new worker for the enrichment of all people concerned. Facilitating a comfortable environment in the company, where intercultural communication and camaraderie are inspired, is a less direct step for the manager to take, but it is one that can certainly be effective and well received.

Discrimination

Under the broad definition of **discrimination**, not one of us can claim to be completely free of prejudice. You like and respond well to some people but not to others. Although most identify the word as applying to reactions to obvious personal attributes, such as race, creed, or color, prejudice often arises from much more subtle interactions—many of them unintentional or subconscious. Prejudice entering into employment activities represents one variety of discrimination.

The Los Angeles bank referred to earlier had an excellent affirmative action hiring policy. Nonetheless, the ethnic group members employed there complained about more subtle, and perhaps unconscious, prejudice.

For example, one noticed that a White male manager spent extra time explaining "how the bank really works" to his protégé—another young White male who went to the same school the manager did. The manager had never shared that information with any ethnic group member employees.

In another instance, a White male department manager posted training opportunities as required but strongly encouraged other White heterosexual men in the department to sign up. He never mentioned them to any women, ethnic group members, or lesbians and gay men.

Prejudice among coworkers is another concern for any business. Some studies show that non-Whites, for example, are more likely to be disciplined or fired for the same offenses.

In schools, teachers find that some African-American students resent discussions of Cinco de Mayo and that Hispanic students feel likewise about observing Black History Month.

Language Use

Traditionally, among immigrants the pattern of learning English has been a three-generation process. New immigrants arrive speaking no English. Second-generation children are urged to learn English. The children of immigrants traditionally are bilingual, living both in the parents' world and in the English-speaking outside world. Perhaps from the strain of a bilingual existence, the second generation encourages its children to speak only English.

On one college campus, students told me they would rather not take a course from a certain professor with a Japanese name. When asked why, they said they wouldn't be able to understand her. The fact is she is a fourth-generation U.S. citizen and I know more Japanese than she does, but students made a judgment based on her last name alone. The pattern of behavior reinforces and continues the pattern that Folb (1994) identified.

This **unconscious prejudice** is, of course, difficult to avoid. The mass immigration of the early 1900s created a turbulent time as will today's immigration. In considering the intercultural communication challenges presented by immigration, you need to recognize how the two time periods are different.

More than before, the United States must learn to cope with diversity. The melting pot no longer exists. You are forced to deal with the challenges of multiculturalism. The question "Can cultures coexist without one imposing its values and communication style on others?" remains as yet unanswered.

ETHNIC DIVISIONS

One result of the fall of Communism has been the rise of ethnic nationalism. As you recall, fewer than 5% of the world's countries are ethnically homogeneous. The world is composed of multinational states. Switzerland is made up of four nationalities and has thrived. Elsewhere in the world, national self-assertiveness is the norm. Serbian and Croatian nationalism destroyed the ideal of ethnic diversity for which the Yugoslav federation stood. "Ethnic cleansing" is again spoken of 50 years after World War II.

Will the intercultural communication challenges of the future be in the economic context of rich versus poor and in the political context of ethnic strife?

A humorous essay in the April 8, 1991, issue of *Time* (p. 84) described the one-culture education of the 1950s in the United States:

There were "Negroes," "whites" and "Orientals," the latter meaning Chinese and "Japs." Of religions, only three were known—Protestant, Catholic and Jewish—and not much was known about the last two types. The only remaining human categories were husbands and wives, and that was all the diversity the monocultural world could handle. Gays, lesbians, Buddhists, Muslims, Malaysians, Mormons, etc. were simply off the map. (Copyright © 1991, Time-Warner, Inc. Reprinted by permission.)

Human beings are more alike than unalike, and what is true anywhere is true everywhere, yet I encourage travel to as many destinations as possible. . . . Perhaps travel cannot prevent bigotry, but by demonstrating that all peoples laugh, cry, eat, worry, and die, it can introduce the idea that if we try to understand each other, we may even become friends.

—Maya Angelou,
Wouldn't Take Nothing for
My Journey Now (1993, pp. 11, 12)

FROM THE INTERCULTURAL PERSPECTIVE

The United States has been described as a multicultural society. In the past, people acculturated (adjusted) to American society by assimilating into the dominant culture. To do this, they lost their old cultures and learned the language and culture of the United States. This was the idea of the "melting pot," where everybody became American. Today, people acculturate to the dominant culture by integrating. They learn the dominant culture and language of the United States but do not lose their original cultures.

If the United States is a multicultural society, is there then a dominant U.S. culture, or are there just a lot of "little cultures"? The answer is that there is a dominant culture and a definite power structure. The dominant culture represents the values of heterosexual White males. Communication aspects of this culture include the use of Standard English, direct eye contact, limited physical contact, and controlled expression of emotions. Economic and political power is generally held in U.S. society by youthful (at least in appearance), healthy (not physically disabled), heterosexual White males. Other people hold power, but they have the same values as the heterosexual White males. The special advantage that White males have in the power structure has been called "White privilege." Nondominant groups find it difficult to share power in this structure.

All people live in and identify with many different groups at the same time. A postethnic perspective recognizes this fact. Instead of having identities based on things like ethnicity (rigid, inflexible), it encourages people to have identities that they choose for themselves and that are based on their affiliations (changing, flexible). The postethnic perspective is idealistic because people still label each other (i.e., give names like Black or Hispanic) and communicate with each other according to these labels.

The special communication problems for multicultural societies come from culture shock, conflicting values, discrimination, and multiple language use. Culture shock can be very difficult as new immigrants learn to "survive" in the new culture and learn the language. It is often hard to tell how much a person has assimilated into the dominant culture, and so there can be misunderstandings about values. New immigrants and minority group members often face discrimination. There is an obvious problem in communicating for people who do not speak each other's languages. However, there is also a problem of unconscious prejudice against people who do not speak the majority language perfectly.

KEY TERMS

discrimination	postethnicity	unconscious prejudice
multiculturalism	salad or stew analogy	White privilege

References

Abrahams, R. D. (1976). *Talking Black*. Rowley, MA: Newbury House.

Adler, P. S. (1975). The transitional experience: An alternative view of culture shock. *Journal of Humanistic Psychology, 15*(4), 13-23.

Adorno, T. W., Frenkel-Brunswick, E., Levinson, D. J., & Sanford, R. N. (1950). *The authoritarian personality*. New York: Harper.

Allen, H. G. (1982). *The betrayal of Liliuokalani: Last queen of Hawaii, 1838-1917*. Honolulu, HI: Mutual Publishing.

Allport, G. W. (1954). *The nature of prejudice*. Reading, MA: Addison-Wesley.

Andersen, K. E. (1991). A history of communication ethics. In K. J. Greenberg (Ed.), *Conversations on communication ethics* (pp. 3-19). Norwood, NJ: Ablex.

Andersen, P. A., Lustig, M. W., & Andersen, J. F. (1987). Regional patterns of communication in the United States: A theoretical perspective. *Communication Monographs, 54*, 128-144.

Angelou, M. (1993). *Wouldn't take nothing for my journey now*. New York: Random House.

Argyle, M. (1988). *Bodily communication* (2nd ed.). New York: Methuen.

Argyle, M., & Ingham, R. (1972). Gaze, mutual gaze, and distance. *Semiotica, 1*, 32-49.

Ariés, P. (1962). *Centuries of childhood: A social history of family life* (R. Baldick, Trans.). New York: Knopf.

Armstrong, K. L. (1999). Nike's communication with Black audiences: A sociological analysis of advertising effectiveness via symbolic interactionism. *Journal of Sport & Social Issues, 23*, 266-286.

Aronson, E. (1988). *The social animal* (5th ed.). New York: Freeman.

Asante, M. K. (1987). *The Afrocentric idea*. Philadelphia: Temple University Press.

Asante, M. K. (1988). *Afrocentricity* (Rev. ed.). Trenton, NJ: Africa World Press.

Asuncion-Lande, N. (1983). Language theory and linguistic principles. *International and Intercultural Communication Annual, 7*, 253-257.

Auletta, G. S., & Hammerback, J. C. (1985). A relational model for interracial interactions on television. *Western Journal of Speech Communication, 49*, 301-321.

Aurand, A. M., Jr. (1938). *Little known facts about the Amish and the Mennonites*. Harrisburg, VA: Aurand Press.

Axtell, R. E. (1991). *Gestures: The do's and taboos of body language around the world*. New York: John Wiley.

Axtell, R. E. (1994). *The do's and taboos of international trade*. New York: John Wiley.

Barer-Stein, T. (1999). *You eat what you are: People, culture and food traditions* (2nd ed.). Willowdale, Ontario: Firefly.

Barna, L. M. (1997). Stumbling blocks in intercultural communication. In L. A. Samovar & R. E. Porter (Eds.), *Intercultural communication: A reader* (8th ed., pp. 337-346). Belmont, CA: Wadsworth.

Baron, D. (1990). *The English-only question: An official language for Americans?* New Haven, CT: Yale University Press.

Barrax, G. W. (1973). Black narcissus. In A. Adoff (Ed.), *The poetry of Black America: Anthology of the 20th century* (p. 223). New York: HarperCollins.

Belay, G. (1993). Toward a paradigm shift for intercultural and international communication: New research directions. In S. A. Deetz (Ed.), *Communication yearbook 16* (pp. 437-457). Newbury Park, CA: Sage.

Berger, C. R., & Calabrese, R. J. (1975). Some explorations in initial interaction and beyond: Toward a developmental theory of interpersonal communication. *Human Communication Research, 1,* 99-112.

Berlo, D. K. (1960). *The process of communication.* New York: Holt, Rinehart & Winston.

Bernstein, R. (1997). *The coming conflict with China.* New York: Knopf.

Berry, J. W., Kim, U., & Boski, P. (1987). Psychological acculturation of immigrants. *International and Intercultural Communication Annual, 11,* 62-89.

Beyer, S. (1974). *The Buddhist experience.* Belmont, CA: Wadsworth.

Bickerton, D. (1981). *Roots of language.* Ann Arbor, MI: Karoma.

Biddiss, M. D. (1970). *Father of racist ideology: The social and political thought of Count Gobineau.* New York: Waybright & Talley.

Bigelow, B. (1980). Roots and regions: A summary definition of the cultural geography of America. *Journal of Geography, 79,* 218-229.

Birke-Smith, K. (1959). *The Eskimos.* London: Methuen.

Black, G., & Munro, R. (1993). *Black Hands of Beijing: Lives in defiance in China's democracy movement.* New York: John Wiley.

Blanchard, F. A., Lilly, T., & Vaughn, L. A. (1991). Reducing the expression of racial prejudice. *Psychological Science, 2,* 101-105.

Bolton, R. (1994). Sex, science and social responsibility: Cross-cultural research on same-sexeroticism and sexual intolerance. *Cross-Cultural Research, 28*(2), 134-190.

Booth-Butterfield, M., & Jordan, F. (1989). Communication adaptation among racially homogeneous and heterogeneous groups. *Southern Communication Journal, 54,* 253-272.

Bosmajian, H. A. (1983). *The language of oppression.* Lanham, MD: University Press of America.

Boswell, J. (1980). *Christianity, social tolerance and homosexuality.* Chicago: University of Chicago Press.

Boswell, J. (1994). *Same-sex unions in premodern Europe.* New York: Villard.

Boucher, J. D. (1974). Culture and the expression of emotion. *International and Intercultural Communication Annual, 1,* 82-86.

Braganti, N. L., & Devine, E. (1984). *The travelers' guide to European customs and manners.* Deephaven, MN: Meadowbrook.

Brislin, R. W. (1988). Increasing awareness of class, ethnicity, culture, and race by expanding on students' own experiences. In I. Cohen (Ed.), *The G. Stanley Hall Lecture Series* (Vol. 8, pp. 137-180). Washington, DC: American Psychological Association.

Bruce, J., Lloyd, C. B., & Leonard A., with Engle, P. L., & Duffy, N. (1995). *Families in focus: New perspectives on mothers, fathers, and children.* New York: Population Council.

Buchanan, P. J. (2002). *The death of the west: How dying populations and immigrant invasions imperil our country and civilization.* New York: Thomas Dunne/ St. Martin's.

Buck, R. (1984). *The communication of emotion.* New York: Guilford.

Burgoon, J. K. (1986). Communication effects of gaze behavior: A test of two contrasting explanations. *Human Communication Research, 12,* 495-524.

Burgoon, J. K., Boller, D. B., & Woodall, W. G. (1988). *Non-verbal communication: The unspoken dialog.* New York: Harper & Row.

Buss, D. M. (1989). Sex differences in human mate preferences: Evolutionary hypotheses tested in 37 cultures. *Behavioral and Brain Sciences, 12,* 1-14.

Buss, D. M. (1994). Mate preferences in 37 cultures. In W. Lonner & R. Malpass (Eds.), *Psychology and culture* (pp. 197-201). Needham Heights, MA: Allyn & Bacon.

Campbell, B. G. (1976). *Human-kind emerging.* Boston: Little, Brown.

Carey, J. W. (1989). *Communication as culture: Essays on media and society.* Boston: Unwin Hyman.

Carliner, D. (1977). *The rights of aliens: The basic ACLU guide to an alien's rights.* New York: Avon.

Carliner, D., Guttentag, L., Helton, A. C., & Henderson, W. J. (1990). *The rights of aliens and refugees: The basic ACLU guide to alien and refuge rights* (2nd ed.). Carbondale: Southern Illinois University Press.

Carroll, J. B. (Ed.). (1956). *Language, thought, and reality: Selected writings of Benjamin Lee Whorf.* New York: John Wiley.

Cavalli-Sforza, L., Menozzi, P., & Piazza, A. (1994). *The history and geography of human genes.* Princeton, NJ: Princeton University Press.

Chance, N. A. (1966). *The Eskimo of North Alaska.* New York: Holt, Rinehart & Winston.

Chang, H.-C., & Holt, G. R. (1991). More than relationship: Chinese interaction and the principle of Kuan-Hsi. *Communication Quarterly, 39,* 251-271.

Chauncey, G., Jr. (1985). Christian brotherhood or sexual perversion? Homosexual identities and the construction of sexual boundaries in the World War One era. *Journal of Social History, 19,* 189-211.

Chen, G.-M. (1989). Relationships of the dimensions of intercultural communication competence. *Communication Quarterly, 37,* 118-133.

Chen, G.-M. (1990). Intercultural communication competence: Some perspectives of research. *Howard Journal of Communications, 2,* 243-261.

Chen, G.-M., & Starosta, W. J. (1996). Intercultural communication competence: A synthesis. In B. R. Burleson (Ed.), *Communication yearbook 19* (pp. 353-383). Thousand Oaks, CA: Sage.

Cherry, C. (1957). *On human communication.* Cambridge, MA: Technology Press of MIT/ New York: John Wiley.

Chesebro, J. W. (1980). Paradoxical views of "homosexuality" in the rhetoric of social scientists: A fantasy theme analysis. *Quarterly Journal of Speech, 66,* 127-139.

Chinese Culture Connection. (1987). Chinese values and the search for culture-free dimensions of culture. *Journal of Cross-Cultural Psychology, 18,* 143-164.

Chu, G. C. (1977). *Radical change through communication in Mao's China.* Honolulu: University Press of Hawaii.

Chu, G. C., & Ju, Y. A. (1993). *The Great Wall in ruins: Communication and cultural change in China.* Albany: State University of New York Press.

Chua, A. (2002). *World on fire: How exporting free market democracy breeds ethnic hatred and global instability.* Garden City, NY: Doubleday.

Chyz, Y. J. (1945, October 13). Number, distribution, and circulation of the foreign-language press in the United States. *Interpreter Releases, 20,* 290.

Clark, K. B., & Clark, M. P. (1947). Racial identification and preference in Negro children. In T. M. Newcomb, E. L. Hartley, & G. E. Swanson (Eds.), *Readings in social psychology* (pp. 169-178). New York: Holt, Rinehart & Winston.

Clough, M. (1997, July 27). Birth of nations. *Los Angeles Times,* pp. M1, M6.

Cobo, J. R. M. (Special Rapporteur). (1987). *Study of the problem of discrimination against indigenous populations.* New York: United Nations Publications.

Cohen, M. N. (1998). *Culture of intolerance: Chauvinism, class, and racism in the United States.* New Haven, CT: Yale University Press.

Collier, M. J. (1988). A comparison of conversations among and between domestic culture groups: How intra- and inter-cultural competencies vary. *Communication Quarterly, 36,* 122-144.

Collier, M. J., & Thomas, M. (1988). Cultural identity: An interpretive perspective. *International and Intercultural Communication Annual, 12,* 99-120.

Cooper, C. R., & Denner, J. (1998). Theories linking culture and psychopathology: Universal and community-specific processes. *Annual Review of Psychology, 49,* 559-584.

Cose, S. (1997). *Color-blind: Seeing beyond race in a race-obsessed world.* New York: HarperCollins.

Costello, E. (1995). *Signing: How to speak with your hands.* New York: Bantam.

Cowan, M. (Ed. and Trans.). (1963). *Humanist without portfolio: An anthology of the writings of Wilhelm von Humboldt.* Detroit, MI: Wayne State University Press.

Cowen, T. (2002). Creative destruction: How globalization is changing the world's cultures. Princeton, NJ: Princeton University Press.

Crawford, J. (1992). *Hold your tongue: Bilingualism and the politics of English-only.* Reading, MA: Addison-Wesley.

Crocker, J., & Major, B. (1989). Social stigma and self esteem: The self protective properties of stigma. *Psychological Bulletin, 96,* 608-630.

Cronen, V. E., Pearce, W. B., & Harris, L. M. (1982). The coordinated management of meaning: A theory of communication. In F. E. X. Dance (Ed.), *Human communication theory* (pp. 61-89). New York: Harper & Row.

Crosby, F., Bromley, S., & Saxe, L. (1980). Recent unobtrusive studies of Black and White discrimination and prejudice: A literature review. *Psychological Bulletin, 87,* 546-563.

Daniel, J. L., & Smitherman, G. (1976). How I got over: Communication dynamics in the Black community. *Quarterly Journal of Speech, 62,* 26-39.

Dannin, R. (2002). *Black pilgrimage to Islam.* Oxford, UK: Oxford University Press.

Darwin, C. (1969). *The expression of the emotions in man and animals.* Westport, CT: Greenwood. (Original work published 1872)

Davis, A. (1992, May 24). Rope. *New York Times,* Sec. 4, p. 11.

Deal, T. E., & Kennedy, A. A. (1982). *Corporate cultures: The rites and rituals of corporate life.* Reading, MA: Addison-Wesley.

de la Garza, R. (1992). *Latino voices: Mexican, Puerto Rican and Cuban perspectives on American politics.* Hartford, CT: Westview.

de la Zerda, N., & Hopper, R. (1979). Employment interviewers' reactions to Mexican American speech. *Communication Monographs, 46,* 126-134.

DeMente, B. (1986). *Japanese etiquette and ethics in business* (5th ed.). Lincolnwood, IL: National Textbook Company.

DeMente, B. (1989). *Chinese etiquette and ethics in business.* Lincolnwood, IL: National Textbook Company.

D'Emilio, J. (1992). Gay history: A new field of study. In J. D'Emilio (Ed.), *Making trouble: Essays on gay history, politics, and the university* (pp. 96-113). New York: Routledge.

de Mooij, M. (1998). *Global marketing and advertising: Understanding cultural paradoxes.* Thousand Oaks, CA: Sage.

Denning, M. (1997). *The cultural front: The laboring of American culture in the twentieth century.* London & New York: Verso.

Developments: Sexual orientation and the law. (1989). *Harvard Law Review, 102,* 1508, 1629.

DeVito, J. A. (1986). *The communication handbook: A dictionary.* New York: Harper & Row.

Dissanayake, W. (1987). The guiding image in Indian culture and its implications for communication. In D. L. Kincaid (Ed.), *Communication theory: Eastern and Western perspectives* (pp. 151-160). San Diego, CA: Academic Press.

Doi, L. T. (1956). Japanese language as an expression of Japanese psychology. *Western Speech, 20,* 90-96.

Doi, L. T. (1973). The Japanese patterns of communication and the concept of *amae. Quarterly Journal of Speech, 59,* 180-185.

Dornberg, J. (1999). Still divided: Germany ten years after the fall of the wall. *German Life, 6*(3), 22-27.

Doty, R. L., Shaman, P., Applebaum, S. L., Giberson, R., Siksorski, L., & Rosenberg, L. (1984). Smell identification ability: Changes with age. *Science, 226,* 1441-1443.

Downing, J. D. H. (1990). Ethnic minority radio in the United States. *Howard Journal of Communications, 2,* 135-148.

Dresser, N. (1996). *Multicultural manners.* New York: John Wiley.

Du Bois, W. E. B. (1903). *The souls of Black folk.* Reprinted in *Three Negro classics* (New York: Avon, 1965).

Dudley, M. K., & Agard, K. K. (1993). *A call for Hawaiian sovereignty.* Honolulu, HI: Na Kane O Ka Malo Press.

Duncan, D. E. (1998). *Calendar: Humanity's epic struggle to determine a true and accurate year.* New York: Avon.

Eastman, C. (Ed.). (1992). *Code switching.* Avon, UK: Clevedon.

Eck, D. L. (1993). *Encountering God: A spiritual journey from Bozeman to Banaras.* Boston: Beacon.

Ekman, P., Friesen, W. V., & Ellsworth, P. (1972). *Emotion in the human face: Guidelines for research and an integration of findings.* New York: Pergamon.

Ekman, P., Friesen, W. V., O'Sullivan, M., Chan, A., Diacoyanni-Tarlatzis, I., Heider, K., Krause, R., LeCompte, W. A., Pitcairn, T., Ricci-Bitti, P. E., Scherer, K., Tomita, M., & Tzavaras, A. (1987). Universals and cultural differences in the judgments of facial expression of emotion. *Journal of Personality and Social Psychology, 53,* 712-717.

Ekman, P., & Heider, K. G. (1988). The universality of a contempt expression: A replication. *Motivation and Emotion, 12,* 303-308.

Emerson, R. W. (1909-1914). *Journals of Ralph Waldo Emerson* (Vol. 7, pp. 115-116). Boston/ New York: Houghton Mifflin.

Epstein, S. (1990). Gay politics, ethnic identity: The limits of social construction. In E. Stein (Ed.), *Forms of desire: Sexual orientation and the social constructionist controversy* (pp. 239-293). New York: Garland.

Essed, P. (1991). *Understanding everyday racism.* Newbury Park, CA: Sage.

Ezrati, M. (1999). *Kawari: How Japan's economic and cultural transformation will alter the balance of power among nations.* Reading, MA: Perseus.

Fairchild, H. H. (1985). Black, Negro, or Afro-American? The differences are crucial! *Journal of Black Studies, 16,* 47-55.

Fejes, F., & Petrich, K. (1993). Invisibility, homophobia and heterosexism: Lesbians, gays and the media. *Critical Studies in Mass Communication, 10,* 395-422.

Fischer, C. S., Hout, M., Jankowski, M. S., Swidler, A., & Lucas, S. R. (1996). *Inequality by design: Cracking the bell curve myth.* Princeton, NJ: Princeton University Press.

Fischer, D. H. (1989). *Albion's seed: Four British folkways in America.* New York: Oxford University Press.

Fisher, B. A. (1978). *Perspectives on human communication.* New York: Macmillan.

Fishman, J. A. (1972). *The sociology of language.* Rowley, MA: Newbury House.

Fitzpatrick, M. A. (1988). *Between husbands and wives.* Newbury Park, CA: Sage.

Fitzpatrick, M. A., Jandt, F. E., Myrick, F. L., & Edgar, T. (1994). Gay and lesbian couple relationships. In R. J. Ringer (Ed.), *Queer words, queer images: Communication and the construction of homosexuality* (pp. 265-277). New York: New York University Press.

Foeman, A. K., & Pressley, G. (1987). Ethnic culture and corporate culture: Using Black styles in organizations. *Communication Quarterly, 35,* 293-307.

Folb, E. A. (1994). Who's got the room at the top? Issues of dominance and nondominance in intra-cultural communication. In L. A. Samovar & R. E. Porter (Eds.), *Intercultural communication: A reader* (7th ed., pp. 131-139). Belmont, CA: Wadsworth.

Fong, M. (2000). "Luck talk" in celebrating the Chinese New Year. *Journal of Pragmatics, 32,* 219-237.

Frable, D. E. S. (1997). Gender, racial, ethnic, sexual, and class identities. *Annual Review of Psychology, 48*, 139-162.

Frank, T. (2000). *One market under God: Extreme capitalism, market populism, and the end of economic democracy.* Garden City, NY: Doubleday.

Frazier, E. F. (1957). *Black bourgeoisie.* Glencoe, IL: Free Press.

Frederick, H. H. (1993). *Global communication and international relations.* Belmont, CA: Wadsworth.

Freire, P. (1992). *Pedagogy of the oppressed* (M. B. Ramos, Trans.). New York: Continuum.

Friedman, T. L. (1999). *The Lexus and the olive tree: Understanding globalization.* Thorndike, ME: Thorndike.

Fukuoka, Y. (1996). Koreans in Japan: Past and present. *Saitama University Review, 31*(1), 1-15.

Furnham, A. (1987). The adjustment of sojourners. *International and Intercultural Communication Annual, 11*, 42-61.

Furnham, A., & Bochner, S. (1986). *Culture shock: Psychological reactions to unfamiliar environments.* New York: Methuen.

Fuss, D. (Ed.). (1991). *Inside/out.* New York: Routledge.

Gao, G., & Ting-Toomey, S. (1998). *Communicating effectively with the Chinese.* Thousand Oaks, CA: Sage.

Garreau, J. (1981). *The nine nations of North America.* Boston: Houghton Mifflin.

Geddes, R. W. (1976). *Migrants of the mountains: The cultural ecology of the Blue Miau (Hmong) of Thailand.* Oxford, UK: Clarendon.

Gerner, M., Perry, F., Moselle, M. A., & Archbold, M. (1992). Moving between cultures: Recent research on the characteristics of internationally mobile adolescents. *Global Nomad Quarterly, 1*(2), 2-3, 8.

Gilbert, D., & Kahl, J. A. (1982). *The American class structure: A new synthesis.* Homewood, IL: Dorsey.

Glendon, M. A. (1991). *Rights talk: The impoverishment of political discourse.* New York: Free Press.

Gonzalez, A. (1990). Mexican "otherness" in the rhetoric of Mexican Americans. *Southern Communication Journal, 55*, 276-291.

Gordon, A. I. (1964). *Intermarriage.* Boston: Beacon.

Gordon, D. R. (1971). *The new literacy.* Toronto, Canada/Buffalo, NY: University of Toronto Press.

Govorchin, G. G. (1961). *Americans from Yugoslavia.* Gainesville: University of Florida Press.

Green, G. D., & Bozett, F. W. (1991). Lesbian mothers and gay fathers. In J. C. Gonsiorek & J. D. Weinrich (Eds.), *Homosexuality: Research implications for public policy* (pp. 197-214). Newbury Park, CA: Sage.

Greenberg, J., & Pyszczynski, T. (1985). The effect of an overheard ethnic slur on evaluations of the target: How to spread a social disease. *Journal of Experimental Social Psychology, 21*, 61-72.

Griffith, J. E., & Villavicencio, S. (1985). Relationships among acculturation, sociodemographic characteristics and social supports in Mexican American adults. *Hispanic Journal of Behavioral Sciences, 7*, 75-92.

Grosjean, F. (1982). *Life with two languages: An introduction to bilingualism.* Cambridge, MA: Harvard University Press.

Gross, L. (1993). *Contested closets: The politics and ethics of outing.* Minneapolis: University of Minnesota Press.

Gudykunst, W. B. (1985). The influence of cultural similarity, type of relationship, and self-monitoring on uncertainty reduction processes. *Communication Monographs, 52*, 203-217.

Guernica, A. (1982). *Reaching the Hispanic market effectively: The media, the market, the methods.* New York: McGraw-Hill.

Hacker, A. (1989, October 12). Affirmative action: The new look. *New York Review*, pp. 63-68.

Haiek, J. R. (1992). *Arab-American almanac* (4th ed.). Glendale, CA: News Circle.

Haiman, F. S. (1994). *"Speech acts" and the First Amendment*. Carbondale: Southern Illinois University Press.

Hall, E. T. (1959). *The silent language*. Greenwich, CT: Fawcett.

Hall, E. T. (1976). *Beyond culture*. New York: Anchor.

Hall, E. T. (1983). *The dance of life: The other dimension of time*. New York: Doubleday.

Hall, E. T., & Hall, M. (1990). *Understanding cultural differences*. Yarmouth, ME: Intercultural Press.

Halman, L. (1991). *Waarden in de Westerse wereld: een internationale exploratie van de warden in de Westerse samenleving*. Doctoral dissertation. Tilburg, the Netherlands: Tilburg University Press.

Hand, L. (1944, July 2). The faith we fight for [Speech in Central Park, NY]. *New York Times Magazine*, p. 26.

Harper, R. G., Wiens, A. N., & Matarazzo, J. D. (1978). *Nonverbal communication: The state of the art*. New York: John Wiley.

Harris, D. (1997). *The rise and fall of gay culture*. New York: Hyperion.

Harry, J., & DeVall, W. B. (1978). *The social organization of gay males*. New York: Praeger.

Hatchett, S. J., & Jackson, J. S. (1993). African-American extended kin systems: An assessment. In H. P. McAdoo (Ed.). *Family ethnicity: Strength in diversity* (pp. 90-108). Newbury Park, CA: Sage.

Hayakawa, S. I. (1978). *Through the communication barrier*. New York: Harper & Row.

Hayes, J. J. (1976). Gayspeak. *Quarterly Journal of Speech, 62*, 256-266.

Hayes-Bautista, D. E. (1992). *No longer a minority: Latinos and social policy in California and redefining California. Latino social engagement in a multicultural society*. Los Angeles: UCLA Chicano Studies Research Center.

Hebdige, D. (1979). *Subculture: The meaning of style*. London: Methuen.

Hecht, M. L., Ribeau, S., & Alberts, J. K. (1989). An Afro-American perspective on interethnic communication. *Communication Monographs, 56*, 385-410.

Hecht, M. L., Ribeau, S. A., & Collier, M. J. (1992). *African American communication: Ethnic identity and cultural interpretation*. Newbury Park, CA: Sage.

Hess, E. H. (1975). *The tell-tale eye*. New York: Van Nostrand Reinhold.

Hickson, M. L., III, & Stacks, D. W. (1989). *NVC, nonverbal communication: Studies and applications* (2nd ed.). Dubuque, IA: William C. Brown.

Hofstede, G. (1980). *Culture's consequences*. Beverly Hills, CA: Sage.

Hofstede, G. (1983). Dimensions of national cultures in fifty countries and three regions. In J. B. Deregowski, S. Dziurawiec, & R. C. Annis (Eds.), *Expectations in cross-cultural psychology* (pp. 335-355). Lisse, the Netherlands: Swets & Zeitlinger.

Hofstede, G. (1984). The cultural relativity of the quality of life concept. *Academy of Management Review, 9*, 389-398.

Hofstede, G. (1991). *Cultures and organizations: Software of the mind*. New York: McGraw-Hill.

Hofstede, G. (1994). Business cultures. *UNESCO Courier, 47*(4), 12-16.

Hofstede, G. (1996). Gender stereotypes and partner preferences of Asian women in masculine and feminine cultures. *Journal of Cross-Cultural Psychology, 27*, 533-546.

Hofstede, G. (1997). *Cultures and organizations: Software of the mind* (Rev. ed.). New York: McGraw-Hill.

Hofstede, G. (1998). Comparative studies of sexual behavior: Sex as achievement or as relationship? In G. Hofstede (Ed.), *Masculinity and femininity: The taboo dimension of national cultures* (pp. 153-178). Thousand Oaks, CA: Sage.

Hofstede, G. (2001). *Culture's consequences: Comparing values, behaviors, institutions, and organizations across nations* (2nd ed.). Thousand Oaks, CA: Sage.

Hofstede, G., & Bond, M. H. (1984). Hofstede's culture dimensions: An independent validation using Rokeach's value survey. *Journal of Cross-Cultural Psychology, 15*, 417-433.

Hoijer, H. (Ed.). (1954). *Language in culture*. Chicago: University of Chicago Press.

Hollinger, D. A. (1995). *Post-ethnic America: Beyond multiculturalism*. New York: Basic Books.

Holm, J. A. (1989). *Pidgins and creoles* (2 vols.). Cambridge, UK/New York: Cambridge University Press.

Hooker, E. (1957). The adjustment of the male overt homosexual. *Journal of Projective Techniques, 21*, 18-31.

Hooker, E. (1965). Male homosexuals and their worlds. In J. Marmor (Ed.), *Sexual inversion: The multiple roots of homosexuality* (pp. 83-107). New York: Basic Books.

Hostetler, J. A. (1980). *Amish society* (3rd ed.). Baltimore: Johns Hopkins University Press.

Hu, H. C. (1944). The Chinese concepts of "face." *American Anthropologist, 46*, 45-64.

Hughes, L. (1961). *The best of Simple*. New York: Hill & Wang.

Huntington, S. P. (1993). The clash of civilizations? *Foreign Affairs, 72*(3), 22-49.

Huntington, S. P. (1996). *The clash of civilizations and the remaking of world order*. New York: Simon & Schuster.

Hurstfield, J. (1978). Internal colonialism: White, Black and Chicano self-conceptions. *Ethnic and Racial Studies, 1*, 60-79.

Infante, D. A., Rancer, A. S., & Womack, D. F. (1993). *Building communication theory* (2nd ed.). Prospect Heights, IL: Waveland.

Ingle, S. (1982). *Quality circles master guide: Increasing productivity with people power*. Englewood Cliffs, NJ: Prentice Hall.

Inglehart, R. (1990). *Culture shift in advanced industrial society*. Princeton, NJ: Princeton University Press.

Inglehart, R., & Baker, W. E. (2000). Modernization, cultural change, and the persistence of traditional values. *American Sociological Review, 65*, 19-51.

Isaacs, J. (1980). *Australian dreaming: 40,000 years of aboriginal history*. Sydney: Lansdowne.

Ivins, M. (1991). *She can't say that, can she?* New York: Random House.

Iwama, H. F. (1990). *Factors influencing transculturation of Japanese overseas teenagers*. Unpublished doctoral dissertation, Pennsylvania State University.

Jahn, J. (1961). *Muntu*. New York: Grove.

Jain, N. C., & Matukumalli, A. (1993, April). *The functions of silence in India: Implications for intercultural communication research*. Paper presented at the Second International East Meets West Conference in Cross-Cultural Communication, Comparative Philosophy, and Comparative Religion, Long Beach, CA.

Jandt, F. E., & Tanno, D. V. (2001). Decoding domination, encoding self-determination: Intercultural communication research process. *Howard Journal of Communications, 12*, 119-135.

Jayasuriya, D. L. (1990). Australian multiculturalism adrift: The search for a new paradigm. *Journal of Vietnamese Studies, 1*, 3-17.

Jones, S. (1993). *The right touch: Understanding and using the language of physical contact*. Cresskill, NJ: Hampton.

Jones, S. E., & Yarbrough, A. E. (1985). A naturalistic study of the meanings of touch. *Communication Monographs, 52*, 19-56.

Jung, C. (1960). *Androgeny*. New York: Guilford.

Kale, D. W. (1997). Peace as an ethic for intercultural communication. In L. A. Samovar & R. E. Porter (Eds.), *Intercultural communication: A reader* (8th ed., pp. 448-452). Belmont, CA: Wadsworth.

Kallen, H. (1915, February 18-25). Democracy versus the melting pot. *Nation*, pp. 190-194, 217-220.

Kallen, H. M. (1970). *Culture and democracy in the United States*. New York: Arno. (Original work published 1924)

Katz, J. (Ed.). (1976). *Gay American history: Lesbians and gay men in the U.S.A.* New York: Thomas Y. Crowell.

Katz, J. H. (1985). The sociopolitical nature of counseling. *The Counseling Psychologist, 13,* 615-624.

Katz, J. H., & Ivey, A. (1977). White awareness: The frontier of racism awareness training. *Personnel and Guidance Journal, 55,* 484-489.

Keesing, R. M. (1988). *Melanesian pidgin and the oceanic substrate.* Stanford, CA: Stanford University Press.

Kidd, J. K., & Lankenau, L. L. (n.d.) Third culture kids: Returning to their passport country. *Syllabus* (a publication of Phi Delta Kappa). Retrieved from http://www.state.gov/m/dghr/flo/rsrcs/pubs/4597.htm

Kim, J. W. (1975). The thought of filial piety. *Research Review of Kyungbook National University, 20,* 239-256.

Kim, M.-S. (1992). A comparative analysis of nonverbal expressions as portrayed by Korean and American print-media advertising. *Howard Journal of Communications, 3,* 317-339.

Kim, Y. Y. (1986). *Interethnic communication: Current research.* Newbury Park, CA: Sage.

Kim, Y. Y. (1988). *Cross-cultural adaptation: Current approaches.* Newbury Park, CA: Sage.

Kirkland, S. L., Greenberg, J., & Pyszczynski, T. (1987). Further evidence of the deleterious effects of overheard derogatory ethnic labels: Derogation beyond the target. *Personality and Social Psychology Bulletin, 13,* 216-227.

Kluckhohn, F. R., & Strodtbeck, F. L. (1961). *Variations in value orientations.* Evanston, IL: Row, Peterson.

Knapp, M. L. (1990). Nonverbal communication. In G. L. Dahnke & G. W. Clatterbuck (Eds.), *Human communication: Theory and research* (pp. 50-69). Belmont, CA: Wadsworth.

Knighton, J. (1999). *Intergenerational transfer and the rise of individualism.* Unpublished paper, Victoria University of Wellington, New Zealand.

Kochman, T. (1981). *Black and White styles in conflict.* Chicago: University of Chicago Press.

Kochman, T. (1986). Black verbal dueling strategies in inter-ethnic communication. *International and Intercultural Communication Annual, 10,* 136-157.

Kohls, L. R. (1984). *The values Americans live by.* New York: Meridian House International.

Kohn, M. L. (1977). *Class and conformity* (2nd ed.). Chicago: University of Chicago Press.

Kraut, A. H. (1994). *Silent travelers: Germs, genes, and the immigrant menace.* New York: Basic Books.

Kraybill, D. B. (1989). *The riddle of Amish culture.* Baltimore: Johns Hopkins University Press.

Krippendorff, K. (1993). Conversation or intellectual imperialism in comparing communication (theories). *Communication Theory, 3*(3), 252-266.

Kushner, H. S. (1982). *When bad things happen to good people.* Boston: G. K. Hall.

Labov, W., Ash, S., & Boberg, C. (1997). *A national map of the regional dialects of American English.* Unpublished research report.

Landis, D., & Brislin, R. (Eds.). (1983). *Handbook of intercultural training* (Vol. 2). Elmsford, NY: Pergamon.

Lau v. Nichols, 414 U.S. 563, 39 L. Ed. 2d 1, 94 S. Ct. 786 (1974).

Lee, W. S. (1994). On not missing the boat: A processual method for intercultural understanding of idioms and lifeworld. *Journal of Applied Communication Research, 22,* 141-161.

Leeds-Hurwitz, W. (1990). Notes in the history of intercultural communication: The Foreign Service Institute and the mandate for intercultural training. *Quarterly Journal of Speech, 76,* 262-281.

Le Play, F. (1884). *L'Organization de la famille.* Paris: Dentu Libre.

LeVay, S. (1993). *The sexual brain.* Cambridge, MA: MIT Press.

Levin, J., & McDevitt, J. (1993). *Hate crimes: The rising tide of bigotry and bloodshed.* New York: Plenum.

Levine, E. S., & Padilla, A. M. (1979). *Crossing cultures in therapy: Pluralistic counseling for the Hispanic.* Monterey, CA: Brooks/Cole.

Lewis, B. (2002). *What went wrong? Western impact and Middle Eastern response.* New York: Oxford University Press.

Liberman, K. (1981). Understanding Aborigines in Australian courts of law. *Human Organization, 40*(3), 247-255.

Liberman, K. (1990a). An ethnomethodological agenda in the study of intercultural communication. In D. Carbaugh (Ed.), *Cultural communication and intercultural contact* (pp. 185-192). Hillsdale, NJ: Lawrence Erlbaum.

Liberman, K. (1990b). Intercultural communication in central Australia. In D. Carbaugh (Ed.), *Cultural communication and intercultural contact* (pp. 177-183). Hillsdale, NJ: Lawrence Erlbaum.

Lipset, S. M. (1990). *Continental divide: The values and institutions of the United States and Canada.* New York/London: Routledge.

Lipski, J. (1985). *Linguistic aspects of Spanish-English language switching.* Tempe: Arizona University Center for Latin American Studies.

Logue, C. M. (1981). Transcending coercion: The communicative strategies of Black slaves on antebellum plantations. *Quarterly Journal of Speech, 67,* 31-46.

Lorde, A. (1984). *Sister outsider.* Freedom, CA: Crossing Press.

Lucaites, J. L., & Condit, C. M. (1990). Reconstructing equality: Culturetypal and countercultural rhetorics in the martyred Black vision. *Communication Monographs, 57,* 5-24.

Lum, C. M. K. (1991). Communication and cultural insularity: The Chinese immigrant experience. *Critical Studies in Mass Communication, 8,* 91-101.

Ma, R. (1992). The role of unofficial intermediaries in interpersonal conflicts in the Chinese culture. *Communication Quarterly, 40,* 269-278.

Maddox, K. B., & Gray, S. A. (2002). Cognitive representations of Black Americans: Reexploring the role of skin tone. *Personality and Social Psychology Bulletin, 28,* 250-259.

Malotki, E. (1983). *Hopi time: A linguistic analysis of the temporal concepts in the Hopi language.* Berlin: Mouton.

Markham, E. (1915). The outwitted. In *The shoes of happiness and other poems.* Garden City, NY: Doubleday.

Masakazu, Y. (1994). *Individualism and the Japanese: An alternative approach to cultural comparison* (B. Sugihara, Trans.). Tokyo: Japan Echo.

Masayuki, N. (1986). Perceptions of self-disclosure in initial interaction: A Japanese sample. *Human Communication Research, 13,* 167-190.

Massey, D. S., & Denton, N. A. (1993). *American apartheid: Segregation and the making of the underclass.* Cambridge, MA: Harvard University Press.

Matthews, S., Polinsky, M., & Comrie, B. (Eds.). (1996). *The atlas of languages.* London: Quarto.

Maurer, D. W. (1981). *Language of the underworld.* Lexington: University Press of Kentucky.

May, L., & Sharratt, S. C. (1994). *Applied ethics: A multicultural approach.* Englewood Cliffs, NJ: Prentice Hall.

Mayer, J. P., revised in collaboration with A. P. Kerr. (1981). Journey to America *by Alexis de Tocqueville* (G. Lawrence, Trans.). Westport, CT: Greenwood.

McClelland, D. C. (1976). *The achieving society.* New York: Irvington.

McCroskey, J. C. (1968). *An introduction to rhetorical communication.* Englewood Cliffs, NJ: Prentice Hall.

McCroskey, J. C. (1990). Correlates of quietness: Swedish and American perspectives. *Communication Quarterly, 38,* 127-137.

McIntosh, P. (1994, Fall). White privilege: Unpacking the invisible knapsack. *Hungry Mind Review,* pp. 12-13.

McWhirter, D. P., & Mattison, A. M. (1984). *The male couple: How relationships develop.* Englewood Cliffs, NJ: Prentice Hall.

McWilliams, C. (1990). *North from Mexico: The Spanish speaking people of the United States* (Rev. ed.). Westport, CT: Greenwood/Praeger.

Mehrabian, A. (1981). *Silent messages: Implicit communication of emotions and attitudes* (2nd ed.). Belmont, CA: Wadsworth.

Meier, M. S., & Ribera, F. (1993). *Mexican Americans/American Mexicans: From conquistadors to Chicanos* (Rev. ed.). New York: Hill & Wang.

Melton, J. G. (Ed.). (1991). *Encyclopedia of American religions: A comprehensive study of the major religious groups in the United States.* New York: Triumph.

Melville, H. (1976). *Redburn.* London: Harmondsworth. (Original work published 1849)

Mendenhall, M., & Oddou, G. (1985). The dimensions of expatriate acculturation. *Academy of Management Review, 10,* 39-47.

Menkiti, I. A. (1984). Person and community in African traditional thought. In R. A. Wright (Ed.), *African philosophy: An introduction* (3rd ed., pp. 171-181). Lanham, MD: University Press of America.

Merriam, A. H. (1974). Rhetoric and the Islamic tradition. *Today's Speech, 22,* 43-49.

Merritt, A. C., & Helmreich, R. L. (1996). Human factors on the flight deck: The influence of national culture. *Journal of Cross-Cultural Psychology, 27,* 5-24.

Meyer, M. (1995). The signifying invert: Camp and the performance of nineteenth-century sexology. *Text and Performance Quarterly, 15,* 265-281.

Milburn, N. G., & Bowman, P. J. (1991). Neighborhood life. In J. S. Jackson (Ed.), *Life in Black America* (pp. 31-45). Newbury Park, CA: Sage.

Miller, D. H. (1998). *Freedom to differ: The shaping of the gay and lesbian struggle for civil rights.* New York: New York University Press.

Miller, L. D. (1982). Attraction and communication style as determinants of interpersonal relationships: Perceptual comparisons between Blacks and Whites. *International and Intercultural Communication Annual, 6,* 47-62.

Miller, M. D., Reynolds, R. A., & Cambra, R. E. (1987). The influence of gender and culture on language intensity. *Communication Monographs, 54,* 101-105.

Miller, N. (1995). *Out of the past: Gay and lesbian history from 1869 to the present.* New York: Vintage.

Mirandé, A., & Tanno, D. V. (1993). Labels, researcher perspective, and contextual validation: A commentary. *International Journal of Intercultural Relations, 17,* 149-155.

Modley, R. (1976). *Handbook of pictorial symbols.* New York: Dover.

Moore, M. M. (1995). Courtship signaling and adolescents: "Girls just wanna have fun." *The Journal of Sex Research, 32*(4), 319-328.

Morris, D. (1979). *Gestures.* Briarcliff Manor, NY: Stein & Day.

Morris, D. (1995). *Bodytalk: The meaning of human gestures.* New York: Crown Trade Paperbacks.

Mott, F. L., & Jorgenson, C. E. (Eds.). (1939). *Benjamin Franklin: Representative selections, with introduction, bibliography, and notes.* New York: American Book Company.

Murdock, G. P. (1949). *Social structures.* New York: Macmillan.

Nafeesi, S. (1986). *Advertising in Saudi Arabia.* Unpublished master's thesis, California State University, San Bernardino.

Nakamura, H. (1964). *Ways of thinking of Eastern peoples: India-China-Tibet-Japan.* Honolulu, HI: East-West Center.

Nash, G. B. (1992). The great multicultural debate. *Contention, 1,* 11.

Nelson, J. (1985). Homosexuality in Hollywood films: A contemporary paradox. *Critical Studies in Mass Communication, 2,* 54-64.

Nisbett, R. E. (1980). *Human inference: Strategies and shortcomings of social judgment.* Englewood Cliffs, NJ: Prentice Hall.

Nisbett, R. E. (1996). *Culture of honor: The psychology of violence in the South.* Boulder, CO: Westview.

Nordenstreng, K., & Schiller, H. I. (Eds.). (1979). *National sovereignty and international communication.* Honolulu, HI: East-West Center.

Oberg, K. (1960). Cultural shock: Adjustment to new cultural environments. *Practical Anthropology, 7,* 177-182.

Obeyesekere, G. (1992). *The apotheosis of Captain Cook.* Princeton, NJ: Princeton University Press.

O'Connor, C. (1991, March). Germany's immigration dilemma. *Europe,* pp. 23-25.

Okabe, R. (1983). Cultural assumptions of East and West: Japan and the U.S. *International and Intercultural Communication Annual, 7,* 21-44.

Oliver, R. T. (1971). *Communication and culture in ancient India and China.* Syracuse, NY: Syracuse University Press.

Omi, M., & Winant, H. (1986). *Racial formations in the United States from the 1960s to the 1980s.* New York: Routledge & Kegan Paul.

Orbe, M. P. (1998). *Constructing co-cultural theory: An explication of culture, power, and communication.* Thousand Oaks, CA: Sage.

Overseas diplomacy: Guidelines for United States Navy. (1979). In D. S. Hoopes & P. Ventura (Eds.), *Cross-cultural training methodologies* (pp. 89-101). Chicago: Intercultural Press.

Owens, K., & King, M. C. (1999). Genomic views of human history. *Science, 286,* 451-453.

Paabo, S. (2001). Genomics and society: The human genome and our view of ourselves. *Science, 291,* 1219-1220.

Pacanowsky, M. E., & O'Donnell-Trujillo, N. (1982). Communication and organizational cultures. *Western Journal of Speech Communication, 46,* 115-130.

Patterson, O. (1991). *Freedom: Freedom in the making of Western culture* (Vol. 1). New York: Basic Books.

Paz, O. (1961). *The labyrinth of solitude* (L. Kemp, Trans.). New York: Grove.

Pedersen, P. (1995). *The five stages of culture shock: Critical incidents around the world.* Westport, CT: Greenwood.

Peters, T. J. (1982). *In search of excellence: Lessons from America's best-run companies.* New York: Harper & Row.

Peterson, R. C., & Thurstone, L. L. (1933). *Motion pictures and the social attitudes of children.* New York: Macmillan.

Pharr, S. (1988). *Homophobia: A weapon of sexism.* Inverness, CA: Chardon.

Philipsen, G. (1975). Speaking "like a man" in Teamsterville: Culture patterns of role enactment in an urban neighborhood. *Quarterly Journal of Speech, 61,* 13-22.

Philipsen, G. (1976). Places for speaking in Teamsterville. *Quarterly Journal of Speech, 62,* 15-25.

Philipsen, G. (1989). Speech and the communal function in four cultures. *International and Intercultural Communication Annual, 13,* 79-92.

Philipsen, G. (1992). *Speaking culturally: Explorations in social communication.* Albany: State University of New York Press.

Piatt, B. (1990). *Only English? Law and language policy in the United States.* Albuquerque: University of New Mexico Press.

Posse, A. (1989). *Perros del paraíso* [Dogs of paradise] (M. S. Peden, Trans.). New York: Atheneum.

Pradhan, G. (1993). *Misery behind the looms: Child labourers in the carpet factories in Nepal.* Kathmandu: Child Workers in Nepal Concerned Center.

Putnam, L., & Pacanowsky, M. (Eds.). (1983). *Communication and organizations: An interpretive approach.* Beverly Hills, CA: Sage.

Rheingold, H. (1999, January). Look who's talking. *Wired, 7,* 128ff.

Richardson, D. (1974). *Peace child.* Marina del Rey, CA: GL Publications.

Riggins, S. H. (Ed.). (1997). *The language and politics of exclusion.* Thousand Oaks, CA: Sage.

Ritzer, G. (1993). *The McDonaldization of society.* Newbury Park, CA: Pine Forge.

Robinson, E. (1999). *Cool to cream: A Blackman's journey beyond color to an affirmation of race.* New York: Free Press.

Rodriguez, A. (1999). *Making Latino news: Race, language, class.* Thousand Oaks, CA: Sage.

Roediger, D. R. (1999). *The wages of whiteness: Race and the making of the American working class.* London and New York: Verso.

Rogers, E. M. (1986). *Communication technology.* New York: Free Press.

Rogers, E. (1999). Georg Simmel's concept of the stranger and intercultural communication research. *Communication Theory, 9,* 58-74.

Rogers, E. M., & Kincaid, D. L. (1981). *Communication networks: A new paradigm for research.* New York: Free Press.

Rogers, E. M., & Shoemarker, F. F. (1971). *Communication of innovations: A cross-cultural approach* (2nd ed.). New York: Free Press.

Rojjanaprapayon, W. (1997). *Communication patterns of Thai people in a non-Thai context.* Unpublished doctoral dissertation, Purdue University.

Rokeach, M., & Ball-Rokeach, S. (1989). Stability and change in American value priorities, 1968-1981. *American Psychologist, 44,* 775-784.

Romaine, S. (1988). *Pidgin and creole languages.* London: Longman.

Romaine, S. (1992). *Language, education and development: Urban and rural Tok Pisin in Papua New Guinea.* Oxford, UK/New York: Oxford University Press.

Ross, M. W. (1989). Gay youth in four cultures: A comparative study. *Journal of Homosexuality, 17*(3-4), 299-314.

Rotello, G. (1998, January 20). Last word: Inside the circle. *The Advocate,* p. 112.

Rothenberg, P. S. (Ed.). (1992). *Race, class, and gender in the United States: An integrated study* (2nd ed.). New York: St. Martin's.

Rushing, J. H. (1983). The rhetoric of the American western myth. *Communication Monographs, 50,* 15-32.

Rushing, J. H., & Frentz, T. S. (1978). The rhetoric of "Rocky": A social value model of criticism. *Western Journal of Speech Communication, 42,* 63-72.

Russo, V. (1987). *The celluloid closet: Homosexuality in the movies* (Rev. ed.). New York: Harper & Row.

Ryan, M. G. (1974). The influence of speaker dialect and sex on stereotypic attribution. *International and Intercultural Communication Annual, 1,* 87-101.

Sabogal, F., Marín, G., Otero-Sabogal, R., Marín, B. V., & Perez-Stable, P. (1987). Hispanic familisam and acculturation: What changes and what doesn't. *Hispanic Journal of Behavioral Sciences, 9,* 397-412.

Said, E. (1978). *Orientalism.* New York: Pantheon.

Said, E. (1981). *Covering Islam: How the media and the experts determine how we see the rest of the world.* New York: Pantheon.

Samovar, L. A., Porter, R. E., & Jain, N. C. (1981). *Understanding intercultural communication.* Belmont, CA: Wadsworth.

Sapir, E. (1921). *Language: An introduction to the study of speech.* New York: Harcourt Brace Jovanovich.

Sapir, E. (1949). *Selected writings in language, culture, and personality.* Berkeley: University of California Press.

Schiller, H. I. (1976). *Communication and cultural domination.* White Plains, NY: International Arts and Science Press.

Schneider, P. (1991). *The German comedy: Scenes of life after the wall.* New York: Farrar, Straus & Giroux.

Scollon, R., & Scollon, S. W. (1991). Mass and count nouns in Chinese and English: A few further Whorfian considerations. In R. Blust (Ed.), *Currents in Pacific linguistics: Papers on Austronesian languages and ethnolinguistics in honor of George W. Grace* (pp. 465-475). Canberra, Australia: Pacific Linguistics.

Sechrest, L., Fay, T. L., & Zaidi, S. M. (1972). Problems of translation in cross-cultural communication. *Journal of Cross-Cultural Psychology, 3*(1), 41-56.

Sedano, M. V. (1980). Chicanismo: A rhetorical analysis of themes and images of selected poetry from the Chicano movement. *Western Journal of Speech Communication, 44,* 177-190.

Segall, M. H., Campbell, D. T., & Herskovits, M. J. (1966). *The influence of culture on visual perception.* Indianapolis, IN: Bobbs-Merrill.

Sennett, R. (1999, Summer). The spaces of democracy. *Harvard Design Magazine,* pp. 68-72.

Shaheen, J. G. (1984). *The TV Arab.* Bowling Green, OH: Bowling Green State University Popular Press.

Shaheen, J. G. (2001). *Reel bad Arabs: How Hollywood vilifies a people.* New York: Olive Branch.

Sharma, I. C. (1965). *Ethical philosophies of India.* New York: Harper & Row.

Sherif, M., & Sherif, C. W. (1953). *Groups in harmony and tension.* New York: Harper.

Shioiri, T., Someya, T., Helmeste, D., & Tang, S. W. (1999). Misinterpretation of facial expression: A cross-cultural study. *Psychiatry and Clinical Neurosciences, 53,* 45-50.

Shipler, D. K. (1997). *A country of strangers: Blacks and Whites in America.* New York: Knopf.

Shome, R. (1996). Postcolonial interventions in the rhetorical canon: An "other" view. *Communication Theory, 6,* 40-59.

Shuter, R. (1979). Gaze behavior in interracial and intraracial interactions. *International and Intercultural Communication Annual, 5,* 48-54.

Slagle, A. (1995). In defense of Queer Nation: From identity politics to a politics of difference. *Western Journal of Communication, 59,* 85-102.

Smith, A. G. (1966). *Communication and culture: Readings in the codes of human interaction.* New York: Holt, Rinehart & Winston.

Smith, C. A. (1991). *The absentee American.* New York: Praeger.

Smith, J. I. (2000). *Islam in America.* New York: Columbia University Press.

Smith, R. C., & Eisenberg, E. (1987). Conflict at Disneyland: A root-metaphor analysis. *Communication Monographs, 54,* 367-380.

Smith, R. R., & Windes, R. R. (1997). The progay and antigay issue culture: Interpretation, influence, and dissent. *Quarterly Journal of Speech, 83,* 28-48.

Smutkupt, S., & Barna, L. M. (1976). Impact of nonverbal communication in an intercultural setting: Thailand. *International and Intercultural Communication Annual, 3,* 130-138.

Snyder, M., & Uranowitz, S.W. (1978). Reconstructing the past: Some cognitive consequences of person perception. *Journal of Personality & Social Psychology, 36,* 941-950.

St. Martin, G. M. (1976). Intercultural differential decoding of nonverbal affective communication. *International and Intercultural Communication Annual, 3,* 44-57.

Stavenhagen, R. (1986). *Problems and prospects of multi-ethnic states.* Tokyo: United Nations University Press.

Stavenhagen, R. (1990). Linguistic minorities and language policy in Latin America: The case of Mexico. In F. Coulmas (Ed.), *Linguistic minorities and literacy: Language policy issues in developing countries* (pp. 56-62). Berlin: Mouton.

Steele, C. M., & Aronson, J. (1995). Stereotype threat and the intellectual test performance of African Americans. *Journal of Personality & Social Psychology, 69,* 797-811.

Steinfatt, T. M. (1989). Linguistic relativity: Toward a broader view. *International and Intercultural Communication Annual, 13,* 35-75.

Stevenson, V. (1999). *The world of words: An illustrated history of Western languages* (Rev. ed.). New York: Sterling.

Stewart, E. C. (1972). *American cultural patterns: A cross-cultural perspective.* Chicago: Intercultural Press.

Stewart, E. C. (1982). Applications of intercultural communication in Japan. *Speech Education, 9,* 4-7.

Stroman, C. A., Merritt, B. D., & Matabane, P. W. (1989). Twenty years after Kerner: The portrayal of African Americans on prime-time television. *Howard Journal of Communications, 2,* 44-56.

Sugawara, Y. (1993). *Silence and avoidance: Japanese expatriate adjustment.* Unpublished master's thesis, California State University, San Bernardino.

Sypher, B. D. (1985). Culture and communication in organizations. *International and Intercultural Communication Annual, 9,* 13-29.

Szalay, L. B., & Inn, A. (1987). Cross-cultural adaptation and diversity: Hispanic Americans. *International and Intercultural Communication Annual, 11,* 212-232.

Szalay, L. B., Moon, W. T., & Bryson, J. A. (1971). *Communication lexicon on three South Korean audiences: Social, national, and motivational domains; Communication lexicon on three South Korean audiences: Domains of family, education, and international relations.* Kensington, MD: American Institutes for Research.

Tajfel, H. (1969). Social and cultural factors in perception. In G. Lindzey & E. Aronson (Eds.), *The handbook of social psychology* (Vol. 3, 2nd ed.). Reading, MA: Addison-Wesley.

Tanno, D. V. (1994). Names, narratives, and the evolution of ethnic identity. In A. Gonzalez, M. Houston, & V. Chen (Eds.), *Our voices: Essays in culture, ethnicity, and communication* (pp. 28-32). Los Angeles: Roxbury.

Tanno, D., & Jandt, F. E. (1994). Redefining the "other" in multicultural research. *Howard Journal of Communications, 5*(1-2), 36-45.

Taylor, D., Dubé, L., & Bellerose, J. (1986). Intergroup contact in Quebec. In M. Hewstone & R. Brown (Eds.), *Contact and conflict in intergroup encounters* (pp. 107-118). Oxford, UK/New York: Basil Blackwell.

Taylor, R. J., & Chatters, L. M. (1991) Religious life. In J. S. Jackson (Ed.), *Life in Black America.* Newbury Park, CA: Sage.

Thernstrom, S., & Thernstrom, A. (1997). *America in Black and White.* New York: Simon & Schuster.

Thompson, H. S. (1966). *Hell's Angels: A strange and terrible saga.* New York: Ballantine.

Ting-Toomey, S. (1985). Toward a theory of conflict and culture. *International and Intercultural Communication Annual, 9,* 71-86.

Ting-Toomey, S. (1986). Conflict communication styles in Black and White subjective cultures. *International and Intercultural Communication Annual, 10,* 75-88.

Tobin, J., & Dobard, R. G. (1999). *Hidden in plain view: The secret story of quilts and the underground.* Garden City, NY: Doubleday.

Tocqueville, A. de. (1945). *Democracy in America.* New York: Vintage. (Original work published 1835 and 1840)

Todd, E. (1985). *The explanation of ideology: Family structures and social systems* (D. Garrioch, Trans.). Oxford, UK/New York: Basil Blackwell.

Triandis, H. C. (1964). Cultural influences upon cognitive processes. In L. Berkowitz (Ed.), *Advances in experimental psychology* (Vol. 2, pp. 1-48). New York: Academic Press.

Tsujimura, A. (1968). *Japanese culture and communication.* Tokyo: NHK Books.

Tsujimura, A. (1987). Some characteristics of the Japanese way of communication. In D. L. Kincaid (Ed.), *Communication theory: Eastern and Western perspectives* (pp. 115-126). San Diego, CA: Academic Press.

Tung, T. M. (1990). Southeast Asia refugee mental health: Fourteen years later. *Journal of Vietnamese Studies, 1*(3), 56-64.

Tylor, E. B. (1871). *Primitive culture: Researches into the development of mythology, philosophy, religion, art, and custom.* London: J. Murray.

United Nations. (1994). *The state of the world's children.* New York: Author.

United Nations. (2000). *The world's women 2000: Trends and statistics.* New York: Author.

United Nations Development Programme. (1999). *Human development report.* New York and Oxford, UK: Oxford University Press.

Useem, R. H., & Downie, R. D. (1976, September/October). Third-culture kids. *Today's Education,* pp. 103-105.

van Dijk, T. A. (1987). *Communicating racism: Ethnic prejudice in thought and talk.* Newbury Park, CA: Sage.

Walker, A. (1983). *In search of our mothers' gardens: Womanist prose*. San Diego, CA: Harcourt Brace Jovanovich.

Walker, A. (1992). *Possessing the secret of joy*. New York: Pocket Books.

Walker, S. (1994). *Hate speech: The history of an American controversy*. Lincoln: University of Nebraska Press.

Wang, X. (1996). Conflict over the role of women in contemporary China: Prospects for liberation and resolution. In F. E. Jandt & P. B. Pedersen (Eds.), *Constructive conflict management: Asia-Pacific cases* (pp. 97-111). Thousand Oaks, CA: Sage.

Warner, M. (Ed.). (1993). *Fear of a queer planet*. Minneapolis: University of Minnesota Press.

Wasserstrom, J. N. (1991). *Student protests in twentieth-century China: The view from Shanghai*. Stanford, CA: Stanford University Press.

Watson, T. J., Jr. (1963). *A business and its beliefs*. New York: McGraw-Hill.

Weber, S. (1985). The need to be: The socio-cultural significance of Black language. In L. A. Samovar & R. E. Porter (Eds.), *Intercultural communication: A reader* (4th ed.). Belmont, CA: Wadsworth.

Weiner, M. (1994). *Race and migration in imperial Japan*. London: Routledge.

Weller, A. (1998, March 12). Human pheromones: Communication through body odour. *Nature*, pp. 126-127.

Westbrook, R. B. (1991). *John Dewey and American democracy*. Ithaca, NY: Cornell University Press.

Weston, K. (1991). *Families we choose: Lesbians, gays, kinship*. New York: Columbia University Press.

Whetmore, E. J. (1987). *Mediamerica: Form, content, and consequence of mass communication* (3rd ed.). Belmont, CA: Wadsworth.

Will, G. F. (1990). *Men at work: The craft of baseball*. New York: Macmillan.

Willis, D. B. (1994). Transculturals, transnationals: The new diaspora. *International Schools Journal, 14*(1), 29-42.

Woodring, A. A. (1995). Power distance and individualism among Japanese university students. *Hiroshima Shudo University Research Review, 11*, 61-75.

Young, B. B. C. (1980). The Hawaiians. In J. F. McDermott, Jr., W.-S. Tseng, & T. W. Maretzki (Eds.), *People and cultures of Hawaii: A psycho-cultural profile* (pp. 5-24). Honolulu: University Press of Hawaii.

Yum, J. O. (1987). Korean philosophy and communication. In D. L. Kincaid (Ed.), *Communication theory: Eastern and Western perspectives* (pp. 71-86). San Diego, CA: Academic Press.

Yum, J. O. (1988). The impact of Confucianism on interpersonal relationships and communications patterns in East Asia. *Communication Monographs, 55*, 374-388.

Yum, J. O., & Park, H. W. (1990). The effects of dxisconfirming information on stereotype change. *Howard Journal of Communication, 2*, 357-367.

Zelinsky, W. (1973). *The cultural geography of the United States*. Englewood Cliffs, NJ: Prentice Hall.

Zenner, W. (1996). Ethnicity. In D. Levinson & M. Ember (Eds.), *Encyclopedia of Cultural Anthropology* (pp. 393-395). New York: Holt.

Glossary

Abaya Long black cloak worn in public by Muslim women

Aboriginal The indigenous peoples of Australia (often applied to indigenous peoples in other countries)

Acculturation An immigrant's learning and adopting the norms and values of the new host culture

Activity orientation Use of time for self-expression and play, self-improvement and development, and work

Adaptation potential An individual's possible success in adapting to a new culture

Afrocentricity Interpreting history, culture, and behavior of Blacks worldwide in terms of dispersion or extension of African history and culture in the context of where it is found

Amae Japanese for a nurturing concern for and dependence on another

Anabaptist 16th-century Reformation movement that insisted that only adult baptism was valid and held that true Christians should not bear arms, use force, or hold government office

Anxiety Diffuse state of being uneasy or worried about what may happen

Appearance Personal appearance, clothing, grooming, and other factors that can be a nonverbal communication message

Arabs Ethnic group that originally spread Islam; the Semitic peoples originally from Arabia and now living throughout the Near East, North Africa, and the Arabian peninsula

Arabic Literary language of the Koran; the language and culture of the Arabs

Argot One term for the specialized vocabulary of subgroups

Artifact Object from a culture

Assimilation An immigrant's giving up the original culture identity and moving into full participation in the new culture

Asylee Person living outside the country of nationality who is unable or unwilling to return because of persecution or a well-founded fear of persecution; the only difference between an asylee and a refugee is that an asylee is applying for admission in the country he or she is already in, whereas a refugee is applying for admission from outside the country he or she desires to enter

Attitude Fairly stable opinion regarding a person, object, or activity containing a cognitive element (perceptions and beliefs) and an emotional element (positive or negative feelings)

Authoritarian personality Type of individual who tends to overgeneralize and think in bipolar terms and who is highly conventional, moralistic, and uncritical of higher authority

Back translation Translating from one language into another and then translating back into the original to compare the result to avoid errors in translation

Beachy Amish Group that divided off from the more conservative Amish over the use of automobiles and modern farm equipment

Biculturalism Ability to function in two cultures

Black English A language of the subculture growing out of slavery and discrimination, providing its speakers with a shared perspective on reality

Call-response Communication practice of punctuating a speaker's statements with expressions from listeners

Cant Specialized vocabulary of any nonprofessional subgroup

Change Substitution of the new for existing

Change agent Person who influences innovation decisions

Change agent ethics Concern for the unanticipated consequences of introducing a new idea or product into a culture

Channel Means by which a message is transmitted

Chicano Term for people born in the United States whose ancestors came from Mexico; often used to represent a nationalist identity and a commitment to disassimilation

Chronemics Study of our use of time

Clothing Can be a nonverbal communication message

Co-culture Term used to convey concept of interdependent and equal subcultures within a society

Code-switching Going from one language to another in the same sentence, as from Spanish to English and then back to Spanish

Collectivism Dimension of culture that refers to interdependence, groupness, and social cohesion

Coming out One's public disclosure of being gay

Communication Process of intentionally stimulating meaning in other humans through the use of symbols

Communication apprehension Fear or anxiety associated with either real or anticipated communication with another person or persons

Conformity Compliance or acquiescence

Confucian work dynamism Dimension of culture that refers to persistence, commitment, and organizational identity and loyalty; relabeled by Hofstede as long-term versus short-term orientation

Confucianism Ethical system based on the teaching of Confucius emphasizing personal virtue and devotion to family and society

Context The physical and social environment in which communication takes place

Convergence A process in which information is shared by individuals who come together over time to a greater degree of agreement

Corporate culture Thinking of an organization as a culture; the values, goals, and priorities that guide policies and procedures of an organization

Creole Language that develops from prolonged contact of two or more languages and acquired by children as their first language

Cross-cultural Comparison of cultural phenomenon in different cultures (e.g., a cross-cultural study of television might compare programming in different countries)

Cultural adaptation An immigrant's learning and adopting the norms and values of the new host culture (*see* **Acculturation**)

Cultural identity Identification with and perceived acceptance into a culture

Cultural invasion Term used by Freire to refer to one group penetrating the culture of another group to impose its own view of the world

Cultural relativism Theory from anthropology that the differences in peoples are the results of historical, social, and geographic conditions and that all populations have complete and equally developed cultures

Cultural Revolution Mao Zedong's attempt to purify China of outside influences and build a Marxist-Chinese culture

Cultural sensitivity Making no value judgments based on one's own cultural values about other cultures' practices or artifacts (i.e., better or worse, right or wrong)

Culture Sum total of ways of living including behavioral norms, linguistic expression, styles of communication, patterns of thinking, and beliefs and values of a group large enough to be self-sustaining transmitted over the course of generations

Culture shock Anxiety, disorientation, and stress that one experiences when in a new culture

Decoding Process of assigning meaning to symbols

Dialect A variety of speech differing from the standard

Diaspora Dispersion of an originally homogeneous people

Diffusion Spread of innovations into a culture

Discrimination Treatment in favor or against a person based on the group to which that person belongs rather than on individual merit

Discursive imperialism Labeling of a group as a dehumanized "other," which facilitates actions taken against it

Ebonics A word created from *ebony* and *phonics* (see **Black English**)

Emic Knowledge learned from the inside, that is, the norms of culture known by its members (*compare* **Etic**)

Encoding Process of putting the communication source's ideas into symbols

Endogamy Marriage in which the partners must be members of the same group (e.g., a religious community)

Equality Being alike or the same in some rank, ability, quantity, and so forth

Esperanto Widely used universal language devised in 1887 based on European vocabularies and Latin grammar

Ethnic group Subgroup identified by shared descent and heritage

Ethnic identity Identification with and perceived acceptance into an ethnic group

Ethnocentrism Negatively judging aspects of another culture by the standards of one's own culture

Ethnography The direct observation and reporting of customary behavior of a culture

Etic Knowledge learned by an outsider, that is, theoretical information about a culture developed by a researcher not a member of the culture (*compare* **Emic**)

Exogamy Marriage in which the partner must be chosen from outside a defined group (e.g., members of the same extended family lineage may not marry)

Expatriate Noncitizen worker in a foreign country

Extended family Family group including parents and their married children

Face In collectivist cultures, public image or reputation that one has achieved (*mian* in Chinese culture); also, the community's confidence in the integrity of one's moral character (*lian* in Chinese culture)

Feedback That portion of receiver response that a source attends to

Femininity Dimension of culture that refers to both women and men being concerned with quality of life, interpersonal relationships, and concern for the weak

Feng shui Chinese art of manipulating the physical environment, such as homes and offices, to establish harmony with nature to achieve happiness, prosperity, and health

Fertility rate Average number of children born alive to a woman in her lifetime; a fertility rate of 2.1 children per woman would eventually result in zero population growth

Four modernizations Deng Xiaoping's economic programs in China in agriculture, industry, science, and technology

Gaijin Japanese for foreigner or "outside person"

Gay Term to refer in a positive way to individuals who are attached to and form primary emotional attachments to members of the same sex and who value one another and similar others

GDP *See* **Gross domestic product**

Gelassenheit German word used by the Amish to mean submission to God

Gender Learned behaviors and attitudes associated with the words *feminine* and *masculine*

Ghutrah Cloth worn by men in Saudi Arabia and some other Arabian countries to cover the head

Global communication Transborder transfer of information and values by groups and governments, the technology used in the transfer, and the issues that arise from the transfer

Globalization The worldwide spread of market economies and democracy

Grammar Linguistic rules governing sounds (or gestures in sign languages), meanings, and syntax of a language

Gregorian Calendar based on the cycles of the sun

Gross domestic product (GDP) The total output of goods and services for final use produced by an economy

Hajj The pilgrimage to Mecca that a Muslim is expected to undertake at least once

Haptics Study of the use of touch to communicate

Hate crime Crime that grows out of a fear of differences and results in hostility toward those who are perceived as different because of race, religion, gender, or sexual orientation

Hate speech Threats or verbal slurs directed against specific groups or physical acts such as burning crosses or placing swastikas on public or private property

Hegemony Predominant influence by one culture over another

Hero A real or imaginary person who serves as a behavior model within a culture

High context Dimension of culture holding that much of the meaning of messages is determined by the context or environment

Hijrah Calendar based on the cycles of the moon

Hispanic Term for people with the capability of speaking and comprehending the Spanish language whose ancestry is based on a Spanish-speaking country and who identify with the subculture

Hmong A people living in Laos who sided with the United States in the Vietnam War and now have resettled in the United States

Homophobia Irrational fear of lesbians and gay men

Homosexual Refers to one's sexual activity with members of one's own sex

Hong Kong British Crown Colony returned to China in 1997

Honorific Form of direct address used in some languages to show respect

Hyperindividualism Excesses of individualism, disregard for others, and withdrawing into individual private shells

Icon Popular symbol that represents a culture

Idiom Expression whose meaning is not predictable from the usual meanings of its words

Individualism Dimension of culture that refers to the rights and independent action of the individual

Ingroup Cohesive group that offers protection in exchange for loyalty and provides its members with a sense of identity

Integration   Maintaining important parts of one's original culture as well as participating fully in a new culture

Intercultural communication   Communication between people and groups of diverse culture, subculture, or subgroup identifications

International communication   The study of the flow of mediated communication between and among countries; the study of comparative mass communication systems; the study of communication between national governments

Interpretation   The step in the perception process referring to attaching meaning to sense data

Iqual   Also known as *agal*, the double ring of black rope or cord used to hold the *ghutrah* worn by men in Saudi Arabia and some other Arabian countries

Islam   World's second largest religion with nearly 1 billion followers that is based on the teachings of the prophet Muhammad, believing in one God, and having a body of law put forth in the Koran and the sunnah

Jargon   Technical language of a professional subgroup

Kinesics   Gestures, body movements, facial expressions, and eye contact

Koran   Holy book of Islam considered to contain the literal words of Allah or God; the Arabic text includes stories, admonitions, verse, and prophetic segments (often spelled Quran)

Kwanzaa   Swahili for first fruits; a celebration of African culture and unity celebrated December 26 through January 1

Language   Set of symbols shared by a community to communicate meaning and experience

Latino   Term for Spanish-speaking individuals who themselves or whose ancestors came from anywhere in Latin America

Lesbian   Term to refer in a positive way to women who form primary emotional attachments to other women

Literacy rate   Percentage of people, age 15 and above, who can, with understanding, both read and write a short, simple statement on their everyday life

Long-term orientation   Fostering of virtues, particularly perseverance and thrift, oriented toward future rewards

Low context   Dimension of culture holding that little of the meaning of messages is determined by the context or environment

Macao   Portuguese colony returned to China in 1999

Majlis   Practice in Saudi Arabia allowing any citizen access to the king and local governors

Marginalization   Losing one's cultural identity and not having any psychological contact with society

Maroons   African fugitive slaves of the 17th and 18th centuries and their descendants living in the West Indies and Guiana

Masculinity   Dimension of culture that refers to distinct traits of being assertive, tough, and focused on material success

Matawain   Public morality committees in Saudi Arabia that ensure compliance with religious requirements

Materialism   Emphasis on material objects, needs, and considerations over spiritual values

Melting pot   Term used to describe the assimilation of early immigrants into a homogenized United States

Message   Encoded ideas of the communication source

Mexican-American   A person from a specific country of origin in assimilation process

Monochronic time   In the use of time, doing one thing at a time in an orderly fashion

Mother tongue   Parent language of other languages or a person's first learned language

Muhammad   Born circa 570, died 632, and the founder of Islam

Multiculturalism   Understanding, acceptance, and constructive relations among people of many different cultures and subcultures

Muslim   Literally one who submits to the will of God; one who practices the religion of Islam

Mutability   State of changeability, variability

Myths   Stories and images representing a culture's values handed down from generation to generation as a guide for living

Need for achievement   Term used by David McClelland to describe the desire to excel because of the feeling of accomplishment it brings

Negritude   Assertion of the importance of the African heritage

New Order Amish   Moderate group of the Amish, accepting some modern conveniences

Noise   External, internal, or semantic limitations on the effectiveness of communication

Nommo   In pan-African culture, the magical power of the word representing the life force of being

Nonverbal communication   Actions and attributes with a socially shared meaning intentionally sent and received

Norms   Standard or model behaviors expected in a culture

Nuclear family   Family group including only parents and children

Nushu   Women's writing developed in rural China as a secret language to communicate with other women

Oculesics   Communication by the eyes

Old Order Amish   The most conservative and strict of the Amish

Oleh (plural Olim)   A Jew immigrating into Israel under the Law of Return

Olfactics   Communication by smells

One-child campaign   China's birth control program introduced in 1979 to encourage most families to have no more than one child

Opinion leadership   Individuals who are able to influence others' attitudes and behaviors

Ordnung   Church rules and values of the Amish

Organization   The step in the perception process referring to organizing sense data in some meaningful way

Ossie   German slang for former East Germans

Othering   The degrading of cultures and groups outside of one's own and creating artificial divisions between cultures and groups by labeling language that emphasizes power relations and domination

Paralanguage   Nonverbal elements of the voice including intensity, pitch, laughter, and so forth

Participant observer   A researcher's orderly and scientific study of a subgroup by actually participating in the group

Peace Corps   U.S. government organization established in 1961 to train and send volunteers abroad to work with people of developing countries in agricultural, educational, and technological projects

Perception   Act of becoming aware of, knowing, or identifying by means of the senses

Pidgin   Mixture of two or more languages to form a new language

Polychronic time   In the use of time, placing a stress on the involvement of people and completion of transactions rather than on adherence to schedules

Postethnicity   Belief that associations or group memberships can be voluntary rather than determined by birth

Power distance   Dimension of culture that refers to the extent to which the less powerful members expect and accept that power, prestige, and wealth are distributed unequally

Prejudice   Irrational suspicion or hatred of a particular group, race, religion, or sexual orientation

Profiling Law enforcement practice of scrutinizing certain individuals based on characteristics thought to indicate the likelihood of criminal behavior

Proxemics Use of fixed space, territoriality, and personal space

Quality circle Employee group working to improve quality during the production process

Race Biologically defined as groups who share some hereditary physical characteristics; sociohistorically defined by unstable social meanings constantly being transformed by debate

Racial profiling Law enforcement practice of scrutinizing individuals based on perceived racial identification

Racism Any policy, practice, belief, or attitude that attributes characteristics or status to individuals based on their race

Ramadan Month of lunar Islamic calendar during which Muslims abstain from food and drink from sunrise to sunset in commemoration of God's revealing the Koran to Muhammad

Rationality Mental powers to form conclusions and sound judgments, intelligent and dispassionate thought

Receiver Person who attends to a communication message

Receiver response Anything the receiver of a communication message does after having decoded the message

Redemptive analogy Something in a culture that can be compared to the Christian gospel

Reference group Group to which one aspires to attain membership

Refugee Person living outside the country of nationality who is unable or unwilling to return because of persecution or a well-founded fear of persecution; the only difference between refugee and asylee is that a refugee is applying for admission from outside the country he or she desires to enter, whereas an asylee is applying for admission in the country he or she is already in

Reverse culture shock Anxiety, disorientation, and stress that one can experience upon return to one's home country

Ritual A socially essential collective activity within a culture

Rules Socially agreed-on behavior; individual guidelines for behavior

Salad or stew analogy In contrast to the melting pot analogy, a description of a culture in which individuals may retain elements of their original culture and still exist together without assimilating

Sapir-Whorf hypothesis Useful way of thinking about the relationship between language and culture (also known as Whorfian thesis and linguistic relativity)

Scientific method Identifying a problem, gathering data, and formulating and testing a hypothesis

Segregation Maintaining one's original culture and not participating in the new culture

Selection The step in the perception process referring to limiting attention only to part of the available sense data

Sensation Neurological process of becoming aware through the senses of stimuli in the environment

Separation Maintaining one's original culture and not participating in the new culture (*see* **Segregation**)

Sex Biological features that distinguish women from men

Sexism Practice of limiting women to traditional women's roles and men to traditional men's roles

Shiite Smaller branch of Islam that has messianic expectations of world justice

Shinto Former state religion of Japan linking the people to ancestors and gods

Short-term orientation Dimension of cultures standing for the fostering of virtues related to the past and present, in particular respect for tradition, preservation of face, and fulfilling social obligations

Silence   Absence of verbal communication that can communicate messages nonverbally

Slang   Term to refer to the specialized vocabulary of subgroups

Sojourner   One who lives in a country for a specific period of time for a specific purpose such as employment and expects to return home

Source   Person with an idea he or she desires to communicate

Spanglish   Mixing Spanish and English words in one sentence

Spanish origin   Term to refer to people who themselves or their ancestors came from a Spanish-speaking country

Spanish-speaking   Term to refer to people who can speak and comprehend the Spanish language as a primary or secondary language

Spanish-surnamed   Term to refer to people with a last name identified as Spanish by the U.S. Census Bureau

Standard Chinese   Mandarin dialect spoken by the majority of people in China

Stereotype   Judgment made about another solely on the basis of ethnic or other group membership

Subculture   Group within a larger society that shares distinctive cultural characteristics to distinguish it from others

Subgroup   Group based on vocation, avocation, or special skills that, like cultures, provide patterns of behavior and values

Sub-Saharan Africa   Countries on the African continent south of the Sahara

Sunni   Largest branch of Islam

Symbol   Verbal and nonverbal language that is used to communicate the idea of a communication source

Syntax   Grammatical rules governing the way that words combine to form sentences

Taiwan   Republic of China located on the island of Formosa off the southeastern coast of China

Taoism   Philosophical system originated by Lao-tzu that advocated a simple life close to nature in order to be in harmony with the Tao or underlying pattern of the universe

Tejano   Person born in Texas of Mexican ancestry

Telemundo   Spanish-language television network

Territoriality   Refers to how space can be used to communicate messages

Thawb   Loose-fitting, ankle-length, usually white shirt worn by men in Saudi Arabia and some other Arab countries

Tibet   A country in South Asia north of the Himalayas under the suzerainty, or overlordship, of China

Uncertainty avoidance   Dimension of culture that refers to the extent to which people are made nervous by unstructured or unpredictable situations

Unconscious prejudice   Institutionalized or patterns of behaviors often unrecognized that do in fact discriminate, favoring one group over others

Univision   Spanish-language television network

Value   A central organizing belief or belief system that shapes a person's goals and motivations.

Wai   Nonverbal gesture used in Thailand to communicate greeting, farewell, respect, and appreciation

Wessie   German slang for former West Germans

White privilege   Advantages that Whites have living in a White culture

Words   Symbols that a language community uses to refer to things

Worldview   Philosophical ideas of being, a culture's beliefs about its place in the cosmos, beliefs about the nature of humanity

Xenophobia   Unreasonable fear or hatred of foreigners

Yang   Bright, dry, warm aspect or principle in Chinese philosophy

Yin   Dark, moist, cool aspect or principle in Chinese philosophy

Index